C000228228

'I was immensely impressed w...
his abilities to disti...

Joyce Yarrow, author of *Sana...*

'A wonderful exploration of the connections that both Russia and the Romanov family had with Britain and the Isle of Wight'

Michael Hunter FRSA, Curator, Osborne House

'The whole story of the connection between the Russian Imperial family and the Royal Yacht Squadron is fascinating. Roman managed to fill in many gaps in my own knowledge of the subject'

HRH Prince Michael of Kent

'There is a separate chapter devoted entirely to the visit of Tsar Nicholas and his family to the Isle of Wight... The story about the murder of the Romanovs is impressive, but also horrific when you find out in Isle and Empires that it could have turned out very differently'

Elma Bruin, *New Royalty World*

'An illuminating and insightful work in which Stephan Roman has gathered together some fascinating episodes in the Romanov's 300-year story which provide many fresh insights into the history of Anglo-Russian relations'

Henry Greenfield, *East-West Review : Journal of the Great Britain-Russia Society*

'Roman makes the atmosphere come alive, and you can almost feel yourself walking with the Grand Duchesses'

Moniek Bloks, Editor-in-Chief at *History of Royal Women*, *Journalist at Royal Central*

'Looking through the prism of the Isle of Wight brings a fresh perspective on the two royal families'

History with Jackson

'Isle and Empires draws on a large and eclectic range of sources to provide not just the bare history but many fascinating details that link to a huge cast of characters – the author has a talent for describing these in an entertaining and enlightening way'

Goodreads Reviewer

'An absorbing read from first page to the last…How different things would have been if the Romanovs had been given refuge in England'

NetGalley Reviewer

'A lively and accessible account of a fascinating relationship between two major powers…Stephan Roman writes in a way that makes this exciting story read more like a thriller. Spies and royals are brought vividly to life'

NetGalley Reviewer

To Jacquie
with best wishes,
Stephan Roman

ISLE AND EMPIRES

Romanov Russia,
Britain and the Isle of Wight

16 April 2024

By Stephan Roman

Medina Publishing

Paperback published in 2022

Isle and Empires:
Romanov Russia, Britain and the Isle of Wight

First published in Great Britain in 2021 by
Medina Publishing
50 High Street
Cowes
Isle of Wight
PO31 7RR

Edited by Eleo Carson
Cover designed by Luke Pajak
Cartography by Stephen Ramsey
Typeset by Alexandra Lawson

Printed in the UK by Clays Elcograf SpA

ISBN (Hardback) – 978-1-911487-39-5
ISBN (Paperback) – 978-1-911487-66-1
ISBN (eBook) - 978-1-911487-44-9

For my parents, Elizabeth and Victor Roman, who brought the British, Russian and Polish sides of our family together, and thus helped create this story.

To my wife, Dorcas, for all her support and encouragement.

Preface

Vladimir Putin and the return of Imperial Russia

This second edition of *Isle and Empires* is being published at a time when relations between Britain and Russia are at their lowest point since the Crimean War of 1853-56 and the difficult days of the Cold War. Russia's invasion of Ukraine has damaged co-operation between the two countries and has once again put the Anglo-Russian relationship under enormous strain.

My aim in writing *Isle and Empires* was to explore the shared history of our two countries during the period of the Romanov Tsars between 1613 and 1918. This was the time when the foundations were laid for the current Anglo-Russian relationship. This shared history was never a smooth and easy one, and it was coloured by frequent misunderstandings and tensions. However, alongside the low points, there were also times when Britain and Russia were allies, such as during the Napoleonic Wars and First World War. It is important that we understand the history of the British relationship with Romanov Russia, if we are to make any sense of what is happening today.

The Russian attack on Ukraine in 2022 has shocked many people in Britain and around the world. Today, as we witness the spectacle of a Russian army invading a sovereign and free European country, it is hard not to feel revulsion and a sense of profound outrage. I write this with a heavy heart. My own grandparents were loyal citizens of the Tsarist Empire, and firm believers in a more liberal Russia. However, exactly a hundred years ago in March 1922, they found themselves refugees in Ukraine, fleeing the oppression of Soviet Russia. I describe their fate – and the fate of millions like them – in the opening chapter of this book. The history of Eastern Europe has too often been written in blood, exile, and violence which tragically repeats itself century after century.

Historical events are often ignored or overlooked by politicians and governments, but in the case of Russia this has always been a big mistake. The Russians have never forgotten their history or its long-term influence and impact. Many of the actions and events that took place in the Romanov period continue to haunt today's world.

Aggression and oppression, both at home and abroad, has frequently been the Russian response to perceived internal and external threats. Some of these threats were very real and threatened Russia's stability and survival such as Napoleon's invasion of 1812. Others were far less existential like the Polish uprisings against Russian imperial rule in 1830 and 1863, which were crushed by the Tsars. The violence of this response shocked liberal European nations such as Britain and France. At other times, such as during the Napoleonic and First World Wars, Russia was a close ally of Britain, and its military victories were widely celebrated by the British public. However, these periods of Anglo-Russian friendship were brief and quickly forgotten, overshadowed as they were by long stretches of mutual suspicion and mistrust.

Vladimir Putin's views on Ukraine are influenced by his nostalgia for the Soviet and Tsarist periods of Russian history. They reveal a fear that modern Russia is losing influence and control of its 'near-abroad', lands that were once seen as a necessary bulwark against foreign invasion. There is no doubt that Putin, and many of those who support him today, are alarmed by the expansion of the European Union and NATO to include several countries that were once in the Soviet sphere of influence. They believe that this is in contravention to assurances they had been given by Western powers at the end of the Cold War – that NATO would not encroach on Russia's borders.

Putin's territorial expansionism feeds off a long-established concern about Russia's geographical vulnerability. The Mongol invasion of Russia and Ukraine in the thirteenth century, which destroyed Kievan Rus' and cities such as Moscow, Ryazan, and Vladimir, led to two centuries of subservience to the 'Golden Horde' of the Mongols and Tartars. This period had a major impact on the Russian national psyche.

The Grand Duchy of Moscow finally threw off Tartar rule in 1480, and its rulers, the Rurik Princes, initiated a period of territorial growth in search of greater national security. This was disrupted by the 'Time of Troubles' between 1598 and 1613. These were years of lawlessness and anarchy when the armies of the Polish-Lithuanian Commonwealth occupied much of western Russia, and it seemed as though Russia itself might not survive. The accession of the Romanov dynasty to the crown of Muscovy in 1613 turned defeat into a national success.

The need to constantly protect and expand territory to secure Russia's borders became a defining feature of Romanov rule. When Peter the Great succeeded to the throne he had two major objectives. First, he decided to modernise Russia and secondly to expand its frontiers. In 1709 he defeated the Swedes, hitherto the pre-eminent power in the Baltic, at the Battle of Poltava. With the assistance of English shipbuilders including Joseph Nye from the Isle of Wight, he went on to create a naval fleet which drove the Swedes out of the Baltic Sea.

Thus began a period of imperial expansion when Russia destroyed its rival, the Polish-Lithuanian Commonwealth between 1772 and 1795, and absorbed large parts of its territories into the Russian Empire. In 1764, Catherine the Great established 'New Russia', a region now in Southern Ukraine, which includes the port city of Odessa. Eastern Ukraine, including Kyiv, had become part of Russia in 1667 following the Treaty of Andrusovo. Acquiring more and more land to achieve national security became a Romanov obsession.

Under the Tsars a new imperial role was shaped, which enabled them to combine territorial acquisitions with becoming the protectors of both Orthodox Christian believers and pan-Slav cultural and ethnic identity. This was not a role that ever found any great favour with the occupied peoples of Poland and Lithuania, but it did resonate with the Serbs, Greeks, and the Bulgarians and it would lead Russia into several wars against the Ottomans in the Balkans, including the disastrous Crimean war of 1853.

Putin sees himself as the inheritor and the protector of this imperial tradition. Although he acknowledges the contribution of the Soviet Union, it is allegedly the Romanov Tsars who fascinate him. He has a particular respect for Peter the Great. Putin has inherited a belief in his country's unique mission in the world, based on promoting Orthodoxy, autocratic government, and a strong

Russian national and cultural identity. All these ideas were originally developed and embellished by the Romanovs.

Like many of his Tsarist predecessors, Putin has a very close relationship with the Russian Orthodox Church. His spiritual advisor and personal confessor is Metropolitan Tikhon, who has written a book about Seraphim of Sarov, the Orthodox saint who was greatly venerated by Nicholas and Alexandra. Tikhon also played a major role in the construction of a church in Moscow near the Lubyanka prison celebrating the 'New Martyrs and Confessors of the Russian Church'. These martyrs include the last Tsar and his family. The inauguration of the church in 2017 was attended by Putin and Patriarch Kirill, the Patriarch of Moscow and the Primate of the Russian Orthodox Church.

Kirill is a very close confidante of Putin, reflecting the close spiritual ties that now link secular power with Russian Orthodoxy. This was also the case in Romanov Russia. It should be noted that the Russian Orthodox Church has refused to condemn the invasion of Ukraine. Putin's quest to unite all Russian speaking peoples under the protection of Moscow, clearly has the spiritual blessing and support of both Tikhon, Kirill and many other Russian church leaders.

Putin has also inherited a powerful sense of national insecurity which dates back to Tsarist times, seeing in the USA, Britain, NATO, and the EU, powers that are seeking to subvert and possibly destroy Russia. These, he believes, are reincarnations of old enemies such as Nazi Germany, Napoleonic France, the Polish-Lithuanian Commonwealth, and the Mongols. He is committed to driving this threat from his country's borders. As part of this pushback Putin is committed to ensuring what he describes as the historic unity of the Russians and Ukrainian peoples.

Britain and France last went to war with Russia in the Crimea between 1853-1856. This was a war initiated by Tsar Nicholas I, who believed that he should protect Christian Orthodox believers from Ottoman Muslim oppression. He believed that the Russian armies would have a quick victory and that Ottoman Turkey was a corrupt and decaying empire. Britain and France came to the support of the Ottomans, and a savage and cruel war was the result. Hundreds of thousands of Russian soldiers died in the three-year campaign. The Russian armies were brought to the brink of total defeat. It was Nicholas's death in 1855, and the accession to the throne of his far more liberal son, Alexander II, which saved the day for the Romanov dynasty.

In his admiration for the Romanov Tsars, it may be salutary for Putin to ponder on the fate of Nicholas I. Launching a war based on the wish to offer Russian protection to the subjects of a foreign government does not always bring the desired outcome. The Crimean War poisoned relations between Russia and Britain and France for over 50 years. It was an unnecessary and destructive conflict, with no positive results, driven by a mistaken sense that Russia could re-order the territory of the Ottoman Empire to suit its own ambitions.

The city state of Novgorod, eventually destroyed by Tsar Ivan the Terrible in 1570, was an example of early civic democracy in Russia. It became an inspiration and beacon of hope to Russian liberals in later centuries.

During the nineteenth century political opponents of the Tsarist regime kept the flame of a more liberal society alive. The Decembrist revolt of 1825, against Tsar Nicholas I, demonstrated that there were strong yearnings amongst the aristocracy and the military elite for a different type of Russia, more closely aligned to European liberal values. From the middle of the nineteenth century many Russian political radicals, men such as Alexander Herzen and Peter Kropotkin, left Russia and sought refuge in countries like Britain and France. Their thinking would eventually contribute to the overthrow of Tsarist autocracy in 1917. Since the middle of the nineteenth century, Britain has played an important role in providing a safe sanctuary and refuge for Russians escaping oppression in their homeland.

There were also two Tsars, Alexander I and Alexander II, who were sympathetic at different times in their reigns to more liberal policies. Alexander II liberated the serfs in 1861 and was widely acclaimed for doing this. Nicholas II, although he can hardly be described as a liberal, worked hard during his reign to promote the cause of international peace. He was the initiator of the First Hague Peace Conference in 1899. He played a key role in overcoming a century of mistrust between Britain and Russia, by strongly supporting the 'Anglo-Russian Convention' of 1907. This was a ground -breaking agreement which created mechanisms for Russia and Britain to diffuse tensions between the two empires in Persia, Afghanistan, and Tibet.

In August 1909 Tsar Nicholas visited the Isle of Wight to set the seal on this new agreement. It was one of the few high points in the Anglo-Russian relationship during the period of the Romanovs and if it had not been for the First World War and the Russian Revolution it may well have laid the foundations for a stronger partnership between the two countries.

The Russian people themselves, stoical, resilient, and determined have often been the unacknowledged heroes and survivors of their fascinating but frequently tragic history. It is important to recognise that the invasion of Ukraine is not being carried out with the full support of the Russian people. There are many Russians who are deeply opposed to what is now taking place. The war has been launched by a leader who seeks to recreate a period of Russian imperial glory and territorial expansion. Whether he achieves his objectives remains to be seen, but the brave resistance of the Ukrainian people could well destroy these plans. The Ukrainians have also inspired those inside Russia who dream of a very different future for their country in the twenty-first century.

As a result of the Russian invasion of Ukraine, it is more important than ever to understand the way in which history has shaped the world in which we now live. This second edition of my book, with its insights into the complex relationship between Imperial Russia and the British Empire, demonstrates that the events of the past continue to echo in powerful and disturbing ways.

Stephan Roman
London, March 2022

Contents

List of Illustrations & Maps

18. Terrorist attack carried out in Tottenham in North London by Russian anarchists. (*The Illustrated London News*, 30 January 1909)

19. The imperial yacht, *Shtandart*, at anchor in the Cowes Roads during the visit by the Tsar and his family in August 1909. (Beken photographic archive, Cowes)

20. Visitors strolling along the Parade in Cowes during the 1909 Regatta. (Hulton Archive/Getty Images)

21. The Tsarina, Alexandra, and her daughters on board the *Shtandart* during their visit to Cowes in August 1909. (Russian State Archive)

22. The state dinner on board the imperial yacht, *Shtandart*, on the evening of Tuesday 3 August 1909. (Russian State Archive)

23. The King's yacht, *Britannia*, during Cowes Week 1909. (Beken photographic archive, Cowes)

24. The Tsar, and King Edward VII relaxing on board the *Britannia* while sailing in the Solent on 3 August 1909. (Russian State Archive)

25. The Romanov children play on Osborne beach with their cousins. (Russian State Archive)

26. Grand Duchesses Olga and Tatiana shopping in Cowes. (Russian State Archive)

27. The Russian and British royal families at Barton Manor in East Cowes. (*The Illustrated London News*, 14 August 1909)

28. Nicholas II and his cousin, George, Prince of Wales, with Prince Edward, and Tsarevich, Alexis. (*The Illustrated London News*, 14 August 1909)

29. The basement room in the Ipatiev House in Ekaterinburg. (Russian State Archive)

30. The Romanov Memorial Cross in Jubilee Park, East Cowes. (Russian Orthodox Church Outside Russia)

Maps

1. Places in Britain associated with the Romanovs (p. xvii)
2. Places on the Isle of Wight associated with the Romanovs (p. 16)
3. Places in Cowes and East Cowes associated with the Romanovs (p. 220)

Note on use of Russian names and dates

Russian names and words are transliterated into English according to the guidelines established by the Library of Congress. When there is a well-known English version of the name, I have used this rather than the Russian name. This is generally the case with the imperial family, where I use their English names rather than their Russian names. For all other Russian names, except in a few cases where the English version is well known, I have used the Russian form. In many cases, particularly when introducing a name for the first time, I have used the full Russian version which includes the patronymic middle name, for example Sergei Yulyevich Witte.

In terms of imperial titles, I have used both Tsar and Emperor, and Tsarina and Empress. These titles are used interchangeably in English. Officially the title of Emperor or Empress was used by all Russian monarchs from 1721 until the end of the dynasty. Several of the foreign princesses who married into the Russian imperial family adopted new names on their marriages. Alexander III's wife, Princess Dagmar of Denmark, became Maria Feodorovna, whilst the wife of Nicholas II, Princess Alix of Hesse, adopted the name Alexandra Feodorovna. Feodor is the Russian version of Theodore, which means 'Gift of God'. Feodor was also a revered name within the Romanov family, as the founder of the dynasty, Michael Romanov, was the son of Feodor Nikitich Romanov. Finally, you will note that I often refer to the last Empress as Alix, as this was the name she liked to use even after her marriage to Nicholas. I use the formal name of Alexandra when referring to her official imperial role.

Between the mid-eighteenth and early twentieth centuries, Russian dates differ from those used in Western Europe. Russia retained use of the Julian calendar until 1917. This means that Russian dates were between eleven and thirteen days behind the equivalent Western date, as established by the Gregorian calendar. In my book, I have used Russian dates when referring to events taking place inside Russia, and Western dates when referring to events taking place in Britain or elsewhere in Europe. In one case, the meeting in June 1908 between King Edward VII and Tsar Nicholas II, I have used the Western dates even though the meeting took place within the borders of the Russian Empire. The new Soviet regime adopted the Gregorian calendar on 14 February 1918 and thereafter Russian and Western dates were fully aligned.

Places in Britain associated with the Romanovs

PART

I

THE PROLOGUE

1

The wreckage of Imperial Russia

Those who survived would never forget the horrific scenes that they witnessed that May afternoon on the shores of the Dniester river in Bessarabia. Thousands of refugees from every class of Russian society crowded on to the banks of the fast-flowing river that marked the frontier between the newly emerging Soviet Union and the Kingdom of Romania. This was like a great wave of fear and desperation, crashing on to the last surviving sandbank of Imperial Russia.

Many of the refugees had been on the road for months and years, fleeing the advance of the Red Army and the agents of the Cheka, the Soviet secret police. Others had fled the violence and terror unleashed by the White armies as they retreated into Southern Russia. Most of those arriving on the banks of the River Dniester were now reduced to a state of poverty, desperation and abject terror. The Russian Civil War, which had started four years earlier in 1918, was now nearing its end. It had been a brutal struggle, leading to the deaths of between eight and twelve million people, through famine, disease, and violent conflict. Millions more were either displaced or had fled into exile.

By the end of 1920, the Bolshevik Red Army of Vladimir Ulyanov Lenin had largely destroyed the opposing White Army, despite the support that the latter was receiving from Britain, France, Germany and the United States. The Whites were a loose confederation of monarchists, socialists and democrats, who were bitterly opposed to the Bolsheviks and led by Generals such as Pyotr Wrangel, Anton Denikin, and Admiral Alexander Kolchak. Between 1918 and 1919 the Whites had made significant advances and successfully captured large swathes of territory across Siberia and Southern Russia. At one point, their armies even threatened Moscow. However, in the autumn of 1919, the Red Army launched a major counter offensive and drove back the White Army.

On 8 February 1920, the seaport of Odessa in the Ukraine fell to the Red Army. This had been a haven for over 500,000 refugees escaping Bolshevik rule. A flotilla of British and French naval ships managed to evacuate around 16,000 soldiers, government officials and civilian refugees. Thousands more gathered on the harbourside but were unable to board the ships as there was not enough space to take them all. As the last ships drew away from the quayside, whole families prayed together and then committed suicide. It was a sight that those on the departing vessels would never forget.

The fall of Odessa was followed by the collapse of White Russian armies across the rest of Southern Russia. The Crimea was their final redoubt but by early November it was clear that the peninsula could no longer be defended. Between 13 and 16 November 1920, a mass evacuation of White soldiers and civilians was ordered by General Wrangel. 146,000 people were transported to safety from the ports of Sevastopol, Yevpatoria, Kerch and Yalta.

Many thousands of White army soldiers and civilian refugees could not reach the boats in time. They were abandoned in the Crimea to fend for themselves. These unfortunates soon found themselves at the mercy of the Crimean Revolutionary Committee, which had been created by the Russian Communist Party and was tasked with bringing revolutionary justice to the region. Heading the Committee were two of the most ruthless individuals in the history of the Bolshevik Red Terror: the Hungarian Bela Kun and his accomplice Rosalia Zemlyachka. Between them, they were responsible for ordering the deaths of 50,000 prisoners of war and anti-Bolshevik civilians in the Crimea. Over the course of the following year another 60,000-70,000 men, women and children were tracked down and executed.

The Red Terror was an organised campaign of political repression which lasted throughout the four years of the Civil War and was responsible for the deaths of anywhere between 200,000 and 1.3 million people. Exact numbers will never be known as the Cheka, the Bolshevik Secret Police, did not keep particularly accurate records of its victims.

Many of those who were killed were members of Russia's former ruling class, including Tsarist government officials, aristocrats, army officers and intellectuals. It was easy for the Cheka to accuse such people of sympathy and complicity with counter-revolutionary activities. Peasants and workers, however, also became victims of the repression, particularly wealthy peasant farmers, or 'kulaks', as well as merchants and workers from the urban areas.

Throughout 1919, as the Red Army consolidated its grip on former White held territories, there were mass executions in Rostov-on-Don, Kiev, Kharkov, and Odessa. In Baku, in April 1920, the Cheka organised what was described as 'the week of the suppression of the bourgeoisie', when thousands of government officials and their families, together with all the officers of the Azerbaijani National Army, were gunned down in batches of a hundred on Nargin Island, a short ferry ride from Baku.

In May 1922 those who now gathered in fear and panic on the Russian side of the Dniester river knew that they could expect little mercy when the Bolsheviks caught up with them. They were desperate to cross the river to safety in Romania.

Amongst them was my grandfather, Emil Konradovich Romanovsky, who had been a senior official in the Tsarist administration, working for the Office of Imperial Posts and Telegraphs. His family were originally from Western Russia and before the Revolution he had been working in St Petersburg, Moscow and Kazan. He was accompanied by my grandmother, Jadwiga Niewierkiewicz, the daughter of an affluent Polish-Lithuanian family from Vilna (later renamed Vilnius) and by their two small children, my aunt Natalia and my father Viktor. They had been refugees since 1919 and were now penniless. During their flight from Moscow they had been threatened with violence, cheated, robbed, and left for destitute. Somehow, they had survived and now sat huddled together, praying that they would find a way to cross into Romania.

My grandparents rarely talked about what they witnessed that May afternoon in 1922. It was as though they preferred to shut from their minds the memories of the tragic scenes that had unfolded around them. They said enough, though, for this eye-witness account of the final tragedy of Imperial Russia to be handed down through the generations.

Any attempt to cross the Dniester and reach the small town of Soroca in Romania was a major challenge for refugees weakened by years of illness, fear and lack of food. Many of them could not swim, and the cold river water would soon claim the lives of those who were not fit and strong.

Entire families took to the waters, roped together and hoping to reach the other side of the river. They had come so far that they would rather die than turn back and face the terror of living in a country in which they no longer believed, and where they felt sure that their lives and their futures would be held forfeit.

There were screams, prayers, and cries for help. Many were swept away by the strong currents, never to resurface. Others used luggage, crates and bundles of clothes to help them float, but too often, these rapidly filled with water and dragged down those clinging to them. A few survivors made it across to the other side and stood gazing back in horror at the heads of those bobbing on the waters, drowning in the middle of a river which in the spring sunshine looked so gentle and benign.

This was the final wreckage of Imperial Russia, the debris and detritus of an Empire that, in the end, could not save itself or protect its own citizens. This was like the sinking of a great ocean liner, or the wreck of a fabulous imperial yacht, where security was an illusion and overweening confidence was tragically misplaced. In this remote south-western corner of the former Empire, the final drama of Romanov Russia was being played out.

Eventually, a few fishing boats appeared from the Romanian side of the river, but this was too late for the many who had long since perished in the water. Some of those that still possessed money or jewels waited for the fishing boats and managed to buy their passage across to the other side of the river. Others were then robbed as they reached dry land and what they had believed to be safety.

My grandparents had decided that they would not risk their lives, or their children's lives, trying to swim across the river. Neither could they afford to pay the extortionate fares demanded by the fishermen. They sat quietly on the riverbank waiting and watching. It would not be long before the Cheka arrived to do their regular sweep of the area and arrest or execute those trying to escape.

It was towards midnight when a small boat appeared. A fisherman from one of the villages near Soroca had spotted the family group huddled together for warmth. He tied up his boat and walked across to them, then asked my grandfather if he could take the family across the river. My grandfather opened his hands in supplication as if to explain that he had nothing to give the fisherman in return. The man stared at him and then, grasping both my grandfather's outstretched hands, he said in a clear and confident voice, 'God will repay in his own way, and in his own time. I require no money from you'.

There was not enough room in the boat for the whole family, so the fisherman tied a rope to one side of the boat and told my grandfather to hold on to this as he ferried them across to Soroca. The moon was high in the night sky as they edged their way across the river. Behind them they could hear gun shots and screams. The Chekist guards had arrived and were executing those refugees who were still waiting to escape.

The water was dark and murky and filled with debris. Bodies brushed against the side of the boat, their heads occasionally bobbing up amongst the weeds. My grandmother saw a beautiful Russian shawl, richly embroidered with red, cream and blue flowers float past her. It reminded her of a precious shawl that she had once owned in her childhood in Vilna, and for a moment she wanted to pick it up and wrap it around her, even though she knew that it would be soaking wet and could provide no warmth or comfort.

A few feet behind the shawl she spotted the body of an attractive young woman, her blonde hair tied in plaits, her arms outstretched in a final gesture of desperate hope. The shawl and the young woman floated on past them, and it seemed to my grandmother that this scene marked the end of every certainty and security that she had ever known. A moment of chance and fortune separated her life from that of the young woman, whose destiny lay now amongst the reeds and mudbanks of the Dniester river.

When they reached the other side of the river, the fisherman insisted that the family come back to his house for food and rest. He could see that they were utterly exhausted, and he did not want them spending the night outside in the cold. They ended up by staying with him for six months. During this time my grandmother fell ill with typhoid fever and lost much of her hearing. In her delirium she conjured up scenes of life that she had known before the Revolution. The baroque churches and cobbled streets of her beloved Vilna, her eccentric aunt in St Petersburg, who insisted on paying for her to become a professional photographer, and her travels to the dark woods and deep blue lakes of the Grand Duchy of Finland.

All these scenes she saw vividly as she lay ill in the fisherman's small wooden cottage on the banks of the Dniester. Every dream ended in a nightmare, though, in which she saw a young woman with a colourful embroidered scarf wrapped around her, crying out and begging to be admitted to the house. When my grandmother awoke there was only the sound of the wind blowing across the river, banging the window shutters noisily against the timber walls of the wooden cottage.

After her recovery, they spent many weeks travelling through Romania and Poland before they finally reached my grandmother's home city of Vilna, where they settled in a large eighteenth-century house used by the family. This stood in the city centre near the former Bishops' Palace. This is where they would stay till the Second World War ripped their lives apart and they once again became refugees, scattered to the various corners of Europe. My grandfather was spared all this. He died in August 1939, on the eve of the German and Soviet invasions of Poland.

Till his dying day, my grandfather never abandoned hope that the Tsars would be restored and that he and his family would then be able to resume the life they had enjoyed in Russia before the Revolution. He would wander the streets of Vilna, tapping on the cobbles with his stick, as he made his way towards the Church of the Holy Spirit: the grandest Orthodox church in the city. He felt an exile and longed to return to his beloved homeland. In the Church, he would light candles to the memory of his sisters and brothers, nephews and nieces, all of them swept into oblivion by the violence of the Revolution and the Civil War. He was never to see any of them again and never knew if any of them had even survived.

It was my father who, escaping Soviet occupation of Eastern Poland in 1946, came to Britain where he settled and married my mother, the youngest daughter of a family then living in Southport, Lancashire. From an early age, my father would tell me stories of our family's lost homelands in Russia, Poland and Lithuania. As I lay safe and secure in my English home, I would dream of snowy landscapes, magical towns with star-spangled cupolas where my ancestors had once lived, and wolves roaming through dark green forests.

Later, as I grew older, I learned about the suffering that my family had experienced as they fled a country in revolutionary turmoil, about the pain and loss of war and exile, and a sense of never quite belonging. On my father's side I needed to go back three generations before I could find any sense of stability or continuity. Both my father and grandfather had lost their homelands.

I tried hard to imagine what it must have been like to flee the country where you had grown up and where you had confidently expected that you would spend the rest of your life. My grandfather was over fifty years old when he decided to flee Moscow. He had had a long and successful career in the Tsarist imperial administration and would have had the prospect of a comfortable retirement ahead of him. Instead, he ended his time in Russia crouching on the banks of a fast-flowing river, fearing death by execution or drowning.

I found myself thinking more and more about Imperial Russia; what had caused its collapse and the impact that this had had on the millions of people who believed it was their home, somewhere they would always belong. They never imagined for a moment that they would one day become refugees, without shelter, sustenance or support.

Here I am, a British citizen, with a grandfather who was born a subject of the Russian Empire and had always imagined that his descendants would live and breathe the same air he did and love the country that he so admired. The Russian revolution changed this forever, as it did for so many citizens of the former Romanov lands.

As I reflected more and more on my family's history, I became increasingly intrigued by Tsarist Russia and its complex and often difficult relationship with Britain. It seemed to me that in this lay the seeds of much of the distrust and suspicion that still colours the partnership between the two countries until the present day.

This book is an attempt to bring together two important themes for me. It is an exploration of the historical relationship between Britain and Imperial Russia during 300 years of Romanov rule, but it is also a personal quest, in that it unites two parts of my own family history and background. As I reflected on the tragic sequence of events that had brought the Romanovsky and Dunn families together, hitherto separated by thousands of miles and completely different cultures and societies, I became fascinated by the fraught relationship that had developed between Imperial Russia and Britain and may have inadvertently led to the collapse of the Tsarist Empire.

2

A tumultuous relationship

In many ways, there was much that could have made the two countries close friends and allies. In the early years of the relationship there were no obvious areas of competition or rivalry. The two countries did not share any land borders and neither sought any territorial, maritime or trade expansion at the expense of the other.

A growing sense of mistrust began to emerge in the eighteenth century but it was another hundred years before it reached its full expression, when Russia and Britain found themselves at war in the Crimea over the decaying Ottoman Empire. This was the only time in their history when the two countries were engaged in a direct military conflict. A growing suspicion of each other's ambitions in Persia and Central Asia clouded the relationship throughout most of Queen Victoria's reign.

These events in themselves do not explain the negative ways in which Russia and Britain viewed each other. Both countries had far more difficult relationships with their immediate neighbours, and these might reasonably have been expected to overshadow the tensions that developed between Russia and Britain during the era of the Romanovs.

This was a thwarted friendship. At every turn, what could have been one of the most powerful alliances of the nineteenth century was destroyed before it could produce any tangible results. Paradoxically, this was also the period when there was a growing fascination with each other's cultures and societies. There was a huge admiration in Russia for British industrial and engineering achievements, literature and democratic values. In Britain there was an appetite to explore the expanding Russian Empire in the east, a land where British investment was creating new opportunities for trade and business partnerships. At the same time, Russian literature, music, theatre and ballet began to exert a powerful influence on the British cultural imagination.

All this was positive and perhaps could have forged the basis for a better understanding between the two countries. However, other forces were at work and these would create a much more negative dynamic in the relationship. For most of the nineteenth century, apart from a few brief years during the Napoleonic Wars, it was as though Russia and Britain constantly misinterpreted and misunderstood each other's motives and ambitions.

Amongst the British ruling class, there was a genuine fear that Russia wanted to seize India and would attempt to control countries like Afghanistan and Persia as an important step towards realising this plan. Fear of Russian ambitions was also fuelled at a popular level, by a growing dislike of Romanov autocracy and its increasingly repressive actions.

From 1830-31, insurgents rose against the Tsarist authorities in those areas of Poland that were under Russian rule. The Polish uprising was brutally suppressed after nearly a year of bitter fighting and thousands of Poles fled into exile, many coming to Britain. Here indignation at the treatment of the Poles fuelled a growing hostility towards the Romanovs. As the century progressed, this combined with a growing resentment of the Tsarist persecution of liberals and intellectuals, and the news of the vicious pogroms launched against the Jews. All these events together created a toxic image of a Tsarist regime that was fundamentally at odds with the values of Victorian Britain. By the 1840s, the caricature of the aggressive Russian Bear had been born, a tangible symbol of this mistrust.

In 1854, relations between Britain and Russia reached their lowest ever point, when the two countries found themselves locked in a bitter and destructive war in the Crimea. This conflict seared itself into the memory of both nations and created an atmosphere of hostility and suspicion that lasted for decades.

It was as a result of this growing climate of hostility towards the Romanovs in Britain, that Russian radicals and revolutionaries were able to find a safe refuge in cities like London. Men like Herzen, Bakunin, Kropotkin, Lenin and many of their followers all spent time in Britain and were able to publish and promote their views to their compatriots back in Russia. The British authorities tolerated or even welcomed them, and they were largely left unmolested, so long as they did not cause any trouble for Britain.

To the Romanovs, and to those Russians who supported the imperial regime, the British position was inexplicable and fuelled fears that Britain was engaged in a subversive campaign to weaken and destroy the Tsarist Empire from within. There was considerable alarm in Russia about British ambitions towards the Ottoman Empire and Central Asia. The British had a reputation in Russia for betraying their friends and allies, and British secret agents were widely suspected to be operating inside Russia to the detriment of the regime. There were rumours that they had even been involved in the murder of Tsar Paul, because of his plans to invade India with Napoleon.

The Romanov regime had never had any compunction in settling scores with its opponents, even if they were living beyond the borders of their homeland. Russian revolutionaries and opponents of the Romanovs living in Britain were therefore seen as legitimate targets. The British authorities may have decided to give these people sanctuary and refuge but in the eyes of the Tsarist authorities these were people who had betrayed their country and were therefore to be discredited, silenced and eliminated where possible.

Thus began a Tsarist campaign of infiltration and subterfuge against Russian revolutionary circles in Britain, that culminated in anarchist-inspired attacks in Tottenham and the East End of London. This febrile atmosphere of political terror and secret police activity roused popular opinion against Russian political refugees, but also against the Russian secret police and the Russian regime.

In 1907 something remarkable and unexpected happened. Russia and Britain signed an agreement to cooperate over Persia, Tibet and Afghanistan. This was the beginning of a new understanding between the two countries that would reach its greatest flowering during the Russian imperial visit to the Isle of Wight in August 1909. For the next ten years, Britain and Russia were close allies, bound together by a fear of Germany and then by their military alliance during the First World War.

During this period, which lasted until the Revolution of 1917, there was a genuine respect and a growing affection between the two countries. It seemed that the misunderstandings that had characterised their relationship during the previous century might finally be over. In Britain, there was huge sympathy and fascination with the new Russia that was starting to emerge. In Russia, people hoped that that the alliance with Britain might herald the start of an era of democracy, and a more liberal century might be within reach.

The Revolution and the Civil War, followed by the murder of the Romanovs in 1918, brought this brief period of friendship to a brutal end. The alliance between Britain and Russia did not survive the creation of the new Soviet State. In the turmoil of these years, there was also a family betrayal. The Romanovs, who had so openly celebrated their ties with the British royal family at Cowes in 1909, were later denied refuge by King George V, a ruler who had been their ally and in whom they had placed their trust.

It was a supreme irony that as the Russian royal family visited the Isle of Wight and celebrated what seemed to be a new era of friendship between the two countries, the political ideologies which would eventually destroy the Romanovs had already been nurtured and promoted by the liberal atmosphere of Victorian Britain. Opponents of the regime had been given the freedom to develop the ideas which would one day lead to the overthrow of Russia's 300-year old imperial dynasty.

The relationship between Imperial Russia and Britain was never an easy one. There were genuine and well-founded grievances and fears on both sides. There were misunderstandings and frequent misinterpretations. Despite all this, there were also periods when the two countries found themselves in step with each other, and these moments produced a brief flowering of friendship and trust - an indicator of what might have been, had events in the twentieth century taken a different direction. As part of this relationship, the Isle of Wight, a small island off the south coast of England, played a fascinating and curious role. This role is worth exploring as part of the wider Anglo-Russian story. Both the imperial family and Russia's revolutionaries are part of this tale and together contributed to putting the Isle of Wight at the centre of the Romanov relationship with Britain in the nineteenth and early twentieth centuries.

Places on the Isle of Wight associated with the Romanovs

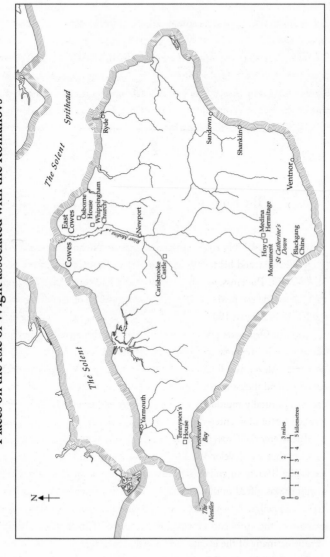

3

The Romanovs and the Isle of Wight

On Saturday 7 July 2018, a memorial cross to Nicholas II, the last Tsar of Russia, and his family was unveiled in East Cowes on the Isle of Wight. The cross, weighing seven and a half tons, stands in Jubilee Park, alongside the road that the Romanovs travelled on their final visit to the Island in August 1909.

Russian Orthodox priests offered prayers at the unveiling ceremony. These were in memory of Tsar Nicholas II, the Tsarina Alexandra, the Tsarevich Alexei, the four Grand Duchesses, Olga, Maria, Tatiana and Anastasia and their maternal aunt, Grand Duchess Elizabeth. All of them had been brutally murdered a hundred years earlier in July 1918, as the Russian Revolution entered a new and deadly phase.

The Memorial Cross by the Russian sculptor, Elena Bezborodova, was a project that was developed and funded by the Grand Duchess Elizabeth Romanov Society in collaboration with the people of East Cowes. The sculpture was gifted to the town by the Society. In return, the people and Town Council of East Cowes made a financial contribution towards the erection of the cross and provided the space for it in Jubilee Park while organising many of the events linked to its unveiling.

The cross was unveiled by the Lord Lieutenant of the Isle of Wight,

General Sir Martin White, and by Prince Rostislav Romanov who was representing the Romanov Family Association. A choir of nuns from the Convent of St Elizabeth in Minsk intoned Orthodox hymns beloved by the imperial family. A gentle and evocative rendering of *Somewhere over the Rainbow* was performed by a group of singers from Wight Harmony, a barbershop harmony club.

The Union Jack and Imperial Russian flags fluttered together over the assembled crowd. Verses of the Tsarist anthem *God Save the Tsar* drew the memorial service to a close, the first time it had been sung in public on the Isle of Wight since the visit of August 1909.

The Island lies only two miles from the English coast but can seem strangely remote, as though inhabiting a different sense of time and space. For centuries, it was the last glimpse of England that many travellers had, as their ships from Portsmouth and Southampton sailed past its white chalk cliffs on their way out to the open seas.

For much of the nineteenth century, the Isle of Wight lay at the heart of the British Empire and the royal residence at Osborne House was the apex of an imperial world. It was to Osborne that Queen Victoria invited Prime Ministers, Kings, Emperors, Princes and Prelates to discuss the major issues of the day. The Island was also where leading writers, artists, and politicians gathered. In the small seaside town of Ventnor, Russian radicals debated and argued. In 1909 this was where the last Tsar and Tsarina, trapped in a claustrophobic world of security and imperial pomp, made their final British visit.

The countryside is still as they would all have known it, a gentle and pastoral place with small towns and villages dotting the landscape. There are rolling hills and wooded valleys, sandy beaches and rocky chalk cliff bays. The river Medina, the longest river on the Island, flows for eleven miles from its source on St Catherine's Down to its mouth on the Solent, where it meets the sea between the twin towns of East Cowes and Cowes.

The history and distinct identities of these two towns are a source of bemusement and controversy to both visitors and residents alike. Although only separated by a narrow stretch of water, they reflect very different and at times antagonistic cultures. In the nineteenth century, East Cowes became a centre of royalty and industry, while Cowes began to develop as a marine and yachting town, its sporting pre-eminence confirmed when the Royal Yacht Squadron moved its headquarters there. To the present day there exists a covert rivalry between the two towns, which is puzzling to outsiders but perfectly natural to those who live on the Island.

Alongside East Cowes and Cowes, the Isle of Wight is now chiefly known for its coastal resorts, towns such as Ryde, Shanklin, Ventnor, and Yarmouth, which were developed in the reign of Queen Victoria, a period when the Island became hugely fashionable due to its close association with royalty. In earlier times, the Island was a major part of England's defence system and castles and forts were built to guard against foreign attack. Carisbrooke Castle, near the county town of Newport, remains the finest castle on the Island but there are forts all along the north coast.

The Island was first settled in Roman times, and from the early sixth century became a Jutish kingdom called Wihtland, Isle of Spirits, with Kings from the House of Wihtwara as its rulers. The Island's links with English royalty were in evidence right from the beginning. The later Wessex kings, particularly the line of King Alfred the Great in the ninth century, could trace their ancestry back to the Wihtwara Kings. Arwald, the last pagan ruler of Wihtland was killed in the year 686, resisting an invasion by King Caedwalla of Wessex. The death of kings has a long association with the Island's story. Caedwalla was acting under orders from Bishop Wilfred, a churchman responsible for converting large parts of Southern England to Christianity.

The Normans invaded the Island soon after their victory over the Anglo-Saxons at the battle of Hastings in 1066. The Norman dynasty of the de Redvers then ruled the Island for around 200 years but in 1293 the last of the family, Countess Isabella de Fortibus, agreed to sell the Island to King Edward I. From that date on, the Isle of Wight became a royal possession.

During the reign of King Henry VIII, the Island was integrated into the overall defence system for the south coast of England. This was intended to be part of the protection against French attacks, particularly on the port towns of Portsmouth and Southampton. Fortifications were constructed on the Island in Cowes and Yarmouth. In 1545 Henry witnessed the greatest maritime tragedy of his reign while on a visit to Portsmouth. This was the sinking of his flagship, *Mary Rose*, which capsized in the Solent within sight of the Isle of Wight,with the loss of over 400 sailors and soldiers.

In November 1647, an episode occurred on the Island which changed the course of British history forever. The English Civil War was reaching its bitter end. King Charles I had been defeated and was imprisoned in Hampton Court Palace. A plan was devised for him to escape from there and head to France. The escape did not go according to plan and he only reached as far as the Isle of Wight.

The King threw himself on the mercy of the Governor, Robert Hammond, whom he believed to be sympathetic to the Royalist cause. Hammond, however, did not turn out to be a friend and Charles was imprisoned in Carisbrooke Castle near the Island's capital of Newport. He was to spend a year on the Island before being taken back to London. In January 1649 Charles was put on trial and executed outside his Banqueting House at Whitehall Palace. This was not to be the last time that a royal ruler destined to be murdered by his own people would visit the Island. 260 years later in 1909, the last Tsar of Russia would step ashore on a final visit to the Isle of Wight, nine years before his own execution in 1918.

Until the beginning of the nineteenth century, the Island was chiefly associated with military defence and with small-scale farming and rural living. However, this began to change as seaside towns became more fashionable in England. This was due to a growing appreciation of the health benefits of living by the sea, and to the influence of the Prince Regent. Through his patronage of seaside towns such as Brighton, the socially ambitious now all clamoured to spend their summers in resorts on the coast.

The architect of the flamboyant Brighton Pavilion was Sir John Nash, who is also justifiably famous for redesigning much of early nineteenth-century London, in a style of architecture that we now call 'Regency'. Nash spent his final years living in East Cowes Castle on the Isle of Wight, and it was during this period that the first resorts began to appear on the

Island. Nash entertained the Prince Regent and other royal guests at his gothic-towered residence in East Cowes. This was the impetus required for fashionable tourism to begin on the Island.

In 1815, the social status of the Island was greatly enhanced by the founding of the Yacht Club in London, which agreed to make Cowes its yachting home. Membership was restricted to those who owned a vessel of at least ten tons, thus ensuring that only the 'best gentlemen' could become members. The Prince Regent was elected a member in 1817. When he became King George IV in 1820, it was renamed the Royal Yacht Club. A few years later, the Club began organising an annual sailing regatta. This became popularly known as the Cowes Regatta, one of the most prestigious yachting regattas in the world.

In 1833, the Club was renamed the Royal Yacht Squadron by King William IV, and from 1858 Cowes Castle, following extensive renovations, became its permanent headquarters. Prior to this, meetings of the members had been held at hotels in East Cowes and Cowes. In 1909, Tsar Nicholas II was formally invited to become a member of the Royal Yacht Squadron. On the evening of 4 August, he was formerly inducted into the Club at a lavish dinner hosted by King Edward VII on board the Royal Yacht *Victoria and Albert III*, while it was moored in the Cowes Roads.

In parallel to the rise of the Island's social reputation and status, new shipping industries started to establish themselves on the Island. These were encouraged by the boom in demand for yachts and naval vessels. Due to the links with the Royal Navy, shipbuilding had been a long tradition there. In 1802, the Kent shipbuilder Thomas White decided to move to Cowes and over the next twenty-five years, he developed a series of major shipyards along both banks of the River Medina.

His grandson, John Samuel White, continued to invest in the shipyards and ensured that East Cowes became the one of the largest construction centres for small to medium-sized vessels anywhere in the world. In 1846, Samuel White was commissioned to build a new imperial yacht for Tsar Nicholas I. This was named the *Victoria*, in honour of the Queen.

By the mid-nineteenth century, the Isle of Wight was moving towards its period of greatest glory. The arrival of Queen Victoria and Prince

Albert in 1844 propelled the Island directly into the centre of British imperial affairs. The Queen had always liked the Island, having spent holidays there as child. She now decided that she would move there on a more permanent basis. In June 1845, the royal couple bought Osborne House, a modest three-storey Georgian house, standing in a secluded spot overlooking the Solent in East Cowes. Over the next six years, between 1845 and 1851, the house was completely rebuilt by Prince Albert in the style of an Italian Renaissance palace.

Victoria adored Osborne and the Isle of Wight. She spent time there whenever she could, usually between three and four months a year. After Albert's death in 1861, it became a very special retreat and her favourite royal residence in England. She never liked Windsor Castle, describing it as 'gloomy' and she longed for the 'cheerful and unpalace like rooms at Osborne House'.

The Island was now the beating heart of the British Empire. If the Queen adored the Isle of Wight so too did many of her subjects. They arrived on the Island in their thousands and stimulated the growth of seaside resorts in Ventnor, Ryde, Shanklin and Cowes.

Charles Dickens rented a house in Bonchurch in 1849, which he compared favourably with 'rainy Paris, dirty Naples and feverish New York'. It was a place where he declared he would be happy to die. He is thought to have written his novel *David Copperfield* while staying in the village. Alfred, Lord Tennyson, who was Britain's Poet Laureate for over forty years, spent long periods of his life living on the Island, in a house that he had bought at the foot of Freshwater Down. Julia Margaret Cameron, a pioneer woman photographer, moved to the Island in 1860 and established her studio at Dimbola Lodge, close to where her friend Tennyson was living. She became famous for her aesthetic portraits, and Victorian celebrities flocked to her studio to be photographed in a variety of artistic costumes and historic styles.

The Russian imperial link to the Isle of Wight stretches back to 1698 when Peter the Great recruited his Chief Naval Carpenter from Cowes, but it was particularly strong in the years between 1847 and 1918. During this period members of the Romanov family visited the Island on a regular basis, both for private and official purposes. Outside Russia's borders this was one of the places where they came most frequently and which, in many ways, still has the most vivid associations with them. For the Romanovs, this became their English Isle.

Imperial Russian visitors to the Isle of Wight included Grand Duchess Maria Alexandrovna (the only daughter of Alexander II), Alexander III and his wife Maria Feodorovna, Tsar Nicholas II, his wife Alexandra and their children, and Grand Duchess Elizabeth, sister to Tsarina Alexandra. Victoria, the elder sister of the Tsarina and her husband, Prince Louis of Battenberg, lived on the Island during the First World War. The last imperial visit in August 1909 was particularly poignant. This was the apogee of the Anglo-Russian alliance, but it was a visit conducted in the shadow of growing security threats to the Tsar and his family and concerns about Germany's increasing power. The Romanovs were one of the most powerful ruling dynasties in the world, but fear of assassination and terrorist attacks stalked their daily existence.

Despite all this, their visit to the Isle of Wight was a chance to experience a rare moment of normality, and for the Tsar's children, it was an opportunity to explore another world. The memory of those summer days on the Island in the English Channel must have often returned to them in those dark days of war and revolution after 1914.

Osborne House, the residence of Queen Victoria, was the focus of Romanov family visits over the years. However, other places on the Island also evoke the memory of Russia's last ruling family. These include Barton Manor, where Nicholas and his family were entertained by King Edward VII in August 1909, the royal church of St Mildred's at Whippingham, where the Tsarina's sister, Victoria, lies buried and where there is a memorial to the Imperial family.

Cowes is where two of the Romanov Grand Duchesses made their first independent shopping trip. It is also home to the Royal Yacht Squadron, which counted two Tsars and a Russian Grand Duke amongst its distinguished members. Across the Medina River from Cowes stands East Cowes, where Victoria, the Tsarina's sister, lived in Kent House. Nearby there is Jubilee Park with its recently erected memorial to the

Romanov family. On St Catherine's Down, in the south-east of the Island, stands a monument commemorating Tsar Alexander I's visit to Britain in 1814. This was erected by a British merchant called Michael Hoy who had established strong trading links with Russia.

On the Solent, the imperial yacht *Shtandart* rode at anchor for four days in August 1909. This is also where the Spithead Review of 1909 took place. It was the last major British Naval Review before the First World War and it was here that Tsar Nicholas II toured the line of battleships and destroyers and took the salute of the British Navy.

The Romanovs were not the only Russians to spend time on the Isle of Wight. Throughout the latter half of the nineteenth century, a stream of Russian visitors made their way across the Solent to enjoy the peace and serenity of the Island. Many of these were curious visitors, eager to see the Island with which their imperial rulers had established a connection. But there were others who saw the Island as a refuge and a haven. Amongst these were Alexander Herzen, described as the father of Russian Socialism, and Ivan Turgenev, who was inspired to write his book *Fathers and Sons* while staying in Ventnor.

Two men who, despite not being Russian themselves, were to change the course of Russian history, also visited the Isle of Wight during this period. Karl Marx and Friedrich Engels both spent time in Ryde and Ventnor and Marx completed the final volumes of his epic thesis on capitalism, *Das Kapital,* while living on the Island.

If East Cowes was the Imperial Russian centre on the Island, Ventnor on the south-east coast became its radical alternative. Within a few miles of each other, two different visions of Russia co-existed on the same English island. One basked in the glory and power of Empire. The other planned its overthrow.

PART

II

THE EARLY ROMANOVS
AND BRITAIN:

Inspiration & Disenchantment

1613-1800

4

Peter the Great: The ship building Tsar

In September 2015, an elegantly crafted wooden frigate sailed into Cowes harbour after a voyage from St Petersburg. It was the Russian youth training ship *Shtandart,* which was on a good will visit around Europe. On board were thirty young sailors and ten officers. A large Russian tricolour in blue, white and red fluttered proudly from its stern.

The *Shtandart* is a replica of the first frigate in Russia's Baltic fleet, constructed in 1703 on the orders of Tsar Peter I. It was built by a Dutch shipwright, Vybe Gyrens, under the Tsar's personal supervision. Like the original ship, it has three masts, and an overall length of 113 feet. The design of the first *Shtandart* was heavily influenced by Dutch and English shipbuilding traditions. It was in England that Tsar Peter I, more famously known as Peter the Great, learned many of his seafaring skills. His *Shtandart* was broken up in 1727 and plans to build a replica were never fulfilled until 1994, when a small group of Russian sailing enthusiasts embarked on a project to recreate the flagship of the Russian Imperial Navy. This was the ship that arrived in Cowes in 2015.

The name *Shtandart* was never forgotten during the years of Romanov rule in Russia. In 1909, Tsar Nicholas II and his family steamed into Cowes on board the imperial yacht *Shtandart.* It was therefore appropriate

Isle and Empires

that over a hundred years later, a Russian ship bearing the same name as the Tsar's yacht and Peter the Great's frigate should arrive in the Isle of Wight. Peter the Great was the first Romanov ruler to visit Britain in 1698 and up to that point, contact between the two countries had been very limited. This was soon to change.

The first Romanovs had ascended the throne in February 1613, when Michael Feodorovich Romanov was offered the Monomakh's Cap - the symbol of Russian autocracy - by the Zemsky Sobor, an assembly composed of representatives drawn from the church authorities and the noble and landowning classes. When Michael received this news, he was in hiding with his mother in the Ipatiev Monastery in Kostroma, two hundred miles from Moscow. He was initially very reluctant to take on the responsibility of becoming a Tsar.

Russia had descended into chaos following the death of Tsar Feodor Ivanovich in 1598 and large parts of the country were under Polish and Lithuanian occupation. It was a period known as 'The Time of Troubles' and by offering the throne to Michael Romanov the Zemsky Sobor hoped to restore legitimacy to the crown and order to the country.

The new Tsar had a tenuous link through his great aunt Anastasia Romanov to the Rurikid dynasty which had ruled the Grand Duchy of Muscovy for many centuries. The Romanov family were chiefly known as being one of the most prominent noble or 'boyar' families in the Grand Duchy. Originally the Romanovs had Lithuanian and Belarusian roots.

Prior to Peter the Great's visit to the West, contact between Russia and Britain scarcely existed. The origins of the relationship stretch back to 1551, when Richard Chancellor, Sebastian Cabot and Sir Hugh Willoughby founded the exotically named *Mystery and Company of Merchant Adventurers for the Discovery of Regions, Dominions, Islands and Places Unknown.* Their plan was to open a north-eastern sea passage to China.

On 10 May 1553, a small fleet of three ships left London under the command of Chancellor and Willoughby. A storm separated the vessels and Willoughby sailed towards Murmansk in Northern Russia where his ship was trapped in the ice and he and his entire crew perished. Their frozen bodies were discovered by fishermen several years later.

28

Chancellor had more success and eventually reached the shores of the White Sea. At this time Russia had no access to the Baltic, and the White Sea region had just been added to the dominions of the Tsar. Although he was over 600 miles from Moscow, Chancellor received an invitation from Ivan the Terrible to make a call on him. This first meeting between a Russian Tsar and an English merchant was a major success. Chancellor immediately spotted opportunities to trade in wool and furs. The Tsar in return was keen to develop links with England and offered trading rights and privileges to English merchants who wished to do business with Russia. He also sent an invitation of marriage to Queen Elizabeth I, which was politely declined.

In 1555, the *Mystery and Company of Merchant Adventurers* was re-chartered as the *Muscovy Company*. The Grand Duchy of Muscovy, with its capital in Moscow, had been the name by which Russia was known until 1547 when Ivan the Terrible assumed the title of Tsar of Russia. In 1556 Chancellor sailed back to England with Osip Nepeya, the first Russian ambassador to the English court. The *Muscovy Company* would survive until the Russian Revolution in 1917, although it was to have a chequered history, particularly in its earlier years.

English merchants now had access to Russian markets and trade became the foundation on which the relationship between the two countries would flourish. In 1649, Tsar Alexei I, appalled by the execution of King Charles I at the close of the English Civil War, expelled all English merchants from his domains. This was a major setback for English trade with Russia. Although some privileges were restored in 1660, following the return of King Charles II to the throne, Dutch merchants had taken advantage of the absence of the *Muscovy Company* to strengthen their control of the Russian market. The Tsar had also grown suspicious of attempts by the English to exclude other European countries from trade with Russia. The mistrust between Russia and England has long roots.

In 1682, Peter Alexeyevich Romanov, popularly known as Peter the Great, was proclaimed Tsar at the age of ten on the death of his half-brother, Fyodor III. Peter's reign was to mark the emergence of Russia as a major European power and laid the basis for a radical shift towards creating a more westernised economic and social culture. This was to have mixed results and the split soul of Russia, torn between its Byzantine and Eastern traditions and its need to adapt to Western economic and cultural norms, would haunt the country's development for centuries to come.

In 1697, Peter decided that Russia would despatch a Grand Embassy to the West. Its mission was primarily diplomatic and was aimed at strengthening the alliance against the Ottomans, as well as building an anti-Swedish coalition which would draw in support from Prussia, Poland, Denmark and possibly England and the Dutch Republic. But it also had another important role. The Grand Embassy was part of Peter's plan to modernise Russia and open the country up to new ideas and new technologies. He decided that he would travel incognito under the pseudonym 'Peter Mikhailov', mainly because he did not want to be burdened with all the protocols of state visits.

This attempt to disguise his identity was only partially effective and may even have been some sort of theatrical ruse. Whenever it suited him, Peter would make his presence known. He enjoyed switching between his different identities and this allowed him the freedom to be the Tsar when he felt this would help him, or opt out when it did not.

In March 1697, the Grand Embassy left Moscow, led by a Swiss soldier, Franz Lefort. He was accompanied by a team of two hundred and fifty people, including pages, dwarfs, servants, trumpeters, musicians, soldiers and physicians. There were also thirty-five Russian volunteers, whose aim was to study shipbuilding and navigation in the Dutch Republic. During this period, the Dutch were considered to be the leading maritime nation in Europe and the vessels of the Dutch East India Company, known as the *Vereenigde Oostindische Compagnie (VOC)*, dominated the shipping lanes between the Netherlands, the Cape of Good Hope, and the Spice Islands of Southeast Asia.

Peter himself was one of these volunteers and carried a letter which stated, 'I am a student, and I require teachers'. This was a truthful statement of his intention to bring back skills and technical knowledge to Russia. He recognised that Russia had fallen behind other European countries. It was viewed as a country that was primitive both at a social and economic level. Peter was determined to change this perspective and make Russia a modern European power. He also had his eyes on the Baltic Sea, which he recognised as being key to Russia's expansion. He needed to transform the Baltic from a Swedish lake into a Russian lake and to do this he had to build a fleet of ships which met the latest naval designs and were equipped with modern fire power.

The Grand Embassy spent most of its time in Brandenburg, Hannover and finally in Holland. There, the Tsar spent four and a half months studying shipbuilding in the dockyards of the VOC, as well as meeting with senior Dutch officials and merchants. He was very impressed by the skills of the Dutch and in later years would claim that he learned the theory of shipbuilding in England but the practical implementation of it in Holland.

In January 1698, Peter received a private invitation from King William III to visit England. During his three months in England Peter worked in the dockyards in Deptford. He proved himself to be an enthusiastic pupil and took a keen interest in English shipbuilding techniques, particularly in the design and mathematics of naval design. He also achieved a rumbustious reputation during his stay in Deptford.

Peter was a huge bear of a man, over six and a half feet tall, and enjoyed practical jokes and noisy entertainments. He had rented a house from the diarist, John Evelyn, which he proceeded to systematically destroy during his wilder bouts of manic fun and drunken revelries. One of his favourite games was to be driven through a hedge in a wheelbarrow. On other occasions he would put his fists through the wooden wainscot panelling of his rented accommodation.

Evelyn was so shocked by the state of his house that he formally called in Sir Christopher Wren, King William's Surveyor to 'view how miserably the Tsar of Muscovy has left my house'. Wren's account of *Goods that are lost, broken and damaged* included 'Three wheelbarrows, broke and lost. Eight feather beds, eight bolsters, and twelve blankets very much dirtied and spoiled'. This was apart from the significant damage to the fabric and brickwork of the house. Evelyn was advised by the King not to bother to pursue any claims. While Peter was a diligent pupil of naval shipbuilding, he was clearly the tenant from hell.

What has been described by some observers as an oddly proportioned and somewhat disturbing statue of Peter the Great, his favourite court dwarf, and his travelling throne now stands in Deptford. It is a gift from the people of Russia and was presented in 1998, on the three hundredth anniversary of the Tsar's visit. The figures are about two times normal life size and are arrayed in rich court costumes. If he were to return, Peter would undoubtedly enjoy this outsized and somewhat bizarre depiction of him and his dwarf companion. He was never a man for observing traditional conventions and always sought to push the boundaries in terms of knowledge, experience, and personal behaviours.

William III and the Tsar established an easy-going friendship. They used to meet regularly at Kensington Palace and often dined together at Lambeth Palace. In February 1698, Peter decided that he would like to commission a painting of himself and present it as a gift to the King. He asked Sir Godfrey Kneller to depict him dressed in a full set of armour, with a white and gold ermine-lined cloak slung across his shoulder, embossed with the double headed eagles of the Romanovs.

The Tsar was a handsome man, a fact which would not have escaped the eye of William III, who had a penchant for good looking young men. The portrait clearly delighted its recipient. William hung it in the Dining Room at Kensington Palace, where he could gaze on what the Russian Ambassador Prince Boris Kurakin described as the 'famed portrait of His Czarish Majesty standing in all his imperial armour and so attractive that I have nowhere seen its equal'.

Peter's voracious and inquisitive interest in his new surroundings took him on visits to the Royal Observatory in Greenwich, to the Royal Society and to Quaker and Anglican Church services. He was elated by his visit to the English Parliament. 'It is good to hear subjects speaking truthfully and openly to their King'. He is reputed to have said on leaving the Parliament building, 'this is what we must learn from the English'. There is no evidence, however, that he ever intended to act on any of these insights.

The one area in which he was inspired to take immediate action was in naval shipbuilding. As a guest of King William III, he made a trip to Portsmouth on 22 March 1698 where he reviewed the English fleet in the Solent, while sailing close to the Isle of Wight. During his visit, Peter carefully noted the number and calibre of the guns of each naval ship, while also studying mock naval battle tactics, logistics and strategies. He was enthralled by what he saw and by the skills displayed by English sailors and naval commanders at sea. By now, East Cowes was already an important centre for the construction of English naval vessels. Joseph Nye was the owner of the main shipyard there. He would go on to become Master Shipbuilder to the Tsar.

In 1696, Nye's Yard, as it became known, had launched a 32-gun battleship HMS *Poole* and this was followed in 1698 by the 48-gun HMS *Jersey*. The shipyard was situated on the eastern shore of the River Medina, close to the Chain ferry which now connects East Cowes and Cowes. Nye was an ambitious man and after hearing about Peter the Great's voyage on the Solent, he travelled up to London, determined to win business from the Tsar. The two men took an immediate liking to one another and so began one of history's most extraordinary friendships, between a Romanov Tsar and an English shipbuilder.

Nye is the only shipbuilder who is mentioned in Peter the Great's financial accounts as receiving money from him on a regular basis. Some have speculated that it was Nye who taught the Tsar the English system of shipbuilding. In June 1698, he moved to Russia, where he joined another English shipbuilder, John Deane, in Voronezh. The two men were commissioned to start building ships of the line for the new Imperial Russian fleet.

In a letter that he wrote from Voronezh, Nye stated that the Tsar preferred the English style of shipbuilding over that of the Dutch. 'His Majesty most admires and is ever praising of our navy' he wrote in his fulsome, flowing style. English shipbuilding was based on scientific mathematical principles which meant that once the principles were understood, it was easy to follow a standard design and construction blueprint. The Dutch shipbuilders had more flair and style, but their skills and knowledge were more individual and less easy to replicate.

Nye, Deane and the Tsar were now close friends and spent a lot of time in each other's company, often locked into heavy drinking sessions.

The English Ambassador to Russia wrote that the two shipbuilders were highly respected and 'caressed by the Tsar and consequently by all the great men of the Kingdom; they partake of his diversions, and on festival days sit at his table when persons of the best quality are bound to stand and wait'. Another report stated, 'their salaries are large and punctually paid. They eat in private and the Tsar hardly goes anywhere or takes any diversion, but they accompany him'. Clearly Peter did not want to lose his English shipbuilders but there was also a genuine friendship between the three men, a mutual respect based on their love and passion for ships.

In 1699, Nye was joined by Richard Cozens, another English shipwright. Deane had died of exposure to the cold during a particularly bitter phase of the Russian winter and Cozens was recruited as his replacement. In 1711, Nye and Cozens moved to St Petersburg, where they worked on building a Russian fleet that would challenge the Swedes for mastery of the Baltic. The Tsar and Nye were often seen deep in conversation as they wandered through the shipyards of St Petersburg, reviewing progress on the construction of the new fleet. The two men wrote frequently to one another, even when the Tsar was absent from St Petersburg.

The knowledge and expertise that Russian ship builders gained from Nye and his colleagues was to prove formative in shaping the new Russian navy. A new generation of Russian master shipwrights soon emerged. Peter also gave orders to recruit more seamen and shipbuilders from England, many of them from Portsmouth and the Isle of Wight. Several of the ships built in Russia in the first half of the eighteenth century bore English names such as *Britannia*, *Portsmouth* and *Devonshire*. Most of the teachers at the new Russian naval academy in Moscow were English.

During his stay in England, King William III presented the Tsar with the *Royal Transport*, one of the most modern ships in the English navy. It became a blueprint for future Russian naval shipbuilding design. The ship was altered and refitted especially for Peter, and it was endowed with additional carved decorations covered in gold leaf.

Peter's time in England confirmed him as a strong Anglophile. Following his return to Russia in 1698, relations with England - known as the Kingdom of Great Britain after its union with Scotland in 1707 - were generally positive. In this early period there were no major issues of disagreement between the two countries. British merchants were encouraged to settle in St Petersburg. The development of Russia's naval fleet depended strongly on British knowledge and skills.

The Great Northern War of 1700-1721 between Russia and Sweden slowly began to change things, as the British government woke up to the expansionist nature of Peter's ambitions. During the war Sweden eventually lost all its territorial possessions along the Eastern Baltic coast, including eastern Finland, and the whole of Estonia and Livonia. In 1703, Peter the Great began building his new capital of St Petersburg on lands previously occupied by the Swedes. This was a major development and confirmed Russia's emergence as both a Baltic and European power. In 1709, the Battle of Poltava, in present day Ukraine, led to Russia defeating the Swedish armies of King Charles XII.

Over the next twelve years, Russian military and naval successes mounted. Britain decided to conclude an alliance with Sweden in August 1719 in order to counter the growing power of Russia. However, this was not backed up by any effective British naval and military support. In 1721, Sweden, under direct threat from a Russian invasion, finally agreed to sign a Peace Treaty at Nystad. This treaty marked the end of Sweden's imperial ambitions and confirmed that a new power had arrived on the Baltic. On 22 October 1721, Peter was proclaimed Emperor of All the Russias. The Tsarist Empire was born.

The new Russian Baltic fleet had been created on the orders of Peter the Great and it played a key role in the victory over Sweden and in the establishment of Russian imperial power. By 1745, the Russian navy had over 130 sailing vessels, including thirty-six ships of the line and nine frigates. There were also 396 oared vessels. Peter's visit to England in 1698 had marked the beginning of this great development.

As Peter the Great gazed at the splendour and might of the English fleet, cruising off the Isle of Wight, it is easy to imagine how this would have inspired him to dream of building a fleet that would rival those of other European powers. In many ways, the origins of his naval ambitions were born in the waters of the Solent and in the shipyards of East Cowes and Deptford.

There was now mounting concern in Britain at the strength of the new Russian navy in the Baltic. The role played by English shipbuilders such as Nye was cited as a prime reason for this. Parliament and the British government viewed the quality and strength of the Tsar's fleet as a growing threat to Britain's seafaring interests. In 1719, Parliament decided to act. Legislation was passed which outlawed skilled British artisans, particularly shipbuilders from the Isle of Wight and Deptford, from going abroad to work for foreign powers and demanded that those already abroad should immediately return to Britain.

The Russians were furious. The British Ambassador in St Petersburg was summoned to a meeting with Tsarist officials and told that this was an ill-judged move. 'This step is now too late, the Tsar's own subjects being able to build ships, and within time accustom themselves to the Sea likewise'. Although under pressure to return to England, Nye and Cozens decided to remain in Russia and continue with their work.

In 1723, in recognition of the contribution that they had made to developing the new Russian navy, both Nye and Cozens were awarded the titles of Captains-Commodores by Peter the Great. This conferred on them the status of being members of the nobility. Joseph Nye's exalted position at the Tsar's court earned him a leading role in Peter's funeral cortège in 1725. He was regarded as such a close confidante of the Tsar that he was asked to hold one of the strings of the canopy that shielded the coffin of the deceased Emperor. Immediately behind him walked the Empress Catherine, Peter's widow, and Alexander Menshikov, one of the Tsar's closest friends and briefly to become the most powerful man in Russia.

Nye was to remain in Russia for over forty years, only returning to England when he was an old man. In 1737, he was awarded a pension of 500 roubles a year, a princely sum by the standards of those days, in recognition of 'his long and faithful services'. The Isle of Wight shipbuilder, who had helped create the Russian navy, ended his days quietly in Deptford, where he died in 1753. The shipyard that he had founded in Cowes would later be bought up by a Kent shipbuilder, Thomas White, whose family would go on to construct the first imperial yacht for Tsar Nicholas I.

Peter the Great's death in 1725 heralded a period of confusion, and frequent change in the line of succession. Peter's son and heir, Alexei Petrovich, had been murdered in the Peter and Paul Fortress in St Petersburg on the orders of his father. The Tsar's grandson Peter II therefore succeeded him, but died after only three years on the throne, aged fourteen.

Peter II was succeeded by Anna Ivanovna who was the daughter of his half-brother and co-ruler, Ivan V. The Romanov dynasty was febrile and unstable in the first half of the eighteenth century and her accession to the throne brought more uncertainty and confusion to Russia's internal and external affairs. Anna was an eccentric and strong-willed ruler, with flashes of cruel humour that bordered on the sadistic.

Anna's death in 1740 cleared the way for Peter the Great's able daughter, Elizabeth Petrovna, to succeed to the throne, deposing the rightful heir, Ivan VI, great-grandson of the hapless Ivan V. Only two months old at the time, Ivan VI was then imprisoned for over twenty years in a remote fortress on the White Sea in Northern Russia. His identity was hidden and he was eventually murdered in 1764 by his gaolers, at the age of just twenty-three. Such were the perils of having a royal lineage in early Romanov Russia.

The Tsarina Elizabeth's reign witnessed an explosion of architecture, arts and culture, and her court became one of the most glamourous and gilded in the whole of Europe. She presided over all this as a gorgeous butterfly, beautifully elegant, resplendent in silks and satins. It is reputed that she owned more than 15,000 dresses and never wore a dress twice.

It was in her commitment to modernising Russia, and in her foreign wars, that she demonstrated that she was in every way the daughter of Peter the Great. During her reign, Russia reached a new peak of confidence and development.

In 1756, Russia became involved in the Seven Years War. This was triggered by a mistrust of the new Anglo-Prussian alliance and a profound dislike of Frederick the Great. Britain and Russia found themselves on opposing sides for the first time since the Great Northern War. Russia, Austria, Spain, Sweden and France were allies against Britain, Prussia, Portugal and Hannover. This was an eighteenth-century version of a world war, as conflicts erupted across Europe but also in the Americas and India. The Prussian defeat at Kunnersdorf in 1759 was a major victory for Russia and a huge set-back for Frederick the Great.

Ultimately however, Britain, Prussia and their allies were to emerge victorious from the war and this was to change the balance of power both in Europe and around the world. Britain became the pre-eminent European power in India and North America. French domination of Europe would not be revived till the age of Napoleon Bonaparte in the early nineteenth century.

Russia and Britain fought on opposing sides throughout the Seven Years War, but at no point did their armies or navies come into direct conflict. Curiously, the Tsarina herself seems to have harboured a deep affection for Britain. This may have dated back to the memory of the warm welcome that her father had received in England during his visit there in 1698. It was probably also to do with the strong trading and naval links that had grown up between the two countries in the early eighteenth century. Russia had no territorial ambitions in either North America or India. Britain was eager to defeat France, not Russia, in the Seven Years War.

Elizabeth's death in 1761 led to the crown passing to her nephew, who became Tsar Peter III. He was the son of Elizabeth's sister, Anna, who had married Grand Duke Karl Friedrich of Holstein-Gottorp, a small German principality centred around Kiel, near the border with Denmark. Although he only ruled for 186 days before he was deposed and imprisoned, Peter III took some important decisions. He withdrew Russia from the Seven Years War, made peace with Frederick the Great, and introduced a range of domestic reforms such as abolishing the secret police, proclaiming religious freedom and beginning a fight against government corruption. This is a far cry from the black legend of the dissolute, drunken, and incompetent ruler that was created about him in the years immediately following his overthrow. There is no doubt that Peter could be a difficult man and although he was prone to fits of rage and had a hot temper, he was no idiot. He was considered to have a sharp wit as well as being a key observer of people.

These skills, however, did not save him from the coup led by his wife, Princess Sophie of Anhalt-Zerbst, and her lover Grigory Orlov in July 1762. She had taken the name Ekaterina Alexeyevna on her marriage to Peter in 1745, and it was under this name that she was proclaimed Tsarina Catherine II of Russia. This was an audacious power grab by a minor German princess who had absolutely no claim to the Romanov throne, but Peter was unpopular at the Russian court. His pro-Prussian sympathies were suspect. The coup succeeded and Peter III was murdered in mysterious circumstances, eight days after his overthrow.

5

Catherine the Great: art, gardens, and porcelain

atherine's reign lasted thirty-four years and is considered the 'Golden Age' of the Tsarist Empire and Russian nobility. This was the era of the Russian Empire's greatest geographical expansion. In the south, the Crimean Khanate was crushed. Russia colonised the territories of Novorossiya or New Russia along the coasts of the Black Sea and the Azov Sea. Ottoman Turkey found itself in retreat. In the east, Russia started to colonise Alaska, and thus established a foothold in the Americas. This would lead to dreams of a Russian Pacific Empire with colonies on the west coast of America.

It was in the west though that Catherine's ambitions changed the face of eighteenth-century Europe forever. Together with the Prussians and the Austrian Hapsburgs, Catherine embarked on a series of three partitions of the Polish-Lithuanian Commonwealth between 1772 and 1795. These partitions destroyed the country. The 'Golden Republic' of Stefan Batory, Jan Sobieski III, and Augustus the Strong had once been the dominant power in Eastern Europe. In the early seventeenth century it had stretched from the Baltic to the Black Sea. By 1795 it had vanished from the map of Europe. Under Catherine, now given the title of 'The Great', the Russian Empire was becoming a European and

Asian power, with ambitions that would soon lead it into war with other European countries.

Russia's military and political expansion was matched by a renaissance in the arts, architecture, the sciences and in education. The Empress was fascinated by the Enlightenment and its new thinking. She maintained a lively correspondence with the French philosopher Voltaire, and their letters covered a whole range of topics and issues ranging from the natural sciences and philosophy through to politics and the events of their time. She encouraged everyone she met to read and study Voltaire. Peter the Great had sought to westernise the Russian nobility through prescription and laws. Catherine sought to do this through learning and education and by example. In their country estates and city palaces, the Russian ruling classes now vied with one another to establish impressive book and art collections. This was the era that the poet and writer Alexander Pushkin would conjure up so elegiacally in his epic poem, *Eugene Onegin*.

Catherine's relations with Britain began in a positive way in the years immediately before her accession to the throne. In 1755, Catherine met Sir Charles Hanbury Williams, who was the British Ambassador to the Russian Court. She was completely charmed by him. It was Hanbury Williams who would introduce her to Stanisław Poniatowski, the young man who would become her lover and whom Catherine helped place on the Polish throne in 1764. Poniatowski sought to strengthen the Polish-Lithuanian Commonwealth but was eventually forced to abdicate in 1795 and returned to St Petersburg where he became Catherine's captive guest.

Hanbury Williams died insane in 1759, three years before Catherine became Empress. However, the memory of their friendship ensured that Catherine remained well disposed towards Britain. This was a sentiment not necessarily reciprocated by the British. During the 1780s, the Prime Minister William Pitt the Younger became increasingly worried by Russia's expansion into Ottoman territories. Its victories in the Crimea were particularly alarming to Pitt, and in 1791 he tried to persuade Parliament to take naval action against Russia for not handing back the key Crimean fortress of Ochakov to the Ottomans. This had been agreed as part of the Russo-Turkish peace treaty, but Russia refused to abide by the clause relating to Ochakov.

The Russian ambassador in this period, Count Semyon Romanovich Vorontsov, was highly influential in British business and political circles. In response to Pitt's plans to go to war, he was able to mobilise public opinion in favour of Charles James Fox, who was Pitt's great Whig opponent in Parliament. Fox argued successfully against Pitt's plans for British support to the Ottomans and these were finally abandoned. In return, Vorontsov negotiated a renewal of the Commercial Treaty between Britain and Russia which was signed in 1793. A war between Russia and Britain had been narrowly avoided due to Vorontsov's skilful diplomacy. Pitt's supporters viewed the ambassador's interference in British Parliamentary debates with great suspicion and there were accusations that Russia was attempting to exert a dangerous influence on the British political system.

Pitt himself was not particularly satisfied with the renewal of the commercial treaty and saw this as a sop to distract Britain from Russian ambitions. He now sought an alliance with the Hapsburgs to contain Russia's growing power in the Eastern Mediterranean and to secure Ottoman territories against future Russian expansion. Pitt's growing fear of Russia was rooted in a concern about maintaining the balance of power in the Eastern Mediterranean and protecting the overland routes to India.

The Ochakov crisis occurred late on in Catherine's reign, and although it was a portent of future troubles in the Anglo-Russian relationship, it was a diplomatic storm that appeared to have blown over by 1793. At the very end of her reign, the growing excesses of the French Revolution would create a closer alliance between Russia and Britain. The two monarchies now found a shared interest in opposing a country that seemed intent on exporting its revolutionary ideology and beliefs to the rest of Europe.

Although Catherine never visited Britain, she was fascinated by its art, science and culture. British landscape gardening, porcelain, and painting were making a huge impression across Europe. The British industrial revolution in engineering and manufacturing was the envy of the world. Catherine was quick to adopt British cultural styles.

She was enthralled by the new garden landscapes that Capability Brown was producing for his aristocratic patrons in Britain. In 1772, she wrote to Voltaire, 'I now love to distraction gardens in the English style. Anglomania rules my plantmania'. She decided that formal baroque gardens were no longer what she wanted and longed for the new English style 'with its gentle slopes, the ponds in the forms of lakes'.

Unable to tempt Capability Brown over to Russia, she did the next best thing and purchased two very expensive albums of watercolours and drawings of the gardens at Hampton Court Palace, produced by Capability Brown's assistant, John Spyers. She intended that these should be used as instruction manuals to redesign the palace gardens at both Peterhof and at Tsarskoye Selo, the royal retreat outside St Petersburg. She never realised that the Hampton Court gardens were classically baroque in style and that Capability Brown had done no more than maintain them. Undeterred, Catherine proceeded to remodel the landscapes in her own interpretation of English garden styles and saw this as a symbol of her liberalism and openness to new ideas.

Collecting English porcelain and pottery was another of Catherine's obsessions. She particularly admired the work of Josiah Wedgwood. In 1773, after significant lobbying by the British ambassador to Russia, she decided to commission one of the most magnificent dinner service sets that was ever made by Wedgwood's Etruria Potteries. This was the 952-piece 'Frog Service', so called because it was ordered for a new palace that was to be built at a place named 'Frog's Marsh'.

Each of the cream coloured plates, soup bowls, dessert dishes and tureens were embossed with the emblem of a green frog inside a four-sided shield. Wedgwood was very excited by Catherine's commission and was convinced that it would seal his reputation in Russia. Despite not having received any payment, he funded the whole production himself, including paying numerous artists to prepare watercolour drawings of 1,244 illustrations of famous scenes in the British Isles. These illustrations were then transferred on to the cream plates and tureens. One of the most famous of these illustrations was that of Carisbrooke Castle on the Isle of Wight.

Ironically, this magnificent dinner service - described as the most famous in the whole of Europe - was only used once by Catherine the Great. It was then hidden away, only to be discovered in 1909 during the reign of the last Tsar. Nicholas II was keen to publicise the Frog collection and allowed every piece to be catalogued and photographed by a British specialist, Dr George Williamson. Several pieces were then sent to an exhibition in London. 1909 was the year of the Tsar's visit to the Isle of Wight and the exhibition of Wedgwood's exquisite pottery, an English product for a Russian Empress, was a fine example of Tsarist cultural diplomacy at work. It was the first time that any of the pieces had been seen in public since 1774 and they created a sensation.

Catherine's greatest coup was the acquisition in 1779 of 204 paintings belonging to the private art collection of Sir Robert Walpole, England's first Prime Minister. It was sold to the Empress by Sir Robert's grandson, who was deeply in debt and needed the money. The sale caused a public outcry and there were furious debates in Parliament about whether a collection of such value should be allowed to leave the country. Ironically, in 1777 Parliament had refused to purchase the collection for the nation, despite the campaign led by the radical English journalist and politician John Wilkes. Walpole's collection, which included works by Gainsborough, van Dyck, Poussin, Rubens, Velázquez and Rembrandt, helped form the core collection of Catherine's Hermitage Art Gallery.

In keeping with her love of art, it is entirely appropriate that one of the most magnificent portraits of Catherine the Great ever commissioned should have found a home in the British royal collection. This is a full-length portrait of the Tsarina by the Danish artist, Vigilius Eriksen. Catherine is attired in a robe of silver brocade and wears the imperial crown, made up of over 5,000 diamonds. Painted in 1765 it was presented as a gift to King George III by the Golitsyns, an influential Russian noble family.

The Empress Catherine the Great died at her palace in Tsarskoye Selo on 17 November 1796. She was succeeded by her son, Paul Petrovich, the only son of Tsar Peter III. Although his paternity was disputed, including by his own mother, Paul shared many of the characteristics of Peter III and earlier Romanov rulers. He was both mercurial and vindictive, but capable of great generosity of spirit and with a strong sense of idealism. Paul was on the throne for only five years. He was murdered in a palace coup in March 1801. It was the death that he had always feared. He had been haunted all his life by the grisly last hours of his father and in the end, a similar fate was to befall him.

6

Tsar Paul, a maverick and an Anglophobe

Paul had a bizarre and difficult upbringing. His relationship with his mother, the Empress Catherine, was cool and distant. He had spent much of his childhood being looked after by a variety of carers who were under the nominal supervision of his Aunt, the Empress Elizabeth. He rarely saw Catherine and when he did, it was almost as though she was determined to humiliate him in public. While she lavished gifts worth thousands of roubles on her court favourites, she would give Paul cheap presents. He grew up with a lasting resentment of both his mother and her lovers. There were strong rumours that Catherine wanted to disinherit her son and pass the crown to her grandson, Alexander. It is obvious that she did not trust Paul. She perhaps saw in him too many echoes of her husband.

Towards the end of her life she openly hinted that Paul was illegitimate, the son of one of her earliest lovers, Sergei Saltykov. He was a descendant of one of Russia's oldest Boyar families and conveniently also had Romanov blood. Catherine seems to have wanted it both ways. An illegitimate son, but in Alexander, a favoured grandson who had Romanov blood and would therefore have the right to ascend the throne.

Almost as soon as he became Tsar, Paul promulgated the *Pauline Laws*, which established a strict principle of primogeniture in the House of Romanov. This stated that the throne must pass to the next male heir. He is also rumoured to have destroyed Catherine's last will, which may have named Alexander as the next Tsar.

He exhumed his father's body from the Alexander Nevsky Monastery, where it had lain for nearly forty years, and reburied it in the Cathedral of the Peter and Paul Fortress, next to the body of his mother. This was a bizarre ceremony complete with a ritual humiliation of those Paul accused of having been involved in the death of his father. Two of the men most closely implicated in the death of Tsar Peter, Count Alexei Orlov-Chesmensky and Prince Fyodor Bariatinsky, were by now elderly and frail, but were forced to march in the funeral procession, one at the head of Peter III's coffin and the other carrying his crown. They were then banished to Siberia.

The actions of Paul's short reign were to prove quixotic and in many cases contradictory. Paul had a huge fascination with all things military, but he was reluctant to send his army to war. One of his first actions on becoming Tsar was to stop the Russian army proceeding with Catherine's plans to attack Persia. The army was recalled. He then set about 'Prussianising', the military. Paul had a huge dislike of the French Revolution and what he believed were destructive, Jacobin ideals that threatened to undermine autocracy in Russia. Catherine's greatest lover, Grigory Potemkin, who had been her favourite since 1774, had introduced new French-style uniforms to the army. These Paul utterly loathed, and in a matter of weeks the entire army was re-clothed in Prussian-style costumes. Paul believed these to be far smarter and more military in appearance. A daily military parade became the centre point of Paul's life, and he took great delight in inspecting his troops in their new Prussian garb.

Paul now decided that the principles of his military parades should be applied to the way that he organised court life. This now became hierarchical and over-structured with strict protocols, rules and regulations. Court assemblies and processions could last for hours, and Paul would demand that everyone approached him on bended knees. True to his contradictory nature, Paul enjoyed light-hearted banter and even playfulness with his closest friends and family. He also had an eye for attractive and pretty young women and a succession of mistresses filled his life, including Anna Lopukhina, described as having 'lively black eyes'.

Paul's closest confidante throughout his life was the enigmatic Ivan Kutaisov, nicknamed Figaro. He was originally a Turkish slave boy captured by the Russian army in Georgia, and then presented to Paul by the Empress Catherine. Kutaisov quickly became Paul's closest friend and then in later years, his most trusted adviser. This strange relationship between a former slave and the Tsar provoked a lot of gossip and curiosity at the Russian court and more widely across Europe. At times it seemed that Paul would do nothing without the advice of Figaro.

Beyond Russia, storm clouds were gathering. By 1795, the French Republic had successfully annexed the Austrian Netherlands, and also invaded the Netherlands and Switzerland. Large parts of Italy were seized in 1796 by a rising new General, Napoleon Bonaparte. Former governments in all these territories were overthrown and replaced by French controlled 'sister republics'.

Due to his deep dislike and mistrust of the French republic, Paul viewed these French military successes with great alarm. Although he was reluctant to involve Russia in any kind of military conflict, he entered an alliance in 1798 with Austria, Britain and the Ottoman Empire to stop further French expansion. He had been particularly upset by Napoleon's seizure of Malta. Paul was devoted to the Order of the Knights Hospitaller based in Malta, and in August 1797 he had been officially declared a 'Protector of the Order'. He was determined to liberate Malta from the grip of French atheists and interlopers.

A Russian army, under the command of General Alexander Suvorov, now played a key role in helping the Austrians drive the French out of Italy. This however was a pyrrhic victory. Losses were heavy and by 1799, the Austrians and Russians had fallen out with each other, as both countries sought to realise different objectives in Italy. The Austrians wanted to acquire territory and the Russians sought to restore traditional monarchies. In October 1799, the alliance was formally terminated.

Paul now turned his attention towards strengthening Russia's alliance with Britain. Plans were laid for a joint invasion of the Netherlands, and which would then lead on to an attack on France itself. In August 1799, the British had defeated a Franco-Dutch army at the battle of Callantsoog, a town in the north of Holland, which was then part of the French-controlled Batavian Republic. It was planned that the Anglo-Russian army would build on this success. The joint force made initial territorial gains but was in retreat by the middle of October. Bad weather and poor planning on the Allied side were largely to blame. The Duke of York, who was in overall command of the invading force, decided to negotiate an honourable capitulation. An armistice was signed, and all British and Russian troops were evacuated by late November.

The Russian troops sailed to the Channel Islands where they spent the next few months on Jersey and Guernsey. Both Tsar Paul and his generals fully expected that they would be called upon by the British to take part in a second invasion of the European mainland when the conditions were right. But the public mood in Britain, where there was increasing anger about the failure of the 1799 expedition to the Netherlands, now turned against any further campaigns. 15,000 Russian troops therefore found themselves stranded on the Channel Islands where their relations with the local population seem to have been reasonably amicable, if somewhat bizarre. There were stories of naked Russian soldiers running through country lanes, much to the horror or delight of the ladies of Jersey and Guernsey, and occasional accusations of thefts from private property. The disputes however were few, and no legal cases were pursued by the British authorities after the departure of the Russian troops.

By January 1800, the Tsar was beginning to suspect British motives and was openly questioning British commitment to the war against the French. In the spring of 1800, he gave orders for the Russian army to return home as he felt humiliated by the way that the Russian troops had been abandoned on the Channel Islands. This was an insult to Russian military pride. The brief Anglo-Russian alliance was at an end.

Paul's mistrust of the British further increased in 1800, when Admiral Horatio Nelson seized Malta from the French, then refused to return the island to the Order of the Knights Hospitaller. It was decided in London that Malta would remain under British rule. To the Tsar this amounted to a final betrayal. Paul took his responsibility as the 'Protector of the Order' very seriously and deeply resented what he perceived as a duplicitous British snub.

In retaliation, he gave orders to seize all British ships in Russian ports. He imprisoned their crews and arrested as many British merchants and traders as could be found inside his territories. He then created an alliance with Sweden, Denmark and Prussia with the explicit aim of closing the entire Baltic to British shipping.

Paul then committed one of the greatest turnabouts of his reign. In 1799, Napoleon Bonaparte had seized power in France and the Republican Directorate was overthrown in a military coup. Napoleon was declared First Consul. This led to the creation of a more conservative French republic. Paul believed that the radical phase of the French Revolution was now over, and in his view, France was returning to a more normal political way of life. This emboldened him to seek an alliance with France against Britain.

Paul decided that a direct attack on Britain would fail. The British navy was too powerful and had direct control of the waters around Britain. However, an assault on British possessions in India might yield successful results. In late 1800, joint plans were drawn up by Napoleon and the Tsar to launch an expedition against the British in India. This was not such a far-fetched plan. France still dreamt about recovering its former possessions in India, lost in 1763 as a result of the Seven Years War. Tipu Sultan of Mysore, a close ally of the French in Southern India, had been defeated only a year previously in 1799. Resentment at Tipu's defeat and suspicion of British imperial designs in other parts of India meant that there would have been a measure of local Indian sympathy and support for a Russo-French attack on the British.

It was planned that 70,000 French and Russian soldiers, supported by a large group of Cossacks, would lead the march on India. The expedition aimed to reach India in September 1801. It was intended that the overthrow of the British should be accompanied by an exploration of the sciences, arts and culture of India, in the style of the scholarly investigation that had followed Napoleon's invasion of Egypt. Savants and scholars were commissioned to accompany the Russo-French forces. It was intended that the liberation of India from British domination would also be an experience for everyone to celebrate. Fireworks and festivities would mark the victory of the French and Russian troops in towns and cities across India.

In the end none of this would come to pass. On 11 March 1801, Paul was murdered in the Mikhailovsky Castle in St Petersburg. The Tsar had only completed the construction of the Castle four months earlier. He did not feel secure in the Winter Palace and he intended that the new building would be a safe retreat for him. His personal apartments were behind high walls and well protected by a moat. The Castle had the look and feel of a medieval bastion of the Teutonic Knights, and this was doubtless intentional. To the very end of his life, Paul was drawn to the spirit of the Prussian military orders.

There were rumours at the time that British secret agents were behind the murder of the Tsar, in order to prevent him from invading India. There is no evidence of this. Paul's murder was carried out by a group of disaffected nobles and military officers who no longer trusted the Tsar and wanted to replace him on the throne with his son and heir, Alexander. It is, however, interesting to speculate as to how far this event may have contributed to the growing Russian suspicion towards Britain. Throughout the eighteenth century, Russia had generally enjoyed good relations with Britain. The dawn of the new century began on a very different note and heralded a period of rivalry, mistrust, and eventually war.

The ringleader of the coup against the Tsar was Count Peter von der Pahlen, a Baltic German who had grown increasingly disillusioned with the capricious style in which Paul dismissed, reappointed and again dismissed key officials. He had personally experienced this several times and believed it to be part of a bitter pattern of misrule which could no longer be tolerated.

Von der Pahlen decided that the time for action had come and Paul must be removed. He approached a group of men who shared his views, amongst them Prince Platon Zubov, and his two brothers, Count Nikolai and Count Valerian, who all agreed to join his conspiracy. Another Baltic

German, General Count Levin von Bennigsen, and the Georgian Prince Vladimir Iashvili, were also to play key roles. Eventually there were over sixty people involved in the plot, most of them holding personal grudges against Paul. It is ironic that Paul, who so loved Prussian culture, would in the end be undone by a conspiracy led and supported by Baltic Germans.

On the night of 11 March 1801, they forced their way into the Tsar's private apartments in the Mikhailovsky Castle in St Petersburg. Most of the attackers were drunk and violent. Paul was so fearful of an assassination attempt that he had securely bolted most of the doors to his bedchamber before retiring for the night. There was no easy way for him to escape once the conspirators had overwhelmed the guards and burst in on him. He hid behind an arras, but was quickly discovered.

It seems that the original plan may have been to arrest Paul and then persuade him to abdicate. In the confusion and disorder of the night, events took a different course. Paul refused to give up the throne and was then violently assaulted and strangled as he begged for mercy. It may have been Prince Iashvili, who had once been violently beaten by Paul, who tied the silk cord around the Tsar's neck. It was a cruel and brutal death.

Von der Pahlen and Count Niklolai Zubov now went in search of the young Alexander. He was found sobbing in bed and crying out that he would forever be blamed for his father's murder. Pahlen's response was direct and to the point. He told him that he was no longer a child and needed to go and start his reign.

The degree to which Alexander was complicit in the coup against his father has long been debated. There can be no doubt that while he was aware of what was being planned, he perhaps never thought that it would result in Paul's murder. While Alexander was content to accept the crown, when it was offered to him on that cold March night in 1801, it seems unlikely that he actively sought his father's death.

Paul's brief reign was a period of contradiction and confusion, both in domestic and foreign policy terms. The failure of the Anglo-Russian campaign in the Netherlands in 1799, then Paul's sense that he had been betrayed by Britain over Malta in 1800, were to create tensions that would last well into the nineteenth century. Although Paul's plans to march on India never became a reality, they created a palpable sense of British insecurity about future Russian ambitions towards the Ottoman Empire and India. This was to have long-lasting consequences.

TSARS ALEXANDER I
AND NICHOLAS I:

Alliance & Conflict

1800-1856

7

The war against Napoleon

Tsar Alexander I was only twenty-three years old when he ascended the throne of Russia. His reign was to witness some of Russia's greatest challenges and triumphs, including the defeat of Napoleon Bonaparte after the retreat of the French army from Moscow in 1812. Alexander also played a key role in settling the peace of Europe through the Congress of Vienna in 1815, and in setting up the Holy Alliance, whose aim was to restrain liberalism and secularism across Europe.

He was the first Tsar to visit Britain since Peter the Great. During his reign, relations with Britain improved as both countries were committed to defeating Napoleon. However, a visit to Britain in 1814 was a setback to the relationship and created a significant amount of ill feeling between the Tsar and George, the Prince Regent.

Alexander was considered, by many who knew him to be a strange and enigmatic man. He was both a liberal and a reactionary and, from 1812 onwards, became increasingly mystical and religious. He saw himself in the role of a holy man who had the responsibility of bringing peace to the whole of Europe. His death in 1825 was equally mysterious. Rumours abounded that he had not in fact died, but had vanished and become a hermit living in Siberia.

Tsar Alexander began his reign committed to a modest level of reform. He appointed Michael Speransky as his chief adviser. He was the son of a village priest and, and a great enthusiast for administrative and constitutional reform. During this period, Alexander created a State Council, and plans were drawn up to establish a new constitution and set up a State Duma or Parliament. Alexander also toyed with the idea of abolishing serfdom, but never acted on this idea. He was a keen supporter of higher education and opened new universities in St Petersburg, Kharkov and Kazan.

The liberal early years of Alexander's reign would not last. As tensions across Europe began to mount, Alexander began to re-interpret his role as Tsar. He became increasingly wary of secular and liberal ideals, and instead recast himself as a defender of orthodox and monarchist values. Speransky fell from favour in 1812 and was ousted from power. He would be rehabilitated in the reign of Tsar Nicholas I.

Alexander's foreign policy reflected a similar ambiguity to his domestic policies. At the start of his reign in 1801, he hastened to make peace with Britain, setting aside the rivalry and mistrust of his father's final years. In 1804 he agreed that Russia would join Britain, Austria and Prussia in the Third Coalition. The aim of the Coalition was to oppose and defeat Napoleon. However, in December 1805, the Russians, Austrians and Prussians were defeated by Napoleon at the Battle of Austerlitz. This was a major victory for the French and led directly to the collapse of the Coalition.

At this point, Alexander decided to make an alliance with Napoleon and in 1807, Russia and France signed the Treaty of Tilsit. Russia joined Napoleon's Continental System, which now included the whole of Europe apart from Portugal and the Balkans. The Continental System was aimed at engineering the economic collapse of Britain. Trade between mainland Europe and Britain temporarily ground to a halt. The British retaliated with maritime blockades and the seizure of Russian ships. There were also some minor naval skirmishes between Russian and British ships in the Baltic Sea, but Alexander did not wish to escalate the conflict with Britain, much to the irritation of the French.

Napoleon believed that the best way to defeat the British was by undermining and weakening their ability to trade with Europe. Once the country's economy had collapsed, he would then be able to launch an invasion. In theory, this was a plausible plan, but Napoleon had not reckoned on two major developments. The first was that the British now succeeded in finding new markets for their exports, particularly in South America. The second, and in many ways the most serious, was that those countries that had agreed to join the Continental System did not feel the need to abide by its rules. This was particularly the case with Russia, which significantly increased the volume of its trade with Britain between 1807 and 1812, and Portugal, which although not a member of the Continental Alliance was expected to support Napoleon's ambitions, but in fact ignored any trading restrictions. Portugal also became a conduit for illegal Spanish trade with Britain.

Napoleon was furious. He warned Portugal that this behaviour would force him to invade. In 1807, a joint Franco-Spanish army attacked Portugal. The British responded immediately, and a military force under the command of Lt General Sir Arthur Wellesley came to the defence of its oldest ally. The war did not go well for the French and in 1808, they declared war on the Spanish. In retaliation, the Spanish allied themselves with Britain and Portugal and the Peninsular War, as it became officially known, was underway. This was one of the most brutal wars that Europe had ever seen and would last for another six years. It led to the loss of over 700,000 soldiers and civilians on both sides and to the defeat of the French in 1814.

Worse was to come. In 1812, while still heavily embroiled in the war in Spain and Portugal, Napoleon decided that he would invade Russia. One of his aims was to force the Russians to stop trading with the British. A secondary aim was the liberation of Poland from Russian rule. This ensured active Polish military and political support for Napoleon. On 24 June 1812, the French 'Grand Army', together with its Polish allies, crossed the River Neman and entered Russia. It numbered around 685,000 men and was equipped with thousands of guns and horses. To many contemporary observers, this was the largest and best equipped army that had ever been assembled in the history of the world. It was an intimidating display of French military might and prowess.

Unlike Hitler in the Second World War, Napoleon had no intention of occupying Russian territory. He had no plans to run a permanent French imperial administration in Russia. He wanted to teach Tsar Alexander I a lesson, and to force him into a humiliating peace treaty which would ensure that Russia remained firmly locked into the Napoleonic system of alliances. Napoleon imagined that a few quick and early victories against the Russian army would bring Alexander to the negotiating table. He did not reckon on the evasive military tactics of his opponents, which would draw him deeper and deeper inside Russian territory.

It was two months before the first major battle of the campaign. This took place at Smolensk between 16 and 18 August 1812 and was a victory for the French and Polish armies. The city itself was burned to the ground and destroyed. This was not a decisive victory, however, and Alexander still refused to admit defeat. The Grand Army pressed on and now drew closer to Moscow. On 7 September 1812, the French reached the small village of Borodino, near Moscow. Here the Russian army, under the command of Prince Mikhail Kutuzov, was waiting. It was to prove the bloodiest battle of the whole Napoleonic campaign, involving around 300,000 men and resulting in over 75,000 casualties.

While Borodino was a narrow victory for the French, it was in no way decisive. Alexander was committed to continuing with the war and the Russian army was growing stronger, not weaker, as more recruits joined his forces. Napoleon knew he only had limited time in which to follow up his victory at Borodino. Autumn was coming and there would soon be a deterioration in the weather. He hoped that he would now be able to pursue the Tsar and his army to the gates of Moscow and trap them there. In this he was badly mistaken, as Alexander had decided on a bold plan. He would abandon Moscow and leave the city to the French, but ensure that in doing so, no food or military supplies would be left behind for use by the invading army. The inhabitants of Moscow had been evacuated a month earlier.

Napoleon entered Moscow a week after his victory at Borodino. The French army's supply lines were over-extended, and his troops were now visibly exhausted. All this might have been manageable, but then a series of fires broke out across the city. It is still debated today as to whether these were deliberately caused by the retreating Russians, or by the carelessness of the French soldiers as they entered the city and looted and pillaged empty buildings. Since much of Moscow was still built of wood, the city was soon ablaze.

A large part of the city, apart from the Kremlin, was destroyed in the fire and contemporary estimates of the damage put total losses at 75% of all the city's buildings. Following the fire, Moscow was manifestly no longer a place in which an occupying army could survive the winter. Napoleon stayed on for as long as he could, hoping that Alexander would agree to sign peace terms with him. The Tsar had absolutely no intention of signing any peace treaty.

On 19 October 1812, Napoleon's Grand Army began its retreat. This was the start of one of history's most tragic military defeats. Over the course of the following eight weeks, the French army was harried and attacked by Russian forces along its entire route. The arrival of winter, along with hypothermia, exhaustion and lack of food took a great toll on those who survived these attacks. The last French and Polish troops numbering 27,000 men finally left Russian soil on 14 December 1812. By this time, Napoleon had already taken flight for Paris. 380,000 men were dead and another 100,000 had been captured. The 'Grand Army' had ceased to exist. Napoleon's great Russian adventure was at an end and Tsar Alexander had emerged as the victor.

Britain and the rest of Europe could only look on in amazement at the unfolding spectacle of the French military collapse in Russia. Napoleon's retreat from Moscow changed the balance of power in Europe forever. The events of June to December 1812 would eventually lead to the defeat of Napoleon and the emergence of a new political order in Europe, in which Tsar Alexander I would play a leading role.

In 1813, Russia joined a new alliance called the Sixth Coalition, which would eventually include Britain, Prussia, Sweden, Spain and Austria. France continued to be supported by its faithful Polish legions, Denmark and the German Rhine Confederacy.

Throughout 1813, Russia and its allies battled with a second, powerful Napoleonic army that had now assembled in Germany. The scale of losses on both sides rivalled those in the Peninsular and Russian campaigns, with thousands dead and wounded as a result of battles across the country. Finally, at the battle of Leipzig in October 1813, the armies of the Sixth Coalition won a compelling victory and the French army hastened back across the Rhine. The German Rhine Confederacy fell apart and Denmark sued for peace, paying a heavy price for having supported Napoleon. It lost all its territories in Norway, which were then awarded to Sweden.

Tsar Alexander was now keen to cross the Rhine and take the war to Paris itself. The Austrians and the Prussians were more cautious, as they were worried this might destabilise both France and Europe. It was Alexander who carried the day. He was now convinced that he was on a sacred and holy mission and that his destiny was to save Europe from the tyranny of Napoleon.

On 31 March 1814, Coalition forces, with Alexander and the Russian army at their head, entered Paris. On 2 April, the French Senate declared that Napoleon was deposed. Four days later, Napoleon abdicated and was exiled to the small isle of Elba. The Bourbons were restored to the throne in the person of Louis XVIII. The first phase of the Napoleonic Wars was at an end and Alexander was widely viewed as the liberator of Europe.

8

Anglo-Russian friendship on the Isle of Wight

It was now that Alexander decided that he would like to visit Britain, a country which had long fascinated him. He was aware that no Russian ruler had been there since Peter the Great in 1698, and he was determined to follow in his footsteps, and if possible, outshine him. At this time, Alexander was very popular amongst the wider British public for the role he had played in defeating Napoleon. However, he was not trusted by the British government or the Prince Regent, who were both wary of his popularity and suspicious of Russian ambitions towards Europe and the Ottoman Empire.

A formal invitation for Alexander to undertake a state visit to Britain was therefore not forthcoming. However, it was decided that he should come over in June 1814, as part of a visit by the sovereigns and generals of the Allied Coalition. The visit was to last for over two weeks between 6 and 22 June and involved Alexander I, Frederick William III, the King of Prussia, and the official representative of the Austrian Emperor, Count von Metternich, together with their victorious army generals and wider entourages.

The Russian delegation accompanying the Tsar included the Foreign Minister, Count Karl von Nesselrode, and two Generals who had played a key role in the defeat of Napoleon, Mikhail de Tolly and Sergei Volkonsky.

The latter would become the inspiration for the character of Prince Andrei Bolkonsky in Tolstoy's great epic *War and Peace*. The star of the delegation, alongside the Tsar, was Matvei Platov, the Altman of the Don Cossacks, who was pursued by admiring crowds wherever he went. A group of Cossacks had earlier toured Britain and so enthralled the British public, that it fuelled a new wave of enthusiasm for all things Russian across the country.

The arrival of the Tsar and his Russian entourage in London was the occasion for an outburst of popular adoration that took the Prince Regent and the government by complete surprise. Contemporary accounts describe how people flocked to see Alexander. The streets of the capital were teeming with people who were determined to catch a glimpse of a man who was described by the Mayor of London as the 'the Almighty Giver of all Victory'. Crowds surrounded the Pulteney, his hotel in Piccadilly, and called out for him to appear on the balcony. When he did so there were deafening cheers and cries of 'Hosanna to Jehovah, Britain and Alexander'. Poems were composed in his honour by Oxford students and professors.

Robert Southey, the Poet Laureate, was sufficiently carried away by the emotion and excitement of the Tsar's arrival in England, to declare that Alexander was 'The Conqueror, Deliverer and Friend of Mankind'. His exuberant Ode praises the connection between Peter the Great and Alexander I:

'Little thought they that in the farthest North
From Peter's race should the deliverer spring
Destined by Heaven to save
Art, Learning, Industry
As little did they (the French) think
That from rude Muscovy the stone should come,
To smite their huge Colossus'

According to the diarist Mary Frampton, London went completely crazy during the Tsar's visit and searching for Alexander became the obsession of the day. She describes how 'cows were too frightened by the constant huzzas to provide milk, people could not get their clothes washed, engagements were broken, and the general confusion beggared all belief'. When the Tsar attempted to leave his hotel, his carriage was surrounded by adoring ladies, who 'rammed bank notes into the Emperor's hand to get them consecrated by his touch or threw themselves with nosegays at his feet'. It was an extraordinary spectacle which alarmed many people. One observer, Mary Russell Mitford, wrote many years later that these scenes made her 'a little ashamed of my country and my sex'.

The Tsar's huge popularity with the British public did nothing to endear him to the Prince Regent, who refused to visit him at his hotel. Alexander was staying at the Pulteney with his favourite sister, Grand Duchess Ekaterina Pavlovna, and he had politely declined an invitation from the Prince Regent to stay at St James's Palace. To add insult to injury, the Prince Regent had had a major falling out with the Grand Duchess Ekaterina, who had arrived in London three months earlier. The two of them had met on several occasions and each time their relationship took a turn for the worse. The Prince made disparaging comments about Ekaterina's physical appearance and the Grand Duchess retorted that the Prince had bad manners. She wrote, 'the Regent, handsome as he is, is a man visibly used up by dissipation and is rather disgusting'.

Ekaterina was quick to inform her brother about her dislike for the Prince Regent and this undoubtedly coloured the Tsar's attitude towards his British host. Alexander's huge popularity with the British public was becoming a source of increasing irritation to the Prince. He received regular reports on the huge crowds cheering the Tsar wherever he went and lauding him as the 'Deliverer of Europe'. None of this might have mattered quite so much, if the Prince Regent had been popular himself. The fact, though, was that he was widely disliked by the British public. Countess Lieven, who was accompanying the Grand Duchess on her trip to London, described seeing the crowds 'hurling mud and stones in the direction of the Prince's carriage'.

It was evident to many contemporary observers that there was a growing coolness between the Prince and the Tsar. The latter was scarcely ever invited to Court and royal events, and instead preferred to attend balls and receptions organised by the Whig opposition, where he was handsomely feted. This did not go unnoticed by the Prince Regent and his party. Supporters of the Prince were critical of Alexander and believed that he had misjudged the situation in Britain and that he was too casual in his dealings with the future ruler of one of Europe's greatest powers. Lady Shelley described the Tsar as 'a dancing dandy, a weak vain coxcomb' while Bishop Edward Stanley thought that 'he had the looks of a country gentleman, not those of an Emperor'.

The Tsar spent his time in London visiting many of the major sights in the capital. He went to Westminster Abbey and the British Museum, and he was glimpsed strolling in Kensington Gardens. He rode in Hyde Park and visited the London Docks. A high point was a naval re-enactment of the Battle of Trafalgar on the Serpentine lake. Models of famous British and French battleships fought one another, with cannon fire echoing across the lake. The French ships were slowly sunk to the sound of the national anthem.

A trip to Oxford now followed, and Alexander and his sister were guests of the university. They stayed at Merton college, and attended a round of official receptions and dinners. Everywhere they went, large crowds gathered to see them. The grand finale of the visit was the award to the Tsar of the honorary degree of 'Doctor of Common Law'. This event took place in the Sheldonian Theatre and was somewhat marred by the Grand Duchess, who suddenly demanded that the Sheldonian Orchestra cease playing all music before the Tsar appeared. It was a strange request which upset many of those involved with the ceremony and seemed to reflect the capricious nature of Russian imperial behaviour.

Alexander's visit started to take on more and more of an erratic nature. He and the Grand Duchess eventually decided to leave Oxford in an open carriage and were caught in a huge thunderstorm. Instead of stopping for the night they continued with the journey, reaching London at two in the morning, utterly soaked. The Tsar then insisted on turning up an hour later at an all-night gathering organised by Sarah Villiers, the Countess of Jersey. She was one of the most attractive and charming women in London society and an invitation to meet her may have been more than enough to keep Alexander racing along in his rainswept carriage. However, there was another reason. She was a known critic of the Prince Regent and the Tsar reportedly enjoyed a long conversation with her about the failings of the heir to the British throne.

The following days were consumed by an exhausting round of visits to St Paul's Cathedral, the Drury Lane Theatre, and the Chelsea and Greenwich Hospitals. On 18 June, the Corporation of London hosted a glittering banquet for the Tsar and the other Allied leaders at the Guildhall, which was attended by the elite of British and Russian society. Generals, diplomats and royalty were all present and Alexander himself invited thirty-six of the guests.

It was now that the Tsar started to reveal his strong interest in spiritual and religious matters. He devoted the entire day on the 19 June to meeting members of the Society of Friends, a Protestant religious movement more commonly known as the Quakers. He became fascinated with the Quakers and had a long private session at his hotel with two of their missionaries, William Allen and Étienne de Grellet. Allen had actively campaigned for the abolition of slavery and was a strong proponent of education for girls. Grellet had once been in the personal bodyguard of King Louis XVI but had converted to Quakerism after escaping France during the revolution. He was strongly committed to prison and hospital reform.

Impressed by his meeting with these two men, the Tsar then decided to attend a Quaker religious meeting in Westminster. He took the Grand Duchess along with him. She too was enchanted by the atmosphere of calm and spiritual humility that she experienced, and would later insist they call on a Quaker couple for further discussions and personal illumination.

Alexander's fascination with Quakerism would continue for several years after his visit to Britain. In 1819, Allen and Grellet were both invited to St Petersburg where they met with the Tsar and continued their discussions. They then went on to visit Southern Russia and the Crimea. At the same time, Alexander was encouraging the British and Foreign Bible Society to open a branch in Russia, so that copies of the Bible in the Russian language could be made available to people at affordable prices.

Six years later, all this work would come to a sudden halt when Nicholas I ascended the throne. He believed that Russian Orthodoxy was Russia's spiritual inheritance and expelled all foreign religious movements from the country.

The Tsar's interest in alternative spiritual experiences would continue until his death in 1825, and it inspired his strong commitment to the Holy Alliance: the coalition of Russia, Prussia and Austria. This was established after the defeat of the Emperor Napoleon with the aim of introducing a new era of justice, love and peace across Europe. Britain resolutely refused to become a member.

Before Alexander returned to Russia, there was one final visit that he decided he must make. This was to Portsmouth, the home port of the British fleet. Unlike his ancestor, Peter the Great, the Tsar had little affinity with the sea and naval ships. However, he showed a commendable interest in the living conditions of the ordinary sailors and asked to be taken below deck, where he insisted on drinking a sailor's daily ration of rum and water. Although Alexander did not cross the few miles of sea that separates Portsmouth from the Isle of Wight, his name is forever linked with the Island due to a man called Michael Hoy, who had been working in St Petersburg for many years.

The story of the Tsar, Hoy and the Isle of Wight is a strange and intriguing episode. Born in London, Hoy was a merchant who had spent many years working in the Russian capital. He first moved there when he was a young man and by 1786, he had become a member of the Russia Company. This company had been operating in Russia for well over two hundred years and was at the heart of the trade and manufacturing relationship between Britain and Russia. Hoy stayed in St Petersburg for another ten years, returning to London in around 1796. He was by now one of the most influential and well-connected of all the merchants in Britain who traded with Russia. He was well regarded by diplomats and businessmen for his knowledge and expertise about the situation there. Hoy appears to have been equally well-respected in Russian trade and court circles.

Soon after returning to London, Hoy set himself up as a Russia Merchant with offices in Bishopsgate. In September 1798, he bought his freedom from the City of London and thus became eligible for public office. He rapidly established himself as one of the capital's leading citizens. His trading business with Russia was flourishing and within a few years he numbered most of the leading London banks and businesses amongst his clients. He was elected a member of the Society of Arts, and he also invested in the rebuilding of the Drury Lane Theatre. In 1812, he became Sheriff of the City of London.

It was during this period that Hoy decided to make a significant purchase of land on the Isle of Wight. By 1810, he owned over 1,700 acres in the south of the Island, near Ventnor and St Catherine's Down. The Island was becoming increasingly fashionable. The Prince Regent's growing interest in the Cowes yachting season was also influencing many in high society to move there. Hoy seems genuinely to have become enchanted with the Isle of Wight and he soon became one of its most prominent citizens. He played a leading role in improving roads around the Island and invested in the Ryde Pier Company. This played a key role in introducing regular packet steamer services between Portsmouth and Ryde.

In order to set the seal on his commitment to the Island, Hoy now built a magnificent house at the foot of St Catherine's Down, which he grandly called the Medina Hermitage. The river Medina has its origins in the grounds of the house, so this was perhaps not an unusual choice of name for his new residence. However, his decision to also call it the Hermitage could indicate his strong Russian affinities and memories of the Hermitage Gallery in St Petersburg, a city which had helped make him one of the wealthiest men in the country.

In 1814, the same year that Alexander visited Britain, Hoy decided to build a monument to commemorate the Tsar's visit. This was to be no ordinary monument but a soaring seventy-two-foot-high pillar of finely carved local Wight stone, resting on a solid square base similar in design to a Roman rostrum. It can be clearly seen from many vantage points around the Island. The Hoy monument stands on a plateau at the northern end of St Catherine's Down, with spectacular views along the coast of the Isle of Wight towards Freshwater Bay and Tennyson Down.

This was never intended to be a modest gesture. Even today, more than two hundred years after it was first erected, the pillar dominates the local landscape. On its base, Hoy had the following words inscribed:

'In commemoration of the visit of his Imperial Majesty Alexander the 1st, Emperor of all the Russias, to Great Britain in the year 1814. In remembrance of many happy years Residence in his Dominions this PILLAR was erected by MICHAEL HOY'.

The relationship between Hoy and the Tsar has never been fully explained. There is no doubt that on Hoy's part there was a strong element of hero worship, a sentiment that was shared by many other people in Britain at that time. However, unlike the majority of those who succumbed to Alexander's charms, Hoy knew Russia well and was a well-connected figure in St Petersburg society. He therefore had no need to prove his credentials. His erection of a monument to honour Alexander may therefore hide more complex and mysterious motives.

None of Hoy's private papers survive, so we have no clear evidence of what propelled him to spend such a huge amount of money building a pillar in the Tsar's honour in such a remote part of the Isle of Wight. It remained the only memorial put up to a Russian Tsar in Britain until the twentieth century. The monument stands directly above where Hoy lived. It was a daily reminder to him of his admiration for the Tsar and his life in Russia. There is a strange twist to the tale in that when Alexander died in 1825, it was widely rumoured that he had not died at all but had in fact gone to live as a hermit in Siberia. Hoy's fanciful naming of his house as the Hermitage, seems to strangely prefigure the future rumours about the mysterious fate of the Tsar.

I visited the Hoy monument on a windswept December day in 2018. The sky was grey and overcast but there was a bleak luminosity about the landscape. Alexander's pillar still stands, tucked into a fold in the hillside. It was restored in 1992 and the plaque to the Tsar was recut by Andrew Morris of Niton, a village close to St Catherine's Down. The unveiling of the restored monument took place in the presence of the Russian Ambassador, Boris Pankin.

The Hoy monument remains to this day an emotional and quixotic tribute from a British merchant living in a remote corner of the Isle of Wight, to a Russian Tsar whom he both respected and admired and who had also clearly enchanted him. Whether Alexander ever knew about the monument is not recorded.

9

Settling the peace of Europe

The Tsar's visit to Britain in 1814 began as a popular triumph but ended as a diplomatic disaster. By the time that he departed for Calais on 26 June, Alexander had managed to alienate not only the Prince Regent but also many of those who had previously considered him to be the heroic saviour of Europe.

The Tsar's flirtation with the political opposition to the Prince Regent and his government was widely resented. Mikhail Kizilov describes how the visit was 'satiated with numerous little conflicts and clashes with the Regent and his immediate entourage. The Regent, who himself was not a particularly tolerant and patient person, in his turn took a most hostile and aggressive stand towards the Emperor'. Lord Grey, one of the Regent's most vociferous opponents, referred to the Tsar's 'vulgar manners and the bad influence that his sister had on him'. The public, which had enthusiastically embraced Alexander on his arrival also seemed to turn against him, resenting the high-handed way in which he behaved towards them.

All this was to have serious diplomatic consequences at the Congress of Vienna, where Britain would side with France and Austria against Russia and Prussia. The Prince Regent had a long memory and did not easily forgive or forget what he perceived as the bitter humiliation that he had suffered at the hands of the errant Tsar.

In November 1814, seven months after the defeat of Napoleon, a meeting of all the major European states involved in the recent wars took place in Vienna. The aim of the Congress of Vienna, as it became known, was to reorganise and reshape the map of Europe, to reward the victors, and to stabilise the continent after the radicalism of the French revolution.

The international gathering was hosted by Prince Metternich, the Foreign Minister of the Hapsburg Empire. He was conservative in his political views and reported every day to the Emperor Francis. The British were represented initially by the Foreign Secretary, Viscount Castlereagh, and latterly by General Arthur Wellesley.

Alexander maintained control of the Russian delegation, although it was officially led by the Foreign Minister, Count Nesselrode. Alexander saw himself as saving Europe from Jacobinism, atheism and liberal values. He believed that he and Prince Metternich would together establish the conservative tone of the Congress.

France was also invited to send representatives to Vienna, and Louis XVIII nominated his Foreign Minister, Charles Maurice de Talleyrand-Périgord, a wily and cunning figure, who managed to ensure that France became central to the negotiations and final settlement. This had not been anyone's intention at the start of the meeting. Altogether over two hundred European States, including many of the small German Principalities and the Papal States, were represented at the Congress. This was clearly not a meeting to be missed and everyone wanted to be there in order to ensure that they did not miss out on any political crumbs falling from the high tables of Russia, Britain, Austria and Prussia.

The Congress of Vienna also turned into one of the most lavish and overblown social events of the nineteenth century. Alexander and the Russians were at the centre of the wild partying that took place. Prostitutes flooded into the city, and all-night balls were regularly held in palaces and grand town houses. It was like an unbridled Roman orgy, a physical manifestation of the relief that most people felt after years of war and violence. Many people commented that the Russians were amongst the worst behaved of all the foreign delegations and seemed to be bound by no rules or social restraints.

If the social atmosphere at the Congress was intense and overwrought, the political discussions were equally fraught. Castlereagh and the British delegation were growing increasingly concerned by the attitudes of the Tsar and by what they perceived as his overweening ambitions. Britain soon made common cause with Austria and France in opposing what they believed to be the dangerous nature of Russia's territorial demands. The Austrians and the British were particularly suspicious of Alexander's plans for Poland.

The detailed negotiations over Poland would drag on for nearly a year. It was finally agreed that Alexander would be made ruler of a new Polish kingdom henceforth to be known as the 'Congress Kingdom of Poland', in recognition of the meeting in Vienna. The plan was that this would be run independently from the Tsar's Russian dominions. The Prussians took the greater part of Saxony with the remaining part surviving as an independent kingdom. A new German confederation of thirty-nine states was established, and these were put under the protection of Austria and Prussia.

A new Kingdom of the Netherlands was established, bringing together the 'Seventeen Provinces' in the Low Countries that had not been united under a single government since the sixteenth century. This arrangement would only last till 1830, when the ten southern provinces rebelled against Dutch rule from the Hague and, with British assistance, set up the new Kingdom of Belgium.

The Congress of Vienna forged a new settlement of European national borders that would last with some modifications till 1914. However, it also created new animosities. British attitudes to Russia hardened after Vienna, particularly in relation to Poland. There was a growing sympathy in Britain for Polish national aspirations and a sense that Russia had not played fairly with the aspirations of the Polish people for self-determination. British popular opinion, hitherto very sympathetic to Tsar Alexander, also soured.

The Treaty of Vienna was finally signed on 9 June 1815. By this time, Napoleon was marching towards Brussels, and General Arthur Wellesley had left the Congress to oppose him. Napoleon's defeat at the Battle of Waterloo on 18 June ensured that the terms agreed in Vienna would survive. A very different political and geographical settlement would have emerged had Napoleon triumphed at Waterloo. Alexander's armies played no direct part in the final victory over Napoleon. This had been a British, Dutch and Prussian success.

On 10 September 1815, Alexander organised a parade of his Russian troops at the foot of Mont Aimé, in Champagne. Over 300,000 soldiers and 85,000 horses took part in this extraordinary demonstration of Russian military power on French soil. Why he chose Mont Aimé for this event will never be known for sure, but there is a possible clue in the history of the hill.

On 13 May 1239, 183 men and women were convicted of being Cathar heretics by the infamous Inquisitor, Robert le Bougre. They were burnt at the top of the hill in a great inferno, which turned their bones to ash. One explanation for why Alexander chose this place for his parade was that he had been told about the history of Mont Aimé by his spiritual adviser, Baroness von Krüdener, and wanted to honour the memory of these medieval heretics. For Alexander, this parade would have been the perfect consummation of his spiritual ideals, linked to a demonstration of his military victory over the French.

Alexander had met Baroness Barbara Juliane von Krüdener, and her colleague, the evangelist Henri-Louis Empaytaz, while staying in Heilbronn in south-west Germany in the spring of 1815. These mysterious individuals now began to confer daily with Alexander and for a time, their prayer meetings became notorious for being the only time Alexander would listen to any direct advice. Krüdener and Empaytaz became the Tsar's guides in his spiritual plans to reshape Europe.

There had always been a streak of mysticism in Alexander's character but perhaps the stresses brought on by Napoleon's invasion of Russia and the subsequent campaigns in Germany and France now led him to a new level of religious devotion and piety, unrivalled by any other Romanov ruler. After meeting the Baroness, Alexander is reported to have wept and declared that a great peace had entered his heart. Given Alexander's well-known susceptibilities to pretty and beguiling young women, it could also be that the allure of the vivacious and attractive Baroness also played its part in his sudden spiritual conversion. She was described as having 'fair, curling hair that fell in soft ringlets around her face, lending her an air of unusual youthfulness'.

The Baroness later claimed that it was she who persuaded Alexander to develop the idea of the Holy Alliance, which in September 1815 united the sovereigns of Russia, Austria and Prussia in declaring their protection for religion, peace and justice through the rule of fraternity and good will.

In late 1815, Alexander and his army returned to Russia. His last years as Tsar were not happy ones. He became increasingly suspicious of what he saw as attempts by liberals inside Russia to undermine the country's political and religious orthodoxy and values. He maintained that 'Liberty should be confined within just limits and the limits of liberty are the principles of order'.

He mistrusted many of those close to him, and not without reason. In 1816, a group of officers who had returned from Paris formed the Union of Salvation. This had the dual aim of establishing a constitutional monarchy but also of assassinating the Tsar. Alexander was warned about the conspiracy but decided to do nothing. This is another example of Alexander's strange duality of character. He could be both a liberal and an autocrat, a man of action but also passive and fatalistic. It is no wonder that many of his contemporaries never fully knew whom they were dealing with and which persona he was adopting on any specific occasion.

By 1825, Alexander was tired and exhausted. He wanted to lay down the burden of being a Tsar. He talked frequently about retiring to the Crimea. In the December of that year he and his wife, the Empress Elizabeth, embarked on a trip to the south of Russia. During the trip he caught typhus and on 19 November 1825, he died in the city of Taganrog.

Even in death the quixotic Alexander did not disappoint. He remained as mysterious and elusive as he had been in his lifetime. For many years there were rumours that the Tsar had not died but had instead become a hermit. Rumours abounded that he was a Russian 'staretz' or holy man called Feodor Kuzmich, who ended his days in Siberia. In 1934, a report appeared in the well-regarded Canadian news magazine *Macleans*, which stated that the Soviet authorities had opened the Tsar's coffin and found it to be empty and weighted with stones.

10

Growing mistrust

Nicholas Pavlovic was the younger brother of Alexander I. In true Romanov style, his ascent to the throne in 1825 was overshadowed by conspiracy and confusion. Alexander had no legitimate male heirs, although he had left a secret message which appeared to state that Nicholas was his successor. His unexpected death in Taganrog had caught everyone by surprise. Tsar Paul's code of succession stated that the throne should pass to the next legitimate male heir. This was Nicholas's elder brother, Konstantin Pavlovich, who at that time was the Russian Governor of the Congress Kingdom of Poland. However, there was a major complication. In 1822, after his marriage to the Polish Countess, Joanna Grudzińska, Konstantin had secretly renounced his claim to the throne and decided to settle permanently inside Polish territory.

On Alexander's death, Konstantin was proclaimed Tsar, but he immediately refused to take up the role. Nicholas was totally bemused as to what was going on and demanded that Konstantin come to St Petersburg and make a declaration in person that he no longer wished to be Tsar. This Konstantin refused to do, perhaps fearing that once he reached the imperial capital, he would be crowned whether he liked it or not. For nearly a month confusion reigned as to which of the two brothers would become Tsar. Nicholas's loyalty to his brother was real and not feigned and he took no steps during this period to claim the throne for himself.

Eventually Konstantin did issue a formal renunciation and Nicholas became Tsar Nicholas I, dating his accession from the death of his brother, Alexander. Konstantin remained in Poland for a further five years, only leaving after the 1831 popular Polish uprising against Russian rule had failed. This was a personal and public catastrophe for him, as he had grown increasingly sympathetic to Polish national aspirations. Sadly, despite all his good intentions, he ended up by being trusted by neither the Russians nor the Poles and died a disillusioned and broken man in 1831.

Amidst all this dynastic indecision, a group of liberal army officers led an uprising against Nicholas in December 1825. Opposition to the Romanovs had been brewing for several years, influenced by the ideals of the American and French revolutions. Tsar Alexander had been warned of the activities of two secret societies which sought radical political, constitutional and social change. The first of these operated amongst the regiments based in St Petersburg and was called the Northern Society. The second, southern group was active amongst regiments based in Tulchin in the Ukraine and was more radical and politically dangerous in its ambitions.

This uprising would eventually be known as the Decembrist revolt, after the month in which it took place. It was a serious military and aristocratic challenge to the Romanov regime and, had it succeeded, it might well have anticipated the Russian Revolution by a century. Nicholas, though, was determined to suppress the uprising and within a few weeks both the northern and southern rebels were defeated. A small number were executed but the majority were exiled to Siberia, where they led reasonably comfortable lives, establishing libraries and schools and helping to create a new intellectual renaissance in Siberian society. Nicholas was only too keenly aware that many of those who had led the rebellion came from the leading families in the Russian Empire. While the individuals responsible had to be punished, this needed to be done in such a way so as not to completely alienate them and their families from the Romanov regime.

The new Tsar was a very different man to his elder brother Alexander. He was described by contemporaries as the most handsome and charming man in the whole of Europe. However underneath the good looks lay a ruthless military figure who was keen to suppress any attempts at reform. It is said that 'Nicholas I came to represent autocracy personified: infinitely majestic, determined and as hard as stone, and relentless as fate'. In 1833, he launched the policy of *Official Nationality* which blended the Orthodox faith, Tsarist government and Russian national identity, into a powerful new state ideology. In many ways, the legacy of this haunts Russia to this day.

The Decembrist revolt had left Nicholas with a deep and permanent sense of insecurity. His reign would be characterised by ruthless oppression at home and by military wars and adventures abroad. At first, these foreign forays produced results and Russia gained new territories from Persia in Georgia, Armenia and Azerbaijan. But, by 1853, Russia found itself in open conflict with Britain and France over the Crimea. This was a war that was to shatter Russian morale and expose its corrupt bureaucracy and underperforming economy.

The reign of Nicholas I oversaw the rapid growth of state power and the creation of an efficient and ruthless police network which infiltrated all levels of Russian society. Police informers became a new and feared dimension of everyday life. Strict new censorship laws were introduced. The management of the country along these lines required a major expansion of government bureaucracy. But this was to be no ordinary bureaucracy. Its staff answered only to the Tsar and his senior Ministers. The nobility and the landed gentry were co-opted into supporting this system of government in return for positions in the new bureaucracy, and a tacit acknowledgement that all their rights and privileges would be maintained.

In 1836, the Russian playwright, Nikolai Gogol, wrote his play *The Government Inspector*, which struck an immediate chord with audiences across the country. This parodied the human greed and extensive political corruption that was now emerging in the new bureaucratic police state. The censors and many government officials saw this play as a threat and wanted it banned. Paradoxically, it seemed Nicholas took a liking to it and insisted that it be staged. Mikhail Shchepkin, Russia's leading nineteenth-century actor, was cast in the main role of the Inspector.

Gogol, however, was no threat to the regime and Nicholas knew this. The writer believed passionately in the role of both the Romanov dynasty and the Russian Orthodox Church, as dual guardians of Russia's identity and future destiny. Nicholas was happy to allow writers like Gogol to flourish, because he knew that ultimately their deeper loyalties lay with the regime.

Gogol would continue to write books that lampooned the more ridiculous aspects of mid-nineteenth century Russian life, but his writings became darker and less forgiving both of himself and of his countrymen. He died in March 1852 after several years of spiritual anguish, during which he had travelled all over Russia and was regularly counselled by his *staretz* or spiritual adviser, Matvey Konstantinovsky. Matvey warned him about the sinfulness of his writings and just before he died Gogol burnt many of his manuscripts. He claimed on his death bed that the Devil had played a last cruel trick on him. This was a final chilling insight into the lost soul of Nicholas's Russia.

The dream of creating a more liberal, pluralistic and constitutional Russia that had briefly emerged during the early years of the nineteenth century had now been shattered. The satirist Mikhail Saltykov-Shchedrin, himself a civil servant, described Nicholas's reign as a 'desert landscape with a jail in the middle: above it, in place of the sky, hung a grey soldier's greatcoat'.

Relations with Britain during the reign of Nicholas I took a serious turn for the worse. It can be said that this was the point in history when paranoia and a fear of Russia really took hold amongst the British ruling classes. There was a growing sympathy among the wider British public for the Poles' struggle against the Russians, as well as a distaste for Tsarist autocratic government. This was linked to a fear over Russian ambitions in the east, and by what many believed to be the increasing threat posed by Russia to British rule in India.

All this combined to create an image of Russia as a country that could not be trusted, with a government that was devious and authoritarian, constantly conspiring against the interests of the British nation. The era of the aggressive and threatening 'Russian Bear' had arrived and it was during the reign of Nicholas I that this image was firmly consolidated in the British popular imagination.

Russian attitudes towards Britain in this period were more nuanced and less hostile. Many Russian liberals looked to Britain as the home of parliamentary democracy, a constitutional monarchy and a free press. There was a lot of admiration for British society and its cultural and social achievements. This was not a view necessarily shared by the Tsar and his immediate circle, though Nicholas himself had a complicated personal attitude towards Britain.

In broader Russian social and political circles there was a sense that Britain could not always be relied upon to deliver what was expected, and a strong feeling existed that the British would always put their own interests first. The perceived betrayals in Malta and the Netherlands as well as Alexander's chequered alliance with Britain still rankled.

It was during the reign of Nicholas I that a new diplomatic and political rivalry between Russia and Britain emerged in Central Asia. This has become known as 'The Great Game'. It began in 1830 with British attempts to gain control of the Emirate of Afghanistan and was to last most of the nineteenth century. If Britain was suspicious of Russian intentions towards India, then Russia was equally worried by British ambitions in Central Asia. The stage was set for mutual recrimination and conflict.

Tsar Nicholas's first direct contact with Britain had been in 1816-17. At that point, he was still a Grand Duke, and as a member of the Russian army he had gained significant experience and credibility as a military engineer. He spent four months travelling around Britain. This was in the wake of the victory against Napoleon and his elder brother's visit in 1814. Nicholas was well received everywhere that he went. In keeping with his military interests, his favourite travelling companion was the Duke of Wellington.

Nicholas displayed an obsessive interest in recording the details of everything that he saw during his visit. This was to become the hallmark of his later behaviour as Tsar, the ruler who saw himself as the military

Inspector General of his Empire. Observing and recording did not, however, build any natural understanding or sympathy for what he was seeing. Nicholas was not impressed by much of British political and cultural life. Parliamentary democracy left him distinctly underwhelmed.

After a visit to Parliament he wrote, 'If some evil genius to our misfortune, transferred to us all these clubs and meetings which produce more noise than substance, I would ask God to repeat the miracle of the confusion of languages. Or even better, to deny the gift of speech to those who put it to such use'.

He seemed only to enjoy the military and naval aspects of his visit, although he had an intriguing trip to New Lanark Village in Scotland in December 1816, where he met the social entrepreneur Robert Owen. He was impressed by Owen's plans for creating new model communities, but disappointed by the poor quality of the music played in his honour by the New Lanark Village Instrumental Band. Before the Grand Duke left, Owen insisted on presenting him with a silver dessert set belonging to his wife. The rest of Owen's family were appalled at this gift to one of the wealthiest monarchs in Europe, as the dessert set was a valuable family heirloom.

11

An unexpected visit

In May 1844, Nicholas embarked on his second trip to Britain. This was the first ever official state visit by a reigning Tsar. Despite their private misgivings, the Queen, together with Prince Albert and the government, went out of their way to welcome Nicholas. It was intended that the visit would build a better understanding on both sides over their differing interests towards the Ottoman Empire, Central Asia and India.

The public reaction to Nicholas's arrival in London on 1 June was distinctly cool, with satirical magazines like *Punch* openly mocking and lampooning the Tsar. Nicholas was seemingly unfazed by the hostility that he encountered and threw himself into all the events of the London Social Season with great enthusiasm. His warmth and unaffected style of behaviour won him many admirers and by the end of his visit the Tsar was being openly cheered by the crowds on London's streets.

The origins of the visit stretch back to January 1844. Both the Russian and British governments were keen to explore ways of improving relations between the two countries. The Tsar himself had fond memories of his earlier visit to Britain and believed that a trip to meet the new Queen would help strengthen the personal friendship between the two monarchs.

Nicholas was also motivated by foreign policy concerns. He was increasingly suspicious of the French government, and of the behaviour of its King, Louis Philippe I. The Tsar was worried by the French occupation of Algeria and by Louis Philippe's growing interest in the affairs of the Ottoman Empire. The idea of developing a new alliance with the British to counter this more aggressive French foreign policy therefore seemed a sensible move.

Nicholas had also never forgotten how Britain and Russia had collaborated during the Greek War of Independence. This had led to their navies inflicting a major defeat on the Ottoman fleet at the battle of Navarino Bay in October 1827. This was a major milestone on the road towards Greek independence which was finally achieved in 1830. Liberating Greece demonstrated the potential for the Russians and British to work closely together but the governments of the two countries drew different lessons from what had happened. The Tsar believed that by working in partnership with Britain that Russia could become the protector of Christian populations in the Balkans and the Danubian Principalities. He saw great potential in enhancing the Anglo-Russian relationship. The British took another view. They saw grave dangers in weakening the balance of power in the region and began to worry about Russia's plans to dismember the Ottoman Empire.

However, putting aside these concerns, the British Prime Minister, Sir Robert Peel adopted a positive approach to the Tsar's overtures. Despite anti-Russian feelings in Britain as a result of the suppression of the Polish uprising in 1830-31, Peel was anxious to invite the Tsar to London. At the annual dinner of the Russia Company in London on 2 March he toasted the Russian Ambassador, Baron Philip von Brunnow, with the words 'eternal friendship between Great Britain and Russia'. The Foreign Secretary, Lord Aberdeen, echoed these sentiments.

At first, Queen Victoria declared that she was 'extremely against the visit'. Her mistrust of the Romanovs had deep roots. However, after discussions with Peel and Aberdeen, she moderated her position and agreed that the Tsar could come in late May or early June, though no precise dates were agreed. Nicholas replied that he would come on the condition that the visit involved little official formality.

It therefore came as a big surprise to the British Ambassador in St Petersburg when he was informed on the 24 May by the Russian Chancellor and Foreign Minister, Count Karl Nesselrode, that the Tsar had already left Russia twelve hours earlier and was now on his way to London. In a curious twist of travel planning, Nicholas had despatched a courier to Queen Victoria with a message that he would arrive in Woolwich on 1 June. He gave strict instructions to the courier that he should not deliver the message before 30 May. This therefore gave the British only forty-eight hours to prepare for the state visit.

All this might have appeared bizarre to those who did not know the Tsar, but Nicholas was known in Russia for his sudden starts and unexpected appearances. There was another good reason for this somewhat strange behaviour. Since the Polish uprising of 1831, Nicholas had become increasingly worried that he might be assassinated by radicalised Polish nationalists. There was a large community of Poles living in London, the majority of whom were political exiles and had no love for the Tsar. The less that was known about his visit, the less time there was for his opponents to prepare an attack on him.

Nicholas travelled to London, disguising himself under the name of Count Orlov. In Britain, apart from the Queen, the Prime Minister, the Foreign Secretary and the Russian Ambassador, nobody else knew that he was coming. Preparations for his arrival were hastily set in motion, including setting aside a special suite of rooms at Buckingham Palace, where it was expected that he would stay.

The secrecy of the visit was helped by the fact that Frederick Augustus II, King of Saxony, was making a visit to London at the same time and so the planning for his visit could be used to cover up the Tsar's arrival. As a result, Frederick Augustus and the Tsar were to form a double act during their time in London and the two sovereigns made joint visits to Windsor, Buckingham Palace, Ascot and Chiswick.

On the clear, moonlit night of Saturday 1 June, the Tsar arrived at Woolwich on the Dutch steamer, *Cyclops*. He was wrapped in a pale grey travelling cloak and was greeted by the Russian ambassador Philip von Brunnow, and by the Commandant of the Woolwich Arsenal. There were no representatives of the Queen to meet him. This is exactly what Nicholas had requested.

He was able to slip away into the night and as his carriage rattled through the darkening streets of London, von Brunnow was able to brief Nicholas on the programme for the visit. It was now that the Tsar decided that he would rather like to stay at the Russian ambassador's home, Ashburnham House in Dover Street, rather than with the Queen and Prince Albert in Buckingham Palace. This total disregard for protocol was typical of how the Tsar behaved and echoed the behaviour of his elder brother, Tsar Alexander I, when he had visited London in 1814.

On arrival at Ashburnham House, Nicholas surprised his host by producing a leather pallet mattress, stuffed with straw, which he declared would be his bed for the duration of his time in London. It was after midnight when he sat down to work on his correspondence. This included sending a letter to Prince Albert, informing him that he had arrived, as planned, and was staying with the Russian ambassador. He also requested a meeting with the Queen at her earliest convenience. He insisted that this message should be delivered to Buckingham Palace, even though it was by now the middle of the night.

The following morning, Sunday 2 June, Prince Albert and the Prime Minister turned up at Ashburnham House to welcome the Tsar to London. The three of them went to Buckingham Palace for lunch with the Queen, and in the evening the Tsar returned for dinner. Victoria and Albert were puzzled, and not entirely enchanted, by their newly arrived guest.

That evening the Queen wrote in her diary, 'There is a strange expression in the Emperor's eyes, one might almost say wild, which is not prepossessing. His manners are dignified and simple. However, he gives me the impression of not being quite at ease. He seldom smiles and when he does it is hardly an amiable expression. Altogether to me he is not fascinating and Albert agrees'.

Victoria's initial view of Nicholas mellowed during the visit, and their time together in early June 1844 gradually softened her opinion of him. She began to see a gentler side to him, particularly in relation to his love for children and his ability to mix in an easy and unaffected way with people of all ranks and classes. However, her suspicions of him did not disappear entirely.

In a letter to her Uncle Leopold, the King of the Belgians, which she wrote shortly after the Tsar's visit, she commented, 'he is certainly a very striking man; still very handsome: his profile is beautiful and his manners most dignified and graceful. He is extremely civil, quite alarmingly so, as he is so full of attention and politesse. But, the expression in his eyes is formidable and unlike anything that I have ever seen before'.

She then goes on to explore the darker side of Nicholas's personality, 'He gives me and Albert the impression of a man who is not happy and on whom the weight of his immense power and position weighs heavily and painfully. He seldom smiles and when he does the expression is not a happy one'. She ends the letter with a rather unexpected observation, 'He is very easy to get on with'.

There is no doubt that Victoria glimpsed a sense of fear and insecurity lurking behind the seemingly confident exterior that Nicholas sought to project to the outside world. This all added to her growing suspicion that the Romanovs were not a stable dynasty, and that this was a fragile crown. These concerns would influence her future relations with the Russian imperial family at various stages of her long life.

On the following day, Monday 3 June, the Tsar decided that he would like to see London Zoo, and was delighted by the sight of the giraffes, exotic creatures that were totally unknown in Russia. The first giraffes had reached London Zoo in May 1836 and proved an instant attraction with the public. They were housed in a special Giraffe House, which was described as looking like a Tuscan barn. The Tsar took a close look at the giraffes and met their keepers, a trio of Sudanese men attired in colourful robes. Nicholas noted approvingly that they appeared to dote on their charges.

That evening, after declining Queen Victoria's offer of a royal escort, he made his way to Paddington station and caught a train to Slough where he was met by Prince Albert. The two men then travelled by carriage to Windsor Castle. Nicholas was greatly impressed by his trip on the railway, and on his return to St Petersburg arranged for a delegation of Russian engineers to visit Britain and learn from the British experience.

The Queen wrote in her diary, 'The Emperor seemed enchanted with Windsor. He is staying in the State Rooms. We dined in the Waterloo Gallery. The Emperor whose civility is immense, and most gallant, led me in. I am now very glad that the Emperor has come'.

The Tsar spent the next four days in Windsor as a guest of the Queen and Prince Albert. Two of the days were taken up with a visit to the Ascot Races, in the company of Prince Albert and the King of Saxony. Nicholas mingled freely with the jockeys in the paddocks and with the race-going crowds who cheered and applauded him. In his enthusiasm to meet people, in as informal an atmosphere as possible, the Tsar would often charge impetuously ahead of his royal companions. On one occasion he lost the King of Saxony, who was trailing behind him. The crowd swallowed up the Tsar so that Frederick Augustus could no longer see where Nicholas had gone. There was a moment of panic as everyone searched for both the errant Tsar and the trailing King.

On his first day at Ascot, Nicholas announced that he would give 500 guineas each year for a cup to be presented at the races. The announcement was loudly cheered by the crowds and doubtless contributed to his growing popularity. The satirical magazine *Punch,* which had adopted a strongly anti-Russian editorial line, commented that the Cup should reflect every possible symbol of Russian atrocities. It suggested to the London silversmiths Mortimer and Hunt, who had been commissioned to craft the Cup, that the symbols on it could include a skull, models of a cudgel used to beat up prisoners, engravings with groups of exiles, the deportation of Jews, and weeping Polish women. Not surprisingly, none of *Punch's* ironic suggestions were adopted in the final design.

Queen Victoria's great fear was that there would be an assassination attempt on the Tsar by Polish émigrés. She was grateful every day for Nicholas's safe return from his various trips. These were real fears, as half-way through the Tsar's time in Windsor, a Polish intruder was caught trying to gain entry to the Castle. Leaflets were also handed round at the Ascot races denouncing Nicholas as a tyrant 'greater than the Roman Emperors Caligula and Nero'. However, these seemed to have little impact amongst the race-goers, who were more interested in cheering the Tsar than in demonstrating against him.

On Thursday 6 June, there was a meeting organised at the National Hall in Holborn to ascertain 'how far the people of England are prepared to welcome to their country the Russian Emperor Nicholas'. Over 1,200 people attended the meeting, while hundreds more were turned away. *The Times* report on the meeting was couched in a decidedly disapproving tone, and it stated that 'the majority of those at the meeting were Poles, Germans, Italians and French. The English were represented by labouring men, mechanics, Chartists, and Socialists'.

The article went on to say, 'the meeting had lasted three hours and was marked by the most violent and rancorous language, the coarsest and fiercest epitaphs'. It seems that Poland was the main issue of the meeting, and various resolutions were passed condemning the Tsar's visit and expressing sympathy for the oppressed and exiled Poles.

In the same week that the Tsar was visiting London, notices were placed in all the major London newspapers advertising a 'Grand Ball' to be held at the fashionable Willis's Room, in St James' Square, in aid of Polish exiles. This was billed as the social event of the season, and the funds raised would be used to support the cause of Polish independence. This ball was clearly timed to irritate the Tsar and embarrass his hosts, Queen Victoria and Prince Albert.

In response to these advertisements, there was a spate of letters to *The Times* and other newspapers attacking the 'Grand Ball' and British popular support for the Poles. A correspondent, identifying himself as 'Philocrates' or 'Lover of the Homeland', wrote a letter of protest that was published in *The Times* on 6 June.

In his letter, the mysterious writer complains about the ball. 'Have we not, Sir, disease and destitution enough amongst the population of the city to claim our sympathies and demand our exertions, without extending them to foreigners who have little claim upon our feelings either from their morality or good conduct?'.

Another letter appeared the following day, again attacking support for the Poles:

'Is it seemly or courteous that a ball for the aid of the Poles should be advertised just as it were in the teeth of the Emperor of Russia who is now honouring our beloved Queen with a visit and is being honoured with the hearty welcomes of a free and generous people?'

The author of this letter again disguises his real name. It is possible that both letters were drafted by genuine British critics of the Polish cause. It is also possible that these letters were sent by officials at the Russian Embassy or by Tsarist agents, to deliberately discredit Polish exiles living in Britain.

The magazine *Punch* meanwhile launched a satirical campaign against the Tsar's visit. It proposed that he should be offered a guard of honour composed of Polish refugees and suggested various toasts that could be offered to the Tsar. These included 'Long life and misery to the exiles of Siberia' and 'To the Extermination of the Poles'. Following Nicholas's visit to London Zoo, *Punch* conjured up an imaginary conversation between the Tsar and a Russian Bear that he meets there. 'The sagacious beast began to growl the very purest Russian, and he was answered in its native sounds by Nicholas'. The bear warns the Tsar of 'rascally newspapers' and not to trust public opinion in Britain or the British ruling classes. A cartoon alongside the article depicts a hunched-up bear, with the face and crown of Nicholas, crouching at the top of a wooden pole and being baited by Queen Victoria. She carries at long sharp stick on which is inscribed the word 'Poland'.

The anti-Tsarist leaflets at Ascot, Polish balls, the satirical jibes of *Punch* and angry protest meetings in London, all seem to have left Nicholas unperturbed. He was enjoying his time with Victoria and her family far too much to let any of this worry him. On Wednesday 5 June, he took part in a magnificent military review in Windsor Great Park, arrayed in the splendid dark green uniform of the Preobrazhensky Imperial Guards. That evening, the Queen hosted another dinner for him and the King of Saxony in the imposing surroundings of the Waterloo Gallery. Victoria wore the red ribbon of the Russian Order of St Catherine in honour of her chief guest.

Alongside all these events Nicholas found time to relax privately with the Queen and her family. The Tsar loved children, something that Victoria noticed immediately about him. His gentle affection for children was a quality that she greatly admired. He seemed to form a particularly strong bond with the young Princess Alice, Victoria's third child, then aged only eighteen months old. He would regularly sweep up Alice into his arms and she would give him a hug and a kiss on the cheek. Alice was always waiting for him to return to the Castle. Nicholas could not have foreseen the destiny that would link them. Fifty years later, Alice's daughter, Alix of Hesse, would marry his great-grandson and the last Tsar of Russia, Nicholas II.

The four days that Nicholas I spent in Windsor were also used for important meetings with the Prime Minister Robert Peel, and the Foreign Secretary Lord Aberdeen. His main obsession in these discussions was the 'Eastern Question' and what to do about the Ottoman Empire. He went over and over the same ground at his different meetings.

He told Lord Aberdeen that 'Turkey is a dying man. We may endeavour to keep him alive, but we shall not succeed. He will, he must, die. That will be a critical moment'. In order to reassure the rather alarmed-looking British Foreign Secretary, he quickly stressed, 'I do not claim one inch of Turkish soil but neither will I allow that any other should have an inch of it'. He could not help himself from criticizing the French, whom he did not trust at all. Nicholas's plan was to create a united force composed of the Russian and Austrian armies and the English fleet, to maintain the peace in the Ottoman territories.

'We should keep the possible and eventual case of Turkey's collapse honestly and reasonably before our eyes. We ought to come to a straightforward and reasonable understanding', was his plea to the British government. Tragically, exactly the opposite would happen. Misunderstanding over the Ottoman Empire would lead Britain and Russia into a direct conflict with each other less than ten years later.

On Friday 7 June, the Tsar returned to London with Queen Victoria, Prince Albert and the King of Saxony. All that afternoon, crowds had been gathering in and around the United Services Club in Pall Mall, then considered to be the most prestigious of London's military clubs. It was only open to those above the rank of Major or Commander in the British Army and Royal Navy.

Rumours had been spreading since the morning that the Tsar would visit the Club. Huge crowds gathered along Pall Mall, anxious to catch a glimpse of Nicholas. The windows of all the clubs were filled with elegantly dressed ladies, waiting expectantly, for the arrival of the Russian Emperor. Carriages lined both sides of the road. As the evening light began to fade, it became clear that the Tsar would not be coming. There was a huge sense of disappointment and the crowds and carriages reluctantly began to disperse.

The following day, people began to converge on Chiswick House, as news spread that the Tsar and the King of Saxony would be the guests of honour at a grand fete being organised there by the Duke of Devonshire. This time, the waiting crowds would not be disappointed. The elite of British society paraded through the gates, eager to meet Tsar Nicholas and King Frederick Augustus. There were dukes, barons, marquesses, viscounts and bishops accompanied by their wives, all richly attired in the latest London and Parisian fashions. It was a riot of colour, perfume and jewellery. *The Times* reported that 'seven hundred members of the principal noble families in the Kingdom were present to meet the Emperor'.

A special tented apartment was set up in the grounds of Chiswick House, its roof emblazoned with the black imperial eagle of Russia and the coats of arms of England. Four giraffes from London Zoo, together with their Sudanese attendants, stood on the edge of the Lake. The Tsar's fascination with these tall, elegant creatures had not been forgotten. The gardens surrounding the eighteenth-century Palladian mansion were perfectly manicured. Bands from the Coldstream Guards and the Royal Horse Guards performed popular tunes throughout the day. The Tsar and his entourage arrived in a group of six carriages. They were cheered along the whole route to Chiswick.

The Tsar moved amongst his guests in a friendly and relaxed manner. In his article *The Emperor Nicholas I in England,* W Bruce Lincoln describes the 'easy freedom in the Emperor's manner, which had the effect of entirely removing any degree of restraint that otherwise might have been felt'. Those who met him that day agreed that he was polite, courteous and interested in everything around him. Many guests found it difficult to reconcile the popular image of the harsh authoritarian ruler with the seemingly sensitive man who stood before them. It was as though they were two completely different characters.

That evening, Nicholas and Victoria went to the Opera to see *The Barber of Seville*. The imperial anthem was played. The audience rose to its feet and applauded the Tsar. At first, he was reticent to acknowledge the warm welcome that he was receiving and had to be encouraged to step forward by the Queen. It was clear that this had been a highly successful visit, and confirmed Nicholas's strongly held view that regular personal meetings between him and Victoria would help build an alliance between Britain and Russia.

Sunday 9 June was the Tsar's last day in London. After lunch with Queen Victoria he had an emotional farewell with the royal family on the steps of Buckingham Palace. There were promises to return and a final hug for Princess Alice. He then left for Woolwich, where a distinguished group was waiting at the Arsenal to greet him. These included the Countess of Pembroke, who despite having seen Nicholas in the morning, clearly could not bear to miss a final chance to say another farewell. There was a full tour of the Arsenal and a close inspection of the new 120-gun ship *Prince Albert* which was then being built at Woolwich. The Tsar was very impressed by what *The Times* described as its 'gigantic appearance'. At the end of the tour, he boarded the *Black Eagle*, for the voyage back to Rotterdam. His second and final visit to Britain was over.

The Times ran an editorial the day after the Tsar's visit had ended 'extolling his unaffected and natural style of behaviour and his friendliness towards ordinary people'. It was clear that he had made a favourable impression. He was praised for his generosity, having agreed to give £500 to help complete the building of Nelson's Column in Trafalgar Square. He had walked past the uncompleted monument during his visit and when he was told that the Nelson Memorial Committee had run out of funds, he offered to make up the shortfall.

Two days after the Tsar's departure, Queen Victoria reflected on the strange and mysterious figure who had spent the last week with her. She was constantly revising her opinions about Nicholas and now that he was gone, her more suspicious and mistrustful view of him began to dominate her thinking. In a letter that she wrote to her uncle King Leopold of the Belgians on 11 June, she summarised her views:

'The Emperor is stern and severe with fixed principles of duty which nothing on earth will make him change: very clever I do not think him and his mind is an uncivilised one; his education has been neglected; politics and military concerns are the only things he takes a great interest in; the arts and all softer occupations he is insensitive to. But he is sincere. I am certain sincere even in his despotic acts from a sense that this is the only way to govern. He asked for nothing whatever, has merely expressed his great anxiety to be upon the best terms with us, but not to the exclusion of others'.

Although the Tsar had not formally asked for anything when he was in Britain, he did have expectations. He clearly hoped that there might now be an alliance between Britain and Russia. Following his return to St Petersburg, the Tsar's Foreign Minister, Count Nesselrode, prepared a Memorandum which summarised the discussions that had taken place at Windsor. The aim was to create a more formal agreement between the two countries, particularly in relation to the future of the Ottoman Empire. The Memorandum proposed that in the event of the Ottoman Empire collapsing, there would be a peaceful partition of its territories between Russia, Britain and Austria. France would be excluded from this carve up. The Memorandum was despatched to London.

The British, for their part, agreed to the Memorandum as being an accurate statement of the discussions that had taken place. However, neither Peel, Aberdeen nor their successors considered that the Memorandum was in any way binding. In their view it certainly was not a formal agreement. This was to be the basis of a great misunderstanding between Russia and Britain, and one which would eventually lead to war between the two countries in 1853.

The Tsar totally misread the British attitude towards him and towards Russia. He believed that his visit had put to rest British suspicions about him as a ruler and Russia as a country. It set the seal, he believed, on a new era of collaboration. It was a fatal misjudgement.

In the immediate years following the Tsar's visit, there was still a residue of goodwill between the two countries. The British government presented Nicholas with the gift of a new imperial yacht, the *Queen Victoria*, which was built in East Cowes. It was constructed by the shipbuilding firm of J. Samuel White. The ceremonial launching of the boat took place off the Royal Yacht Squadron's slipway on 10 June 1846 in the presence of the Russian Consul, Temzensky. The ship was luxuriously appointed in rosewood and maple and had a saloon which measured 23 feet in length. This extended across the yacht's full beam with almost seven feet of headroom under the beams.

The *Queen Victoria* was an elegant and graceful vessel which set the standards for all future Russian imperial yachts. It left Cowes for Kronstadt, the naval base of St Petersburg, in the autumn of 1846. The yacht became a great favourite of both Nicholas I and Alexander II and was used by the imperial family until 1881.

In recognition of the Tsar's new yachting links with the Isle of Wight, Nicholas was invited to become a member of the Royal Yacht Squadron. However, he resigned his membership in 1854, the year that Britain and Russia went to war in the Crimea.

Much to his fury, the Tsar learned that the Royal Yacht Squadron had despatched several of its yachts to help provision the British troops besieging Sebastopol. These included the schooner *Fairy* which sailed to Balaclava in 1854 where according to *The Times* 'she unloaded comforts and luxuries to alleviate the sufferings of British soldiers in the trenches in front of Sebastopol'. She was accompanied by several other yachts from the Squadron, including *Esmeralda* and *Claymore*. When Tsar Nicholas received this news, he immediately cancelled his membership.

The Tsar, in his turn, was lavish with his gifts to the Queen. Franz Krüger's magnificent portrait of Nicholas, completed in 1847, was presented to Victoria in the same year by the Russian ambassador, von Brunnow. It is a fine full-length depiction of the Tsar, resplendent in a striking red uniform of the Russian cavalier guard, with the white enamel badge of the Order of St George. The painting hung in Buckingham Palace until it was sent to Windsor Castle in 1922 and was then rolled up and put away for over eighty years.

Nicholas also despatched an enormous gilded vase to Victoria. This was produced by the Imperial Porcelain Factory of St Petersburg and was decorated with large scale paintings of the palaces of Peterhof and Tsarskoye Selo. The vase and its pedestal arrived in eight large cases aboard the steamer *Mermaid* in December 1844. The Queen described the vase as 'splendid and immense' and later wrote to Nicholas to let him know that the 'vase, which is superb, is in the drawing room [at Windsor], where we spend our evenings. It is admired'.

Three years after Nicholas had visited Britain, his second son, Grand Duke Konstantin Nikolaevich, arrived at Woolwich on 22 May 1847. He spent several weeks in England as a guest of the Queen. During his stay he visited Victoria and Albert at Osborne House on the Isle of Wight. They declared that he was a delightful guest and the three of them enjoyed musical evenings together. He was the first Romanov to step foot on the Island, although Peter the Great, Alexander I and Nicholas I all had previous connections to it. In recognition of this visit, Konstantin was also invited to become a member of the Royal Yacht Squadron, an invitation that he took up in 1850. His schooner, *Volna*, was part of the Squadron's fleet until 1888.

12

At war in the Crimea

The Tsar's visit to Britain in 1844, for all its good intentions, would not prevent the slide to war between Britain and Russia. Concerns over Russian ambitions in India and Central Asia continued to mount. There were also growing worries about Russian attitudes towards the Ottoman Empire. The fragility and decay of the Ottoman Empire was now dominating the foreign policy thinking in the Chancelleries of Europe's great powers, an issue that became known as the 'Eastern Question'.

Russia had long harboured a desire for direct access through the Black Sea and the Bosphorus to the Eastern Mediterranean. Britain and France now suspected that Russia intended to take advantage of growing Ottoman weakness to make territorial gains at the expense of the Ottomans. There were even fears that Russia might try and seize Constantinople and restore the city to its original role as an Orthodox stronghold. Russia believed that it was the guardian of Orthodoxy in the East, so this was not such a far-fetched suspicion.

It seems that Nicholas wanted to reach an agreement with Britain over how to handle the Ottoman Empire and did not see any reason for conflict. In January 1853, the British Ambassador to Russia, G.H Seymour, had a private conversation with the Tsar in which Nicholas is reputed to have said:

'Turkey seems to be falling to pieces, the fall will be a great misfortune. It is very important that England and Russia should come to a perfectly good understanding and that neither should take any decisive step of which the other is not appraised'. He then makes the famous statement 'We have a sick man on our hands, a man gravely ill and it will be a great misfortune if on one of these days he slips through our hands, especially before the necessary arrangements are made'.

There was no shared agreement however as to what those 'necessary arrangements' should be. Britain's view was that the Ottoman Empire should be propped up and supported. There was no desire to imperil the existing status quo. Russia, however, believed that there was now an opportunity for the European powers to reorganise the map of the Balkans and the Eastern Mediterranean to suit their own strategic needs. It may well be that Nicholas intended to organise a conference of all the European powers which would agree the future of the 'Sick Man'. The Congress of Vienna, which had redrawn the map of Europe after the defeat of Napoleon, provided a precedent for this.

The immediate causes of what would later become known as the Crimean War lay in the conflicting approaches between France and Russia over the rights of Christian subjects in the Holy Land, then part of the Ottoman Empire. The French, now under the rule of the Emperor Napoleon III, were keen to promote the rights of Roman Catholics for control of the Holy Sites, while the Russians backed the Orthodox Church. Arguments between the Roman Catholics and Orthodox communities in Jerusalem about the position of a ladder or the use of a key in a religious building may seem trivial and banal but reflected more dangerous power rivalries. These were to have devastating consequences.

In a bid to outmanoeuvre the French and the Ottomans, Nicholas now issued an ultimatum that all the Orthodox subjects of the Ottoman Empire should be placed under his protection. This was a direct violation of the territorial authority of Sultan Abdul-Mejid I, and the Russian request was immediately rejected. Britain entered the fray and sought to mediate between all the parties involved, in the hope of maintaining the peace.

Nicholas was now in a position where he could not back down. He decided to prepare for war against the Ottomans. In July 1853, Russian troops occupied the Danubian Principalities, now part of modern Romania. These territories were nominally part of the Ottoman Empire. The Turks were able to halt the Russian advance on the Danube at the port city of Silistra, but at the same time Russian troops launched an attack on the fort of Kars, in Eastern Anatolia. Turkish attempts to relieve the fortress were thwarted by a superior Russian force. The Ottoman Empire formally declared war on Russia on 4 October 1853.

The British and the French looked upon this unfolding drama of Russian military expansion with growing concern and alarm. On 29 March 1854, they declared war on Russia. Russia had refused to respond to their joint ultimatum to withdraw troops from the Danubian Principalities and there was a growing realisation that Russia was using the war with the Ottomans to reshape the map of the Balkans in its favour.

British and French troops were sent to Gallipoli and then moved north to Varna, a major port on the Bulgarian Black Sea coast. The aim was to check any further Russian moves into the European territories of the Ottoman Empire. The Russian army appeared reluctant to engage the British and French and the result was a phoney war in which both sides held back from initiating any attack on the other.

Public opinion in both Britain and France was now turning decisively against the Russians, and there were calls for a much more active campaign to be launched in support of the Turks. Karl Marx, never one to miss an opportunity to mock the imperial powers, wrote, 'There they are, the French doing nothing and the British helping them as fast as possible'.

In September 1854, over six months after they had entered the war, British, Ottoman and French troops attacked Russia's main naval base at Sevastopol on the coast of the Crimea. Although the Allies won the initial battle of Alma on 20 September 1854, the subsequent battles of Balaclava on 25 October and Inkerman on 5 November were inconclusive victories for the Allies. This led to an eleven-month long siege of Sevastopol, which was characterised by brutality and sickness. Thousands died on both sides, many of them from disease and illness due to the poor sanitary and medical conditions. The ill-fated Charge of the Light Brigade at Balaclava came to represent the pointless sacrifice of young men on the altar of an incompetent military command.

Britain lost 2,755 men in action but another 19,427 died of their wounds or of disease. It was the efforts of Florence Nightingale and her team of nurses in caring for the thousands of injured and dying soldiers during the Crimean war that highlighted the need for better nursing and medical care. The French and Turkish casualty figures were even more horrific. While 18,490 were killed in military action, another 121,000 died of wounds and disease. This was a war without glory. It was fought with modern technologies, and for the first time since the Napoleonic Wars, exposed the backwardness of Russian military capabilities. Due to photography and telegraph reporting, it was the first war that was fought under the public gaze. Military setbacks and medical incompetence, alongside the ineptitude of their military high command, horrified the British and French publics, who became increasingly disillusioned by what they read in their newspapers.

The photographs of Roger Fenton were the first shocking images to emerge from the Crimean War and came to define the pointless tragedy of the conflict. Fenton spent four months in the Crimea between March and July 1855, and he was the first photographer to document a war for public consumption. Many of his works depict the tired and strained faces of soldiers in the field, but it was his haunting *Valley of the Shadow of Death*, which seared itself into the popular imagination. This was photographed in the bleak valley through which the Light Brigade had made its fatal charge and conveyed a scene of utter desolation.

If the Crimean War was an unfolding tragedy for the Allies, it was a disaster for the Russians. 35,000 soldiers were killed in battle with over 400,000 dying from wounds and disease. For Nicholas this war now represented a major strategic error, a huge loss of life, and an unsustainable drain on the Empire's finances. He fell into a gloomy depression.

In January 1855, Nicholas caught a chill and a month later he died. The Tsar who had sought to unite his country around autocracy, the Orthodox

Church, and renewed sense of Russian identity was gone. He left behind a bitter legacy which had brought Russia close to military defeat. The Crimean War revealed a country that was economically bankrupt, and one that was falling further and further behind other major European powers in its technological, social and political developments.

The war would continue for another year, and it was not until January 1856, that the new Tsar, Alexander II, agreed to negotiate peace terms. By this time, the public in Britain and France was also becoming increasingly anxious for a settlement. Although Sevastopol had finally fallen in late 1855, this seemed to be a pyrrhic victory. The Russians had sunk their entire fleet, so that this blocked the entrance to the harbour and the city lay in ruins.

The Crimean War marks the only time in history when British and Russian troops confronted each other in a land war. There had been several naval conflicts, particularly during the Napoleonic Wars, but before 1854 the armies of the two countries had never fought face to face as enemies. The reign of Nicholas I and the Crimean War fundamentally changed British perceptions of Russia. Before Nicholas, there had certainly been a great deal of wariness towards Russia. This was tempered however by the memory of the joint struggles against Napoleon and the collaboration following the war that had brought lasting peace to Europe.

This all now changed. The Crimean War was a conflict of brutality and cruel fiasco and a negative archetype of Russia firmly embedded itself into the British national consciousness. There would be later periods in the Anglo-Russian relationship when this archetype would be challenged and even modified. However, these were fleeting moments and the British view of Russia and its authoritarian regime that was shaped during the mid-nineteenth century, has persisted in various forms until the present day.

On the Isle of Wight, Tsar Alexander I's monument now bore a new inscription. This was commissioned in 1857 by Henry William Dawes, a man who owned the house where Michael Hoy had once lived. It read, 'In honour of those brave men of the Allied Armies who fell on the Alma at Inkerman and at the siege of Sevastopol. AD 1857'

Dawes felt strongly that a monument built to glorify one Russian Tsar should now be amended to reflect the iniquities of another. This was not the legacy which Nicholas I would have wanted to leave behind, in a country which he had loved and admired in so many ways.

Three years earlier, on 2 December 1854, the Poet Laureate, Lord Alfred Tennyson, had been walking across the Downs near his house at Freshwater Bay on the Isle of Wight. It was here that he composed the verses of what became the most famous war poem of the nineteenth century, *The Charge of the Light Brigade*.

Over 100 men were killed and more than 160 were injured in a misjudged attack on the Russian gun positions at the battle of Balaclava on 25 October 1854. The 660 cavalry men of the Light Brigade, led by the Earl of Cardigan, were caught in a death-trap: a narrow valley which Tennyson called the *Valley of Death*. Russian cannons and guns mowed them down as they made their fatal charge into the valley.

In Britain there was outrage at what had happened at Balaclava. *The Times* ran a report on the battle in which it used for the first time the words 'someone has blundered'. This was the spark that Tennyson needed. As he wandered on the windswept cliffs, above the cold winter sea, he conjured up the verses that would come to haunt the nation in its hour of grief:

'Half a League, half a league
Half a league onward
All in the Valley of Death
Rode the Six Hundred
"Forward the Light Brigade!
Charge for the guns" he said
Into the Valley of Death
Rode the six hundred'

Tennyson himself, despite his mistrust and suspicion of Russia, would go on to have a curious relationship with the Romanovs. In 1883, he was asked to join a gathering of the British and Russian royals and read from a selection of his poems. Both Tsar, Alexander III and his wife, Maria Feodorovna, were present. Tennyson, being rather short sighted, did not recognise the Tsarina, and mistook her for one of the royal ladies-in-waiting. When she thanked him for his readings, he affectionately patted her on the shoulder, exclaiming as he did 'My dear girl, that is very kind of you, very kind'. The Tsarina could not resist a smile, but the Tsar was completely taken aback by this unexpected display of over-familiarity towards his wife.

It seems though that the Imperial couple were not at all upset by what had happened and later presented the poet with the gift of a Siberian wolfhound. Tennyson named the wolfhound, Karenina, after the novel *Anna Karenina*, which he greatly admired, and the two of them would be seen regularly striding across the Downs on the Isle of Wight. Friends of Tennyson called it 'a beautiful and picturesque creature, the constant companion of its master'. A cast bronze statue of Tennyson and Karenina, sculpted by George Watts, still stands outside Lincoln Cathedral.

PART

IV

WIGHT RUSSIANS

13

Radical Russia in Ventnor

The repressive nature of Nicholas I's rule was to result in the small seaside town of Ventnor on the Isle of Wight becoming one of the most creative and radical centres of nineteenth-century Russian political and literary life in Britain. Between 1855 and 1860, Ventnor discovered that it had become a favoured summer retreat for many Russians who were seeking a political and creative freedom denied them in their homeland.

During these few heady years, Ventnor became the prototype of an alternative Russia. Socialist thinkers such as Alexander Herzen and the political activist Nikolay Ogaryov spent summers by the sea at Ventnor, as did the novelist Ivan Turgenev and the popular poet, Count Alexei Tolstoy. By the year 1860, Ventnor was considered by many in England to have become virtually a Russian seaside resort. It would retain this appeal for Russians late into the nineteenth century and its radical charm lingered long after the departure of Herzen and Turgenev, attracting visitors such as Karl Marx and Friedrich Engels.

Marx and Herzen were friends and at his suggestion Marx made three visits to the Island between 1874 and 1883. On the last two occasions that he spent the winters in Ventnor, Engels decided to explore the Island after hearing about its appeal from Marx. It is a strange irony of history that the final political dramas of the Russian Empire were played out not only at home in Russia, but also in this far-away island in the English Channel.

While the Romanovs were to be associated with Cowes and Osborne, the political radicals who would eventually contribute to the overthrow of their dynasty are forever linked with Ventnor, only fourteen miles away. The two towns reflected very different political communities with conflicting perspectives on the future of their homeland. During the latter half of the nineteenth century, it was as though the Isle of Wight mirrored all the ideological tensions of Russia, played out in a scaled-down version of the Empire.

The first Russians to arrive in Ventnor in the early 1850s felt that they had discovered a small and remote seaside town, far-removed from the prying eyes of both the British and Russian establishments. At that time, it was only connected to the rest of the Island by a stagecoach and occasional steamers. There was no railway, as this did not reach Ventnor till 1866.

The town today still retains the remote and unspoilt appeal that initially attracted visitors like Alexander Herzen. It is situated in the far south-east of the Island, with a coastline dominated by striking cliff scenery. The town rises through a series of south-facing terraces from the wide and attractive Ventnor Bay to St Boniface Down, which contains the highest point on the Island.

It was the publication in 1830 of James Clark's popular book *The Influence of Climate on Disease* which transformed Ventnor's fortunes. Up till this point, Ventnor had been a small fishing village, with a few simple cottages by the sea. In his book, Clark enthused about the health benefits of Ventnor's superior climate, which he claimed could help cure people from chest infections, particularly consumption. This bold claim came at a time when the Island was gaining modest popularity as a summer resort, due to the patronage of both King George IV and his successor William IV. When Queen Victoria bought Osborne House in 1845, the Island's appeal was assured.

Royal patronage, and Clark's praise for Ventnor and its healthy climate, ensured that the resort grew rapidly. The 'Undercliff', a stretch of coastline which runs from Ventnor along to Blackgang Chine, has one of the driest and sunniest climates in Britain and the area is well sheltered from wind and rain. By the time that the first Russian visitors began to appear in the 1850s, the fishing village was already being transformed into an elegant seaside resort, with its own newspaper, the *Ventnor Times*, fashionable hotels, and a pier.

It is difficult to pinpoint the exact year when Ventnor first started to appeal to radical Russians. Alexander Herzen, the 'father of Russian Socialism', first visited the town in September 1854. He came with his family, and the group included the redoubtable Malwida von Meysenbug, who acted as housekeeper, governess and surrogate mother to Herzen's children. His wife, Natalya, had died in Geneva in 1852, just before Herzen's decision to move to London.

Malwida came from a well-established German family living in Hesse, but she had rejected her conventional upbringing, moved in with a radical community in Hamburg, and then emigrated to London where she met Herzen. Their lives were entwined for many years, although her exact relationship with him is difficult to unravel. Herzen himself had been emotionally scarred by his failed marriage to his first cousin, Natalya Zakharina, whom he had secretly married in 1837 after eloping with her. He was deeply in love, but the relationship soured, and she had had a passionate affair with the German poet George Herwegh, before dying of consumption in the best romantic tradition.

By the time that Herzen first appeared in Ventnor in September 1854, he had already been in exile for seven years, living in Italy, France and Switzerland before moving to London. There was no prospect of any immediate return to his homeland. Herzen was well known to the Tsarist authorities, both as a political radical and an open critic of both Nicholas I and his style of autocratic government.

Relations between the two countries also made any return for Herzen very difficult. Russia and Britain were now engaged in a brutal war in the Crimea, then the lowest point in the complex and fraught relationship between the two countries. The war had already been raging for nearly a year and there was no end in sight to the conflict. In the same month that Herzen arrived in Ventnor, British and French troops attacked the Russian army defending the Alma Heights - a key strategic target for the Allies - on their way to capturing Sevastopol, the chief port in the Crimea.

Initially, Herzen hoped that the war would lead to the fall of the Romanovs and he was convinced that it would expose the rotten and corrupt nature of Russian autocracy. His political attacks on the Tsar and his government had now reached new levels. In June 1853, soon after his arrival in London, Herzen had launched the *Free Russian Press*, a printing and publishing house which, he boldly announced, would become the uncensored voice of a liberated Russia. Its leading publication was an openly revolutionary periodical called *The Polar Star*. This was followed by a series of deliberately inflammatory brochures and pamphlets calling for the liberation of the Russian peasantry, and for Poles and Russians to work together in launching a common revolutionary front against the Tsarist regime.

However, Herzen was frustrated by the seeming lack of response to his publications from within Russia itself. In 1856, his friend the political activist and poet Nikolay Ogaryov joined him in London and persuaded him that the *Free Russian Press* needed to start appealing to a much wider cross section of the Russian public, if it was going to enjoy any success. This was a turning point for Herzen. Soon after Ogaryov's arrival, a new periodical called *Voices from Russia* was launched and this adopted a less obviously revolutionary stance. It had an immediate impact on the wider Russian public and encouraged a flood of contributors from inside the country.

In 1857, Herzen and Ogaryov decided to publish a new journal. This was *Kolokol*, or the *Bell* and it became one of the most popular of all nineteenth-century Russian radical publications. It was banned in Russia itself, but despite this, had a major impact on public opinion inside the country with its calls for the liberation of the peasantry, land reform and the abolition of censorship. It may well have influenced the new Tsar, Alexander II, to embark on his plans to emancipate the serfs and introduce wider governmental reforms.

The *Bell* put Herzen at the centre of radical Russian thinking and he began to mix with a wide range of political revolutionaries and writers. He became closely involved with the *International Working Men's Association,* which was founded in 1864 in London and aimed to unite socialist, anarchist and communist groups into a single movement. Through his involvement with movements like this he became friendly with Karl Marx and Mikhail Bakunin, the Russian revolutionary anarchist. Writers like Ivan Turgenev also sought him out and would also become part of the Russian circle that gathered on the Isle of Wight.

In 1854, when Herzen first reached Ventnor, much of this fame still lay in the future. What brought him to the Isle of Wight? He seems to have been attracted to the place both by its growing reputation as an escape from the pressures of life in London, but also because Ventnor was already becoming a favoured destination for other European political radicals like the Hungarians Lajos Kossuth and Ferenc Pulszky.

Both Kossuth and Pulszky had fled into exile in Britain with their families after the failure of the Hungarian uprising against the Hapsburgs in 1848. This had been suppressed with the help of Tsar Nicholas I. Herzen was appalled by his government's involvement in the destruction of the Hungarian fight for freedom and this drew him close to Kossuth and Pulszky. These two men and their families were already spending their summers in Ventnor and it seems likely that this is what may have persuaded Herzen to make his first visit.

Malwida von Meysenbug vividly describes the family's arrival in Ventnor in her memoirs. 'We took the boat over to Wight island' she writes, 'the natural beauty of which I had long wanted to see. On the journey across the Island to the little city of Ventnor on the southern side, Herzen and his son sat atop the stagecoach, the children and I sat inside. Delighted by the glorious road, I called up to them: Isn't that beautiful, Wasn't I right in suggesting this? Laughingly, Herzen called down 'I didn't want to tell you, but yes you were right. It's glorious and I am glad that we came'.

According to Sarah J Young who has researched Herzen's visits to Ventnor, the family passed their days very agreeably, either swimming in the sea, or strolling along the coast. Malwida appears to have been something of a bathing fanatic, and she was clearly an early proponent of the health benefits of saltwater immersion. Herzen was greatly amused by her constant forays in the bathing machines that were already becoming such an established feature of the mid-Victorian beach landscape.

The evenings were spent mainly with the Kossuths and the Pulszkys, engaged in lively political discussions about the Crimean war. Malwida wrote, 'Herzen, more so than the others, was very excited. He prophesied the Russian defeat and wished for it, since he believed that it would lead to the downfall of autocracy'. That same week, over 8,500 Russian and Allied soldiers lay dead or dying on the battlefield of Alma in the Crimea. The terrible reality of the war was now dawning on both the Russian and British publics.

Herzen was sufficiently pleased with Ventnor to propose to Malwida that they return to Ventnor the following summer, this time for several weeks. They rented St Augustine's Villa, an imposing neo-Gothic mansion with commanding views of the sea. It still stands today in the centre of Ventnor. Malwida wrote, 'We rented a comfortable home on the ocean, and the wonderful sea air and charmingly beautiful coast revived our good spirits. The Pulszkys were also there again. They frequently came in the evening'.

Twelve months on from their last visit, the Ventnor radicals were all much more subdued about what was happening in both Russia and the Crimea. The siege of Sevastopol had been raging for nearly twelve months, leaving over 200,000 dead. Tsar Nicholas I had died the previous March and had been succeeded by his son, Alexander II, who was clearly seeking a way to end the war. The new Tsar also appeared to be infused with a more liberal political spirit. It was Alexander who had appealed to his father in 1837 to free Herzen from internal exile in the north-eastern Russian city of Vyatka.

Malwida wrote, 'News reached us [in Ventnor] about the taking of Malakoff. This meant that Sevastopol would probably fall, and the war would be over. We rejoiced at the news, not only out of consideration for human life, but especially for Russia, since it could be assumed that the new Emperor would attempt domestic reforms after the close of this war that he had inherited'.

The family occupied themselves that September of 1855, in swimming and taking long walks. Herzen, in a letter to the German political activist Reichel, writes that 'for three days, the weather has been like June and I have been bathing recklessly in the sea'. However, he also complains bitterly that 'there were four days of storms, rain, and bitter cold'. He appears to have enjoyed Ventnor but there is an acerbic aside: 'if it were not so boring, I would live here but there are no resources at all'. Malwida, however, was enchanted by the small seaside town and in her memoirs enthuses about the beautiful coastal paths and the surrounding landscape.

Following the two summers spent by the Herzen family in Ventnor, word began to spread amongst the Russian exile community in England and amongst liberals in Russia about the appeal of Ventnor. Here was a charming seaside resort in a country which many of them admired, but also a place where intellectuals could meet and exchange views in safety and security. From the late 1850s, Russians began to arrive on the Island in increasingly large numbers, and most of them headed directly to Ventnor.

In 1859 these visitors included the literary critics, Vasily Botkin, and Pavel Annenkov as well as the journalist Mikhail Katkov, all of whom were sympathetic in varying degrees to the cause of liberal reform in Russia and considered themselves part of Herzen's inner circle.

Botkin, amongst his many other literary achievements, introduced Friedrich Engels to the Russian reading public, although he later regretted this as he became more and more conservative in his old age. Annenkov, who was both a close friend of Herzen, and of the Russian revolutionary anarchist Mikhail Bakunin, engaged in a lively correspondence with Karl Marx and followed the writer Nicholas Gogol around Germany. He would also be responsible for introducing his great friend Ivan Turgenev to Ventnor.

Katkov became a classic example of a liberal who turned into a reactionary. When he visited Ventnor and strolled along the promenade, he considered himself to be a political radical, in favour of introducing British-style political democracy to Russia. By the end of his life, he had abandoned this early liberalism in favour of adopting a hard line Slavophile philosophy, and he rejected the emerging aspirations of national minorities within the Empire.

Another visitor to Ventnor that summer of 1859 was the Ukrainian writer, Marko Vovchok. She became famous for her wonderfully evocative Ukrainian folk tales, which attracted the attention of writers like Turgenev and Tolstoy. Much acclaimed for her grace and style, she was an early advocate of Ukraine's emerging national identity, though she was damned as a political radical in the eyes of the Tsarist regime.

Comfortably ensconced in Vale Cottage in the High Street in Ventnor was Viktor Kasatkin. He was closely associated with Herzen's *Free Russian Press* and had been an early advocate of the 'Land and Freedom' movement. Despite these excellent credentials, he seems not to have been popular with many of his Russian compatriots and was actively disliked by the writer, Ivan Turgenev when they met during the latter's visit to Ventnor.

By the summer of 1860, Ventnor was akin to a Russian colony anchored in the English Channel. The entire resort was crowded with Russian visitors and many of the hotels and villas available for rent were occupied by families from St Petersburg and Moscow, as well as by Russian exiles living in England. In its weekly editions of August and September that year, the *Ventnor Times* recorded the comings and goings of the Russian liberal elite.

Paradoxically Herzen had decided to avoid Ventnor after hearing that it was overrun by Russians. He went instead to Bournemouth. Annenkov however was back in residence, as was Count Alexei Tolstoy. He was a second cousin of the novelist Leo Tolstoy and would go on to become Russia's most important historical dramatist with his epic works *The Death of Ivan the Terrible* and *Tsar Boris*.

Two brothers, Nikolai and Dimitri Goubarev, were renting Woolton Cottage in Church Street while a Mr Korsakov was staying at Burnhill Cottage. Little is known about the Goubarevs, but Korsakov may well have been the radical A. S Korsakov, who later became infamous for his involvement in conspiracies against the Tsar. Mr and Mrs Mordvinov were in residence at Montebello House in Victoria Street. A man called Nicholas Mordvinov would later be arrested in Russia for circulating

Herzen's writings and it is likely that this was the same man listed as staying at Montebello House in 1860.

Leon and Lady Krivochapkine and family were at Prospect House in Grove Road. Leon was an open admirer of Herzen and his political views, but he was never fully trusted by men like Annenkov and other friends of Herzen's. There is no evidence that he was in any way a police informer, set up in Ventnor to spy on the activities of the Russians staying there, but Annenkov was suspicious of him and uncomfortable in his presence. He omits any mention of him in his memoirs. Colonel Nikolai Rostovtzev and his wife were at Somerset Cottage, also in Grove Road. This road was almost becoming the 'Russkiy Prospekt' of Ventnor due to the large number of Russians living there. Rostovtsev was a known liberal sympathiser, and the son of Yakov Rostovtsev, the man who was responsible for drawing up the statutes that would lead to the liberation of the serfs in 1861.

Down on the sea front, Prince Victor and Princess Maria Bariatinsky together with Countess Chreptonvitch were all comfortably settled together in the Esplanade Hotel. The Princess was later to become a close friend of Ivan Turgenev and has been described by Patrick Waddington in his book *Turgenev in England* as 'an extraordinary woman, fascinating and perplexing in her sphinx-like beauty and demeanour'. She was known in liberal circles for combining charm with political radicalism.

Perhaps one of the more intriguing Russian visitors to Ventnor that summer was Nicholas Kruze. He and his wife were staying at a house called Primrose Bank in Grove Road. Kruze had been the darling of St Petersburg's literary society. He was a well-known social activist and liberal who paradoxically also held the post of a government censor. When he was dismissed from this role because of his reluctance to censor any books or journals, he was accorded a grand farewell celebration by the St Petersburg intelligentsia.

He later became a member of the St Petersburg Provincial *Zemstvo* until this was dissolved by Alexander II in 1858 on the grounds of insubordination. Given his impeccable reputation as a committed liberal, it is rather surprising to discover that Herzen did not have a high opinion of Kruse. He described him as a 'puny, vapid man' whom the St Petersburg intelligentsia had elevated far above his actual talents and capabilities. Herzen's sarcastic nickname for Kruse was 'Robinson Kruse' indicating that here was a man adrift and alone in his own world of liberal incompetence.

Towering over the Russian community in Ventnor that August in 1860 was one of the country's greatest literary figures, the writer Ivan Sergeyevich Turgenev. It was while he was staying in Ventnor that Turgenev was inspired to write his ground-breaking novel *Fathers and Sons*, considered by many literary critics to be one of the greatest stories ever conceived. He was the first of the Russian nineteenth-century classical novelists to receive major recognition in Britain.

Turgenev was born in 1818 into a noble family living in the Oryol Oblast, a province located around two hundred miles south-west of Moscow. He was given a liberal western education and the young Turgenev soon became fluent in German, French and English. He studied at the universities of both Moscow and St Petersburg, before moving to Berlin in 1838, where he continued his higher education in philosophy and history at Berlin University.

Turgenev was a moderate liberal in his political views, and while he opposed serfdom, he preferred a cautious approach to political change. He corresponded with and considered himself to be a friend of Alexander Herzen, but unlike Herzen he was not a political radical. It is therefore ironical that in *Fathers and Sons*, first published in 1862, he created one of the most revolutionary characters in Russian literature, the provincial doctor, Yevgeny Bazarov.

Bazarov is a man who lacks a belief in anything around him, and who completely rejects the old order. This philosophy became known as Nihilism and Bazarov was, in many ways, its inspiration. By the end of the nineteenth century, Russian Nihilism had become a byword for political and revolutionary terror. The character of Bazarov was created in Ventnor. It might therefore be said that Nihilism first emerged into the light of day from this small seaside town, with Bazarov springing fully grown from the dark fantasies and terrors of Turgenev's imagination.

Turgenev had decided to leave Russia in 1845, ostensibly in protest at the growing oppression of the Tsarist regime, but more likely because he had fallen madly in love with the French opera singer Pauline Viardot. He had heard her exquisite rendering of *The Barber of Seville* at a theatre in Russia in 1843. He eventually moved in with her and she became his close confidante and friend. It is not clear if they were ever lovers, but their relationship appears to have been platonic rather than sexual in nature.

Turgenev would spend the rest of his life moving backwards and forwards between Russia and Western Europe, and he spent a lot of time in France and Germany with Pauline and her family of four children. However, he could never abandon Russia completely. It was lodged deep in his soul and psyche. He became increasingly disillusioned by the way he was criticized in his homeland, particularly after the publication of *Fathers and Sons*. Turgenev was acknowledged as a great writer in Western Europe long before he was ever given this accolade in Russia.

When he arrived in Ventnor in 1860, he was already an author with a growing reputation. His short story collection called *A Sportsman's Sketches* had been published in 1852, and this had been followed by several novels. These included *Rudin*, a story about an intellectual man from a poor gentry background who is indecisive and ineffectual, despite having the best of intentions. Turgenev saw this as a commentary on the generation of the 1840s, young Russians trapped in an increasingly stultifying political and social environment. It would be a short step from here to the Nihilism of Bazarov.

Turgenev arrived in Britain in early August 1860 and first went to stay with Herzen and Annenkov at Herzen's temporary home in London. It was at their recommendation that Turgenev set out for the Isle of Wight, arriving in Ventnor on 12 August. He rented rooms in Rock Cottage, Belgrave Road, a house that was destroyed by bombing during the Second World War. The landlady was a prim woman of strong, non-conformist religious beliefs and was quick to criticize anything that she disliked in the behaviour of her Russian guest.

During the first few days of his stay, the sun shone out of a clear blue sky and Turgenev was enchanted by what he saw. 'What a delight this island is', he wrote to the Ukrainian folk story novelist Marko Vovchok, 'it is impossible to convey it! Trees, flowers, cliffs, the scent of freshy mown hay and the sea, in a word, luxury!'

Pavel Annenkov joined him on the 19 August and also rented rooms in Rock Cottage. However, their landlady was not at all happy with Annenkov's smoking habits and ordered him out of the cottage. Annenkov proposed to find a hotel in town and promised Turgenev that he 'would appear before his door each day and not puff any ungodly smoke about within the walls of the hallowed abode'.

Turgenev was furious at the censorious attitude of their landlady and headed down to the Esplanade where he managed to rent rooms in Belinda House for the two men. This remained their base for the rest of their stay in Ventnor, a good location as it was close to where many other Russian visitors were staying and was very near the seafront.

The weather took a turn for the worse just before Annenkov arrived. Clouds and heavy rain lashed the Isle of Wight and it was grey and chilly. On the 18 August, Turgenev wrote to his great friend, Countess de Lambert, that he enjoyed watching the 'bottle green, cold northern waves and seeing the straight-backed figures of English people out for a stroll on the damp, firm seaweed-striped sand'.

This poor weather persisted throughout the rest of the month. It may well have contributed to Turgenev's decision to spend his time indoors working with Annenkov and other Russians in Ventnor to launch a new initiative to support primary education for the rural masses in Russia.

As Richard Freeborn argues in his article *Turgenev in Ventnor,* this was a curious development. Turgenev had never shown any real interest in educational reform before he arrived on the Isle of Wight and would never do so again. It seems that the combination of bad weather, Annenkov's arrival, and the small colony of Russian radicals living in Ventnor may have tipped Turgenev into devoting time to what became, possibly to Turgenev's own surprise, a very radical project.

The summer of 1860 was a period of ferment and liberal idealism across both Russia and Europe. In Italy, Garibaldi was on the march and a new spirit of freedom was in the air. This optimism extended to Russia, where Tsar Alexander II was overturning the repressive government of his father and was on the verge of declaring freedom for the serfs.

Russian exiles in London, led by Herzen and Ogaryov, were already active in developing new ideas for a more liberal Russia. On 1 August 1860, an article was published by Ogaryov in the *Bell* called *Letters to a Compatriot*, which argued that the Russian nobility should now actively work in partnership with the peasantry to promote a strategy for communal land ownership. This would be the precursor to the complete democratisation of Russian society, which would rid the country of Tsarist bureaucracy and create self-governing peasant communes.

Ogaryov saw education as key to this process. He argued that 'it is necessary to prepare teachers, propagators of knowledge for the people, itinerant teachers or *Apostles* who would carry useful and practical knowledge from one end of Russia to the other'. Annenkov was fully familiar with these ideas when he arrived on the Isle of Wight.

In Ventnor he met a restless Turgenev, anxious to do something practical and useful with his time, now that the weather had taken a turn for the worse. It therefore did not take too much effort to persuade Turgenev of the important role that education could play in helping modernise Russia. The result was a decision to develop a draft programme for the establishment of a 'Society for the Propagation of Literacy and Primary Education'.

It seems to have been Turgenev who developed the aims for the Society and who corralled other members of the Russian community in Ventnor into getting actively involved in agreeing the draft programme. Kruze and Rostovstev were key members of the group, along with Turgenev and Annenkov.

Richard Freeborn describes 'many arguments, corrections, and adaptations' before the draft was finally presented to the Russian colony in Ventnor for their endorsement. The proposal was to establish a society that would teach 'people to read and write and to disseminate primary education. This would be a private initiative that would be carried out with the support of the Russian propertied and educated classes'.

This was a bold idea and it was fully in line with Ogaryov's proposal in the *Bell*. While Turgenev may not have perceived its revolutionary nature, many others certainly did. The Society's manifesto was circulated to artists, writers, and influential figures in both Russia and Britain. The proposal was viewed as too radical within Russia and gained little support at government level. Education for the rural masses was still viewed with suspicion, despite the more liberal nature of Tsar Alexander's regime.

The Ventnor manifesto on education, if it had been implemented, could have enhanced the lives of Russia's rural poor and made a significant contribution towards creating a literate peasant class half a century before the Bolshevik Revolution. Instead, Herzen and Turgenev later fell out over the work that had been done on the Isle of Wight that summer.

Herzen accused Turgenev of being a dilettante, without any long-term commitment to supporting genuine democratic change, and attacked him in various articles in the *Bell*. In 1862, he wrote to Turgenev, 'I never considered you to be a political person, and I don't consider you one now, despite the fact that along with Robinson Kruze on the Isle of Wight you talked about the alphabet for two weeks'.

Turgenev was stung by these criticisms and attacked what he saw as the unrealistic revolutionary socialism of Herzen, Ogaryov and Bakunin. Increasingly he mistrusted the political radicalism of the Russian exiles in Britain. The irony of the situation is that Turgenev, despite his political timidity, would in many ways have a major impact on Russia's revolutionary future both through his novel *Fathers and Sons* and through his commitment to educating the peasantry as a precursor to political action and change. The 'Alphabet of Revolution', bringing literacy to the masses, would be a strategy that the Bolsheviks would later adopt.

On 27 August, Annenkov decided that it was time to return to London, but he first wanted to call on Herzen who was then staying at his country cottage called the 'Eagle's Nest', located close to Poole in Hampshire. Turgenev was not ready to leave Ventnor but felt that a short break with Herzen in Poole would suit him very well, and so agreed to accompany Annenkov on the trip.

Turgenev and Annenkov's plans soon went completely awry. Herzen had a poor sense of geography, and before their departure from London, he had provided them with a highly inaccurate hand drawn map about the route to Poole. He placed Ventnor on the north coast of the Isle of Wight opposite Southampton and Bournemouth, when it in fact lies on the south-east coast, and he showed Bournemouth and Poole as being directly south of Southampton, when they both lie to the west of the port city. His house was illustrated by a bizarre sketch showing two tents with the words 'This is where I am setting up camp' scrawled underneath. The result was that Turgenev and Annenkov got completely lost in the suburbs of Southampton looking for the route to Poole.

Annenkov wrote later in his *Literary Reminiscences*, 'Turgenev and I wandered about on various roads for the whole day and then came to a stop close to Southampton, where we found a public stage coach and reached by nightfall the hill [near Poole] with the little house on top of it'. The hill was close to the sea and bore the proud name of the 'Eagle's Nest'. Turgenev was highly amused to discover that 'there was no eagle here, with the exception of the host, whose jovial laughter greeted us at the door'.

Herzen's poor map making skills were overlooked in the joy of the reunion. The three Russians appear to have spent an enjoyable two days together and doubtless discussed in enthusiastic terms the 'Society for the Propagation of Literacy and Primary Education'. At this stage, they would have had high hopes for its future success. Buoyed up by their time in Poole, Turgenev returned to Ventnor and Annenkov travelled on to London. The second half of Turgenev's stay on the Isle of Wight was to lead to the birth of his greatest novel.

The dark, stormy weather that he experienced in Ventnor that summer left an enduring impression on Turgenev's imagination. It was during his walks along the windswept cliffs at Blackgang Chine, a few miles south of Ventnor, that he conjured up the spirit of Ellis - the powerful and mystical force that would find full expression in his short story *Phantoms*. At the same time, the destructive and shadowy figure of Yevgeny Bazarov - the man who believed in nothing, not even his own value and worth - began to stir, taking shape in his mind.

Blackgang Chine, once a notorious haven for smugglers and wreckers, is a rocky ravine on the south-east coast of the Isle of Wight, which plunges sharply down into a wild stretch of sea. Above it rears St Catherine's Hill, crowned at its far end by the monument to Tsar Alexander I. It is a grim and sinister stretch of the Island's coastline, haunted by the memories of the many seamen and ships lost under its ragged cliffs.

Turgenev would walk across the hills from Ventnor to Blackgang Chine so that he could gaze at the foaming and raging sea, as it crashed on the rocks beneath him. Here was an elemental force, a seething and violent creation of nature that could not be subdued. In *Phantoms* which he wrote several years later, he recalls the scene that he saw.

'Overhead are heavy smoky clouds: they crowd together, they run, like a herd of wicked monsters... and there below is another monster: the enraged, literally enraged sea, white foam flickers and bubbles on the surface in mountains of water, and rearing up its ragged waves, it beats with a coarse thundering against an enormous rock, as black as tar. The wailing of the storm, the chilling rise and fall of the teeming depths. Everywhere death, death and horror... my head began to spin, and horror-struck I closed my eyes

'What is it? Where are we?'

'On the south coast of the Isle of Wight before Blackgang Rock' came the reply, 'where ships are so frequently broken to pieces'.

'Take me away, away from here... take me home, take me home!'

Out of this chaotic and primeval maelstrom, Turgenev saw a monstrous vision: 'I dreamed of a dark, wild, huge figure, half grown from the earth, strong, wicked, honest and nevertheless doomed to perish because it still stands on the threshold of the future'.

In that moment Turgenev conjured up the man from the future, the man who was already crushed and dying, the man who had fallen beneath the wheel. This was the inspiration for the tragic figure of Yevgeny Bazarov, the nihilist, who lived life without spiritual or emotional comfort in the belief that his entire existence was ultimately worthless. In this dark vision there was no place for love or affection, for artistic sensitivity or for culture and refinement.

Fathers and Sons shocked, disturbed and inspired an entire generation of young Russians. It seemed to be a cry emanating from deep within their soul and their culture. It echoed their political impotence, stifled by the bureaucracy and servitude of their homeland.

Turgenev's novel would help inspire a new revolutionary movement in Russia, Nihilism, which took the character of Bazarov as its guiding star. This was a movement conjured up by a man who had never actually existed. It was the ultimate rejection of the reality imposed on Russia by the Tsarist state. In the eyes of the Nihilists, this state had no authenticity, reality or legitimacy.

The Nihilists ran a campaign of terror across Russia in the last years of Tsarist rule, leading to the assassination of many government officials. Nihilism spawned movements such as the Circle of Tchaikovsky, the People's Will, and Land and Liberty. Their most famous victim would be Tsar Alexander II, assassinated in 1881 on the very day that he had approved new constitutional reforms.

To many Russians, the murder of Alexander II seemed cruel and pointless, striking at a ruler who was seeking to liberalise the country and improve the conditions for ordinary people. To the Nihilists however, this was the natural culmination of a struggle inspired by a complete rejection of feeling, empathy and emotion.

In early twentieth-century Russia, the appeal of Nihilism lingered long after the movement had been crushed by the Tsarist secret police. The Marxist revolutionary philosopher and journalist, Vladimir Alexandrovich Rudnev, adopted the name Bazarov in 1896 as an underground pseudonym. He would later develop the economic strategy for the new Soviet state.

Turgenev feared the power and destructive nature of Bazarov from the moment that he had summoned him into existence. He realised, with growing horror, that this was a spirit over which he had no control. There is a scene set on the sea front in Ventnor in Tom Stoppard's play *Salvage*, about Herzen and other Russian revolutionary exiles in the West. The play was first performed in London in 2002. Turgenev falls into conversation with a Russian doctor who is also holidaying on the Isle of Wight. The man turns out to be called Bazarov and tells Turgenev that the time has come 'to believe in nothing, Niente, Nihil'.

Turgenev protests, 'You don't believe in progress, morality or art?'. The doctor replies, 'especially not in progress, morality or art. Only the authority of facts. Everything else is sentimentality'. Turgenev shudders as it dawns on him that this is the man for whom he has been searching all his life. 'I have been looking out for you without knowing it', he tells Bazarov. 'The other day, the day that we had the storm, I went to look at Blackgang Chine. Have you been? It's not far from here'. The Russian doctor remains silent.

Turgenev continues, 'In that place, I realised that there is no hope for us. And there was a man in my mind suddenly, a dark nameless figure, strong, with no history, his ill intention complete. I knew that he was the future arrived before his time and that he too was doomed'. The scene in Stoppard's play ends with Turgenev asking the young doctor what to call him.

The doctor replies, 'Call me Bazarov'.

Half a century after Turgenev had created Bazarov, the last Tsar of Russia and his family made their final visit to the Isle of Wight. They spent their time in Cowes only a few miles from Ventnor and Blackgang Chine. It is doubtful that they made any connection between their visit and Turgenev's novel. However, within a few years they would all be murdered by men who, like Bazarov, dealt in harsh revolutionary facts and accepted that brutal acts needed to be carried out without compassion or regret. Nihilism and its gratuitous disregard for life spawned the violence of the Russian revolution, and the last Romanovs were destined to become the most famous victims of that monstrous creature summoned up out of the depths of the raging seas around Blackgang Chine.

One final link connects Ventnor with revolutionary Russia. That link was provided by Karl Marx. Although Marx was not a Russian, his seminal works *The Communist Manifesto* (published in 1848) and *Das Kapital* (the first volume of which appeared in 1867) were both to have a major influence on Russian political thinking, and would be adopted by the Bolsheviks as their ideological blue print for violent revolutionary change.

When the first Russian version of *Das Kapital* appeared in 1872, the Tsarist censors did not believe that it posed any threat to the regime. They considered it to be a tedious scientific political text, which would be read by only very few people, and understood by even smaller numbers. As a result, the censors did not place it on their list of banned titles. Within a few years they realised their mistake, but by then it was too late. The Russian version of *Das Kapital* sold faster than any other translation in the world. 3,000 copies were bought in its first year and numerous reprints were soon running off the presses in St Petersburg, Moscow and other major cities. Marx soon became aware of the huge interest that Russians were showing in his writings, and he began to regularly correspond with men like Herzen and Bakunin.

In 1883, there was a split in the popular Russian socialist revolutionary movement Land and Liberty, and the terrorist organisation People's Will was suppressed after the assassination of Alexander II. These events gave the opportunity for Marxism to emerge as an alternative revolutionary movement in Tsarist Russia. Marx, though, did not live long enough to see this happening, as he died in London on 14 March 1883.

During his time in England, Marx visited the Isle of Wight three times. He went first to Ryde in 1874, but on his subsequent visits in the winters of 1881 and 1882 he transferred his affections to Ventnor. Its reputedly healthy climate may have appealed to him, and the fact that many Russians continued to visit there, even in the colder months, would also have been an attraction. By the early 1880s he was fully aware of the strong appeal that his writings were making on Russian political radicals.

Marx was enchanted by the charms of the Island. In a letter to Friedrich Engels, written in 1874, he described how he sailed around the Island by boat, and called it 'a little paradise'. He did not return for another seven years, but in the autumn of 1881, with his health failing, he decided to spend that winter in Ventnor.

He rented lodgings at 1, St Boniface Gardens, a large and substantial house owned by a Scottish lady called Miss McClaren. It had a generously sized garden with good views over the sea. The house still stands to this day. Ventnor clearly impressed Marx. In a letter to Engels he wrote, 'One can stroll here for hours enjoying both sea and mountain at the same time'.

Marx settled comfortably into a daily routine. He was still writing the second, third and fourth volumes of *Das Kapital*. He went for regular walks by the sea, and he enjoyed wandering along the Downs which rise steeply behind Ventnor. Every Sunday he would walk along a footpath to the village of Bonchurch.

He returned to the same house in St Boniface Gardens during the winter of 1882. By this time, he was a sick man and would make frequent calls on the local doctor, Mr Williamson. Marx was now suffering from pneumonia and pleurisy, compounded by his long-standing liver problems and neuralgia. Williamson prescribed him quinine brews, morphia and chloroform, as well as equipping him with a respirator.

These growing health problems did not deter Marx from enjoying his walks in the fresh air. When he was not exploring the Downs, he continued to work on *Das Kapital* and found time to correspond with a wide variety of revolutionary thinkers across Europe. He was fascinated by mathematics, anthropology, history, politics and, for some reason, electricity, and enjoyed discussing and writing about all these subjects. He followed international political developments very closely but was also intrigued by local issues and court cases involving Ventnor.

Marx died in London in March 1883, a few weeks after returning from Ventnor. It was left to Engels to edit his final writings and prepare Volumes Two and Three of *Das Kapital* for publication. These appeared in print in 1885 and 1894. In Russia, the new Tsar, Alexander III, was reversing the limited reforms of his father. As Marx spent his final days in Ventnor, he observed Russia sinking back into a period of political repression. His last volumes of *Das Kapital*, composed as he sat in St Boniface Gardens, would be eagerly read by a new generation of young Russian radicals keen to destroy the entire power structure and society of Imperial Russia. Marx's political and economic thinking would directly contribute to the overthrow of the Romanov dynasty and the emergence of Soviet Russia.

TSARS ALEXANDER II
AND ALEXANDER III
AND ROYAL FAMILY TIES
1856-1894

14

Politics, liberation, and love

The death of Tsar Nicholas I in 1855 was followed by the accession of his eldest son, Alexander, popularly known as the Tsar-Liberator due to his decision to abolish serfdom in 1861. Ironically, despite this act of emancipation, he was to die violently at the hands of anarchist assassins, an event which would have long-term and tragic consequences for the final years of Romanov rule in Russia.

Alexander was the eldest son of Nicholas I and inherited the crown at a time when Russia was deeply embroiled in the Crimean War. One of his first decisions in 1856 was to end the war and agree to peace terms, even though these were not advantageous to Russian interests. Alexander recognised that the war was going badly, and that the Russian army was not in any fit state to continue fighting. He was also sensible enough to see that popular opposition to the war was growing inside Russia and this was undermining confidence in the Tsarist regime.

Alexander's foreign policy was relatively cautious. He sought to work in close collaboration with other major European powers. His primary aim was to avoid a repeat of the disaster that had befallen Russia in the Crimean war. This approach ensured that Alexander was able to achieve some major international successes, particularly over Bulgaria, where the

Tsar's skilful diplomacy following the Russo-Turkish War of 1877-78, led to the *Treaty of Berlin* and the establishment of an independent Bulgarian state for the first time since 1396.

Alexander's support for Bulgarian independence was not matched, however, by any similar sympathies for separatist movements within the Russian Empire. The Polish Uprising of 1863 was harshly suppressed. Poles, Lithuanians and Byelorussians were placed under martial law for the next forty years and a cultural and religious war now took place. The Russian language became the official language of these territories and the Orthodox faith was given preference, particularly over Roman Catholicism. This policy contrasted strongly with the Tsar's approach to the Grand Duchy of Finland, which was now given increased autonomy and treated as a favoured territory within the Empire.

Relations with Britain improved during Alexander's reign, compared to the low point that they had reached during the Crimean war. There was positive collaboration in relation to Bulgaria and the Ottoman Empire. In Central Asia, there was a new attempt to align British and Russian policies so that the interests of both powers were protected, particularly over Afghanistan, Tibet and Persia. Wherever possible, Alexander sought to avoid any direct confrontation with Britain.

In 1874, the Tsar's only daughter, Grand Duchess Maria Alexandrovna, married Queen Victoria's second son, Alfred, Duke of Edinburgh. This was the only time that a Romanov would marry into the British royal family. It was Alexander's hope that this dynastic marriage might improve ties between the two countries.

Despite these positive developments, mistrust and suspicion remained the defining features of Anglo-Russian relations during Alexander II's reign. The suppression of the Polish Uprising in 1863 confirmed the British view of the Tsar as an authoritarian and oppressive ruler. The memory of the Crimean War was still fresh and bitter in the minds of many in Britain. There was much concern over Russian ambitions in Central Asia and India. The image of the Russian Bear, claws outstretched and teeth bared for attack, remained a popular caricature of the Russian Empire throughout this period.

Alexander II visited Britain twice during his life. His first visit was in 1839. This was intended to be part of his broader education. Tsar Nicholas, despite his own conservatism, was keen that his son should enjoy a liberal education and learn as much as possible about Russia and the wider world.

In 1837, together with his tutor, the poet Zhukovsky, Alexander undertook a six-month tour of Russia. This included a visit to Siberia where he encountered some of the Decembrists and managed to intervene successfully on their behalf. He also met the writer and thinker Alexander Herzen, who had been exiled to the city of Vyata in north-eastern Russia for his radical political and social views.

Alexander took immediate steps to ensure that Herzen was released from detention in Vyata, and the writer was appointed to a senior position in the Ministry of the Interior in Moscow. Ultimately this was not a role that Herzen could tolerate and he eventually left Russia and settled abroad. Some have credited Herzen's political views with having influenced Alexander's decision to liberate the serfs in 1861, but there is little evidence for this.

In 1839, the Tsarevich Alexander arrived in London to spend a month in Britain as a special guest of the Queen. The young Victoria had only recently ascended the throne, and she was still unmarried. The Tsarevich was handsome, charming and a year older than the Queen.

In a whirl of balls, receptions, horse races and picnics, Victoria and Alexander became increasingly close. Victoria described Alexander as 'having a fine open countenance, fine blue eyes, and a pretty mouth with a sweet smile'. In a demonstration of Romanov extravagance, he brought with him a trunkful of diamond-inlaid boxes and enormous diamond rings which he handed around to anybody he liked or who had impressed him. This caused a lot of comment amongst some members of court society, with many seeing this as a vulgar display of Russian ostentation. Others fell under his spell and were impressed by his generosity and effortless style and vied for his attention. The Romanovs, it seems, could simultaneously both appal and attract their publics.

Alongside his diamond gifts, Alexander also made a generous donation to the Jockey Club, the largest commercial horse racing organisation in Britain. The £300 he gave was used to establish the *Cesarewitch*. This horse race was named in honour of the Tsarevich, and it has been run every year since 1839 at Newmarket in Suffolk. It is one of the longest major flat races in the country.

Victoria, for her part, had fallen for the young Grand Duke's charms from the moment that she had first met him. She now decided to invite him to stay with her at Windsor for three days as her personal guest, an invitation which scandalised many in the British establishment. At a ball held on the first evening of his stay, the young couple danced until three in the morning. Victoria wrote 'I think we are great friends already and get on very well: I like him exceedingly'. Back in London, during a visit that they made to the opera, the Tsarevich visited Victoria in her private box, and it was noted that the curtains were soon tightly closed.

Those in the Russian entourage accompanying the Tsarevich could no longer ignore the increasingly close relationship between Victoria and Alexander. A secret despatch was sent to Tsar Nicholas which reported, 'The Queen is clearly enjoying the society of His Imperial Majesty. Everyone is saying they are an ideal couple. Were the Grand Duke to make a proposal to the Queen, it would be accepted without hesitation'.

Victoria was falling for the handsome Russian Prince. She confided to her close companion, Baroness Louise Lehzen, that she was experiencing deep and passionate feelings for him. It seems that these were partly reciprocated, although Alexander's initial description of Victoria in his private diary was perhaps less than chivalrous. He wrote, 'she is very short, with a bad waist, uncomely face, but speaks charmingly'. However, Alexander told his aide-de-camp that he was in love with Victoria and was convinced that she felt the same way about him.

On both the Russian and British sides, there was growing unease about where this liaison was heading. Tsar Nicholas immediately ordered his son home to St Petersburg. It was made clear to Alexander that were he to marry Victoria he would have to give up the Russian throne and there was clearly no way that Victoria would have agreed to move to Russia and abandon her throne.

It is fascinating to speculate though what might have happened if Victoria and Alexander had married and reigned as two co-equal sovereigns. Would the nineteenth century have been dominated by a grand Anglo-Russian alliance? Maybe the Crimean War would have been avoided and the long era of rivalry and mistrust that has characterised relations between the two countries would never have occurred.

In her diary, Queen Victoria described their parting in words that convey the emotional experience it was for both of them. 'The Grand Duke took my hand and pressed it warmly. He looked pale and his voice faltered, as he said 'I do not have the words to describe how I feel for you… he hoped to return again and he trusted that all this would only tend to strengthen the ties of friendship between England and Russia. He then pressed and kissed my hand, and I kissed his cheek, upon which he kissed mine in a very affectionate manner. I felt sad to take leave of this dear amiable man with whom I really think I was a little in love'.

For several days after Alexander's departure, Victoria consoled herself by playing his favourite quadrilles. A few weeks later came the news that Alexander was engaged to marry a German Princess, Princess Maximiliane Sophie Marie of Hesse-Darmstadt. Alexander and Victoria were not to meet for another thirty-five years. In 1874, following the marriage of his daughter Maria to Alfred, Duke of Edinburgh, Tsar Alexander came on a state visit to Britain. By this time Victoria was a widow and Alexander was unhappily married and involved in a long- term relationship with his mistress, Princess Ekaterina Dolgorukaya.

Who can really know what Victoria and Alexander felt when they met again after so many years apart? It is possible that a spark of the old romance still lingered. The Queen noted in her diary that the Tsar looked 'terribly altered, so thin, and his face looks so old, sad and careworn'. There is a note of concern and sadness in her comments. On a positive note, as a result of the marriage between their son and daughter, they were to share grandchildren.

15

A Romanov Grand Duchess and Queen Victoria

Grand Duchess Maria Alexandrovna was the only Romanov to marry into the British royal family. Born in October 1853, she was the sole surviving daughter of Tsar Alexander II and his wife, Marie of Hesse-Darmstadt. Photographs and paintings of the Grand Duchess, even from an early age, show her to be a strong and determined character. It is easy to see that she drew on the same gene pool as her autocratic and authoritarian brother, the future Tsar Alexander III. Pretty and beguiling in her youth, Maria would go on to develop a full, rounded face, with a clear and steely gaze.

Her father adored her. She was intelligent, lively and took a keen interest in everything around her. From an early age, she reportedly used to read all her father's diplomatic and consular correspondence. According to Diana Mandache, who has edited the writings of Grand Duchess Maria, 'her personality was a distinctive mix of dominant behaviour and imperial outlook tempered by an astute, realistic perception of the world'.

In 1868, the young fifteen-year old Princess was visiting relatives in Hesse-Darmstadt, when she first met Alfred, Duke of Edinburgh, the second son of Queen Victoria. He was then aged twenty-four and was serving in the Royal Navy. Three years later, they met again and there was an immediate and mutual attraction. They decided that they wanted to marry but both families were against the match. The Tsar was very closely attached to his only daughter, and he did not want to see her moving abroad. He was also aware that there was still a lot of anti-British sentiment in Russia in the aftermath of the Crimean War. From the British side, Queen Victoria was also not in favour of the marriage. She felt that there would be complications in permitting a Russian Princess to marry into the British royal family and her old mistrust of the Romanovs resurfaced.

There were frantic attempts on both sides to postpone any move towards an official engagement and the Tsar lined up a bevy of prospective suitors for Maria. She declined to meet any of them. Alfred, meanwhile, declared his undying love for his Russian Princess. He refused to believe the rumours that were circulating in both the British and Russian courts that she had had an affair with a Russian nobleman.

In June 1873, the Tsar and Tsarina finally consented to a meeting with Prince Alfred. A month later, the young couple were engaged. Alfred wrote to his mother requesting her blessing on their union. Queen Victoria sent her congratulations but confided her worries to her diary on 11 July 1873, 'Not knowing Maria, and realising that there may still be many difficulties, my thoughts and feelings are rather mixed'.

The Tsar gifted his daughter a very generous dowry amounting to over £100,000 (worth over £11 million in today's money) plus an annual allowance of £32,000 a year. In addition, he gave his daughter some of the most famous Romanov jewels, including a diamond and ruby parure set made up of a necklace, earrings, brooch, bracelet and tiara. It was a lavish and extravagant gesture, but it did not please the Queen, who had always disapproved of what she perceived as the Romanov penchant for vulgar excess. To round things off with a flourish, Alfred was also made an Honorary Chief of a Russian Guards regiment and had a Russian battleship named after him. This was appropriately called the *Herzog Edinburgsky*.

Tensions between Queen Victoria and the Tsar were not slow to emerge. First, the Tsar refused to bring his daughter to Balmoral to meet with Victoria. She then turned down a request from the Russians that the two families meet in Cologne, describing this as a 'simply impertinent' suggestion. She felt that she was the senior monarch in Europe, having ascended to the throne twenty years before Alexander.

On 23 January 1874, the marriage between Prince Alfred and Grand Duchess Maria took place in St Petersburg. At the request of Queen Victoria, there were two wedding ceremonies, both held in the Winter Palace. The first was a Russian Orthodox celebration, presided over by the Metropolitans of St Petersburg, Moscow and Kiev. The second was an Anglican service which was conducted by Arthur Stanley, the Dean of Westminster. The Queen herself did not make the journey to Russia for the double wedding but she was represented by the Prince of Wales and his wife, Alexandra.

The double wedding in St Petersburg was a glittering and lavish occasion, and both the Russian and British guests were dressed in full imperial and military uniforms. Grand Duchess Maria wore a mantle of crimson velvet trimmed with ermine, and a coronet which sparkled with rubies and diamonds in the light of a thousand flickering candles. The British guests invited to the two ceremonies were overwhelmed by the scale of the Russian celebrations and by the magnificence of all the entertainments that accompanied the marriage. They were whisked from one exotic location to another in gilded sleighs, wrapped in expensive furs, welcomed inside grand palaces where meals for five hundred guests would be routinely served up, and where the dancing lasted till dawn. It was easy to be seduced by the excess and glory of Imperial Russia and more than a few of the British guests found themselves turning into convinced Russophiles.

That day, in London, the Queen celebrated her son's wedding in a more sober and restrained manner. In honour of the Romanov Princess who was marrying into the British royal family, she wore the Imperial Russian Order of St Catherine. This consisted of a scarlet sash embroidered with silver, a jewelled badge in the shape of a cross, and an eight-pointed, silver-set star with diamond-encrusted rays. She raised a toast to the newly wedded couple.

The Tsar was described as looking pale and sad throughout the wedding celebrations in St Petersburg. He was very close to his only daughter, and the thought of losing her to Britain was almost too much for him to bear. He continued to hope that Maria and Alfred would decide to make their permanent home in Russia. Until his death seven years later, he insisted that their honeymoon suite should be preserved for the young couple in case they should ever decide to return.

Grand Duchess Maria and her husband arrived in England in early March 1874 and travelled first to Windsor where they were met at the station by the Queen. The town was colourfully festooned with both Imperial Russian flags and Union Jacks. A nervous Maria was warmly embraced by Victoria who wrote in her diary, 'I took dear Maria in my arms and kissed her warmly several times'.

Unexpectedly, the Queen found that she was falling for her son's new bride. 'She has a very friendly manner, a pleasant face, beautiful skin and fine bright eyes'. The more she saw of Maria, the more she was impressed. 'She has a serious intelligent mind, and her occupation and interest in everything makes her a most agreeable companion. Everyone must like her'. Despite her initial opposition to the Russian marriage, the charm of the Romanovs was now working its old magic on the Queen.

After a public entry into London on 12 March, where thousands of curious people lined the route from Paddington to Buckingham Palace to welcome their new Russian Princess, the couple settled into Clarence House, which became their main residence. They were also given a 2,500-acre country estate at Eastwell Park, near Ashford in Kent.

Maria's reactions to her arrival in England were tinged with homesickness and disappointment. She thought that London was a rather dull and boring city and compared it unfavourably with the glamour and imperial grandeur of St Petersburg. She found the capital's social scene tedious and considered most of the royal family to lack any serious intellectual interests. She thought that the Princess of Wales was a 'light minded and foolish woman'. To cap it all, the weather in Britain was abominable and she felt constantly cold in the unheated palaces and royal residences where she was required to stay. She particularly disliked Balmoral.

Maria found the separation from her beloved father and from her homeland very difficult to deal with, and she returned to Russia at every opportunity. Many years later, in a private letter that she wrote to King

Carol I of Romania on the eve of her daughter's marriage to his son, she confessed, 'For years I suffered from homesickness of the highest degree, not only a simple longing for my own country, but a longing more than anything else for the environment in which I was born and bred. The homesickness sometimes became a true illness.'

She went on to write, 'the only thing which sustained me on this painful journey was the frequent visits I was able to make to Russia. I would never have been able to bear the long months in England without the hope of the frequent outings and several months spent with my family and in a Russian environment among my family, friends, and acquaintances. Each time they gave me the strength and courage to return to England and do my duty. After almost twenty years, I have finally mastered those feelings'

It was soon after her arrival in Britain that the newly married couple were summoned down to the Isle of Wight and it was here that Maria found that she would spend more and more of her time. At first, she and Alfred were lodged in Osborne House but later she took up residence in Osborne Cottage, a comfortable and spacious house in the grounds of the royal estate.

Increasingly she found the Queen's company at Osborne irksome and oppressive, and she did not enjoy talking late into the night with her. In letters to her father she described the Queen as a 'silly, obstinate old fool', and 'a capricious old lady'. Tensions between the two of them soon began to rise. Maria herself was no fool and despite her private concerns about Victoria, she also recognised that it was important that she try to maintain as positive a relationship as she could with the most powerful Queen in the world. On several occasions, however, this willingness to compromise wore thin and there were open disagreements between Victoria and her Russian daughter-in-law.

Maria's high-handed attitude also alienated many of Victoria's courtiers. They were appalled by what they perceived as the arrogance and lack of respect exhibited by the Grand Duchess. Maria would regularly smoke in public, even in the presence of the Queen, and no attempt to dissuade her from doing this had any effect at all. In this regard, she displayed the worst aspects of Romanov obstinacy.

As the leading Grand Duchess in Russia, Maria insisted that she should take precedence over everyone at Court, apart from the Queen. This included the Princess of Wales, a woman whom she did not like or respect. There were regular squabbles with Victoria about her position at official functions and dinners, which drove both women to the brink of public showdowns.

In order to outshine the British princesses, Maria would regularly turn up wearing her most magnificent diamonds and rubies. Victoria was furious and whenever Maria appeared like this, it was clear that the Queen did not hide her feelings. She was described as looking at Maria with 'her mouth drawn down at the corners in an expression which those who knew her had learned to dread'. The Queen's crosspatch face did not appear to worry Maria.

In later years Maria wrote, 'The English court regard me as a real curiosity because I don't intrigue and don't get involved in the petty intrigues of the Ladies-in-Waiting and the servants. I also keep my suite and my servants away from these English court intrigues. This is why the English family is not fond of me.'

She went on to have some interesting reflections about whether her marriage had helped improve Anglo-Russian relations and decided that it had made no difference at all. 'Before my own marriage, in Russia and above all in England, there was so much shouting in celebration of the enormous political importance of the union and what have been the results? None whatsoever'.

Maria was an astute and sharp observer of what was going on at the British court and she was under no illusions about how she was perceived. Her only close friends at court were the Queen's youngest daughter, Princess Beatrice, who was later to become Governor of the Isle of Wight, and the young Prince Leopold who was to die of haemophilia at the age of thirty-two. Her friendship with Beatrice blossomed and turned Maria's summer visits to Osborne Cottage into enjoyable and relatively carefree events. The two women were often seen in each other's company and Beatrice's personal dedication to Victoria earned Maria's admiration and eventually softened her critical attitude towards the Queen.

Two months after Maria's arrival in Britain, her father decided he would like to make a trip to see her. On 13 May 1874, Alexander II arrived in Dover at the start of an official three-day state visit, the last ever made by a Russian Tsar. The 1909 visit by Nicholas II was never formally accorded the status of a state visit.

The Russian press was ecstatic at the prospect of the Tsar being received by Queen Victoria. A leader article in *Golos Moskvy*, one of Russia's politically moderate newspapers, reported that the visit marked a turning point for Russia's international reputation.

'While serfdom existed Russia was strong, yet more dreaded than loved by her neighbours. Now that we are free and have entered on a more judicious and promising path, we are regarded by Europe as a progressive Power interested in the maintenance of peace and the friend of liberalism rather than reaction as formerly was the case'.

There would have been many inside and outside Russia who would have questioned this rather over optimistic interpretation of Russia's new commitment to freedom and liberal values. However, there is also no doubt that there were people in Russia who genuinely believed that Alexander II's reign had ushered in a new spirit of constitutional government. There was everything to hope for in this more open environment.

The *Golos* article went on to extol the new Anglo-Russian friendship and how it might benefit Russia. 'There is no doubt that our present satisfactory relations with England, now cemented by family ties, and rendered still more intimate by the forthcoming state visit, will not remain without its fruit'. Conjuring up the memory of the visit by Peter the Great to England 176 years earlier, the newspaper stated that while Russia had profited in 1698 from the shipbuilders of Deptford and the Isle of Wight, it would now benefit from adopting the British respect for liberty, the law, and civic duty. These virtues would 'embed the recently won liberal reforms into the heart and soul of Russian society'.

The Tsar had originally intended to arrive in Gravesend on the north coast of Kent. The town was ready and waiting, and a public holiday had been declared. Imperial Russian Flags and Union Jacks were hanging in all the streets. Thousands of tickets had been sold to visitors who were eager to greet the arrival of the Tsar and his entourage. Prince Arthur of Connaught, Victoria's third son, had made his way to Gravesend, resplendent in the blue and gold uniform of the Queen's Seventh Hussars.

The Corporation of Gravesend had sent a formal request to the Admiralty that the entire Channel fleet should be moored off the town. This request had been endorsed by the Harbourmaster, who said that there was enough water in the Gravesend Roads to permit this. The Admiralty did not agree to this request but instead sent HMS *Triumph*, a 6,000-ton armoured ironclad battleship - one of the newest in the Channel fleet - to salute the Tsar on his arrival. In the meantime, workmen were busy at the North Kent railway station, from where the Tsar would depart for London, turning the whole building into a conservatory with shrubs, flowers and elegant garden furniture.

The official welcoming party, composed of the Prince of Wales, the Duke of Cambridge and Grand Duchess Maria, was on board the royal train at Charing Cross station and waiting to leave for Gravesend when news arrived that a mishap had befallen the Russian imperial yacht, *Derzhava*. It had run aground on a sandbank close to Flushing, due to the incompetence of the Dutch pilot who was guiding the boat. The Tsar and his entourage were stranded until the next high tide, which meant that the *Derzhava* would not reach Gravesend in time to catch the high water there. This would result in a further delay. It was decided that in order to save time, the *Derzhava* would divert to Dover, from where the Tsar could make a quick journey by train to London.

The *Daily Telegraph* commented wryly, 'A Dutch mud-bank yesterday upset the arrangements of two Empires, disappointed countless people, and held the Tsar of All the Russias, the most powerful and autocratic of potentates, a helpless prisoner amidst the crabs and periwinkles of the Flushing coast'.

There was a sense of widespread disappointment in Gravesend, as the news that they had lost the Tsar to Dover filtered through to the assembled dignitaries and waiting crowds. The Prince of Wales sent an immediate message of consolation to the town. This thoughtful action did not assuage the Mayor's anger. He felt that Gravesend had been badly let down and he did not refrain from expressing his irritation that Dover had profited from his town's misfortune as a result of a muddy Dutch sandbank.

In Dover, a hastily laid out red carpet was quickly produced, so that the Tsar would feel he was receiving some sort of official welcome when he descended the gangplank from the imperial yacht. Flower shops were raided, their floral displays stacked alongside the quayside and in the station waiting hall. An official address written on vellum was also rather miraculously conjured up and 'finished off with a pendulous seal of the hue and size of a Chichester lobster'.

It was after 10pm in the evening when the Tsar's train finally reached Windsor. The Queen and the welcoming party had been anticipating the Tsar's arrival since the afternoon and were tired and exasperated by the delay. 'What a contretemps!' noted Victoria in her diary. 'We only sat down to dinner at a quarter to eleven'. Over dinner, which was hosted by Victoria in the Oak Room of Windsor Castle, a selection of waltz and ballet music by Meyerbeer and Rossini was played by the Band of the 1st Lifeguards.

The following day was spent exploring Windsor Castle and Virginia Water. The Tsar, accompanied by the Prince of Wales, the Duke of Edinburgh and by Prince Arthur, first visited Frogmore where they saw the tomb of Prince Albert. This was almost akin to a sacred rite for any high-ranking dignitary who was a guest of the Queen. The tomb is housed in the Royal Mausoleum, built in the shape of a Greek cross, with granite and Portland stone walls and a roof covered with Australian copper. Albert had been buried in a huge monumental tomb, hewn out of a single piece of grey Aberdeen granite, which stood under a recumbent marble effigy of the Prince. Alexander's thoughts on seeing this extraordinary tribute to Victoria's dead husband were never recorded.

After visiting Frogmore, the Tsar returned to the Castle, where he was welcomed by the Reverend Gerald Wellesley, the Dean of Windsor, who conducted him on a tour of the Wolsey Chapel, which was then being turned into a memorial chapel for Prince Albert. Alexander showed a great deal of interest in the magnificent sculptures and mosaics that were being installed, and he examined these carefully.

The afternoon was spent with the Queen touring Windsor Great Park. Alexander and Victoria travelled in a carriage together with Grand Duchess Maria and the Princess of Wales. They first stopped at the Flemish Farm, where they assisted in the trial of a new steam threshing machine. This may seem an odd thing for the Tsar to have done, but Alexander was committed to constantly improving the productivity of Russia's agricultural sector. He was a great believer that the future wealth of Russia lay in efficiently exploiting the land and enhancing industrial farming methods. *The Times* reported the following day that 'if the machine in question becomes as popular as it promises to be, it must make a most material increase in the wealth of Russia by giving an extraordinary impulse to agriculture and commerce'. Alexander was never slow to spot new opportunities.

From the Flemish Farm, they proceeded to Virginia Water, a large man-made lake complete with artificial waterfalls and classical ruins. Alexander appeared to enjoy his time wandering amongst the Corinthian columns and stone archways of the Temple of Augustus, rescued from Leptis Magna, the great Roman city in Libya. The afternoon ended with a trip on the lake in a barge, crewed by a team of rowers sent up specially for the occasion from Gosport in Hampshire.

The steam threshing machine and the ruins of Leptis Magna perfectly sum up the character of the ruler that they called the 'Tsar Liberator'. Alexander was, in many ways, the last great hope of Imperial Russia, combining a love of the arts with a commitment to limited political reform, emancipation from serfdom and industrial progress.

That evening, the Queen hosted a State banquet for the Tsar in St George's Hall. It was a magnificent affair and no expense was spared in impressing the Imperial Russian visitors. Victoria sat between the Tsar and his son, Grand Duke Alexei, then third in line to the throne. A band of the Coldstream Guards played a selection of Russian dances together with music by Strauss and Meyerbeer. There were toasts to the Tsar and the Queen, and the glittering company rose to salute the anthems of both countries.

The following morning, Alexander and his entourage travelled to London on a specially chartered train of the Great Western Railway company. They reached Paddington station around midday and took carriages to Buckingham Palace, under the escort of the Royal Horse Guards. That afternoon the Tsar received members of the British government in the Bow drawing room at Buckingham Palace.

The Conservative Prime Minister, Benjamin Disraeli, was the first to be greeted by Alexander. Although he had been an energetic opponent of Russia during the Crimean War, he was one of the first British politicians to call for peace and was generally well disposed towards building stronger ties with Russia. In May 1874, the Conservative party had only been in power for four months and Disraeli had led the Conservative party to its greatest election victory since 1841.

The Tsar was intrigued by this Jewish political outsider who, despite all the odds and difficulties stacked up against him, had managed to claw his way to the top of a political party dominated by aristocrats and industrialists. He contrasted this with the prejudices and discrimination that still prevailed in Russian political and business circles and confided to a friend that he longed to see his own country become as tolerant as Britain, so that a man like Disraeli could rise to the very top of government.

In the evening, the Tsar and his party attended a ball at Stafford House, now known as Lancaster House. In 1874, this was one of the grandest private residences in London, eliciting the comment from Queen Victoria when she had first visited it, 'I have come from my House to your Palace'. The Tsar's hosts were the Duke and Duchess of Sutherland, both well known for their support of liberal causes in Britain and around the world.

Amongst their friends were the factory reformer Lord Shaftesbury, the anti-slavery campaigner Harriet Beecher Stowe who had visited them in 1856, and the Italian revolutionary leader Giuseppe Garibaldi. The latter had stayed with them in 1864, combining this with a visit to both Alexander Herzen and his great friend and supporter Charles Seely on the Isle of Wight. The invitation from the Sutherlands to the Tsar was deliberately intended to send a signal to British and Russian society that they considered Alexander to be on the side of reform and political freedom.

There was a special bond between the Tsar and the Duke of Sutherland. The latter had been a keen advocate of restoring full diplomatic ties between Russia and Britain following the Crimean War. In 1856, he attended the coronation of the new Tsar in St Petersburg, one of the first people in Britain to visit Russia following the cessation of hostilities between the two countries. This had been noted by Alexander and he was therefore keen to repay the Duke's friendship by appearing at the Stafford House Ball during his visit to London.

Over eight hundred people were invited as guests that night, all of them eager to meet the Tsar. Alexander arrived at around eleven in the evening, in the company of the Prince and Princess of Wales and the Duke and Duchess of Edinburgh. He led the way up the grand staircase with the Duchess of Sutherland on his arm, while the Guards Band in the hall struck up the notes of the Russian imperial anthem. Alexander was quick to take to the dance floor and partnered the Duchess of Sutherland in a lively quadrille.

The Russian party stayed for over two hours, enjoying the hospitality and adoration of London society. Anglo-Russian relations had reached a high point not seen since the visit of Tsar Alexander I in 1814. The marriage between the two royal families and the Tsar's state visit seemed to have set the seal on a new era of cooperation between the two Empires.

Sadly, this optimistic spirit was not to last. In 1877, only three years after Alexander's visit to Britain, there was a huge diplomatic confrontation between the two countries over the future of Turkey's territories in Europe. Russia had invaded the Balkans with the aim of liberating Romania and Bulgaria from Ottoman rule. This had long been a Russian objective and it was a strategy of expansion that Britain had always resisted. The Queen sent a series of aggressive telegrams to the Tsar, threatening him and his country with dire consequences if Russia persisted in its actions. Russia and Britain teetered on the brink of war.

Grand Duchess Maria was horrified by what the Queen had done, and never forgave Victoria for the hostility shown to her native country and to her father. From this date on, Maria is rumoured to have become a convinced Anglophobe and never again trusted her adopted country.

Increasingly, Maria found ways to distance herself from life in Britain. For several years she accompanied her husband on his posting to Malta as the Admiral of the Royal Navy. From 1887 the couple also spent an increasing amount of time in Coburg, where Alfred was now the official heir to the throne of the Duchy of Saxe-Coburg and Gotha. They lived in what became known as the Edinburgh Palace, an elegant building that stood opposite the Duke's official residence.

Alfred succeeded to the title of Duke in 1893, and from that time on, Coburg became their main home. Maria enjoyed life there. It appealed to her cultural and intellectual sensibilities, and she felt that she had an important role to play in the life of the Duchy. She spent her time in helping restore the castles scattered across the Ducal estates and she also supported various charities. This included opening an establishment for the mentally handicapped, work for which she received a great deal of praise. Opera, music, and stimulating conversation were also her passions and she found plenty to entertain and occupy her in her new adopted home.

Despite now living far from Queen Victoria, the tensions between the two women persisted. In February 1896, Maria wrote to her daughter, Marie, and told her how she had managed to avoid being summoned back to the Isle of Wight for the funeral of Prince Henry of Battenberg. The Court at Coburg, however, had to observe official mourning for a week. She described this as 'very unfortunate, as we cannot give any balls now and no theatre is allowed'. She went on to write, 'Granny [Victoria] is terribly fussy, thinking the whole time that we are going to neglect the mourning'. The relationship between the Queen and her Romanov daughter-in-law remained tense and prickly till the end.

As a Romanov she had never felt fully accepted by the British court but in Coburg things were different. There was a long history of German ducal princesses marrying into the Russian imperial family, and the local population took pride in the fact that they had a Russian princess now living amongst them. She encountered no suspicion and mistrust from her new German subjects.

Maria's great passion was her family. She and Alfred had five children. A son, also called Alfred, and four daughters, Marie, Victoria Melita, Alexandra and Beatrice. She was devoted to her children, although this did not prevent her from spending long periods away from them during her increasingly frequent trips to Russia, Germany and Denmark. This was an opportunity, though, for the children to visit their grandmother, Queen Victoria, on the Isle of Wight, where they were usually accommodated at Osborne Cottage. There they mixed with their Hesse cousins, including Alix and her sister Elizabeth, both of whom were destined to marry into the Romanov family.

All five of Maria's children grew to love the Island, although it was the eldest daughter, Marie (nicknamed Missy) who seems to have developed the closest affection for her life there. In later life, when she was Crown Princess of Romania, Missy and her husband Prince Ferdinand would spend holidays at Osborne. In a letter to her mother dated July 1900, Missy described it as 'Our dear Osborne' and lamented the fact that Queen Victoria had not invited them to spend the summer with her.

Life, though, had its difficulties. Grand Duchess Maria's relationship with her husband deteriorated. He was unfaithful on several occasions and from the early 1880s it was clear that he was increasingly drifting into alcoholism. She described her role as being no more than Prince Alfred's 'legitimate mistress'. In 1881, her beloved father Alexander II was assassinated in St Petersburg. Maria was devastated and returned to Russia for his funeral, staying on for the coronation of her brother, Alexander III. Throughout her life, Maria made frequent visits to Russia in order to see her family and enjoyed immersing herself in the gossip and intrigue of the imperial court.

She proved to be a sharp observer of what was happening with the Romanov family and as the century drew to its close, she became increasingly concerned by what she perceived as the withdrawn behaviour of her nephew Tsar Nicholas and his wife, Alexandra. Maria sympathised with the flamboyant and extravagant nature of Russian imperial rule where public show was everything, and she did not like or understand the quiet, subdued approach adopted by the young Tsar and his wife.

In October 1897 in a letter to her daughter, Marie, she described an afternoon with the Tsarina. 'She is no doubt most excellent but is most dull. I had to sit with her a whole afternoon and at the tennis where she would not move but only looked on'. In August 1898, she observed that, 'Nicky and Alix shut themselves up more than ever and never see a soul. Alix is not a bit popular'. Her concerns about the way that the Tsar and Tsarina were isolating themselves from the mainstream of Russian life were shared by many other members of the Romanov family, by wider Court circles and, increasingly, by the Russian public.

Sadly, in later life, Maria's own children would also create problems for her. Prince Alfred, her eldest child, died at the age of twenty-four in mysterious circumstances. He was an emotionally unstable young man, and it appears that he tried to shoot himself following a family argument over his love life. He died in February 1899 at a sanatorium in Austria-Hungary.

Maria's daughter Victoria Melita, nicknamed Ducky, divorced her husband Ernest Louis, the Grand Duke of Hesse, in 1901, after discovering that he was involved in a succession of homosexual relationships with footmen and servants working at his court. The divorce created a scandal across the whole of Europe, though Maria openly supported her daughter's decision.

In 1905 Ducky married Kirill Vladimirovich, a Russian Grand Duke, who was a first cousin of Tsar Nicholas II. This marriage also provoked a scandal. As they were first cousins this was in contravention of Russia's dynastic legislation, which explicitly forbade marriage between two cousins. The Tsar exiled them both from Russia. Nicholas's reaction could also be partly explained by the fact that Victoria Melita's first husband, Grand Duke Ernest of Hesse, was the only brother of Tsarina Alexandra and she was hugely protective of her brother and his reputation.

It was with her eldest daughter Marie, who became Crown Princess of Romania in 1893, that Grand Duchess Maria would form her closest family relationship. Mother and daughter maintained a long-standing correspondence over many years and shared confidences on a whole range of issues. The letters make many references to Osborne and Queen Victoria.

The twentieth century brought little happiness for Grand Duchess Maria. The Russian Revolution destroyed the power of the Romanov dynasty, and she lost many close relatives, including her nephew Tsar Nicholas II and her brother, Grand Duke Paul Alexandrovich. Her personal fortune was confiscated by the Bolshevik government. Although she had supported Germany in the First World War, she was driven into exile because of her strong links to both Russia and Britain. Angry mobs regularly surrounded her car in Coburg and she eventually fled from Germany to seek shelter in Switzerland.

In 1918, the Duchy of Saxe-Coburg and Gotha was officially abolished. Deprived of both her Russian and German income, and dependant on a small annual payment from Britain, she slipped into penury and genteel poverty. The last surviving daughter of Tsar Alexander II died in her sleep in Zurich in October 1920, aged sixty-seven. In her last days, she believed that the British royal family had committed an act of gross betrayal in not saving the Tsar and his family and this was one final grudge that she would hold against her adopted country till the end.

16

Reform and terror

Alexander II has often been described as the last great Tsar. During his reign Russia enjoyed a greater measure of political freedom and economic prosperity than at any time hitherto. This was also a new golden age of culture and art, comparable in its achievements to the reign of Catherine the Great. The abolition of serfdom in 1861 was part of an overhaul of Russian society that Alexander felt was long overdue. Almost as soon as he became Tsar, Alexander lifted many of the restrictions imposed by his father. Censorship was eased, foreign passports were issued, and there was a reform of the army, the police and government bureaucracy.

Newly liberated serfs would become a powerful factor in the economic transformation of Russia and the rise of a new middle class. At the same time, Russia was industrialising and a new urban proletariat was emerging. All this was to have a major impact on the future of Russia in the late nineteenth and early twentieth centuries. Political and social forces were being unleashed which it would be increasingly difficult for the traditional Tsarist power structures to control.

Alexander's commitment to these changes was cautious. He recognised that there was a need for political, judicial and constitutional reforms, but he was committed to doing these in ways that preserved Russia's internal stability and social cohesion. Alexander was in no sense a liberal. He was prepared to consult with a wider group of the aristocracy and gentry in the running of the country, but he was not prepared to broaden that consultation to other sections of Russian society.

In 1864 Alexander approved new forms of self-government at district and provincial level. Significant legal reforms were introduced, including trial by jury and public hearings. There were also plans for constitutional changes, but these were never introduced. In 1866, a young man, Dmitry Karakozov, attempted to assassinate the Tsar. This was a huge shock to Alexander and from this point on he began to adopt a more conservative and repressive domestic policy.

Alongside the limited political and economic reforms introduced in this period, there was now a flowering of Russian art and culture. Russian writers, composers and painters sought to widen the appeal of their works beyond the aristocratic elites who had been their traditional patrons. The aim of authors like Tolstoy and Turgenev, and composers like Tchaikovsky and Rimsky-Korsakov, was to reach larger audiences, both amongst the growing middle classes in the cities and the increasingly prosperous peasant families in the rural areas.

Russia was changing, and this new spirit of cultural creativity and controlled political reform seemed to augur well for the last decades of the nineteenth century. However, there were also worrying signs that social and political tensions were starting to emerge and these would gather pace as the century neared its end.

The Tsarist system, despite its attempts to modernise and reform, was still seen as autocratic and corrupt by the more radical elements in Russian society. Intellectuals were growing impatient with the pace of change in the country and frustrated by what they saw as Alexander's limited commitment to reform. Socialist study circles began to emerge across Russia in the 1870s, particularly amongst students. These were heavily influenced by the writings of men like Alexander Herzen, Pyotr Lavrov and Alexander Bakunin.

Various populist movements tried to translate this thinking into action. In 1874, a mass movement of intellectuals, students, doctors and teachers emerged, which aimed to start spreading socialist and revolutionary ideologies through working and living with the peasantry in the countryside. At its peak, perhaps as many as 2,000 people were involved in this movement, which was given the name of 'Going to the People'. 1,600 of its members were soon arrested and the movement collapsed.

This failure radicalised the political opposition to Tsarism and laid the foundations for the revolutionary terrorism that was to become a hallmark of the last years of Romanov rule in Russia. In 1876, a new, secret revolutionary organisation appeared. This was founded in St Petersburg and was called 'Zemlya I Volya' (Land and Liberty). Its avowed aim was violent revolution, and its programme argued for direct action against the Tsarist regime. The days of dialogue and talk appeared to be over.

In 1879, the movement split. The members who argued for a peaceful approach to revolution set up a new organisation called 'Black Repartition'. Those committed to terrorism as the only means of achieving their aims created what was to become the most feared terrorist organisation operating inside Imperial Russia. This was known as 'Narodnaya Volya', the People's Will. Although this movement set out its own political manifesto, its primary aim was to create maximum terror, and to break the Tsarist system through acts of extreme violence. One of its first formal acts was to sentence Tsar Alexander to death in August 1879.

A series of terror attacks now took place, with the direct intention of killing the Tsar. There were attempts to sink a ship in which he was sailing, and then to blow up the royal train. The most serious attack was in February 1880, when the dining room in the Winter Palace was destroyed by a bomb. Eleven people were killed and fifty-six injured. The Tsar had been held up waiting for a delayed guest. Otherwise he would certainly have been a victim of the blast. There had been attempts on Alexander's life as far back as 1866, but the campaign mounted by the People's Will was the most sustained and, ultimately, the most successful.

Alexander became a nervous and withdrawn man. In the last few months of his life he barely left the safety of his palaces. On 13 March 1881, members of the People's Will struck again. A bomb was thrown at his carriage in St Petersburg. He was not injured in the explosion but climbed out of the carriage to assist the wounded and dying. This was the opportunity for a young revolutionary, Ignacy Hryniewiecki, to throw a second bomb directly at the Tsar. The explosion seriously injured Alexander, blowing off both his legs. Although he was immediately taken back to the Winter Palace, and the doctors were hastily summoned, he died within a few minutes of his arrival there, surrounded by shocked and horrified members of the Romanov family.

Hryniewiecki has been described as the world's first suicide bomber. He accepted that he would not survive the attack. In a letter that he wrote on the night before the assassination, he penned the ominous words, 'Alexander II must die. He will die and with him, we, his enemies, his executioners will die too.'

It is one of the great ironies of history that Alexander was assassinated on the very day that he had finally approved a range of constitutional and administrative reforms. These were proposed by his specially appointed Minister, Count Mikhail Loris-Melikov. The new decrees were intended to address some of the concerns that underlay popular discontent towards the Tsarist regime, particularly amongst the elite sections in Russian society. A limited role for a consultative assembly dominated by the nobility was envisaged. It is interesting to speculate whether this may have evolved into a broader, consultative body which might have moved the country towards a more representative form of government earlier in its history.

A memorial church was built in St Petersburg on the site of Alexander's assassination. The 'Church of the Saviour on the Spilt Blood' became a chilling reminder of the violence that had now reached into the very heart of Imperial Russia. The new Tsar, Alexander III, and his son, Grand Duke Nicholas Alexandrovich, were both scarred by the events that they had witnessed on that bloody March day in 1881. From then on, they would both mistrust any move towards greater democratisation of Russian government and society. The actions of the People's Will ensured that Alexander's planned reforms did not proceed in any form. They also laid the foundations for the revolution that was to come a generation after Alexander's death.

17

The return of autocracy and repression

The new Tsar, Alexander Alexandrovich Romanov, was a very different man to his father. He was in every way a larger than life figure, physically a giant, who towered over both his family and his nation. He was a political autocrat and he detested all attempts to move Russia towards democracy, however limited these might be. His first act as Tsar was to bring a halt to all the constitutional and administrative reforms that Alexander had been planning to introduce.

Many people considered him to be a rough and ready man, with the tastes and style of a peasant rather than a monarch. But, beneath this tough exterior was a man driven by a vision of the Russia that he wanted to create. He had high personal moral standards and was devoted to his Danish wife, Maria Feodorovna, and to his immediate family. Unlike earlier Romanov rulers he never took a mistress.

Alexander III had never expected to become Tsar. His elder brother, the Tsarevich Nicholas, died suddenly in 1865 from cerebral meningitis. On his death bed, it is reported that the Tsarevich had expressed the wish that Alexander should marry his fiancée, Princess Dagmar of Denmark. The young Grand Duke was now the heir to the Russian throne, but he was in no way prepared for this. He had not had the broader education required for a future Tsar. He was also deeply in love with his mother's lady-in-waiting, Princess Maria Elimovna Meshcherskaya, whom he had nicknamed Dusenka. The young couple were devoted to each other and had planned to marry.

The Tsar soon made clear to his son where his duties now lay, and with great reluctance the new Tsarevich broke off his relationship with Dusenka in late 1865. A year later, on 9 November 1866, Alexander married Princess Dagmar in the church of the Winter Palace in St Petersburg. She was the second daughter of King Christian IX of Denmark and she took the name of Maria Feodorovna on her marriage. Alexander never saw Dusenka again. She left Russia in March 1867, and a few months later married the wealthy Russian diplomat Pavel Pavolovich Demidov. She tragically died giving birth to her baby son in 1868.

The marriage of Grand Duke Alexander and Princess Dagmar was the second step in a series of marriages that would cement the alliance between the British and Russian royal families. In 1863, Dagmar's elder sister, Alexandra, had married the Prince of Wales, later to become King Edward VII. The children of these two marriages were therefore closely related through their royal Danish mothers. The future Tsar Nicholas II and King George V were first cousins and bore an extraordinary physical likeness to one another. These two marriages, combined with that of Grand Duchess Maria to the Duke of Edinburgh, created an interlocking set of relationships between the British and Russian royal families. These marriages would draw Russia and Britain closer together in the years before the First World War.

In the years before his accession to the throne, the Tsarevich Alexander kept a low profile. He was seen little in public. During this period, he studied law and administration under the direction of the jurist Konstantin Pobedonostsev, who was Professor of Law at Moscow University, and latterly became Chief Procurator of the Holy Synod of the Orthodox Church in Russia.

Tsar Alexander II appointed Pobedonostsev as his son's tutor in the mistaken belief that the jurist had reformist sympathies. This had in fact been the case in the earlier part of the tutor's career, when he had been a strong supporter of the Tsar's reforms. But by the 1860s his views were changing. Increasingly disillusioned with where Alexander's rule was leading Russia, he became a champion of an orthodox and autocratic Russia. He believed that any form of liberal reform was alien to Russian political culture and society. He argued that religious dissent and political diversity should be suppressed in the interests of creating a sense of national harmony. This would be based on authentic Russian values and a deep respect for the Tsar as God's representative on earth.

The young Tsarevich was very comfortable with Pobedonostsev's teachings. He also began to make it increasingly clear that he was not happy with his father's views. When he succeeded to the throne in 1881, the time had come to implement a new much more conservative ideology.

Pobedonostsev now became Tsar Alexander III's leading adviser. He set out his principles in his book, *Reflections of a Russian Statesman*. He denounced representative democracy, trial by jury, freedom of the press and secular education. He was ferociously anti-Jewish and argued that there need to be a solution to the Jewish question in Russia. Jews should either be driven into exile, forcibly converted to Orthodox Christianity, or starved to death.

Under Pobedonostsev's influence Alexander III sought to build a future for Russia based around orthodoxy, autocracy and 'narodnost', a belief in the moral and spiritual integrity of the Russian people, their culture and values. This however was to lead him and the country towards a dark and intolerant future. Russification of minorities in the Russian Empire became a central part of government policy. This was linked to the persecution of non-Orthodox religious minorities. The darkest aspect of these policies were the pogroms against the Jews.

The assassination of Alexander II in 1881 was the initial trigger for a virulent outburst of anti-Jewish riots. There was a suspicion that Jews had been involved in the Tsar's assassination and while there was no serious basis for this, it was an opportunity for agitators to vent their economic and social grievances on a defenceless minority. The first pogroms broke out in Ukraine and then spread across Southern Russia. Although the authorities did try and intervene, the anti-Jewish riots continued for three years. The new Tsar blamed both revolutionaries and the Jews for the riots and in 1882, a series of harsh restrictions were imposed on them.

The Tsar's anti-Semitic views soon became fashionable amongst larger sections of the Russian population, both in the rural and urban areas. The Jews were blamed for a whole range of misfortunes, both economic and social. This growing hostility convinced many Jews that they had a very limited future in Russia. Many now decided to emigrate to countries in Western Europe such as Britain and Germany and to the United States.

If Alexander was harsh on his Jewish population, he was equally ruthless in his behaviour towards political terrorists and extremists. The full might of the Okhrana, the Russian secret police, was launched against members of the People's Will and other radical political groups, particularly the Socialists and the Anarchists. Many fled into exile in the West, but others were caught and executed. Amongst these was Alexander Ulyanov, the elder brother of Vladimir Lenin. He was hanged in May 1887, along with four other members of the People's Will, all of whom had been planning to assassinate the Tsar.

This led to a period of crisis in the movement and to its collapse. With many of its members in prison, or in exile, it would be another fifteen years before the movement could reorganise. When it did, it would not be the People's Will that would arise from this repression but a new political party. This was the Socialist Revolutionary Party which would itself embark on a fresh round of political struggle and terror, culminating in the Russian Revolution of 1917-18.

Despite the autocratic nature of Russian government and society under Tsar Alexander III, the country flourished in unexpected ways. The economy continued to grow, industry and private business expanded and there was a push to modernise the country's infrastructure. School, vocational and university-level education became available to wider sections of the population. The middle classes, although still very small in numbers, started to exert a greater influence on society.

The strict censorship of Alexander's reign and the growing power of the Orthodox Church had a negative impact on Russian literature.

Writers no longer felt they had the freedom to express themselves as they had done under the previous regime. Russia entered a period of literary gloom and retrenchment. The only significant writer to emerge during this period was Anton Chekhov. His short stories and plays reflect the ennui, boredom and frustrations of life in provincial Russia. They also accurately reflect the literary suffocation that was taking place across the country.

Surprisingly, this was not the case in the performing arts. Alexander's decision to end the monopoly on theatrical production held by the Imperial Theatres in 1882, and to close the Italian Opera in 1885, soon led to a growth in private theatres and opera houses across the country.

This was the era of Pyotr Ilyich Tchaikovsky, one of the greatest of all Russian composers. He was a favourite of the Tsar and, in 1884, was personally honoured by Alexander and awarded a lifetime pension. Most of Tchaikovsky's greatest ballets and operas appeared during the reign of Alexander III. His music reflected the glory of the Imperial Russia that Alexander sought to create. However, beneath the soaring and romantic compositions lurk darker undertones, a sense of menace and evil, of a society and a culture that was itself on the brink of destruction.

Tchaikovsky himself was drawn towards a beauty and a sexual power that he feared could one day destroy him and his reputation. His homosexual longings were never openly acknowledged, despite the rumours about his private life. In 1893, he died of cholera. There were suspicions that he had committed suicide, fearing that he might be exposed after an affair he had had with the son of a Tsarist Minister.

Under Alexander's patronage there was a revival in traditional art and architecture. This reflected a nostalgia and a rediscovery of what were believed to be fundamental Russian spiritual and cultural values. The architecture of the Memorial Church to Alexander II in St Petersburg is a perfect example of this. Here, in the middle of Peter the Great's capital replete with its Western-style classical buildings, emerged an extraordinary Church which more closely resembled the colourful and sinuous splendours of St Basil's Cathedral in Moscow or the Byzantine glories of Kievan Rus.

Alexander, however, will long be remembered for his one very personal contribution to Russian imperial culture. This was the commissioning of the first Fabergé egg, as a present for his wife, Maria Feodorovna in 1885. The Hen Egg, as it became known, had a delicate white enamelled shell, which opened to reveal a yellow inside yolk. This then revealed a golden hen with a diamond replica of the Russian imperial crown.

Maria's delight at this present led to Peter Carl Fabergé being given a special appointment as goldsmith to the imperial Crown. Over the course of the next thirty-two years, until the revolution of 1917 brought a halt to all production, a Fabergé egg was presented every Easter to the Romanov family. Altogether, there are fifty of these imperial eggs, including an exquisite model of the *Shtandart* crafted in 1909, the very same year that the yacht sailed to the Isle of Wight with the Russian royal family on board. This is made of transparent hollowed out rock crystal, inlaid with green enamel and diamonds. It is currently to be seen in the Kremlin Museum in Moscow.

In 1903, Fabergé opened a branch in London. This was his only shop outside Russia. It soon became a prominent part of the city's glittering retail offer and the haunt of royalty, aristocrats, socialites, and financiers. The close ties between the British and Russian royal families made London a natural base for Fabergé. King Edward VII and Queen Alexandra were already keen collectors of his works, and he was quick to adapt his productions to suit British tastes. There was a strong focus on beautifully enamelled animals and racing horses, snuff, and cigar boxes for the British market. On 5 November 1908, Grand Duke Michael Alexandrovich, who was on a visit to the London branch, bought a nephrite cigar box with a sepia enamelled view of the houses of Parliament, which he presented to King Edward VII.

During his lifetime, Alexander was called 'The Peacemaker'. This was an accolade bestowed on him by many of his subjects, who were grateful for the chance to get on with their lives in relative peace and security. Russia was not involved in any foreign wars during Alexander's reign and the Tsar pursued a skilful diplomatic path which ensured that Russia avoided military conflict but increased its international influence.

In this, Alexander was indebted to Nikolay Girs, his pragmatic and sensible Foreign Minister who was instrumental in persuading the Tsar to resolve tensions through compromise and negotiation. Girs passionately believed that peace was essential for the imperial regime to survive. Jews and political opponents of the regime were, of course, excluded from this vision of a safe and secure Imperial Russia, at peace with itself and the wider world.

In the early years of Alexander's reign, Russia had been in an alliance with Bismarck's Germany. However, the growing power of a united Germany and its secret alliance with Austria-Hungary and Italy in 1882 alarmed both the Tsar and Girs. Increasingly, Russian and French interests began to coincide and in 1891 the Franco-Russian Alliance was signed. This had a strong economic basis to it, as the French were prepared to be a lot more liberal than the Germans with their loans to Russia.

The Franco-Russian alliance was to lead to a fundamental realignment of Russian foreign policy, which now moved away from Germany and Austria-Hungary and towards France and Britain. In 1907, Britain and Russia signed the Anglo-Russian Entente and together with France, this formed the 'Triple Entente', an alliance which would endure until the revolution of 1917 destroyed the Tsarist regime.

Alexander handled his relations with Britain in a careful and cautious way. The two royal families were now linked by marriage and by increasingly shared international interests. Alexander visited Britain only once during his lifetime. This was in 1873, when he was still the Tsarevich. Alexander and his Danish born wife Maria Feodorovna were invited to London as guests of the Prince and Princess of Wales, the latter being the older sister of Maria. They arrived with their two sons, Georgy and Nicholas, and spent much of the summer with the British royal family.

The visit included a naval review at Spithead, several military parades, and a visit to Parliament. In contrast, Maria and her sister, dressed in identical costumes, visited the slums of the East End, where they called on charities supported by the Princess of Wales which offered refuge and help to the poor. Maria was so inspired by these visits that she decided to set up similar charitable organisations when she returned to Russia.

During his time in London, the Tsarevich expressed a strong interest in the British judicial system and was invited to spend an afternoon at the Court of the Lord Chief Justice. Here he attended the trial of a man who maintained that he was Roger Tichborne, heir to a large fortune, who had mysteriously vanished at sea in 1854, but had now returned to claim his family wealth. This case fascinated the public, who were divided as to whether the claimant was a fraud or the genuine heir. The Tsarevich was completely caught up by the drama of the case and followed the story in the newspapers for many weeks after his visit. After a trial lasting 188 days the jury ruled that the claimant, now identified as a man called Thomas Castro, was a fraud and an imposter. He was sentenced to fourteen years in gaol.

In early August the Romanov family made an extended visit to the Isle of Wight, where they stayed at Osborne Cottage and enjoyed the delights of Cowes Week, alongside spending time with the Queen at Osborne House. It was while they were at Cowes that the French society artist, James Tissot, painted his masterpiece *The Ball on Shipboard*, which in recognition of the Tsarevich's visit, depicts a party of well-dressed visitors dancing on the upper deck of a grand yacht with Tsarist imperial flags draped above them.

The increasing rapprochement between the two royal families was not, however, matched by any growing sympathy for the Tsarist regime amongst the wider British public. Reports of anti-Jewish pogroms, the persecution of religious minorities, and the harassment and imprisonment of political dissidents, did little to endear the British people to the Tsarist regime during this period. Financial institutions in Britain were also reluctant to make loans to Russia on the scale of their French equivalents, due to their dislike of the Tsar's discriminatory policies towards the Jews.

Russian exiles were now increasingly visible in London and other cities in Britain. The anarchist philosopher Prince Peter Kropotkin spent much of his life in exile in Britain and worked hard to promote a view of the Tsarist regime as corrupt and oppressive. He was a co-founder of the London journal *Freedom* and between 1892 and 1894, parts of his anarchist manifesto *The Conquest of Bread* were serialised in the journal.

His writings did much to increase liberal and socialist hostility towards Russia. He became a friend of George Bernard Shaw and William Morris and spent his time in Bromley and Brighton.

The popular press in Britain was quick to demonise Russia and there was little sympathy in presenting a more nuanced understanding of where the country was heading as it approached the twentieth century. Queen Victoria's hostile views towards the Tsar, whom she personally disliked, and the Romanovs in general were reciprocated by many of her subjects.

Russian attitudes towards Britain were more complex. There was still a legacy of mistrust dating back to the Crimean and even Napoleonic Wars, but this was largely dissipating as British industrial, engineering and business investment became much more visible. This was the era when British railway, textile, and agricultural engineers flocked to Russia along with British manufacturers and industrialists. Many married Russian wives and founded prominent family businesses, which flourished until the revolution of 1917. Alongside this, British style and culture were also increasingly influencing the Russian upper and middle classes. The era of the British nanny, a major feature in the lives of many Russian aristocratic and gentry families, had also arrived.

This was the period when a fascination with English literature and culture began to sweep across Russia. The novels of Walter Scott and the poetry of Lord Byron had originally influenced writers like Pushkin and Lermontov. However, by the end of the century, Russia was consumed by a mood of Anglophilia. The writings of Oscar Wilde became particularly popular, and the art of Aubrey Beardsley influenced an entire generation of Russian artists, designers and ballet choreographers. Amongst the young generation of the 1890s, it became fashionable to dress and pose as an English dandy.

At a diplomatic and political level, a lot of energy was expended on managing the rival British and Russian spheres of interest in Central Asia. This was a part of the world where there was huge potential for conflict between the two countries. Alexander III, however, decided to continue the conciliatory policies of his father and actively sought to defuse tensions between the two countries. He sought to expand Russian domination and influence in the region but in such a way as to avoid upsetting Britain.

In 1885, early on in Alexander's reign, there was a major crisis between the two countries when Russia captured an Afghan border fort in the small town of Panjdeh. Britain saw this incursion into Afghanistan as a direct threat to its rule in India. For a while neither side would back down, but in the end a diplomatic solution was reached. This was a short but sharp lesson for Alexander. Russian expansion towards India now stopped and the north-west border of Afghanistan was clearly defined, so that no further misunderstandings should occur between the two countries. In compensation, it was agreed that Russia would keep the fort at Panjdeh, which became part of the southern boundary of the Russian Empire. It now sits inside Turkmenistan.

Tsar Alexander died unexpectedly of kidney failure on 20 October 1894, at the age of forty-nine. A railway accident in 1888 was blamed as a contributory factor in his death. The imperial train had been derailed at Borki in the Ukraine due to travelling at excessive speed on the line. The roof of the dining car, in which the Tsar and his family were travelling, had collapsed. Alexander, with his prodigious physical strength, held up the roof of the carriage till everyone escaped safely. However, in doing this he had damaged his kidney. Six years after the accident he developed a terminal kidney disease.

Alexander's death left both the country and the dynasty in disarray. He had been such a dominating figure that many in Russia felt totally bereft without him. The twenty-six-year-old Tsarevich Nicholas wept openly on hearing the news of his father's death and declared that he was not ready to rule the country. There was a strong sense that Russia was approaching the twentieth century with an inexperienced and possibly inept new Tsar on the throne. The certainties of Alexander III's rule, for good and for bad, were now to be replaced by indecision, ineffective autocracy, and a retreat from political reality. The reign of the last Tsar, Nicholas Alexandrovich Romanov, had arrived.

PART

VI

BUILDING A NEW
ANGLO-RUSSIAN
ALLIANCE
1894-1907

18

Nicholas and Alexandra: The last Romanovs

Contemporaries were baffled by the character of the man who now occupied the Russian throne. He was considered by many to be a mystery and a psychological phenomenon. Nicholas projected a shy and gentle image, a ruler who was sensitive and keen not to offend or upset those around him. Yet, he was also viewed as being inflexible, autocratic, and with a limited ability to understand alternative viewpoints. Many of his decisions as Tsar were both contradictory and confusing. His quixotic role during the events of Bloody Sunday in January 1905, when the police opened fire on unarmed demonstrators in the heart of St Petersburg, lost him much sympathy and support.

Nicholas was an avid diarist, and so we should know more about his personal thoughts than we do about many of the other Romanov Tsars. His diary entries, however, are curiously opaque and pedestrian, revealing very little about the character of the man who now presided over the destiny of millions of people across the Russian Empire.

His reign began in gloom and despondency. The death of Alexander III was a shock to both the Romanov family and to the wider Russian public. Grand Duke Alexander Mikhailovich describes in his memoirs how on realising his father was dead 'Nicholas could not collect his thoughts. He knew that he was Emperor now, and the weight of this terrifying fact crushed him'. In desperation, Nicholas appealed to his uncle, 'What am I going to do, what is going to happen to me, to you, to Xenia, to Alix, to mother, to Russia? I have no idea of even how to talk to Ministers'.

It was a depressing start to his reign, though other Tsars like Alexander I had found themselves in similar predicaments when they first ascended the throne, then rallied to become confident and effective rulers. Nicholas, however, never seemed to recover. He believed all his life that he had been born under an unlucky sign, that of the Biblical Job who had suffered and been tested by God in the most extreme ways, losing all those most precious to him. In his darker moments Nicholas believed that it was his destiny to share the same fate as Job.

Nicholas had been brought up by his parents in a straightforward and practical way. The Tsar and his wife, the Empress Maria, did not believe in spoiling their children. Furnishings and home comforts at both the Gatchina and Anichkov Palaces, where they primarily lived, were sparse and simple. Summer holidays were usually spent in Denmark, where the Romanov children would mingle with their English cousins in King Christian's summer residence at Bernstorff. This was a simple white-washed building that stood in a park by the sea and where both royal families could feel relaxed and at ease. It was here that Nicholas and his first cousin, Prince George, later King George V, would regularly meet, and where they formed a friendship that would endure till the Tsar's overthrow in 1917.

The young Tsarevich pursued a relatively carefree life. It was not anticipated that he would become ruler any time soon, as his father was still in the prime of his life. Little preparation was therefore made for his ascent to the throne. Nicholas made a trip around the world in 1890-91, which ended badly when he was attacked by a Japanese madman and suffered serious head wounds. Years later, these wounds were still evident on his skull and were part of the identification markings used to prove that the human remains found in the woods outside Ekaterinburg were those of the last Tsar.

Nicholas, like many in his family, was of a romantic and emotional nature and soon fell in love. His most famous liaison was with the Polish ballerina,

Mathilde Kschessinska, a star of the Imperial Ballet in St Petersburg. This intense relationship lasted three years and only came to an end in the months prior to Nicholas's marriage to Princess Alix of Hesse in November 1894. On her marriage she took the name Alexandra Feodorovna.

Alix was born in 1872, the sixth child of Louis IV, the Grand Duke of Hesse and his wife, Princess Alice, the daughter of Queen Victoria. The Grand Duchy had been founded in 1806, and although it was one of the smaller Princely states, it was already linked through marriage to the Romanovs. Princess Marie of Hesse, the Aunt of Grand Duke Louis, had married Tsar Alexander II in 1855.

Alix had a happy early childhood and was nicknamed 'Sunny' because of her cheerful disposition and friendly manner. However, in 1878, all this changed. On 3 September of that year, the Thames paddle steamer *Princess Alice,* named after Alix's mother, was returning to London from a day trip to Sheerness in Kent. It was crowded with hundreds of men, women and children enjoying a late summer trip to the seaside. As the evening light faded, the *Princess Alice* was cruising off Woolwich when it was rammed by the collier *Bywell Castle.* The pleasure boat sank within a few minutes, drowning over 650 passengers and crew. Alix's mother, at her home in Darmstadt, was very shaken when she was told of the disaster, believing that the sinking of the ship, which carried her name, was an omen of ill fortune and looming tragedy.

Only three months later, in December 1878, diphtheria swept through the Ducal Court. Princess Alice tended to the whole family with selfless care and devotion. Alix's beloved younger sister, Marie, was the first victim of the epidemic at the age of only four. There was worse to come. Princess Alice herself fell ill and died on 14 December, the anniversary of Prince Albert's death. She was only thirty-five. Her mother's death was a huge shock to six-year-old Alix, and one from which she never fully recovered throughout the rest of her life. She now became shy and withdrawn, a lonely little girl, often neglected by her father.

There was one person, however, to whom she would always turn. This was her beloved grandmother, Queen Victoria. Alix and her sisters, Victoria and Elizabeth, would henceforth spend long periods in Britain, either at Windsor or on the Isle of Wight, in the care of the Queen. Osborne House became a second home for the Hesse children, and Victoria took on the role of a surrogate mother. She was particularly devoted to Alix, who was possibly her favourite granddaughter. It therefore came as a shock to the aged Queen when Alix asked her permission to marry Nicholas in 1894.

In 1884, the Tsarevich had met Alix for the first time when she came to St Petersburg for the marriage of her elder sister, Elizabeth, to Grand Duke Sergei, Nicholas's uncle. Elizabeth, known as 'Ella', by all those who loved her, was a woman of rare physical and spiritual beauty. After her husband's assassination in 1905 by members of the terrorist wing of the Socialist Revolutionary Party, she withdrew from public life and became a nun. Three years later, she founded the *St Martha and Mary Convent of Mercy* in Moscow, which was devoted to the care of the homeless and hungry. At its peak, the convent had nearly a hundred nuns and served thousands of meals a week to the poor and dispossessed. Ella dedicated all her energies to her new religious life and in seeking forgiveness for her husband's murderers. She herself would later be murdered by the Bolsheviks, the day after her sister and her family were put to death.

Nicholas was only sixteen and Alix was twelve when the two of them first met. Nothing was to come of this meeting, but it is reported that Nicholas made a lasting impression on the young German Princess. In 1892, Alix returned to visit her sister, and spent several weeks in St Petersburg. It was now that the young couple fell deeply in love. In December 1891, Nicholas confided in his diary, 'My dream is to marry Alix of Hesse'. The only issue preventing this was Alix's reluctance to convert to the Russian Orthodox faith. She was a devout Lutheran and her religious beliefs meant a huge amount to her.

At first, Tsar Alexander III and his wife resisted Nicholas's plans to marry Alix, as they felt that the young Tsarevich could make a much more advantageous match, possibly with a French Princess. Empress Maria was particularly opposed. She described Alix as 'awkward, disagreeable, impolite and abominably dressed' and the Ladies of the Court took their cue from the Empress. Alix was snubbed and side lined by almost everybody apart from her sister Ella, her husband Grand Duke Sergei and, most importantly, by Nicholas. He was now completely enthralled by Alix's ethereal beauty, by her elegant tristesse, and by her strange remoteness and spirituality.

Nicholas's determination to marry Alix eventually won the day and the Tsar and the Empress agreed that he could propose to her. The first opportunity to do this came in April 1894, when one of the grandest royal gatherings of the late nineteenth century took place in Coburg, to celebrate the marriage of Princess Victoria Melita of Saxe Coburg-Gotha to Ernest-Louis, the Grand Duke of Hesse. Both were grandchildren of Queen Victoria, and Princess Victoria Melita was also a niece of the Russian Tsar Alexander III. The Queen had announced her intention of being at the wedding as she saw herself as responsible for the event. She had worked hard to bring the young couple together and was delighted that the wedding was now taking place.

This was an opportunity for royal families from all over Europe to descend on Coburg, including the Tsarevich and Kaiser Wilhelm II. At the apex of all the festivities and celebrations stood the looming figure of Queen Victoria, the matriarch of European royalty, wrapped in an old-fashioned dress of black bombazine. Nicholas described her rather unkindly as 'a round ball on shaky legs'. He was under no illusions that she was in favour of Alix marrying him, knowing that she had actively opposed any engagement. Victoria believed that the Romanovs occupied a dangerous and unstable throne.

There was an added poignancy for the Queen in returning to Coburg. This was the town where Prince Albert had grown up. They had both visited frequently before his death in 1861. When she arrived in the city on 15 April 1894, she had not been back there for nearly twenty years, and she nervously fondled the miniature of her beloved Albert as she rode in her carriage from the train station to the Palace.

The possible engagement of Nicholas and Alexandra was the talk of Coburg's royal circles. It was widely rumoured that the young couple were deeply in love. Alix's reluctance, however, to convert to Orthodoxy was still a stumbling block. In desperation, Nicholas suggested that she meet with the Tsar's spiritual Confessor, Father Yanishev, who had made the trip to Coburg with him. She agreed to do this but after listening carefully to what he had to say, she was still not convinced. Despite her love for Nicholas her intuition was warning her not to marry him. She felt uneasy about what a marriage to a future Romanov Tsar might entail. Doubtless, Queen Victoria's warnings rang in her ears but there may have been a deeper sense of unease and foreboding.

Family pressure was now brought to bear on Alix. Her sister, Ella, married to Grand Duke Sergei, talked at length with her about why she need not compromise her Lutheran faith. Her cousin Kaiser Wilhelm of Germany, also interceded on Nicholas's behalf. He was keen for a German Princess to marry the future heir to the Russian throne and told her that it was her duty to marry the Tsarevich. Her brother Ernest, whose marriage they were all attending, also implored her to follow her heart and marry the man she so loved. In the end all this was too much for Alix. She now decided that she was ready to accept Nicholas. She could no longer resist the love she felt for him and felt that she would be able to create her own spiritual pathway that combined her Lutheran faith with Russian Orthodoxy.

When she told Nicholas, he burst into tears with joy. 'Oh God, what happened to me then' he wrote to his mother, 'I started to cry like a child and so did she, only her expression immediately changed: her face brightened and took on an aura of peace'.

Later that night, he confided in his diary, 'I remained the whole day wrapped in a kind of cloud, and I could not realise what really had happened to me. I cannot believe yet that I have a bride.'

Reports of the engagement soon filled the press. The British public were mesmerised by the news and lapped up every detail of the story. This seemed like a fairy tale brought to life with a beautiful but sad looking young Princess, in love with a handsome and dashing Tsarevich. Although Queen Victoria gave her blessing to the engagement, she was uneasy about doing so. She felt that Alix was a fragile and emotionally insecure woman and feared for her future in Russia. Her premonitions were not misplaced.

After a few quiet days together in Coburg, where Nicholas and Alix spent their time wandering together through the gardens and crooked lanes of the old town, they parted for a few weeks. Alix returned to England and Nicholas went back to Russia. They promised each other that they would meet again within a couple of months.

In Russia, Nicholas was congratulated by his parents and the wider Romanov family. It seemed that the earlier mistrust felt towards Alix was dissipating. However, the Empress Maria still had her reservations about the Hesse Princess who was now to become her son's wife and, ultimately, her successor on the throne. Their relationship, difficult at the beginning, was soon to sour and the Empress would eventually make no attempt to disguise her dislike of Alix.

Back at Windsor Castle, Alix devoted herself to learning the Russian language and to studying the Orthodox faith. There was an intensity of purpose about the young Princess, which meant that once she had decided on a course of action, she would devote herself completely to following it through. While this was in many ways an admirable characteristic, it also revealed a determination not to tolerate any deviation or obstruction to her plans. Nicholas was much less decisive and more willing to change his mind. The combination of these two personalities would ultimately prove fatal to the Romanov dynasty.

The emotional strain of the weeks she had spent in Coburg now took their toll. Alix's health had always been fragile, and she suffered a serious attack of sciatica soon after returning to Windsor. It was decided therefore that she should go to Harrogate, a spa town in Yorkshire, where she could take the waters and relax without having to worry about court life and official protocol.

In May 1894, Alix arrived in Harrogate, under the assumed name of 'Baroness Starckenburg'. She was accompanied by her lady-in-waiting, Baroness von Fabrice. She had chosen the name of Starckenburg because it was one of the lesser titles that she could use, and referred to the historical area around Darmstadt, her home city in Hesse.

Alix moved into Cathcart House, a rather stern looking nineteenth-century boarding house built of dark brown Yorkshire stone. It still stands near the centre of Harrogate. The owners of the house were a Mr and Mrs Allen, who knew the real identity of the mysterious Baroness, but were fully complicit in maintaining her secret. It did not take long, though, for rumours to start spreading around Harrogate that the future wife of the Tsar of Russia was living in the town. Soon it became difficult for Alix to go out, without curious onlookers ogling her every move, and crying out, 'It's her!' whenever she entered a shop or walked in the town's Valley Gardens.

'Of course, it is in all the papers that I am here' Alix wrote to Nicholas. 'The rude people stand at the corner and stare; I shall stick my tongue out at them the next time'. Alix's dislike of being in the public eye was already apparent in these comments. She was already displaying the traits that would drive her and Nicholas into almost total social seclusion during their reign in Russia. This need for privacy and isolation was acceptable as the wife of a private citizen. It was not acceptable, though, as the wife of the Tsar and would do enormous damage to the role and profile of the monarchy in the years leading up to the Revolution.

During her time in Harrogate, the landlady gave birth to twins, who were named Nicholas and Alix, in honour of the family's distinguished guest. Alix asked to become godmother to the children and attended the christening which took place in the nearby Anglican church of St Peter's. Crowds of strangers swarmed into the church, none of them interested in the christening, but all of them determined to get as good a view of the Princess as they could.

Alix took her role as godmother to the two children very seriously. She scoured the shops in Harrogate for suitable gifts and on her return to Russia continued to send them presents every year on their birthdays. This continued until 1915. The presents included two silver enamelled cutlery sets, made by the Russian imperial silversmiths the Grachev Brothers, and sent to the children on their first birthday on 21 May 1895. In 1910, the Tsarina gave the son, Nicholas Allen, a pair of gold Fabergé cufflinks and pins.

Although Alix was happy staying with the Allen family, she became more and more edgy about the public scrutiny that she now experienced in Harrogate. Soon after the christening she noticed a strange woman, who was waiting for her whenever she went outside, and would always try and

1. The author's grandparents, Jadwiga and Emil Romanovsky, at their wedding in Moscow in 1916.

2. Jadwiga and Emil Romanovsky during their flight from Soviet Russia in 1920. It took the author's grandparents two years to reach safety in Romania.

3. Tsar Peter the Great by Sir Godfrey Kneller, painted during the Tsar's visit to England in 1698. It hung in the Drawing Room at Kensington Palace for many years from 1700.

4. Tsar Alexander I, painted by George Dawe in 1824.

Suprised and pleas'd, the docks survey'd
Those mighty monuments of trade,
Where the proud God of commerce is
Throned in his hundred palaces,

5. Cartoon published by Thomas Tegg of Cheapside in 1814 depicting Tsar Alexander I's review of the British fleet at Portsmouth. The Tsar was hugely popular with the British public and was called the 'Liberator of Europe' much to the irritation of the Prince Regent. Coloured etching by C. Williams.

6. The Tsar and his sister, Grand Duchess Ekaterina Pavlovna, being cheered by the London crowds.

Took notes—set off—and thought to Jog
Home to my own abode incog
But was discover'd on my road
And follow'd with a general shout.

7. The monument to Tsar Alexander I at St Catherine's Down, Isle of Wight. This was erected in 1814 by Michael Hoy, an English merchant, who had spent many years living in St Petersburg and decided to create a permanent memorial to the Tsar and his achievements. It remains one of only three public monuments ever erected to the Romanovs in Britain.

8. A view of Ventnor in the mid-nineteenth century at a time when the seaside resort on the Isle of Wight was enjoying great popularity amongst visiting Russians. The building with the tower in the foreground was called St Augustine Villa, and was where the Russian socialist and political writer, Alexander Herzen, spent several summers between 1855-1859.

9. 'The latest arrival at the Zoological Gardens'. This was a cartoon from the satirical magazine, *Punch*, lampooning Tsar Nicholas I during his state visit to Britain in June 1844. *Punch* was a vociferous critic of the Tsar and the illustration shows Queen Victoria baiting a bear-like Tsar, with a lance bearing the word 'Poland' on it, in protest at the Russian treatment of occupied Poland. The Tsar had spent time at London Zoo during his visit.

THE LATEST ARRIVAL AT THE ZOOLOGICAL GARDENS.

THE "MONTAGNE RUSSE."—A VERY DANGEROUS GAME.

10. 'The "Montagne Russe"- a very dangerous game'. A wood engraving by John Leech published in Punch in 1854, during the Crimean War. This satirical cartoon shows Tsar Nicholas I hurtling towards the edge of a precipice on a sledge labelled 'Despotism'.

11. Valley of the Shadow of Death. A photograph taken by Roger Fenton, on 23 April 1855, during the Crimean War depicting the supposed valley through which the Light Brigade charged to their deaths in October 1854. This became one of the most famous photographs ever taken during the Crimean war and came to symbolise the bleak futility of the conflict.

12. A 1867 portrait of Alexander Herzen by Nikolai Ge, an early Russian realist painter. Herzen was a radical opponent of Tsarist autocracy and spent many years living in exile in London. He and his family visited the Isle of Wight several times during the 1850s. He is widely credited for popularising Ventnor as a summer resort for Russian visitors.

13. A portrait of the writer Ivan Turgenev painted by Ilya Repin in 1874. Turgenev spent the summer of 1860 at Ventnor where he began work on his greatest novel, *Fathers and Sons*. This conjured up the character of the nihilist doctor, Yevgeny Bazarov, who would inspire an entire generation of revolutionaries in Russia.

14. Tsar Alexander II with his only daughter, Grand Duchess Maria. She married Queen Victoria's second son, Prince Alfred, the Duke of Edinburgh, in 1874. The Tsar was very close to Maria and greatly missed her when she left to live in Britain. Maria had an uneasy relationship with the Queen and her visits to Osborne House were marked by tensions with other members of the British royal family.

15. A nineteenth century illustration of Osborne House, which became the favourite retreat of Queen Victoria and Prince Albert. The original house was purchased by the royal couple in 1845, and this was then replaced by a new Italianate style residence completed in 1851. Several members of the Romanov family, including Tsar Alexander III and Nicholas II, visited Osborne House.

16. In 1894, Nicholas and Alix, were officially betrothed. In the July of that year they stayed with Queen Victoria at Osborne House, and while on the island they were photographed by the royal photographers, Hughes and Mullins of Union Street, Ryde.

17. In 1896, the newly crowned Tsar Nicholas II, together with his wife, Alix and their baby daughter Olga, visited Queen Victoria and the Prince of Wales at Balmoral Castle. This was to be the last meeting between the Queen and the Russian Imperial family, as she died five years later in 1901.

THE ILLUSTRATED LONDON NEWS.

REGISTERED AT THE GENERAL POST OFFICE AS A NEWSPAPER.

No. 3641.— VOL. CXXXIV.   SATURDAY, JANUARY 30, 1909.   With Coloured Supplement: SIXPENCE.
        Miss Irene Vanbrugh.

The Copyright of all the Editorial, Matter, both Engravings and Letterpress, in Strictly Reserved in Great Britain, the Colonies, Europe, and the United States of America.

"Jacob."   Charles Wyatt.   Hefeld (Firing from the Back of the Car).

MURDERERS ON A TRAM PURSUED BY POLICE ON A TRAM: THE REMARKABLE RUNNING FIGHT IN THE TOTTENHAM AFFAIR.

DRAWN BY CYRUS CUNEO, FROM MATERIAL SUPPLIED BY CHARLES WYATT, WHO DROVE THE CAR.

One of the most remarkable features of the five-miles running fight between the Russian Anarchists who ran amok at Tottenham, the police, and the crowd of helpers, was the commandeering of an electric tram by the murderers, and the pursuit of it by police on another tram. The driver got on to the top of the car, and the conductor, Charles Wyatt, was forced to drive in his stead by the man known as "Jacob," who held a pistol to his head. The other desperado fired on the car that brought police in pursuit from the back platform of the car.

18. The *Illustrated London News* front cover for January 1909, reporting on the terrorist attack carried out in Tottenham, North London by Russian anarchists. A tram was seized, a policeman and a ten-year old boy were killed, and many others injured. This provoked a lot of anger and hostility towards Russian refugees living in Britain in the months before the Tsar's visit to the Isle of Wight.

19. The Imperial yacht, *Shtandart*, at anchor in the Cowes Roads during the visit by the Tsar and his family in August 1909. The yacht is dressed in a full array of maritime flags in celebration of the Imperial family's arrival to the Isle of Wight.

20. Visitors strolling along the Parade in Cowes during the Regatta. Cowes Week was the high point of the international yachting calendar, and the Tsar's visit in 1909 added extra lustre and glamour to the occasion.

21. The Tsarina, Alexandra, and her daughters on board the *Shtandart* during their visit to Cowes in August 1909.

22. The state dinner on board the imperial yacht, *Shtandart*, on the evening of Tuesday 3 August. The Tsar and Tsarina hosted King Edward VII and Queen Alexandra to a sumptuous six-course dinner where toasts were exchanged in celebration of the new friendship between Britain and Russia.

23. The King's yacht, *Britannia*, during Cowes Week 1909. The Tsar and Tsarina were guests on Tuesday 3 August and spent much of the day watching the races.

24. The Tsar and King Edward VII relaxing on board the *Britannia* while sailing in the Solent on 3 August 1909.

25. On the morning of 3 August, the Romanov children went to play on Osborne beach with their British royal cousins.

26. On the afternoon of 3 August, Grand Duchesses Olga and Tatiana went for an informal shopping trip in Cowes. It did not take long for them to be recognised and soon a huge crowd was following them along the High Street, much to the alarm of the British police and Russian security, who soon whisked them away.

27. The Russian and British royal families met for tea at Barton Manor in East Cowes on the afternoon of 4 August. This was the last time that the two families would meet before the Russian revolution of 1917. The Tsar and King Edward VII sit at the centre of the gathering, with Queen Alexandra next to the Tsar and the Empress Alexandra next to King Edward.

28. Nicholas II and his cousin, George, Prince of Wales, are photographed together at Barton Manor on the afternoon of 4 August 1909. The Tsar is standing next to Prince Edward, the future King Edward VIII, while the Prince of Wales has his hands resting on the shoulders of the five-year old Tsarevich, Alexis.

29. The basement room in the Ipatiev House in Ekaterinburg where the Imperial family and four of their servants were brutally murdered on the night of 16-17 July 1918, this bringing to a close 300 years of Romanov rule in Russia.

30. The Romanov Memorial Cross in Jubilee Park, East Cowes commemorates the Russian Imperial family and their last visit to the Isle of Wight in August 1909. The memorial was unveiled on 7 July 2018 in the presence of Prince Rostislav Romanov, a direct descendant of Tsar Alexander III. The Memorial Cross was funded by East Cowes Town Council and the Grand Duchess Elizabeth Romanov Society.

get as close to her as possible. The woman's menacing stare was frightening and unsettling.

Eventually the tension became unbearable. Alix started to dread walking out into the street and was forever scouring the horizon for any sight of the woman. Though the police were alerted, no action was ever taken, and the identity of the stranger remains a mystery to this day. This episode has more than a touch of Henry James about it, an echo of ghost stories and repressed desires and fears. Was this woman a figment of Alix's imagination? It was always Alix who noticed the woman first, though others claimed they had also seen her. Perhaps, in the lonely menacing figure that daily crossed her path, she saw an image of her own future, and a chilling harbinger of the difficult life that lay ahead.

On 20 June, Nicholas finally arrived in England and a delighted Alix was able to leave Harrogate. It was Nicholas's third visit to England, having visited most recently in 1893 for the marriage of his cousin Prince George to Princess Mary of Teck. The couple were reunited in Walton-on-Thames, where they stayed in a house called Elm Grove, then owned by Victoria, Alix's older sister. She was now living in England and married to Prince Louis of Battenberg.

Nicholas was charmed by Elm Grove and called it a 'Cosy Cottage', although it had three storeys and numerous public and private rooms. For the young couple, these few days in Walton were to be amongst the happiest and most carefree time of their lives, and one that they would later look back on with affection and nostalgia. They spent their time enjoying picnics, taking boat trips along the river, and relaxing in the warm summer sunshine.

On 24 June, Nicholas and Alix moved from the private and charmed existence of Elm Grove to the more formal environs of Windsor Castle. Here they were under the strict surveillance of the Queen and a busy round of social events including garden parties and official banquets now followed. Alix's lifelong friend, Baroness Buxhoeveden, later wrote, 'Victoria had strict ideas on chaperonage and never left the engaged couple alone for a moment, which must have been rather trying for the Tsarevich'.

A few days later, Nicholas managed to slip away to spend a couple of days with his aunt, Alexandra, and Bertie, the Prince of Wales, at their house in Sandringham in Norfolk. He loved the location of the house, appreciating the woods and the 'delightful fresh breeze from the sea'. Bertie had arranged a trip to a horse sale near King's Lynn, where they sat in a large tent in the company of over 200 farmers and horse dealers. Nicholas decided to purchase two chestnut mares and was loudly cheered by the assembled crowd. However, in a letter he wrote to Alix later that day, he complained bitterly about how cold and windy it was sitting in the tent. Back at Sandringham, he had an attack of neuralgia, but persevered with the tour of the gardens and stables that had been arranged for him. Later that day he played skittles and was pleased to win against his Uncle Bertie.

On Nicholas's return to Windsor, Queen Victoria held an eleven-course dinner in honour of his visit. Later that evening, she wrote in her diary, 'The dinner table looked very handsome and was covered in roses. Nicky was very affectionate and attentive to me. Princess Alicky looked lovely, as always'.

In July, the young couple travelled to the Isle of Wight and Osborne House. To Alix, this was a return to a favourite retreat, a second home to her ever since the death of her mother, Princess Alice. Now, she was coming back for a last visit before she became the wife of the heir to the imperial throne of Russia.

Many observers noticed that there was a strange melancholy about Alix during those summer days on the Isle of Wight. It was as though she sensed the burden of the responsibility that she had taken on, and her spirit was already recoiling from what lay ahead. She and Nicholas spent time on the small secluded beach at Osborne House where they sat on the sands, gazing out over the Solent, and talked about their future lives together in Russia. She teased Nicholas about the English grammar books that he had brought with him in order to improve his grasp of English. They went swimming in the sea.

They were photographed by Hughes and Mullins of Ryde, the Queen's official photographers. Nicholas stands staring confidently ahead, but Alix looks nervous and haunted. Her hands are tightly clasped. She is composed, and sits upright, but there is a sense in her expression that this is the end of a way of life that she has known and what lies ahead is a future that is dark and unfathomable. This is the final photograph of Princess Alix of Hesse before her departure to Russia.

Even as the young couple enjoyed each other's company on the Isle of Wight, events in Russia were taking a worrying turn. The Tsar's health was seriously concerning his doctors. It was therefore agreed that he should spend time at his estate at Livadia on the Black Sea, where he could rest and recuperate in the mild and warm southern air. Nicholas returned to Russia at the end of July, on board the imperial yacht *Polar Star*. It was a difficult parting from Alix. The Queen wrote in her journal, 'Nicky gave us some lovely presents and took leave of me in the Hall, thanking me much for all my kindness, and kissing me affectionately. Alicky looked very sad'

'Ever strong and ever loving, faithful pure and strong as death' were the words that Alix wrote in Nicholas's diary on the night before he sailed away from the Isle of Wight. Her favourite song was a melancholy lament for a nightingale which she is reported to have hummed to herself as she watched the imperial yacht disappear over the horizon.

The day after Nicholas's departure she wrote a letter to him. 'Sweet Love, every moment I think that the door will open, and your sweet face will appear. Could I but fly over to you and throw my arms around your neck and press you to my gently beating heart and gently kiss you on the brow. I can only kiss your photos and the ring you gave me'.

Once he was back in St Petersburg, it soon became apparent to Nicholas that his father was gravely ill. He cancelled all other plans and immediately hurried down to the Crimea to join the Tsar in Livadia. An urgent message was sent to Alix, requesting that she travel to join him as soon as possible.

Within a week of her arrival, Alexander died on 20 October 1894. Nicholas, aged twenty-six and Alix, aged twenty-two, were the new rulers of Russia. They were both totally unprepared to take on these demanding roles. Their inexperience meant that they were at the mercy of those at the Court who pursued their own personal agendas. Alix could not expect any support from or guidance from her mother-in-law, the Empress Maria, as she was completely immersed in her own grief. Nicholas found himself surrounded by his father's brothers, a formidable group of four Grand Dukes who all had strong and often contradictory views on almost every subject.

Confusion reigned while the young Tsar spent his days closeted away in total isolation, attending endless prayers for the Dead, and unable to make a single decision. Meanwhile, no arrangements had been made for the transportation of Alexander's body to St Petersburg and it was rotting away fast in the sultry air of the Crimea.

It took the arrival of reliable Uncle Bertie, the Prince of Wales, and his Danish wife, Alexandra, to sort out this mess. They had been alerted to the Tsar's illness some days earlier and set out immediately for Livadia, fearing the worst. They arrived two days after Alexander's death to find the Romanov court in total chaos, unable to deal with the simplest issues. If one Grand Duke issued an order, it was immediately countermanded by one of his brothers. Nicholas and Alix were helpless, bewildered and lost in this maelstrom of emotional disorder, grief and family turmoil. Nicholas's reign had begun as it would end twenty-three years later, with a withdrawal from responsibility and a failure to face up to the reality around him.

It was Uncle Bertie who steadied everyone's nerves and organised the funeral cortège, which set out on the five-day long train journey to St Petersburg. On 7 November, the stinking and by now rapidly decomposing corpse of Tsar Alexander III was finally buried in the Peter and Paul Fortress.

A week later, Alix and Nicholas were married. Many in Russia saw this marriage as an omen of ill fortune. This was a bride who only a few days earlier had been dressed in a black mourning dress and had entered St Petersburg behind the coffin of a Tsar. She was now decked out in a lavish white wedding outfit, like a ghost at her own wake. All this added to Alix's sense of melancholy and fatalism. Unknown to anyone, the marriage had also brought the seeds of illness and death into the Romanov family. Alix was carrying the fatal haemophilia gene. While this would not directly affect any daughters born to Nicholas and Alix, it could cripple any son and would very likely lead to his early death.

Crowds gathered outside in the streets to acclaim the newly wedded couple. They milled around, pressing ever closer to the Winter Palace. After the wedding ceremony, Nicholas and Alix drove to the Kazan Cathedral to pray before the Feodorovskaya Icon of the Mother of God, the patron Saint of the Romanov family. When they came out of the Cathedral, the crowds were so numerous that they now blocked the route of their carriage. The royal couple were trapped like creatures in a cage. Curious faces pressed against the windows, pawing at the glass. For Alix this was a terrifying moment, and a brutal awakening to the role that she had now assumed. Were the crowds friendly or might they be murdered at any moment?

Alix would never forget this experience and what should have been a joyous day ended on a note of fear and terror, as they waited inside their gilded coach to be rescued by the police. The rescue never came and in the end the coachman had to force a way through the seething mass of people, who were crying out for their Tsar and Tsarina. Eventually, after what seemed an interminably long drive, they reached the safety of the Anichkov Palace. Outside the crowds danced in the streets, in celebration of the wedding of their new rulers.

If people had forebodings about the ill fortune being brought to Russia by Alix of Hesse, then these were amply confirmed by the Coronation of the Tsar and Tsarina eighteen months later on 14 May 1896. What should have been a day of joy and happiness tragically turned into a nightmare that would cast a long shadow over the reputation of Nicholas and Alexandra.

As part of the celebrations being laid on for the coronation, a large crowd gathered at the Khodynka Field in Moscow on 18 May. News spread that free sausages, pretzels and gingerbread were to be distributed to everyone, along with special coronation mugs. Food tents, a funfair and theatres had also been erected and these added to the festive atmosphere

Estimates of the numbers of people that were present vary, but there could have been anywhere up to 500,000. In the rush to get the free food and mugs, the crowds pushed forward and then panicked. Thousands of people were trampled to death or seriously injured in the ensuing stampede. The final death toll was announced as being around 1,360 but this was felt by many people to be a serious underestimation

That evening a ball was being held in the Tsar's honour at the French Ambassador's residence. Given the scale of the tragedy at the Khodynka Field, Nicholas's first instinct was not to attend, but he was overruled by his uncles. They told him in no uncertain terms that this would be perceived as an insult by the French. He went to the ball, and though he and Alix did not stay long, the damage to his reputation had been done. From now on he was condemned as callous and uncaring, the Tsar who danced on the graves of his subjects.

In his diary that night, Nicholas referred to what had happened at Khodynka Field as a 'great mishap and awful to say around 1300 people were trampled!! [his exclamations]. I went to the ball at the French Ambassador's. It was very nicely arranged but the heat was unbearable'. This was his sole diary reference to an appalling tragedy which had resulted in large number of his subjects now lying in morgues all over Moscow.

The events at Khodynka Field and his attendance at the ball earned the newly crowned Tsar the nickname of 'Bloody Nicholas', and a reputation for callous indifference that would last for the rest of his reign. There is no evidence that Nicholas was in fact cold hearted or indifferent to the tragedy that had taken place that afternoon in Moscow. He did make efforts to visit the injured in hospital and he also set up a fund to help families that had lost their breadwinners. Later in his reign, he claimed that he regretted being persuaded to attend the ball that night, but by then the damage had been done.

19

Anglo-Russian tensions

Nicholas inherited the throne of a country that was experiencing enormous economic, political and cultural changes. The liberation of the serfs had created a new class of peasant landowners. There were many other poorer peasants, however, who now drifted away from the countryside, forced out of their traditional way of life by the changing nature of agricultural production and land ownership. Many of these poured into cities like St Petersburg and Moscow, where new industries were soaking up hundreds of thousands of workers.

There were huge imbalances within the Russian economy, which, although it was now expanding very fast, suffered from poor infrastructure, restrictions on worker mobility, and a lack of coherent national planning and investment. This was an unbalanced and divisive economy, where the new urban and rural elites were benefiting at the expense of the majority of the population. Most people in the Empire still earned a living from the land but there were increasing numbers of industrial workers. These made up a new urban proletariat that was being influenced by radical new political ideas, demanding the violent overthrow of the Tsarist system.

There was also an emerging and increasingly prosperous middle class. Although it was relatively small, at no more than two to three million people out of a total population of 125 million, this was an articulate and educated group of people who were now demanding greater freedoms and more political rights. They were broadly loyal to the Tsarist system, but they wanted to see more rapid change in the country's constitutional and social systems. Many were increasingly unhappy with the huge inequalities in Russian society.

A bolder and more confident Tsar might have taken the opportunity to launch a series of economic and political reforms which would have set Imperial Russia on a different path for the twentieth century. Tragically, Nicholas lacked any real understanding of the Empire that he had inherited. He sought reassurance in a mythical golden past of Russian autocracy and spiritual orthodoxy, believing that he could create a mystical union between the peasantry and their 'Little Father', the Tsar. His opposition to democratic reform echoed the views of his own father.

At his accession, Nicholas's most influential Minister was Sergei Yulyevich Witte, who had been appointed to the important post of Minister of Finance by Alexander III. Witte was a powerful political figure and sought to drive through a major programme of modernisation and industrial change for Russia. He had come from humble origins and rose to power through his work on the railways.

Nicholas did not trust Witte and was always suspicious of his motivations and attempts to introduce constitutional change, industrial development and economic reform. There was always a certain disdain and arrogance in the Tsar's attitude towards Witte, whom he would sometimes treat as a jumped-up railway clerk. On his death bed, Alexander III had advised his son to work closely with Witte and to listen to what he had to say. This advice was not heeded.

Nicholas was instead attracted to men like the notorious reactionary, Konstantin Pobedonostsev, the Procurator of the Holy Synod and a key adviser to Alexander III. It was Pobedonostsev who was responsible for Nicholas's first major speech as Tsar in January 1895, when he lambasted the 'senseless dreams of those who favour democratic reform'.

This was a major disappointment for the intelligentsia and all those who had been hoping that the reign of the new Tsar would usher in a period of liberal change. It also was a signal to more extreme elements in Russia that change, if it was ever to come, would need to be achieved through violence and revolution.

In 1895, Nicholas and his family left St Petersburg and moved to Tsarskoye Selo, a complex of royal palaces and private residences thirty miles from the capital. There they decided to take up residence in the Alexander Palace, a classical style building which had been erected by Catherine the Great in 1796. Here the imperial family withdrew into their own private world, increasingly isolated from the politics, gossip and social whirl of St Petersburg. They created an environment that reflected the Tsarina's love of all things English, as though she was reaching out for the security of the times that she had spent in Windsor and on the Isle of Wight. Ultimately, this move to the Alexander Palace was to do the monarchy enormous damage, as it isolated them from their natural circles of aristocratic support and made them appear distant and remote to broader sections of the Russian population.

The private apartments of the imperial family were filled with plumped up sofas and armchairs covered in English calf leather, many strewn with Persian rugs. Everywhere there were souvenirs, family photographs and porcelain vases. Paintings by Russian artists like Ilya Repin hung in heavy gilt frames on the walls. The image conjured up was of a rather gloomy middle-class English home in the closing years of the Victorian period. This was the décor and style of Osborne House, recreated for Imperial Russia.

It was here that the first child of Nicholas and Alexandra was born on 3 November 1895. Grand Duchess Olga grew to become a strong-willed and passionate young woman, often at odds with her mother, but utterly devoted to her father. In quick succession, three other daughters were born.

Grand Duchess Tatiana was born on 29 May 1897. She was considered the most elegant and refined of all the Tsar's daughters, tall and slender with dark auburn hair and deep blue eyes. She had the closest relationship of all the girls with the Tsarina and the two seemed to instinctively understand and empathise with one another. Tatiana later emerged as the natural leader of the Romanov children.

Grand Duchess Maria, the third daughter, was born on 14 June 1899. She was in some ways the most Russian of all the children with a broad, open Slavonic face, and a generous and tolerant attitude towards everyone she met. She was also considered the best behaved of the Tsar's daughters and very rarely put a foot wrong.

The Tsar and Tsarina continued to hope that their next child would be a son. There had been Romanov Tsarinas on the throne in the eighteenth century, including the redoubtable Catherine the Great, but her son Tsar Paul had ensured that after him only male rulers could succeed to the Russian throne.

There was therefore disappointment in court circles when a fourth daughter, Grand Duchess Anastasia was born on 5 June 1901. She was the mischief maker in the family, lively and cheeky, but also a charmer, and was forgiven by her parents on numerous occasions for her bad behaviour. Anastasia, it seemed, was always getting herself into scrapes but would always survive these. After her death at the age of seventeen, Anastasia would be transformed into a living legend, and would become a symbol of survival for all the Romanov children, the one whom everyone wanted to believe had escaped the massacre at the Ipatiev House.

At last on 30 July 1904, in the middle of the war with Japan, a son was born. The Tsarevich, Alexei Nikolayevich, was named after his distant ancestor, Tsar Alexis, who had reigned in the seventeenth century. The cannons at the Peter and Paul Fortress boomed out on the news of his birth. Crowds rejoiced in the streets despite the gloomy news of military and naval setbacks in the Far East. A new male heir now guaranteed the succession of the Romanov dynasty well into the twentieth century.

The Tsarina was now increasingly immersed in a world of Orthodox spirituality, her private rooms at the Alexander Palace festooned with icons and religious art. Her strict Lutheranism seems to have been subsumed in an extraordinary outpouring of devotion to Russian saints and mystics. She now firmly believed that her son's birth was due to the blessings of St Seraphim of Sarov, a holy man whose canonisation the family had attended the previous summer.

Alix's belief in spiritual guides was becoming more and more evident. Both she and Nicholas had fallen under the influence of a French mystic and hypnotist, Philippe Vachod, who had been introduced to them through Princess Anastasia and Princess Milica, the two daughters of King Nikola I of Montenegro. They had both married into the Romanov family and had become friends of the Tsarina.

Feeling lonely and isolated, the Tsarina had been drawn into a friendship with these two strange sisters. 'The Black Montenegrins', as they had become known, were disliked by the wider Romanov family, who saw them as both sinister and untrustworthy. It was Milica and Anastasia who recommended Philippe Vachod to the Tsarina. He, in turn, advised her to pray to Saint Seraphim of Sarov for a son, and told her that if she did this, her deepest wishes would be granted.

Alexei's birth therefore seemed to confirm the Tsarina's growing belief in her new-found Orthodox spirituality. Philippe led a shadowy life, always hovering on the edge of scandal, and eventually left Russia, dying in France in 1905. Before his departure, however, he told Alix that there was one who would come after him, a holy man who would prove to be the saviour of the imperial family.

The way was now paved for the arrival of Grigori Yefimovich Rasputin, the man with whom the last rulers of the Romanov dynasty would always be fatally linked. He would first appear in their lives in early November 1905, as the imperial family desperately sought help in dealing with the haemophilia of their beloved son.

Around the imperial family, trapped in their own interior and private world, events were now moving in new and frightening directions. The Tsar's poor grasp of political reality led him to put increasing trust in reactionary figures like Vyacheslav von Plehve. He had risen through the ranks of the Imperial Russian Police to become its Director. He was also responsible for the Department for Protecting Public Order and Security, the Okhrana. This was the secret police force of the Russian Empire, first created in 1866, an organisation which soon acquired a sinister and ruthless reputation both inside and outside Russia.

In 1899, Plehve was appointed a Privy Counsellor and Finnish Minister-Secretary of State. His ruthless administrative efficiency was greatly appreciated by the Tsar, who chaffed under the liberal conservativism of men like Witte and the Minister of the Interior, Dmitry Sergeyevich Sipyagin. In 1902, Sipyagin was assassinated in the Mariinsky Palace by the Socialist-Revolutionary Stepan Balmashov.

This cleared the way for Plehve to be appointed Minister of Interior in Sipyagin's place. He brought to his new role a reputation for harsh and intolerant actions against all those whom he believed now threatened the Tsar's autocratic rule. This included revolutionaries and terrorists, but also liberals who challenged the regime. His anti-Jewish measures led to pogroms across Russia, which earned the country a shameful international reputation. In a notorious speech in 1903, he claimed that in Western Russia 90% of those involved in revolutionary and terrorist activities were Jewish. 'If you do not deter your youth from the revolutionary movement' he threatened Jewish community leaders, 'we shall make your position untenable to such an extent that you will have to leave Russia, to the very last man'.

In 1891, Plehve was involved in the expulsion of all Jews from Moscow. From 1903 onwards, pogroms became part of the official policy of the Russian Empire, the most shocking of these being in Kishinev in present day Moldova. Thousands were killed and eventually over two million Jews would flee Russia. It was while Plehve was Minister of the Interior that one of the most notorious anti-Semitic documents ever to appear was first published in Russia. This was the *Protocols of the Elders of Zion*, a fabricated treatise which purported to be the minutes of a meeting organised by Jewish leaders, in which they set out their plans for global domination through the subversion of national economies and cultures. This hoax document was widely disseminated and created a justification for the persecution of Jews well beyond the borders of Russia.

Plehve's malign influence was soon felt in other ways. In February 1904, Russia and Japan went to war over rival imperial ambitions in Manchuria and Korea. It was widely believed at the time that Plehve was responsible for encouraging the Tsar to ratchet up tensions with Japan. These tensions then spilled over into an outright military and naval conflict, when Japan suddenly attacked the Russian Eastern fleet stationed in Port Arthur on the Pacific coast. Many people at court claimed that Plehve had often talked about the benefits to the Empire of fighting 'a small war', which would deliver quick and easy victories for the regime.

He could not have been more mistaken. The Russo-Japanese war would last for over eighteen months, and it resulted in 200,000 Russian dead and wounded. There were savage battles in Mukden and Yalu, and the important naval base of Port Arthur fell after a long and bloody siege. Both the Russian Eastern and Pacific fleets were destroyed. It was a catastrophe for the regime and seriously damaged the credibility of the imperial government, as well as undermining public confidence in the Tsar himself.

Plehve himself was assassinated on 28 July 1904, when a bomb was thrown into his carriage by a member of the Socialist-Revolutionary Combat Group, a young man called Yegor Sazonov. Few people in Russia mourned his passing. The Jewish Lithuanian journalist, Theodore Rothstein, then living in exile in London, wrote Plehve's epitaph in the journal *The Social Democrat:*

'Blood at the beginning, blood at the end, blood throughout his career, that is the mark Plehve left behind him in history. He was a living outrage on the consciousness of mankind'.

It was a damning indictment of one of the Tsar's most trusted confidantes. The war could have been even more dangerous as it brought Russia and Britain to the verge of open conflict. Britain and Japan were allies and although Britain had remained neutral during the war, tensions began to escalate when British journalists in Port Arthur were accused of being spies. Matters then got a lot worse when the Russian Baltic Fleet, sailing from St Petersburg to Port Arthur, opened fire on what it believed to be Japanese battleships at Dogger Bank in the North Sea on the night of 21 October 1904. These turned out to be British fishing vessels, part of a trawler fleet from Hull. Three British fishermen were killed, and several others injured.

In the confusion that followed the attack, Russian battleships also opened fire on their own fleet, and two cruisers, the *Aurora* and the *Dmitri Donskoi,* were badly damaged, with several of their crews being killed and injured.

The British media and public were outraged. *The Times* thundered against the incompetence of the Russian navy. The popular press described the Russians as pirates and demanded action by the government. The Royal Navy prepared for war and twenty-eight battleships were ordered to sea. For a few days it looked possible that Britain and Russia might go to war. In the end, hastily arranged diplomatic negotiations and a promise by Russia to thoroughly investigate the incident averted what could have turned into a very serious international crisis.

The Russian Baltic fleet continued its journey south, past the Isle of Wight, where observers on Tennyson Down noted how closely British naval vessels were shadowing their Russian counterparts. Seven months later, the fleet, now renamed the Russian Second Pacific Squadron, reached the Sea of Japan, where it was largely destroyed by Admiral Togo in the Straits of Tsushima on 27/28 May 1905. This defeat effectively marked the end of the war and the Russians were forced to sue for peace.

To many people in Russia, this careless international adventurism and the humiliating defeat inflicted on Russian imperial forces in the Far East exposed the rotten heart of the regime. The stage was set for the 1905 Revolution which came close to destroying the Tsarist system. In Lenin's view, it also laid the foundations for the successful Revolution that came twelve years later in 1917.

While the Russo-Japanese war was the trigger for the disturbances that began in January 1905, a whole range of political, social and economic factors contributed to the breakdown of law and order that now took place across the Empire. There was a widespread sense of impending doom and catastrophe at all levels of Russian society.

The Tsar's cousin, the poet and playwright Grand Duke Konstantin Konstantinovich, wrote in his diary on 18 November 1904, 'The Tsarist authority is shaky. All our misfortunes stem from the Emperor's lack of will. The disturbance is increasing, and one senses ahead something unknown, but inescapable and terrible'.

20

Russian exiles and revolutionaries

The assassination of Tsar Alexander II in 1881 meant that terror became the order of the day. A bleak, encroaching terror that would gradually envelop the whole of Russian society from the Tsar and his senior officials of State through to ordinary workers in the factories and peasants in the fields. This was a terror that would numb the intelligentsia, and drive thousands of political opponents of the regime into long-term exile in France, Britain and Germany. It was a twin headed terror perpetuated by both the State and those who sought its overthrow, trapped together in a mutual embrace of fear and destruction.

Tsar Alexander III launched a ferocious and determined drive against the political opponents of the Romanov regime. Russia was stunned by the murder of the Tsar-Liberator. It seemed to many ordinary people that a terrible new frontier had now been crossed and a dark act of infamy and shame stained the Russian soul. The writer Leo Tolstoy heard the news of the Tsar's murder, and wrote to Alexander III, expressing his horror and shock at what had happened. He then begged that the Tsar should forgive the terrorists who carried out this abominable crime because 'Punishing three or four criminals only gives rise to thirty or forty more. Evil begets evil'.

There was to be no forgiveness, no attempt to understand the rage that was now seething below the surface of society. Repression was the answer to revolutionary terror. The organisation that was responsible for the assassination of the Tsar, the 'People's Will', was brutally suppressed, many of its members being executed or sent to prison in Siberia. Many other opponents of the regime fled in to exile in western Europe, where they would keep alive the torch of resistance till it could be passed onto the next generation. By 1884, the once feared revolutionary organisation was no more. It had dissolved itself, beset by internal dissension and demoralisation, public hostility and state terror and repression.

There now followed a period of apparent calm in Russia. The impetus for radical political and social change seemed to have passed. The reign of Alexander III, based on the twin pillars of harsh autocracy and an unswerving suppression of liberal ideas, brought a brief respite from revolutionary terror. However, beneath the surface new movements were beginning to stir, aided and abetted by the strong Russian exile community abroad.

By the mid-1890s, the Tsarist secret police, the Okhrana, became aware that new revolutionary cells and political movements were springing up across Russia. The Okhrana's aim was to keep these different cells weak and disunited, and above all prevent the re-emergence of any terrorist movement that harked back to the days of the 'People's Will'. Tsarist secret agents infiltrated radical circles both in Russia and in the émigré communities abroad and on many occasions successfully managed to create rivalry and dissension between the various groups. This strategy was to have considerable success until the turn of the twentieth century, when several new political movements began to emerge. These included the Russian Socialist Revolutionary Party and the Marxist-leaning Russian Social Democratic Labour Party. These began to unite the various socialist factions, both inside Russia and in the West, around more coherent ideologies and revolutionary strategies.

Exposure to Western Marxist, Socialist and Anarchist ideas was changing the nature of Russian revolutionary politics. The 'People's Will' had been a movement that was essentially focused on the political and social needs of an agrarian society. However, Russia's massive industrialisation, from the 1880s onwards, was creating a new urban proletariat with different needs and demands.

It was now that new thinkers like Viktor Chernov emerged. These were men who were to have a profound influence on creating the new style of revolutionary politics that would transform Russia. Chernov had been involved in radical movements from the early 1890s, was imprisoned, and then fled into exile in Switzerland. It was here in 1901 that he joined the newly launched Socialist Revolutionary Party and became the editor of its paper *Revolutionary Russia*. This became the instrument for forging a new and dynamic ideology, that fused traditional Russian revolutionary thinking about land reform with Marxist ideas that were of wider appeal to the emerging industrial working classes.

The Socialist Revolutionary party led the way in creating what became known as known as 'Revolutionary Populism'. By 1917, it was the largest socialist party in Russia, with over one million members. The future, however, would not belong to it, but to a smaller political grouping - a much more explicitly Marxist party that had emerged in 1898. This was the Russian Social Democratic Labour Party. One of its key figures was Vladimir Ilyich Lenin who had entered revolutionary politics after his elder brother was executed for involvement in a plot to kill Tsar Alexander III.

The 1890s was the decade that Marxism and revolutionary socialism entered the Russian political consciousness in a meaningful and influential way. The consequences for the Romanov regime were to be catastrophic. In 1844, Karl Marx and Friedrich Engels had met and become close friends. They were both committed to revolutionary socialism as a means of reshaping politics and economics and decided to begin work on what would turn out to be their most famous and influential work, *The Communist Manifesto*. This was published in early 1848, as Europe slipped into revolution.

A year later, Marx would move to London which became his home until his death. It was there that he wrote the first volume of *Das Kapital*. This was a searing critique of the capitalist economy and was to provide the political framework for revolutionary socialism for the next hundred years. Marx and Engels anticipated that the revolution against bourgeois economic control would take place in countries with advanced capitalist economies, such as Britain and Germany. They never imagined that it was Russia where their ideas would be adopted. Nor, it seems, did the censors in Tsarist Russia, who famously described the book as so boring that there was no need to ban it from circulation.

Marxist ideas, however, caught the imagination of the Russian intelligentsia. It was the radical young journalist, Pyotr Struve, who now did much to popularise Marxism amongst the urban populations in the Russian Empire. He had established the first Marxist student circles in 1890. The historian Mikhail Zygar describes Struve as a 'political rock star', whose lectures on Marxism 'were attended by legions of fans'.

These developments were certainly causing problems for the Tsarist authorities. However, the political situation was suddenly about to get a lot more worrying. In 1902, one of the original founders of the Socialist Revolutionary Party, Grigory Gershuni, decided to revive the use of terror as a means of hastening the overthrow of the Tsarist regime. He established a new wing of the party, called the Socialist Revolutionary (SR) Combat Organisation, which embarked on a reign of violence across Russia. This group targeted Tsarist officials and senior members of the imperial family, assassinating the Minister of the Interior Dmitry Sipyagin in 1902, and the Governor of Ufa in 1903.

Their most spectacular victim though was Grand Duke Sergei Alexandrovich, the Governor of Moscow, who was killed by a bomb on 4 February 1905. His carriage was blown into thousands of pieces and very little of his body was ever recovered. His wife, Grand Duchess Elizabeth, who was the sister of the Tsarina, heard the explosion and rushed out to try and help him. She spent the next few hours on her knees in the snow pathetically trying to piece small fragments of his remains together. Only a part of his skull and the tips of his fingernails were ever recovered. Revolutionary terror had well and truly returned to Russia.

The Okhrana worked hard to infiltrate the SR Combat Organisation and in Evno Azef, they pulled off one of their most spectacular coups. He had been originally recruited to join the Okhrana in 1893, in order to spy on fellow Russians in Germany. When he joined the Socialist

Revolutionary party, he seemed to be genuinely committed to its values and beliefs. The Okhrana was keen that he become a member of the SR Combat wing, which he agreed to do. Over a period of several years, he rose to the top of the organisation, and from this position of power was able to delay and disrupt many planned terrorist attacks inside Russia. However, other attacks, including the assassination of von Plehve, went ahead as scheduled. There were doubts expressed in some quarters of the Okhrana about whether Azef could be trusted and where his true loyalties lay. Azef's career was to end in spectacular exposure, in a scandal that rocked both the Tsarist establishment and the revolutionary parties.

If there was one country in Europe which the Romanovs and their officials blamed more than any other, for aiding and abetting revolutionary politics and terror, that country was Britain. Due to its liberal political atmosphere, it was increasingly seen as a haven for Russian exiles, with anarchists and socialists being particularly prominent amongst the political refugees who settled there. The British state showed complete indifference to these new arrivals. As far as the British authorities were concerned, Russian political exiles could do whatever they wanted, so long as they did not cause any problems for the British public and went about their business in a peaceful and orderly manner. This attitude greatly irritated the Tsarist Government, which believed that many of these people were dangerous revolutionaries and radicals who needed to be closely monitored, if not imprisoned.

One of the first of the political Russian exiles to arrive was the agrarian socialist Alexander Herzen, who settled in London in 1852. Another was the anarchist Prince Peter Kropotkin who, having escaped from imprisonment in the Peter and Paul Fortress in St Petersburg, reached Britain in 1876. After further wanderings around Europe, he settled in London in 1881. Kropotkin became a leading proponent of anarcho-communism, and his writings included books such as *The Conquest of Bread* and *Fields, Factories and Workshops*.

Anarchist exiles and British Socialists flocked to meet him at his modest villa in Bromley, which became a centre for free political thinking, intellectual debate and radical politics. His fierce opposition to the Russian imperial state was well known. In January 1905, following the Bloody Sunday massacre in St Petersburg, his cottage was besieged by journalists who wanted to interview him and learn about events in Russia. He did not feel well that day and so sent down a note to the growing crowd of reporters which simply read, 'Down with the Romanovs!'

Between 1881 and 1891, thousands of Russians sought refuge in Britain. Large numbers of these were Jews escaping the pogroms and persecution of their homeland, but there were many socialist and anarchist exiles amongst them, too. Parts of the East End of London suddenly seemed to become Russian revolutionary enclaves. This imposed a huge strain on the social and economic fabric of these areas, and it was not long before the popular press and media began to decry the threat to the British way of life and jobs that was posed by this sudden and huge influx of foreigners.

It was now that events began to spiral out of control. The brutal murders committed by Jack the Ripper in the Whitechapel area over the years 1888-1891 fuelled a lot of fear and tension in the East End. There was a growing resentment towards Russian refugees and exiles. Russian Jews, Socialists, and Anarchists were all suspected of being implicated in the murders, and many Jews were directly threatened and abused by large and unruly crowds, who shouted, 'No Englishman could have perpetuated such horrible crimes!'

Anti-Russian feeling in connection with the murders took a new twist when a shadowy Russian anarchist called Nikolay Vasiliev was held responsible for the murders. Nobody could identify who this man was, and nobody had even seen him, but many people were sure that he was to blame. It seems now that he was a totally fictitious character and there is a strong suspicion that the rumours about him being Jack the Ripper may well have been created by the Okhrana in order to discredit Russian revolutionaries living in London.

The rumours about Vasiliev were largely fuelled by a mysterious Russian émigré called Olga Alekseyeva Novikova, who settled in London in 1868, having previously run an elegant salon in St Petersburg. She was to emerge as one of the most celebrated and notorious Russian women living in Britain in the nineteenth century. Soon after her arrival, she embarked on a high-profile career as a writer and journalist and her pro-Russian comments and opinions were soon being widely reported by all sections of the British media.

The British public, along with many senior figures in government, including the Prime Minister, William Gladstone and the campaigning journalist William Stead, were fascinated by this glamorous Russian aristocrat who seemed to have connections at all the right levels of British and Russian society.

Novikova claimed that it was her duty to work towards improving Anglo-Russian relations and she therefore wrote passionately on a wide range of political and social matters. It seems very likely, however, that she was in the pay of the Okhrana and one of her roles was to promote news stories that supported Tsarist Russia while at the same time undermining opponents of the regime. Many of these stories had little basis in truth. In the Ripper case and the creation of the 'fanatical anarchist' Vasiliev she may well have scored one of her most spectacular successes.

Despite the growing British suspicion and hostility towards Russian political émigrés and refugees, many more continued to arrive in the early years of the twentieth century. In 1902, Vladimir Lenin moved to London. He chose to stay in Bloomsbury, where he mainly divided his time between researching and writing at the British Museum, and editing a revolutionary journal called *Iskra* ('Spark').

In August 1903, Lenin, Leon Trotsky, and around fifty other members of the Russian Social Democratic Labour party organised a congress in London which was to have a profound impact on the future of Russia. This was the key moment when the Russian revolutionary movement split into the two rival factions of Bolsheviks and Mensheviks. The Bolsheviks, led by Lenin, argued for a much tighter, centralised party, while the Mensheviks supported a looser, and more broadly-based alliance of revolutionary forces. The terms derived from the way that the voting split between a majority group, the Bolsheviks, and a minority group, the Mensheviks. Lenin narrowly lost the vote. The future battle lines of the Russian Revolution and the new Soviet state were being drawn.

The London congress had originally been due to be held in Brussels, but it was moved because of harassment by the Belgian authorities. The British were known to have a much more lenient approach towards troublesome Russian revolutionaries. The congress took place in several different locations in the East End, in order to avoid detection and infiltration by Tsarist agents. Lenin's notes of the meeting seem to indicate that the furious arguments that led to the crucial split between the two wings of the party took place at the *Three Johns* pub in Islington.

In the same period that Lenin was forging the future of the Bolshevik party, Nicholas and Alexandra were bathing in the waters of the Sarov River, praying for a male heir to the Romanov throne. They had gone there on the instructions of their spiritual guide, Father Philippe. Relics of St Seraphim, the holy man of Sarov, were laid before them. They joined the monks for a simple monastic supper. They were surrounded by thousands of people who had come to gaze on their rulers. Later that evening, in complete secrecy, they went to the source of the Sarov river and immersed themselves in its sacred waters. Their son, Alexei, would be born in July 1904, a year after their visit to Sarov. He was destined to be murdered on the orders of the man then sitting in an obscure pub in Islington, far from those healing waters.

21

The 1905 Revolution

From the start of 1905, Russia was convulsed by disorder and disturbance. The war in the Far East was a disaster, and there was increasing economic and political chaos in Russia itself. The Tsar dithered, unable to face up to the reality of what was happening around him. The imperial family increasingly withdrew into its own private world, shocked into a silent grief by the news that the young Tsarevich was a victim of haemophilia.

On the streets of St Petersburg and other major cities, crowds demonstrated and rioted. The police and army seemed unable to keep order. In the countryside, peasants attacked the manors of the gentry, leading to hundreds of deaths. It was as though this was a time for settling old scores that had festered for years.

Russia's defeat in its war with Japan triggered a popular outburst that took both the regime and its opponents by surprise. All the elements were there for a full-scale revolution, but fortunately for the regime, these elements did not fully coalesce and the Romanov dynasty would manage to survive for another twelve years.

Several factors provoked the 1905 Revolution. There was a growing consciousness amongst the urban working class of their rights, and a resentment of the way that they were being treated by an oppressive industrial-capitalist system. Amongst the rural masses there was a sense that they were not sufficiently benefitting from the agrarian reforms that they had been promised. Across the Russian Empire there was growing hostility amongst its minority ethnic populations towards the continued imposition of Russian culture and religion. Finally, there was a political radicalisation of students and the intelligentsia, many of whom were strongly influenced by Marxist and Socialist ideologies.

The Revolution broke out in December 1904, when a strike began at the Putilov factory in St Petersburg, which supplied equipment for the railways and the army. Sympathy strikes then broke out across the city. By late January 1905, nearly 400 factories were on strike and large parts of the city had come to a halt, with no transportation and many shops closed.

It was in this period that an event occurred which was to leave an indelible stain on the Tsar's reputation and turn what had hitherto been a local disturbance, largely confined to the capital, into a full-blown revolutionary situation that directly threatened the stability of the whole Empire.

On Sunday 9 January 1905, thousands of men, women and children, many of them carrying portraits of the Tsar and singing Orthodox hymns, converged on the Winter Palace. The crowd was made up of workers and their families and their aim was to petition the Tsar for better living conditions. Unbeknownst to the crowd, the Tsar no longer spent much time at the Winter Palace. He now mainly stayed at the Alexander Palace in Tsarskoye Selo, and he was therefore ignorant of the events unfolding in St Petersburg.

The marchers were led by the enigmatic and mysterious Father Georgy Gapon, who was later to be exposed as a Tsarist agent. It is clear though that Gapon felt great loyalty and commitment to the revolutionary cause, with which he was now so closely associated. He was an Orthodox Priest with conflicting beliefs and was dedicated to achieving his personal aims for a fair and just society by working with both the government and the revolutionaries. This he sincerely believed would deliver the best outcome for everyone.

Events soon took a tragic turn. A detachment of Cossacks attacked the crowd as they reached the Winter Palace. Soldiers stationed in front of the Palace fired into the massed ranks of demonstrators. In the panic, men, women and children were trampled underfoot. People fled in all directions, as fear and disorder spread throughout the centre of the city, and students and workers joined in the fray. Military regiments were despatched to take control of the situation, but the fighting continued for two days. At the end of it all, hundreds lay dead, with thousands more injured. The final casualty figures were never fully revealed, and many believed that the government had covered up the true death toll and secretly buried many victims in mass graves.

In his palace at Tsarskoye Selo, Nicholas was virtually isolated from what was taking place in his own capital city. The reports reaching him were few, and often incoherent. 'There were serious disturbances in Petersburg as a result of workers wishing to reach the Winter Palace', he wrote in his diary: 'the troops were forced to open fire in several parts of the town. Lord, how painful and how sad!'. As if all this had nothing to do with him, he then went on to write about how he'd had lunch with his mother and the family and then gone for a walk with his brother, Grand Duke Michael.

In the days following 'Bloody Sunday', as it became known, the Tsar made no attempt to return to St Petersburg, or to visit the wounded in hospital. His puzzled and bemused cousin, Grand Duke Konstantin, reflected what many must have asked at the time, 'What does the Emperor really think?' He wrote, 'I heard that he [Nicholas] was not inclined to take the disturbances seriously and thought that they had been greatly exaggerated'. At a time of national crisis, which called for a ruler who would unite his fractured people, Nicholas was completely absent from the political scene. Into this void, others would now step, and events would unfold at a bewildering pace.

The tragic events of 'Bloody Sunday' provoked great outrage across Russia as well as in Britain, where the Liberal and Socialist movements united in their condemnation of 'Nicholas the Bloody'. This cursed title was now well and truly established and would follow Nicholas into his grave.

As news of what had happened in St Petersburg spread across the Empire, there was a huge public reaction to the slaughter. Hundreds of thousands of workers in Russia, Poland, Finland and the Baltic provinces went on strike. These strikes soon spread to the Caucasus. In response, the authorities hit back with violence and repression. All the universities were closed, and soldiers were given orders to fire on strikers.

In order to defuse the revolutionary situation, the Tsar began to make political concessions. In early August 1905, he agreed to the issuing of the *Bulygin Constitution*, scripted by his Minister of the Interior, Alexander Bulygin. This promised to introduce a limited number of constitutional reforms and democratic changes. These included the creation of a State Duma of the Russian Empire with consultative powers, and nods towards free speech and religious tolerance. These concessions were not enough. The first St Petersburg 'Soviet' (council) representing over 200,000 workers was set up, and it soon threatened to escalate the strikes and opposition to the regime.

Throughout the summer of that year, trouble continued to spread across the Empire. There were peasant uprisings and land seizures. On the Black Sea, the crew of the imperial battleship, *Potemkin,* mutinied and murdered several of their senior officers in protest at poor living conditions at sea. The red flag was hoisted, and the *Potemkin* sailed into Odessa harbour, hoping to encourage other ships in the Black Sea fleet to follow their example and mutiny. Odessa was in chaos with a general strike taking place in the city and the crew of the *Potemkin* did little to support the strikers.

Several days later, with naval vessels loyal to the Tsar sailing towards Odessa, the crew of the *Potemkin* decided to head for Constanza in Romania, where they surrendered their weapons and the ship. After the 1917 Revolution, the events in Odessa would be immortalised by Sergei Eisenstein in his 1922 epic film *Battleship Potemkin,* which became a paean of praise to revolutionary heroism and sacrifice, even if the events that had taken place did not quite match the myths depicted on screen.

By October 1905, over two million workers were on strike, and all transport had ground to a halt. Clashes and rioting became a feature of everyday life in all the major cities. There were attacks on the Jews, particularly in the Ukraine.

In the middle of this growing chaos, the Tsar reluctantly agreed to sign a *Reform Manifesto* that had been presented to him by Sergei Witte, and Dimitri Obolensky. In October 1905, Witte had become the Chair of the Council of Ministers, a position that made him equivalent to Prime Minister. He was now the most important politician in the country. For several years, he had been warning the Tsar about the need for constitutional reform and the political catastrophe which faced the regime if no action was taken. Nicholas neither liked nor trusted Witte, but faced by the scale of the disorders now engulfing the Empire, he felt that he had no choice but to approve the *Reform Manifesto*, which set out a range of new constitutional reforms.

At the heart of these reforms was the creation of an Imperial Duma, which would be elected through a democratic franchise, and would have legislative powers. Civil liberties including freedom of expression would be granted and there would be an end to censorship, as well as to imprisonment without trial. The army was ordered to stop confronting demonstrators and strikers. Criminal investigations would be carried out to identify those responsible for the recent pogroms against the Jews.

The aim of Witte's reforms was to move Russia towards becoming a constitutional monarchy, with Russians eventually enjoying the same democratic freedoms as their compatriots in Britain and France. Through these reforms, Witte was also seeking to split the liberals from the revolutionaries and create a broad-based coalition of support for a new, moderate political settlement.

It was a bold and courageous vision, but from the beginning the Tsar never really accepted it. He was increasingly uncomfortable with what he saw as his personal political humiliation. The Tsarina criticised him for not preserving the imperial inheritance that had been granted to him by his own father. The ghosts of Imperial Russian autocracy cast a long shadow. Nicholas wrote in his diary soon after approving the new constitution that he felt 'sick with shame at this betrayal of the dynasty. The betrayal was complete'.

The announcement of the *October Constitution* went a long way towards calming the unrest across the Empire. Many strikes collapsed and liberal opponents of the Tsar demonstrated in his favour and declared their willingness to work with the regime. Preparations were soon launched for elections to the Imperial Duma. Now began a period known as the 'Days of Freedom', an extraordinary six weeks of political and press freedom. Nothing like it had ever been seen before in Russia. All censorship was removed, new political parties and labour unions were established. Public demands were openly made for the overthrow of the Tsarist regime.

It was clear that events were beginning to take a revolutionary turn and the regime was nervous. Revolutionary and socialist political leaders also realised that the mood of the government was changing and decided to pre-empt any attempts to curtail their newly won freedoms. In early December, a general strike was called which led to bitter street fighting between workers and government troops. It was not until 18 December that the uprisings could be put down in St Petersburg and Moscow, and the violent phase of the 1905 Revolution finally came to its close.

In the middle of all this turmoil, the Tsar received a telegram from Grigori Rasputin. It read, 'Little Father Tsar! Having arrived in St Petersburg from Siberia, I would like to bring you an icon of the Blessed St Simon Verkhotursky, the Miracle Worker, who is so revered among us; with faith that the Holy Saint will preserve you for all the days of your life and help you in your service for the good and happiness of your devoted sons'. A few days later, on 1 November, Nicholas and Alexandra went to the Palace of Sergievka, where they had tea with the so-called 'Black Princesses' of Montenegro, Milica and Stana. There they met Father Grigori for the first time.

By the end of that year, it was clear that although the government had survived, its reputation and political authority had been seriously damaged. The 1905 Revolution had been a severe shock and a warning to the imperial regime that reform was long overdue. Although the Tsar may have wanted to retrench and avoid implementing much of what he had agreed in the *October Manifesto*, it was clear that he was no longer in any viable position to do so.

In April 1906, a new Constitution was ratified by the Tsar, in which he formally agreed to share power with an elected assembly. There was provision for a new two-chamber parliament, which had to approve all laws enacted in Russia. The Upper Chamber was to be known as the State Council and many of its members were to be directly appointed by the Tsar. The Lower Chamber would be called the State Duma and all its members were to be elected by Russian voters. The Tsar, however, was determined not to give his powers away quite so easily. The Duma, as it soon became clear, had relatively limited rights to challenge the Tsarist government. The Tsar retained the right to veto any legislation with which he did not personally agree. He could also dismiss the Duma and call fresh elections if he was not happy with the way the elected chamber was behaving.

Despite these restrictions, though, the election of the first Duma marked a milestone in Russian political history. A limited form of democratic accountability had now been imposed on the Tsar. This marked a palpable erosion of the autocratic system of government as it had existed prior to 1906. Although the official opening of the Duma was greeted by the Tsar and his family with considerable emotion and relief, it was not long before Duchess Xenia, the Tsar's sister, wrote in her diary, 'The Duma is such filth, such a nest of revolutionaries, that it is disgusting and shaming for the rest of Russia in front of the whole world'. Autocracies do not easily surrender their privileges and their power.

22

A new Anglo-Russian alliance

After a century of suspicion and conflict, Anglo-Russian relations slowly improved during the reign of Tsar Alexander III. The Tsar was keen not to antagonise Britain over Central Asia and strong efforts were made to find areas of common agreement over Afghanistan, Tibet and Persia. Although the issue of the Ottoman Empire remained a constant source of tension between the two countries, there was a gradual rapprochement in foreign affairs. Russia's new alliance with France and the need for Britain to contain the growing power of Germany also meant that the two countries increasingly shared strategic international interests.

Despite the many political and diplomatic difficulties that Nicholas II experienced with the British government, there is no doubt that throughout his life he felt a great sense of personal warmth towards Britain as a country, and towards his British relations. This was strengthened in 1896 by his marriage to Alix of Hesse.

On 20 September 1896, four months after their coronation in Moscow, Nicholas and Alix (now officially referred to as Alexandra Feodorovna since her coronation) arrived in Scotland to stay with Queen Victoria at Balmoral. Their visit was to last ten days. For the Tsarina, this was a homecoming and the time spent with her grandmother was always precious to her. The visit was something of an ordeal for Nicholas, who disliked the wet, windy weather and the stuffy protocol of Victoria's court.

On their first day in Balmoral, the Queen could not resist putting on a small exhibition to commemorate the defeat of the Russians at Sevastopol in 1855. This included trophies that had been won from the Russian Imperial Army. It was reported that the imperial couple viewed the exhibits with 'humourless solemnity'. There was certainly a mischievous side to Victoria, and she clearly did not want to pass up the opportunity of tweaking the tail of the Russian bear.

The visit, however, was in no way intended to be political and was very much billed as a family event. Nicholas stolidly ate his way through plates of Scottish porridge, went stalking with the family (during which he was completely unsuccessful in shooting any stags), and sat through a round of tedious tea parties and luncheons.

He managed to avoid any serious political discussions with his 'Uncle Bertie', but could not avoid having them with Queen Victoria, who cross questioned him about Russian intentions towards the Ottoman Empire. As they bumped along in the carriage, she suggested that closer Anglo-Russian cooperation might be in the best interests of both countries. Nicholas refused to be drawn into the discussions and his diary for that day is blank apart from mentioning the lunch and dinner that he appeared not to have greatly enjoyed.

The visit came to an end on the evening of Saturday 3 October, and Nicholas and Alexandra left by overnight train to Portsmouth where they boarded the imperial yacht *Shtandart*, which was moored in the Solent, off Portsmouth. Nicholas was relieved to have left Balmoral.

The following day, they sailed past the Isle of Wight on their way out to the Channel, and then on to France where they were to make a five-day official visit to Paris and Versailles. This was the last time that Nicholas and Alexandra would see Queen Victoria. On 22 January 1901, less than five years after their time together in Balmoral, she died at her beloved Osborne House.

It was the end of what had been a difficult era in Anglo-Russian relations. Following the accession of King Edward VII, a new and more positive phase was about to begin, though echoes of the old difficulties and suspicions would still cast their long shadows into the new reign.

King Edward VII believed strongly that Britain and Russia should find a way to resolve their differences and build a new international partnership in the twentieth century. There was now concern in Britain about the rising power of Germany. Under Kaiser Wilhelm II, a new, more confident Germany was beginning to assert itself on the world stage. German industry was now outperforming British industry. There was also a naval race now underway with Germany, which many in the Royal Navy viewed with increasing alarm.

The Kaiser's interventions on behalf of the Boers in the South African War of 1899-1902 and German propaganda about the British concentration camps in which Boer women and children were interred, had inflamed British attitudes towards Germany. It was becoming increasingly clear that France and Russia were no longer the threat to British interests that they had appeared to be in the previous century. A new, more dangerous power had emerged on the European stage and increasingly, British foreign policy strategies focused on how to contain German ambitions both in Europe and around the world.

Germany had now become the bogeyman and the German threat began to haunt the British public imagination. Popular literature reflected this concern. Novels like Erskine Childers' *The Riddle of the Sands* exploited these fears, conjuring up images of a German invasion force that was preparing to cross the North Sea and invade Britain from the mud flats of the Frisian Islands.

King Edward himself was wary of the Kaiser. His Danish wife, Alexandra, actively disliked Germany and had never forgiven or forgotten the defeat of her father's armies at the hands of the Austro-Prussian troops in 1864. This was a resentment that increasingly coloured Edward's attitudes towards his nephew Kaiser Wilhelm II, after the latter ascended the throne in 1888 and embarked on a more aggressive foreign policy.

Hitherto, German foreign policy ambitions - under the careful stewardship of the Chancellor Otto von Bismarck - had been more moderate and conservative in tone. All this now changed and with

Bismarck's resignation in 1890, the young Kaiser was able to give free reign to his plans for industrial, military and territorial expansion.

The Kaiser's hostility towards Britain, Russia and France, three countries that he believed were denying Germany its legitimate position as an international power, now drove Russia and France into a new alliance. This was formally agreed in 1894. Following his accession in 1901, King Edward VII and his government, while reluctant to commit Britain to this alliance, sought to draw closer to both countries.

In May 1903, Edward VII made an historic visit to Paris, which led to the signing of the *Entente Cordiale*, a series of foreign policy agreements between France and Britain which set Franco-British relations in a new and more positive direction. The visit that he made to Paris was at his own instigation and was largely kept secret from the government. French attitudes towards Britain in 1903, both at a public and governmental level, were at best indifferent, at worst hostile. The King's charm, diplomatic sensitivity and friendly attitude towards everyone he met transformed these negative perceptions. The ground was now prepared for the biggest shift towards friendly collaboration between the two countries in over eight hundred years. The Entente was signed on 8 April 1904, less than a year after the King's visit, and was a tribute to his commitment to turning old rivals into new allies.

Edward was determined to build on the French alliance with Russia to improve the British relationship with the Tsar and his government. However, international events would soon make this a risky and difficult step to take. Since 1902, Edward had made it one of his key objectives to cultivate good relations with the newly appointed Russian Ambassador to London, Count Alexander von Benckendorff. He was a Russian diplomat who was a passionate Anglophile and believed that it was in his country's best interests to build an alliance with Britain. At his Embassy in Kensington, Benckendorff entertained on a lavish scale and it was rumoured that he spent more money and time on entertaining than any other foreign ambassador. He and Edward soon became close friends, and he was frequently invited to royal house parties at Balmoral and private gatherings in Windsor.

The outbreak of the Russo-Japanese war in 1904 put an enormous strain on the relationship between Britain and Russia. Britain was officially an ally of Japan, but it chose not to enter the war. However, British intelligence was passing secret information to Tokyo and this help undoubtedly aided the Japanese war effort. The Kaiser was quick to exploit the situation, writing to the Tsar and directly blaming the British for Russian defeats in the Far East. Tensions rose between St Petersburg and London. There was a lot of anti-British rhetoric in the Russian press and a wave of Anglophobia swept the country.

During the unfolding crisis of 1904-05, Edward and Benckendorff worked tirelessly to address any misunderstandings between the two countries. Edward was regularly in touch with the Tsar, assuring him of his understanding and support, and Benckendorff went to great lengths to ensure that the Russian government fully grasped the importance and value of building a more positive relationship with Britain.

By 1905, with Russia embroiled in revolution, and the war with Japan drawing to its close, the diplomatic crisis between Britain and Russia had passed. The last fourteen years of Tsarist rule would be marked by an increasingly close partnership between the two countries. Although there were still problems, relations between Russia and Britain started to improve. Both governments saw real value in working together more closely, not only to deal with tensions in Central Asia and the Balkans, but also to limit the growing power of Germany.

This more positive British government attitude towards the Tsarist regime was not initially supported by the wider British public, or by the trade unions and the Labour and Liberal parties. They all continued to be strongly critical of what they saw as the oppressive nature of Tsarist government. These hostile attitudes would be given full expression during the Tsar's visit to the Isle of Wight in 1909.

In 1907, the governments of Russia and Britain signed what became known as the *Anglo-Russian Convention on Persia, Afghanistan and Tibet*. This aimed at reducing tensions between the two countries in a part of the world where there had been much jealousy and rivalry. The *Great Game*, with its spies, conspiracies and military skirmishes, had helped to create a suspicious atmosphere on both sides. For the British, the protection of the empire in India was central to its imperial strategy. Combating growing Russian influence in neighbouring countries, particularly Persia, Afghanistan and Tibet, was therefore of paramount importance.

The 1907 Convention was not a military alliance. Its main aim was to define British and Russian spheres of interest and influence and chart the ways in which the two countries would work together to ensure that these respective interests were better protected. This was a breakthrough in Anglo-Russian collaboration. It also marked the start of long-term British interference in Persia's domestic affairs.

The threat of a Russian invasion of India, which had dominated British imperial military planning since the reign of Emperor Paul in 1800, was now finally lifted. Secret papers prepared for the British Cabinet, even as late as 1905, were still assessing the likelihood of a Russian attack on India and how best to prepare for this. After 1907, no such papers were issued.

The *Anglo-Russian Convention* helped create the *Triple Entente*, which brought Britain, Russia and France together in a loose partnership. The *Triple Entente* was never in itself a formal alliance but built on a series of bilateral partnerships: the *Dual Alliance* between France and Russia, the *Entente Cordiale* between Britain and France and the *Anglo-Russian Convention*. Europe was now divided into a competing set of geographical pacts as Germany, Austria-Hungary and Italy were officially united in a military pact, the *Triple Alliance*. The scene was set for the confrontations that would lead to the First World War.

In Britain, the *Anglo-Russian Convention* was viewed with considerable suspicion by both the press and by Parliament. The agreement had been signed on 31 August 1907 when Parliament was on holiday, and many months were to pass before the Government allowed a debate on it in the House of Commons. It was almost as though the British government was ashamed of the deal. In Russia, by contrast, there was a widespread sense of hope that the 1907 Convention marked the start of a new era of collaboration with Britain. In this spirit of optimism, the Tsar invited his uncle, King Edward VII, to make an official visit to Russia in the early summer of 1908. Edward was happy to accept. It would be the first ever visit by a ruling British sovereign to Russia.

In fact, Edward never stepped foot on Russian soil. It was decided that the security risks were too great for both the King and the Tsar to be on dry land together. Terrorist attacks in Russia were now a frequent occurrence and plots to kill the Tsar and his senior officials were being regularly thwarted.

Two recent successful attacks had been the assassination of the Tsar's uncle, Grand Duke Sergei, in February 1905, and the bomb attack on the residence of the Prime Minister Pyotr Stolypin in August 1906. This killed and injured over thirty people, though Stolypin himself survived on that occasion. Five years later, in September 1911, he was murdered in Kiev by a disgruntled police officer.

Although Edward himself had been the victim of an anarchist assassination attempt in Brussels, he was not unduly concerned about his personal safety. In Britain he led a relaxed and relatively free life with minimum protection. He was therefore keen to visit St Petersburg which, as Prince of Wales, he had last seen in 1894 following the death of Alexander III. However, these were tense and much more dangerous times in Russia.

The Tsar was horrified by Edward's insouciance and seeming lack of concern about his personal security. 'In England' he wrote, 'the King is used to strolling around wherever he wants and will do the same here. I know him. He will walk to the theatre and the ballet and probably go and inspect some factories and shipyards'. Eventually, a decision was made by both the Russian and British security services that the two monarchs would meet at sea, close to the city of Reval - now called Talinn - in modern-day Estonia.

The visit was presented as a family reunion rather than as an official state visit. This was to soothe the anger of many British Members of Parliament, who strongly opposed the trip and saw it as condoning the Tsar's oppressive regime. Only a day before King Edward set sail for Reval, the House of Commons debated whether it should even go ahead. Out of the 284 who were present, fifty-nine MPs voted against the visit. Ramsay

MacDonald called the Tsar 'a common murderer'. Keir Hardie, the Labour party leader, denounced the visit and claimed that it gave 'official approval to the atrocities and crimes committed by the Tsar'.

In order to ameliorate the situation, the Foreign Secretary, Sir Edward Grey, assured Parliament that he would not be accompanying the King to Reval and that no new treaties or conventions would be signed. He announced that Charles Hardinge, who was Permanent Under Secretary of State for Foreign Affairs, and a man greatly liked and trusted by the King, would accompany the royal party.

In Russia, there was greater enthusiasm for the visit. In May 1908, Hugh O'Beirne, a Counsellor at the British Embassy in St Petersburg and one of the most able diplomats of his generation, wrote to Sir Edward Grey to reassure him of the positive Russian press and parliamentary reaction to Edward's arrival.

'The great majority of the Russian papers attach the highest political importance to the forthcoming visit, which they regard as setting the seal on the recent Anglo-Russian Convention. It will, they consider, lead to the further development of relations now established between the two countries'.

He mentioned that the opposition to the visit was generally confined to traditional opponents of Britain such as the journal *Sviet*, which O'Beirne described as a 'reactionary paper of little standing' or *Russkoe Znanie*, which 'indulges in virulent attacks on Great Britain and her policy and is the discredited organ of the violently reactionary *Association of the Russian Peoples*'. O'Beirne's critique of *Russkoe Znanie* may have been rather too harsh as it had a distinguished panel of contributors including the writer, Maxim Gorky'.

O'Beirne noted that the German language press in St Petersburg was universally cool towards the visit. The *Petersburger Zeitung* protested at what it believed to be the over exaggeration of the importance of the meeting, while the *Herold* deplored the Anglomania that was sweeping the imperial capital.

Most Russian politicians welcomed the King's visit. There was a genuine belief that an increase in English influence could only benefit the liberal cause in Russia. The aggressively anti-Tsarist British newspaper *Daily News* had been whipping up a popular media campaign against the Reval meeting. This was regretted by many Russian political leaders and parliamentarians who believed that this type of campaign only suited the interests of the revolutionary parties. 'Less extreme politicians in Russia consider this campaign to be extremely disadvantageous to the interests of liberalism in their country', O'Beirne wrote in his despatches to London.

After a very rough and uncomfortable crossing on board the royal yacht *Victoria and Albert III* due to strong gales blowing in the North Sea, the King reached Reval and anchored close to the Tsar's imperial yacht *Shtandart*. The King's yacht was accompanied by two armoured cruisers, HMS *Minotaur* and HMS *Achilles*, and by four British destroyers.

On their way to Reval they had called in at the German port city of Kiel, where they were entertained to dinner by Prince Henry of Prussia, who made a speech expressing friendship towards Britain and disclaiming any aggressive intentions on the part of the German Navy. He asked that these views be understood and spread throughout Britain.

The King and his party, however, did not fail to notice the whole of the German North Sea fleet riding at anchor in the port, together with a flotilla of new torpedo boats. This obviously intentional display of German naval might was not lost on the British naval officers on board the King's yacht. They were quick to remark that this was an important warning for them about the strength and efficiency of the German navy.

The port city of Reval had been part of the Russian Empire since 1710, when it was seized from the Swedes during the Great Northern War. It was one of the most attractive cities in the Empire, with an historic centre crammed with narrow cobbled streets, fortified walls and great gothic churches. During the latter half of the nineteenth century there had also been rapid industrialisation. The King, however, was to see none of this, except what he managed to glimpse from the deck of his royal yacht.

On this trip, Edward was accompanied by his wife, Queen Alexandra, and by their daughter, Princess Victoria. The Tsar travelled with the Tsarina, his five children, and with his mother, the Dowager Empress,

Maria Feodorovna. She was Queen Alexandra's sister and so it was felt that she would be helpful in smoothing relations between the two families.

Security for the visit was very tight. Among the numerous warships guarding the Tsar in Reval was the *Aurora,* the only surviving naval vessel from the ill-fated battle of Tsushima in 1905. In 1917, the *Aurora's* guns would be trained on the Winter Palace at the start of the Bolshevik Revolution.

The Tsar had travelled to Reval on board his private train and the entire route was lined by thousands of soldiers. No unauthorised personnel were allowed access to the royal yachts. The British were shocked by the paranoia that they witnessed on the Russian side. This was a level of security that went beyond anything they had ever experienced at home. General Alexander Spiridovich was now the Head of the Tsar's Personal Police Guard, and he took extreme measures to ensure that there would be no mishaps during this important meeting between the rulers of two of the world's greatest Empires.

This would lead to one of the most farcical episodes of the whole visit, when members of an Estonian Ladies Choir were threatened with being strip searched by the Tsar's security police, before being allowed to sing in front of the King. Sir Frederick Ponsonby, the King's Equerry, was appalled when he heard that this was about to happen. He wondered what the reaction would be in England if the 'Russian Emperor came to England and some ladies' choral society asked leave to serenade him, and our police insisted on stripping and searching them'. After hasty discussions between the heads of the two security services, the Russians agreed to abandon the plan and the ladies sang in front of the King without being required to undress.

At 11.30 on the morning of 9 June, the Tsar and his family came on board the *Victoria and Albert.* The Tsar was dressed in the uniform of the Scots Greys. In 1894, Nicholas had been appointed Colonel-in-Chief of the regiment by Queen Victoria in honour of his marriage to her granddaughter, a role that he took very seriously. The fact that the Tsar chose to make a call on the King was in breach of traditional protocol. It should have been Edward's responsibility to call on the Tsar as he was the guest in Russian waters. However, this was an important statement of how much Nicholas respected his 'Uncle Bertie'.

During the two days that the King and the Tsar were together in Reval, the city was bathed in sunshine and the sea was calm. Had they arrived only a few days earlier the two yachts would have been tossing about in high winds and rough seas and the crews would have been coping with clearing snow and ice from the decks. This would certainly have made for a far less comfortable and enjoyable royal rendezvous.

The King and the Tsar took the opportunity to have important discussions about a range of international issues in the Balkans, Persia and Afghanistan. This was Edward at his best. He was the consummate diplomat and put Nicholas at his ease, complimenting him on his Scots Guards uniform and treating him as an equal in all ways. There was none of the bullying that Nicholas had come to fear whenever he met Kaiser Wilhelm.

Edward listened carefully to everything that the Tsar and his Ministers told him about the situation in Russia. His discussions with the Russian Foreign Minister, Alexander Izvolsky, and the Tsar's Prime Minister, Pyotr Stolypin, were particularly productive and made a strong and positive impression on both men. Although Edward was a natural conciliator and always sought to smooth out any areas of difference, he was not afraid to raise difficult questions.

In a private meeting with Stolypin, he registered his concerns over the treatment of Jews in Russia and particularly about the pogroms that had occurred in the Ukraine and Bessarabia two years earlier. While we cannot doubt Edward's sense of personal revulsion at the treatment of Russia's Jews, there may also have been other reasons as to why he raised the issue. Since 1881, many Jews had been fleeing persecution in the Russian Empire and heading towards Britain. The arrival of so many refugees was starting to put pressure on poorer communities in London and other major cities and there was a growing sense of anger about the number of immigrants arriving in the country. This had the potential to create serious social and political disorder in many British cities. Edward was aware of these tensions and the fact that, if the pogroms continued, this would lead to even larger numbers of refugees arriving in Britain.

Only two days after the Reval meeting had finished, Sir Charles Hardinge wrote a secret memorandum to the British Foreign Secretary Sir Edward Grey, detailing all the issues discussed with the Tsar and his Ministers. He described it as a 'satisfactory visit, which should be productive of the best possible results in the future'.

The Balkans dominated a lot of the discussions. The 'Macedonia Question' was now uppermost in the minds of governments across Europe. Macedonia was at that time under Ottoman control, but this was an increasingly beleaguered and ineffective rule. Russia and Britain were both wary of the ambitions of the Austro-Hungarians and Germans and their plans for expansion in the Balkans. The meeting in Reval provided an opportunity to discuss how to maintain the peace in the region and restrain the two Central Powers.

Looming over all the discussions was the growing power of Germany. Everyone at Reval agreed that Germany needed to be treated with the utmost care and caution. The Tsar was keen not to provoke the Kaiser and regretted that the Russian press was now adopting an increasingly anti-German attitude. Hardinge told Izvolsky about the growing alarm in Britain at the scale of the German naval programme and where this might lead. Hardinge predicted that 'a critical situation might arise with Germany in seven or eight years from now' and that Britain may then have to call on Russia to be the arbiter in resolving the crisis.

The Russians raised the issue of Persia and their concerns about German intrigues in the region. Both the Russian and British governments were committed to keeping the Shah on the throne. They mistrusted German ambitions in the region, and they certainly did not like German plans for building a railway line from Istanbul to Baghdad. Railway systems were a major way of projecting international power during this period. There was a real fear that German control of the railway system across the Ottoman Empire and into Persia might one day threaten the British Empire in India.

Throughout the discussions in Reval, the Tsar was 'repeatedly expressing his great satisfaction at the visit of the King and Queen' which he claimed had 'sealed and confirmed the intention and spirit of the Anglo-Russian Agreement'. He expressed his 'profound conviction that the friendly sentiments which now prevail between the two governments could only mature and grow stronger with the progress of time to the mutual advantage of both countries'.

He reiterated that 'the Russian press of all shades and opinions showed conclusively how extremely popular throughout Russia the King's visit had become, and how it was welcomed as a visible sign of a new era in Anglo-Russian relations'.

Alongside the diplomatic discussions there was also plenty of time at Reval for family reunions over lunches, teas and dinners. The two royal families could move between three royal yachts, *Victoria and Albert*, the *Shtandart* and the Dowager Empress's yacht *Polar Star*.

On their second evening in Reval, the Tsar entertained the King and Queen to dinner on the imperial yacht. There were warm words of welcome from the Tsar, and an affirmation of his strong support for the new partnership between Russia and Britain. Edward reciprocated with equally cordial words and concluded his speech by saying, 'I most heartily endorse every word that fell from Your Majesty's lips. I believe that it will serve to knit more closely the bonds that unite the people of our two countries'.

After dinner the guests gathered on the deck of the *Shtandart* where they were entertained by groups of local singers. The *New York Times* reported that boatloads of German, Estonian and Russian singers sailed out to the imperial yacht and serenaded the royal visitors with national folk songs. Edward's reaction is not recorded. However, according to some observers, he spent a long time fiddling with his pocket watch and not displaying a huge amount of interest in the melodic offerings.

The following day, Edward returned to the *Shtandart* and appointed Nicholas as an 'Admiral of the Fleet in the British Navy'. Now, the Tsar of Russia had both naval and military uniforms to wear whenever he met with the King of Great Britain. It seems that Nicholas was immensely pleased by this unexpected honour. That evening, when he and the Tsarina joined the King and Queen for a State Dinner on board the *Victoria and*

Albert, Nicholas returned the favour by inviting Edward to become an Admiral of the Russian fleet.

The following morning, the King's yacht weighed anchor and set sail for home. The Reval meeting was over and general opinion was that it had been a resounding success. Hugh O'Beirne, writing from St Petersburg to Sir Edward Grey one week after the visit, noted that he had been assured 'from many widely different quarters of the excellent effect on Russian opinion by the Reval meeting'. The King's toast to the 'welfare of the great Russian Empire' had been very well received, not only among politicians but also in Court circles, 'where narrower views are apt to prevail'.

O'Beirne also alluded to the growing anti-German sentiments now emerging throughout the Russia Empire and how the Reval meeting had encouraged these to flourish more openly.

'I believe' he wrote, 'that one of the principal causes underlying the general satisfaction with which Russia, as a nation, has seen the friendly meeting between the Tsar and the King is due to the deep-seated dislike of the Russians for Germany'. While the Tsar and his Ministers sought to maintain a harmonious relationship with Germany, popular public opinion was now shifting against the Kaiser. Anglomania was firmly in fashion and the British alliance was now seen as the best way of preserving Russia's future security.

The Reval visit was to lead directly to the Tsar's visit to Cherbourg and the Isle of Wight in 1909. These two meetings would set the seal on Russia's Triple Entente with France and Britain and would confirm the worst fears of Germany and Austro-Hungary. The Central Powers now awoke to the real threat of encirclement. The growing anti-German mood in France, Russia and Britain could also no longer be ignored. Popular opinion in these three countries began quite openly to treat Germany as an enemy.

PART

VII

THE 1909 RUSSIAN IMPERIAL VISIT TO THE ISLE OF WIGHT

Places in Cowes and East Cowes associated with the Romanovs

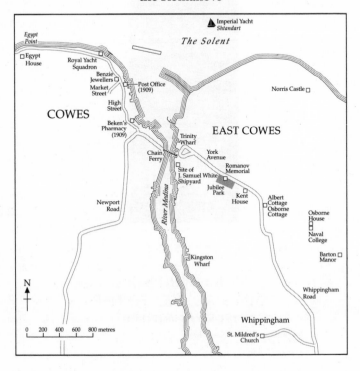

Imperial Yacht
Shtandart

The Solent

Egypt
Point

Egypt
House

Royal Yacht
Squadron

Benzie
Jewellers

Market
Street

Post Office
(1909)

Norris Castle

High
Street

COWES

Beken's
Pharmacy
(1909)

Trinity
Wharf

EAST COWES

York
Avenue

Chain
Ferry

Romanov
Memorial

Site of
J. Samuel White
Shipyard

Jubilee
Park

Kent
House

Albert
Cottage

River Medina

Newport
Road

Osborne
Cottage

Osborne
House

Naval
College

Barton
Manor

Kingston
Wharf

N

Whippingham
Road

0   200   400   600   800 metres

Whippingham

St. Mildred's
Church

23

A family invitation

On Monday 2 August 1909, the imperial yacht *Shtandart* reached the Cowes Roads, after a short voyage from Cherbourg. The Tsar and his family had been guests of the French President, and the visit to France was intended to affirm the strong alliance between the two countries. The sea crossing had been smooth and the weather was set to be fine, after early thunder and rain had cleared.

The Tsar was looking forward to spending a few days in the company of his British royal cousin Prince George, his aunt Queen Alexandra, and his uncle King Edward VII. The Isle of Wight had very special memories for both Nicholas and Alexandra. In many ways, this was a homecoming for the two of them.

Here at Cowes, they could enjoy the most famous yachting regatta in the world, review one of the largest ever gatherings of the British fleet, and celebrate the growing alliance between their two countries. Though few could see it at the time, this visit was to mark the final meeting in Britain between the two royal families. Ahead lay war, revolution, and a final family betrayal that would haunt King George V and his successors for many years afterwards.

The imperial visit was not formally trumpeted as being a state visit, but to all intents and purposes it came close to being one. The Tsar's visit had aroused a lot of controversy and opposition in Britain when it was first announced in January 1909. There were genuine fears that, if the Tsar came to London, there would be demonstrations and possible riots encouraged by Socialist and Labour party agitators.

The Prime Minister Herbert Henry Asquith and his Liberal government were also very uneasy about appearing to welcome the Tsar, given the autocratic and oppressive reputation of his regime. There were also worries that Russian anarchists and revolutionary terrorists, now well entrenched in Britain, might launch an attack on the imperial family. All these factors conspired to make a visit by Nicholas a sensitive issue, and a problem that nobody really wanted to own. However, Russia was now an ally of Britain, and despite the historic tensions between the two countries, it was recognised that a visit by the Tsar would undoubtedly help strengthen this important new partnership.

To avoid the embarrassment and security risks associated with a full state visit, the King and the Prime Minister agreed that Nicholas and his family would be invited to spend a few days as the personal guests of the British royal family. The Royal Yacht Squadron Regatta in Cowes, and the Naval Review in Spithead, were both being held in early August 1909. These two events were clearly the perfect opportunities to entertain the Tsar, in an appropriate style, but in a secure location.

The Tsar was keen to take up the invitation. Both he and Alexandra liked the Isle of Wight, and the idea of sailing there appealed to them. Travelling in their own yacht and remaining on board throughout their visit would also help address the worries of the British and Russian security services and was a perfect solution for all parties. A visit to London would undoubtedly have provoked demonstrations and increased the chance of a terrorist attack.

The Tsar could come to Britain, which he wanted to do, and this would allow for important discussions to take place in a safe environment. Necessary protocol could be observed with the Tsar attending both the Cowes Regatta and the Royal Naval Review. It was also hoped that this meeting between the two royal families would strengthen the Anglo-Russian alliance in a deeper and more personal way.

Edward VII treated his nephew with affection and respect throughout the visit. He recognised that the Tsar was not the strongest or most decisive of rulers. However, he also knew that with Germany posing an increasing threat to British influence and power, his country needed Russia as an ally and friend.

Nicholas, on his part, was respectful towards his uncle but also wary of him. Suspicion and mistrust of Britain and its motives was strongly engrained in the Romanov psyche. However, he also acknowledged that it was in the interests of Russia to build a closer alliance with Britain. Russia's relations with Germany were strained, even though Kaiser Wilhelm II was keen to woo Russia away from the French alliance. Nicholas did not trust the Kaiser or his motives, so his natural instincts therefore drew him closer to Britain, now also a friend of France.

24

Public protest and anarchist terror

The year 1909 had opened with a major crisis in the Balkans which came close to plunging Europe into war. All the tensions that were to lead to the outbreak of the First World War five years later were now in place. On this occasion, skilful diplomacy avoided a full-scale conflict. The new alliance between Russia, Britain and France survived its first major test, although there were important lessons for all three countries to learn in noting the key role that Germany had played in the crisis.

In early October 1908, only four months after the Reval meeting, Austria-Hungary had formally annexed the Ottoman province of Bosnia-Herzegovina. This had been officially under Austro-Hungarian administration since the Treaty of Berlin in 1878, but the Emperor Franz Josef now felt it was time to legitimise this occupation and grant the Bosnians a new constitution within the Empire. Bosnia's neighbour, Serbia, was outraged by what it saw as a flagrant landgrab by the Hapsburg Empire. Relations between Serbia and Austria-Hungary were poor, and this tipped the situation in the Balkans into an international crisis.

On 7 October, Serbia mobilised its army and demanded that the Austro-Hungarians rescind the annexation, which they refused to do. Germany backed Austria-Hungary. There was little practical action that

Serbia could take without military support from Russia. The crisis now engulfed Europe, and all the major powers became involved. The British government trod warily, as it did not wish to provoke Germany and Austria-Hungary, but it made clear to Vienna that it expected the situation with Serbia to be handled in a peaceful manner. France supported the British position.

Russia was blackmailed by Austria-Hungary into withdrawing its support for Serbia. The Austrian Foreign Ministry threatened to expose a whole set of diplomatic documents between the two countries dating back to 1878. In these Russia agreed to let Austria-Hungary have a free hand in dealing with Bosnia-Herzegovina. Russia's foreign policy had changed a lot since these documents were first produced, but they would still have constituted an enormous embarrassment for the Russians.

In Britain the popular press whipped up a mood of fear and hysteria about the ambitions of the Central Powers in the Balkans. Newspapers thundered against 'German sabre-rattling' and denounced 'the new Masters of Europe, Germany and Austria-Hungary'. One headline for 29 March 1909 talked about a 'Dangerous Peace' in which Germany was openly accused of 'threatening the balance of power in Europe and grinding small states into the dust'.

On 31 March, under pressure from Russia, Britain and France, Serbia backed down and accepted the annexation of Bosnia-Herzegovina. However, the Russians had been humiliated and this was a lesson that they would never forget. The next time there would be a crisis in the Balkans involving Serbia and Austria-Hungary, there was going to be no retreat by Russia.

The crisis of 1908-09 underscored the importance to Britain of strengthening its new alliance with Russia and France. It was becoming clear to the British government that Germany was now a growing danger to European peace and was going to use its economic power and military strength to shape a future that promoted its own national interests, even if this meant plunging Europe into war.

It was in this highly charged and over-wrought international atmosphere that an invitation was extended to the Tsar to make a visit to

Britain in the summer of 1909. It was agreed that he would also make an official visit to France at the same time. It was felt that this trip would set the seal on the Triple Entente.

Both the King and the British government were very reluctant to announce the visit. There was considerable nervousness about how Parliament and the public would react to the news. On 4 May 1909, a question was raised in Parliament by Arthur Henderson, the Leader of the Labour Party, about whether the Tsar would be making a visit to Britain. The Foreign Secretary Sir Edward Grey was evasive in his reply, knowing full well that many members of the Labour Party would oppose such a visit.

At this point discussions were taking place between the King and the government about whether the Tsar should be invited to London or kept out of the capital. A few weeks later, a formal statement was made to Parliament that the Tsar would be coming to Britain but spending all his time at sea, close to the Isle of Wight. The visit was presented as primarily a private meeting between the two royal families and a chance for the Tsar to attend the yachting regatta at Cowes.

Parliamentary discomfort at the visit of the Tsar was not long in emerging. On 22 July, less than two weeks before the Russian imperial family was due to arrive, Henderson directly accused the Government of deliberately misleading the House of Commons as to the true nature of the Tsar's visit. 'It is perfectly obvious' he stated, 'that this visit is of a public and official character. To represent this visit in any such character seems to me to mislead. This is carrying international etiquette a little too far. It is a policy which is repulsive to multitudes of our people'.

He attacked the British alliance with Russia, which he said had not produced any improvement in the Russian human rights record. Quoting from a recent book by the Russian anarchist, Prince Pyotr Kropotkin, he stated that there were currently over 181,000 prisoners in detention in Russian gaols, living in conditions of tremendous squalor and overcrowding. He challenged the Foreign Secretary to dispute these figures, which he claimed Kropotkin had obtained directly from secret sources in Russia. He then demanded that the invitation to the Tsar to visit the Isle of Wight should be withdrawn and that the alliance with Russia be formally abandoned.

Henderson's belligerent attitude towards the Tsar's visit took Sir Edward Grey and other members of the government by surprise. More worrying was that Henderson's views seemed to be supported by a larger group of MPs than the government had anticipated. There were jeers and catcalls from the opposition benches as Grey rose to reply. He rejected the figures about prisoners that Henderson had produced. He said that demonising the Tsar's government was not helpful. The Russians were involved in an international war on terrorism. Attacks inside Russia had claimed the lives of over 6,000 people. He reminded members of Parliament about the recent terrorist attack in London in January 1909, which had claimed British lives, and stressed that Russia's war on terrorism also ensured the future safety and security of British civilians.

Grey went on to say that the constitutional reforms taking place in Russia proved that the Tsar was committed to improving democratic freedoms in the country. These should be supported and not undermined. British criticism of the regime would only strengthen the hands of those reactionaries, still influential in the government, who sought every opportunity to halt liberal reforms. He emphasised how important it was that Britain cultivate friendly relations with Russia. He recalled the long history of mistrust between the two countries and the need to overcome this. He appealed to the House of Commons to extend a warm welcome to the Tsar.

There now followed several speeches by MPs declaring strong support for the new Anglo-Russian partnership. Hilaire Belloc, the Liberal MP for Salford South, declared that Parliament should 'not turn to the bitter writings of Russian exiles, many of whom are the enemies of their country'. He felt sure that any attempts to prevent the visit of the Tsar to Britain would be widely resented by the majority of decent, law-abiding Russians.

Labour MPs were not slow in responding to this provocation and Keir Hardie now directly questioned the figures that Sir Edward Grey had produced about the 6,000 people killed by terrorist attacks in Russia. He did not accept these figures, and argued that these deaths had in fact often been caused by Russian police agents posing as terrorists in order to discredit opponents of the Tsarist regime. In Keir Hardie's opinion the Tsar's regime, far from protecting its own citizens or civilians in countries like Britain, was promoting terrorist attacks both at home and abroad. He refuted Sir Edward Grey's thesis that the Tsar was committed to extending democratic freedoms in Russia. He accused the Tsar of bad faith in arresting members of the Second Duma.

He also accused the government of inviting the Tsar to the Isle of Wight only to support the interests of the financial sector in Britain. 'I venture to tell the government and the Foreign Office' he thundered, 'that if the interests of these same financiers lay in not receiving the Tsar, he would not be invited to Cowes, or anywhere else to meet the head of the British Empire'.

Keir Hardie's final plea was to reject the invitation to a ruler who was the representative of 'an official despotism that has few parallels in history, ancient or modern', an autocrat who stood at the head of a police state endorsing the crimes of the 'Bloody Hundred', the gang responsible for the anti-Jewish pogroms and numerous other crimes against Russian democrats, liberals and socialists. He went on to claim that 'every section of the advanced movement in Russia, from the extreme Socialists to the mildest Liberals, regard the visit of the Tsar to this country as to some extent throwing back their cause by giving him official recognition by a great state'.

The debate about the Tsar's forthcoming visit to the Isle of Wight raged on through the afternoon and long into the evening. It evoked huge passions on both sides, including a curious intervention by John David Rees, a former Indian colonial administrator who was the Liberal MP for Montgomery. He took everyone by surprise when he stated, 'if I was a convicted prisoner in Russia, I would rather spend the term of my sentence in Siberia than in any prison I have seen in the world'. He claimed that prisoners were perfectly free to go wherever they wanted so long as they did not leave Siberia.

This observation outraged many other MPs, who spoke out vociferously against what Rees had said. John MacNeil, the Irish Nationalist MP for

South Donegal, quoted evidence that large numbers of prisoners were confined in very restricted spaces and fed small amounts of food. He stated that deaths from typhus fever were endemic and physical violence was common. This was a very different picture to that painted by Rees, who seemed to be harking back to a gentler period of Russian prison history, when aristocratic opponents of the regime had been allowed to rent private houses during their exile in Siberia.

It soon became clear that although some MPs did have strongly expressed misgivings about the Tsar's visit, the majority were convinced that the visit should proceed in the interests of strengthening the friendship between the two countries. Several recalled the long history of mistrust that had existed between Britain and Russia. 'I can remember a time' one of them said, 'when there was the gravest danger of war between this country and Russia because of the constant attitude of suspicion that was always being fostered in England against Russia'. He believed that the new rapprochement with Russia would be of great service to Britain.

The Government won the subsequent vote with a majority of 108 votes and, to the relief of the Prime Minister and the King, parliamentary approval was given for the Tsar's visit to proceed.

The Tsar's visit took place against a backdrop of rising public and governmental concern in Britain about Russian refugees and Russian inspired terrorism. Russian anarchists and socialist revolutionaries had sought refuge in London and other cities in Britain since the middle of the previous century. At first, they had been mainly aristocrats and intellectuals, fleeing the autocratic regime of Tsar Nicholas I. Exiles like Prince Peter Kropotkin and Alexander Herzen even became the darlings of certain sections of the British political establishment.

However, from 1881, larger numbers of political and ethnic refugees began to arrive from the Russian Empire. This diaspora was fuelled by the anti-Jewish pogroms in the Ukraine and the suppression of independence movements in the Polish, Finnish, Lithuanian and Latvian territories of the Empire. There was a growing resentment, particularly in the poorer urban areas of Britain where most of these refugees settled, about this large-scale migration and the impact this was having on local communities, jobs and housing.

The Whitechapel murders of 1888-1891 provoked the first ugly reactions to this, when mobs attacked Russian and Latvian Jews in the East End of London, believing erroneously that they were responsible for the killings. In this overwrought atmosphere of fear and resentment, it was easy to blame Russian immigrants for the economic and social pressures that working-class British people were now experiencing.

Many refugees were instinctively hostile towards the Tsarist regime because of what they had suffered in Russia, but were primarily concerned with making new lives for themselves in Britain rather than getting involved in radical politics. However, in this febrile and unsettled milieu of exile and poverty, anarchist and socialist revolutionary politics did find a solid niche. Well-respected anarchist exiles like Kropotkin were hugely influential in the wider refugee community but argued strongly against the use of violence as a means of achieving political objectives. However, more radical elements were now appearing, who argued that terrorist violence in Britain was a legitimate way of provoking revolutionary turmoil and chaos. In Russia, the Combat Organisation wing of the Socialist Revolutionary Party had shown the way by engaging in a full-scale terrorist assault on the Tsarist State to considerable success.

There was also a worrying link between terrorism and criminality and the two shaded into each other, so that it was becoming more difficult to disentangle where one began and the other ended. Russian criminal gangs were active in London in the early years of the twentieth century. Few of these criminals were politically active, but criminal money was always available to fund potential terrorist activities. There were also anarchist exiles who were prepared to resort to criminal violence in order to achieve their political aims.

In this lethal brew of political terrorism and criminality, the Tsarist secret police, the Okhrana, was also active. There was widespread suspicion about its covert activities. Okhrana agents were infiltrating anarchist and revolutionary movements and then encouraging terrorist attacks in order to discredit the attackers in the eyes of the wider public.

The Times reported on 20 January 1909 that the double agent Evno Azef had been exposed. Here was a man who had been in the pay of the Okhrana but 'held the threads of the whole Russian terrorist organisation in his hands'. Azef was responsible for approving a range of terrorist attacks inside Russia but each of these attacks had been agreed with the Head of the Russian Secret Police. Russian security and terror were therefore all linked in a web of duplicity, subterfuge and double dealing. In the eyes of the British public, anarchist terror, criminals, and the Russian secret police were all mixed up in one unholy brew, which fuelled increasing hostility towards the Russian refugee community in their midst.

The growing fear about the threat from Russian terrorism in Britain was perfectly captured in the novels of Joseph Conrad. Originally named Konrad Korzeniowski, he was Polish by birth and came from a family that had a long history of resistance to the Russian occupation of Poland. His father, Apollo, was fiercely patriotic and struggled all his life for the re-establishment of Poland as an independent country, free from Russian control.

Conrad spent most of his early career as a seaman, working for the French, Belgian and British merchant fleets. This was a life that took him all over the world and gave him ample material and inspiration for many of his future novels, set in exotic locations in the Far East and Africa. Conrad was reluctant to return to life in the Tsarist Empire. He therefore applied to become a British citizen and once he had achieved this, renounced his Russian citizenship in 1889. Five years later, he gave up his career at sea, due to increasing ill health, and concentrated on his growing interest in writing. His first novel, *Almayer's Folly,* was published in 1895. It was to be the first of more than twenty novels that he would write over the next thirty years.

Conrad never forgot his experiences in Russian-occupied Poland. In many ways, he was haunted by his decision to become an exile in Britain and his love for his native land never left him. He became increasingly fascinated by the refugee communities in London, and by their daily struggles to survive in an alien environment.

In 1907 he published *The Secret Agent*, a novel which took as its main theme the subject of anarchists, a double agent, and a terrorist attack on the Greenwich Observatory. The hapless lead character, Adolf Verloc, is part of a circle of rather ineffectual anarchists living in London. However, Verloc is also in the pay of an unnamed foreign embassy and is persuaded by one of its diplomats, Mr Vladimir, to carry out a terrorist attack to prove that he can be trusted. The meetings between Verloc and Vladimir take place in a building which appears very similar to the Russian Embassy in London as it existed in the 1880s. This was a place that Conrad knew well, from the time when he was still a citizen of the Russian Empire and used to visit the Embassy on a regular basis.

Vladimir tells Verloc that in his view, Britain is far too lenient in dealing with anarchists, and this is a threat to his own country. Therefore, it is important to carry out a terrorist attack which can then be linked to the anarchists, so that the British authorities will start to take a much harsher line with revolutionary groups in London. The *Secret Agent* ends in tragedy, and the terrorist attack destroys Verloc, his family, and his anarchist friends. The cynical and ruthless Vladimir has achieved his objectives.

In 1911, Conrad's novel *Under Western Eyes* appeared, and became a touchstone for many people who were following events in Russia. The story is a searing indictment of the way that ideas can destroy innocent people. Its main theme is again concerned with revolutionary ideals, betrayal, and secret agents, set against the backdrop of Russia, Switzerland and Italy. Conrad's writings in this period accurately captured the mood of unease in Britain about the way that political tensions in Russia were spilling out into the wider world.

On Saturday 23 January 1909, an incident occurred in the North London suburb of Tottenham which would crystallise all these fears. It was the first of three terrorist linked events carried out by Russian anarchists between 1909 and 1911 that were to negatively alter British attitudes towards foreign immigrants.

The 'Tottenham Outrage', as it became known, horrified Edwardian Britain. The two principal protagonists were Paul Helfeld and Jacob Lepidus, two Jewish immigrants from Latvia, then part of the Russian Empire. Such was the confusion about who they were that some reports described them as Polish refugees, while others said that they were Russian Tsarist agents.

The Times, in its report of 26 January, firmly described Helfeld and Lepidus as anarchists and headlined its story as 'The Shooting Outrage: Anarchist Society of Tottenham'. There could be no doubting the message from the Press.

On that fateful Saturday morning the two Latvians, armed with semi-automatic pistols, arrived outside the gates of the Schnurmann Rubber factory in Chesnut Road, Tottenham. There they lay in wait for the arrival of the factory wages clerk, Albert Keyworth, and his driver, Joseph Wilson, who were bringing the weekly wages for the factory staff from the local bank. This amounted to about £80 in gold, silver and copper coins.

A violent struggle took place in front of the factory gates following the arrival of Keyworth and Wilson. Both men were shot by the Latvians but survived. Two police constables had by now heard the gunfire and rushed to the scene. They were too late to prevent Lepidus and Helfeld escaping but decided to set out in hot pursuit of the armed robbers. A frantic chase through the streets of Tottenham now took place, which culminated in an exchange of gunfire in Tottenham Marshes. This ended in the death of one of the constables, William Tyler, who was shot through the head by Helfeld.

The two Latvians then hijacked a tram, and then a horse and cart, shooting wildly at the passengers on board. They were now being pursued by over forty police officers and a crowd of several hundred furious civilians. Helfeld was cornered by the River Ching. He then shot himself in the eye. He was taken to the nearby Prince of Wales Hospital where he subsequently died of his injuries. Lepidus managed to stay ahead of his pursuers for a little longer and hid in a cottage in Hale End, where he was eventually tracked down. He committed suicide rather than submit to being captured alive.

The casualty list was shocking. Twenty-five people had been injured in the aftermath of the robbery, several of them seriously. Most of these were civilians who had been gunned down randomly by the two Latvians as they fired at their pursuers. Tragically, the casualties included a ten-year-old boy, Ralph Joscelyne, who died in the arms of a bystander before he could be taken to hospital.

The national reaction to what soon became known as the Tottenham Outrage was overwhelming. The funerals of Police Constable Tyler and Ralph Joscelyne took place on Friday 29 January. It was virtually a State occasion. Three thousand police officers lined the route of the cortège, accompanied by men from the Scots Guards and the Royal Garrison Artillery. A crowd of half a million people turned up to watch the procession, which extended for over two miles. The young boy's coffin was drawn by white-plumed horses, while black-plumed horses drew the coffin of Constable Tyler. The *Daily Mirror's* headline for the following day trumpeted 'Police Constable Tyler who was murdered by Alien Terrorists, at Tottenham, given a Hero's Funeral'.

The tragic events in Tottenham confirmed the mistrust and suspicion felt by large sections of the British public towards foreign immigrants and their links to Russian terrorism. In the weeks immediately following the Tottenham Outrage there were angry scenes in the East End of London, where large numbers of refugees from the Russian Empire were living. Those refugees suspected of having links to anarchist terrorists were attacked, and their houses and businesses were trashed. The mood towards 'Aliens', as they were then termed, was turning ugly.

A dangerous undercurrent of anti-Jewish propaganda was also swirling around in the popular British press and it now found a new energy and voice. In the public mind, refugees, Jews, anarchists, and Russians were all conflated into a single group, who had become a major threat to the security of the British homeland.

The *Daily Chronicle* reported, 'there is a large Alien colony in Tottenham. The news of the murders has been received by them with various feelings; some have openly rejoiced over the exploits of their comrades, and one of them remarked that he wished he had enough money to buy champagne in which to drink to the memory of these two soldiers of the Revolution'.

What the *Daily Chronicle* chose not to report was that much larger numbers of refugees living in Tottenham had openly expressed their horror at the events of 23 January and disassociated themselves completely from the actions of Helfeld and Lepidus. This did not fit the emerging anti-immigrant narrative that was now sweeping the country.

In response to these growing concerns, Parliament had already passed the Aliens Act of 1905. This was the first ever recorded attempt in Britain to introduce immigration controls and registration. It was largely driven by the arrival of over 150,000 Russian Jews fleeing Tsarist pogroms. In 1905, The *Manchester Evening Chronicle* had thundered against 'the dirty, destitute, diseased verminous and criminal foreigner who dumps himself on our soil'. For many people, Tottenham proved, once and for all, that much more drastic measures now needed to be taken if the threat of immigration and terrorism was to be finally curbed.

A letter to the Editor of *The Times* on 26 January from a London businessman, Mr Charles Lee, expressed his astonishment 'at the ease with which the roughest-looking aliens continue to land on our shores. The only qualifications for admission to England appears to be good clothes, as every obstacle in the way of anarchists coming over here is now being rapidly removed'.

Public outrage at what had happened in Tottenham led to a Parliamentary debate in the House of Commons on 25 February 1909. The debate was opened by Claude Hay, the Conservative MP for Hoxton, who wanted to draw the attention of MPs, to 'the manner in which a most undesirable class of Aliens are able to gain access to this country, despite the barrier which the Aliens Act was supposed to present to them'.

Hay openly accused the government of a gross failure to control immigration and claimed that the numbers of foreigners arriving on British shores was rising all the time, from 93,707 in 1906 to 112,809 in 1908. He demanded to know what the government proposed to do about this. A heated Parliamentary debate then followed on the ruling party's immigration policy, which the government won by a majority of 133 votes.

There was no doubt that the Tottenham Outrage had created a mood of national insecurity about foreigners, particularly Russians, and this event had seriously rattled the confidence of the government. There were regular reports in the British press that various Russian terrorists or spy-chiefs had been seen visiting London. In March, there were numerous newspaper articles which stated that the notorious double agent and perpetuator of many shocking terror attacks in Russia, Evno Azef, had been spotted in Aldgate in central London and positively identified by two men who knew him well.

This was the mood in Britain on the eve of the Tsar's visit. Radicals, socialists and many liberals loathed the Tsar's regime, for persecuting its Jewish population and oppressing its political opponents. Nonetheless, they were still keen to offer sanctuary to refugees whom they believed were genuinely in fear of their lives. They wanted to maintain Britain's reputation as a country where anybody facing persecution, for whatever reason, could find a home. However, an increasing number of British people now distrusted and feared these same refugees. It is likely that, had it not been for the First World War and the Russian Revolution, these opposing attitudes to immigration would have seriously polarised political and social views in Britain and created a major national crisis.

Two further terrorist acts would be carried out following the Tsar's visit to the Isle of Wight and would confirm the public's perception that Russian anarchists threatened the country's peace and security. On 16 December 1910, three heavily armed Latvian anarchists including a man called George Gardstein tunnelled their way into a jeweller's shop in Houndsditch, not far from Aldgate Station. They were members of an Anarchist group that met regularly in Stepney. Neighbours heard a series of explosions, the police were called, and a gunfight ensued. The three Latvians escaped but three unarmed policemen were killed and two others seriously injured. Gardstein later died of his injuries. His two accomplices vanished.

A major manhunt was launched to find them. On 1 January 1911 an informer passed information to the police that two anarchists were hiding in a house in Sydney Street, in the East End of London. On 3 January the police cordoned off the house and the siege began. The Latvians were heavily armed while the police only had outdated weapons. It was an unequal struggle and the police eventually had to call in the army to help them. Winston Churchill, who was then Home Secretary in the Liberal Government, visited Sydney Street while the fighting was taking place and was barracked by people gathered at the end of the street. 'Oh, let them in!' the crowd shouted, mocking the Liberal government's support for immigration.

Six hours later, there was a huge explosion and the house collapsed. Inside the burned-out building the badly charred bodies of the two terrorists were discovered. At first it was thought that one of these might be the mysterious Peter Piaktow, also called 'Peter the Painter', an anarchist who was famed across Europe for planning and executing terrorist attacks.

The Painter's identity remains unknown to this day and much about him is rumour and conjecture. There are doubts that he even existed and may have been a composite cover name for various Latvian anarchists, such as the artist and revolutionary Gederts Eliass or the Latvian far leftist Janis Zhaklis.

To add further confusion, the *New York Times* ran an article in May 1911, in which Peter the Painter was identified as a Tsarist double agent called Peter Straume. It was claimed that Straume was in the pay of the Okhrana, and that he was posing very successfully as an anarchist terrorist. In order to maintain this cover, he had planned the Houndsditch Robbery and then betrayed his fellow anarchists to the British police. He had then sought refuge at the house of the Russian ambassador in London from where he had been secretly smuggled out of the country. The article ended on an ominous note:

'Where is he now? I have no means of knowing. I only feel certain that hand will be shown wherever it is to the advantage of the Russian Government to force a campaign against the revolutionaries under the guise of an attack against anarchy. It may well be that he will return to London. It may be that he will find in New York a new field for operations'.

The threat that there might be a terrorist attack against the Tsar during his time in Britain haunted the minds of both the British and Russian security services in the months before the visit. It was only six months since the Tottenham Outrage and Russian anarchists as well as members of the Combat Organisation of the Socialist Revolutionary Party were known to be active in London. Terrorist attacks were now a regular feature of life in Russia. Following the events in Tottenham it was conceivable that similar attacks could be mounted in Britain against the Tsar and his family.

British security for the Tsar's visit that year was co-ordinated by the Committee of Imperial Defence, working in close collaboration with the Metropolitan Police Service and the Home Office. On the Russian side, security was handled by Alexander Spiridovich, who had been appointed Head of Nicholas II's secret personal guard in 1906. Before taking up this role, Spiridovich had been Chief of the Kiev Section of the Okhrana, Russia's secret police.

Kiev was notorious as a centre for the terrorist activities of the Socialist Revolutionary Party and Spiridovich was a target for their assassins. In 1905 he had narrowly escaped death when a Bolshevik activist, Peter Rudnenko (who also worked for Spiridovich as a double agent), shot him twice at close range. He survived but had to take an extended period of recuperation. His dedication to rooting out terrorism in Kiev now came to the attention of the Tsar, and he was asked to take on the role of the Tsar's Head of Security. He would be the man who would accompany the imperial family to the Isle of Wight.

In preparation for the Tsar's arrival, Russian police agents now began to appear in Britain. They did not always work in close cooperation with their British counterparts in the Metropolitan Police, and this was sometimes a cause for considerable concern and confusion.

On 20 July, Will Thorne, the Trade Unionist and one of the first Labour Members of Parliament, raised a question in the House of Commons. He asked whether the Government was aware of the activities of Russian secret agents and quasi police officers who appeared to be operating in Cowes and its vicinity under the auspices of the Russian Embassy. He enquired whether these agents would be permitted to carry on their operations in Britain and, if so, 'whether the Government intends taking any steps to protect British subjects from their operations?'

Herbert Gladstone, the Secretary of State at the Home Office, replied that he had 'no knowledge of the presence in this country of the agents to whom Mr Thorne refers, but if they exist, they have the same right to visit this country as any other foreign subjects.'

It was clear, though, that Gladstone knew more than he was admitting, as he then went on to try and justify the presence of Russian secret agents in Britain. 'The protection of sovereigns when travelling abroad is often carried out in part by the officers of their own country. Our own countrymen are not in any danger from the operations of such agents.' Then to prevent any further questions being raised, he closed the whole topic:

'I do not consider that any further steps require to be taken in this matter'. That was the end of the issue as far the Government was concerned.

In the weeks before the Tsar's visit, Russian terrorists, revolutionaries and secret police agents dominated the popular imagination and the popular press. To many people in Britain they were the same characters operating in different guises. Suspicious-looking Russians were now spotted by eagle-eyed observers travelling in all parts of the country, but particularly on the Isle of Wight. Here they were believed to be posing as tourists, craftily decked out in sinister straw boaters and striped sports jackets.

The fact was that there were many Russians visiting the Isle of Wight that summer. It was a favourite resort for wealthy Russians because of its association with the Romanovs. There were undoubtedly secret agents amongst these visitors, but most of the Russians were innocently enjoying the summer attractions of Cowes, Ventnor and Ryde, exactly like their British counterparts.

In the final weeks before the arrival of the Tsar to the Isle of Wight, there were many public protests against his visit, which culminated in a major demonstration in Trafalgar Square on 25 July. Between 6,000 and 7,000 people attended this event. The protestors were led by Keir Hardie, a founding member of the Labour Party, and a bitter opponent of the Tsarist regime. Ramsay MacDonald, who was to become Britain's first ever Labour Prime Minister, and the dramatist Bernard Shaw were also present.

The writer and politician Henry Hyndman, who was the first author to popularise Marx's writing in the English language, was also very prominent at the demonstration, along with a number of Russian politicians such as Aleksei Feodorovich Aladin, who was the leader of the Russian Peasants party Trudoviks.

Aladin had been a member of the 1906 Duma and after its dissolution he had fled to Britain. He returned to Russia after the Revolution, but quickly found that he was not in favour with the new Bolshevik regime and so came back to Britain, a country which he had grown to like and respect. Trotsky later referred to him contemptuously as a 'man who never removed an English pipe from his mouth'.

The *Daily Telegraph* described the crowd which assembled in Trafalgar Square that day as being 'mainly of the working classes' and it accused the main speakers, men like Keir Hardie and Ramsay MacDonald, of making a series of 'violent speeches' against the Tsar. *The Times* reported the demonstration in a much more measured and balanced fashion. It painted a picture of a lively and boisterous crowd, marching behind brass bands and under banners which denounced the Tsar. They were inscribed with messages such as, 'A Message from Hell: Welcome Little Father Tsar', 'Down with Nicholas the Tyrant', and in a pointed reference to the events of 'Bloody Sunday' in January 1905, 'Shall we grasp this bloody hand?'

Hyndman denounced the 'Scoundrel going to Cowes' and said that he should be tumbled into a sewer, and never come out of it. 'Let the King kiss him, let Mr Asquith beslobber him, and let Sir Edward Grey lick his boots. The People spurned the Tsar and spat in his face for the scoundrel that he was'.

There were many references by agitated speakers to the '181,000 Russian prisoners, of whom 100,000 were political prisoners' and the increase in executions from 144 in 1906 to 835 in 1908. Aladin, to huge cheers from the crowd, said that if there was a war, most of Russia's vast troop numbers would never be sent to the front but would be used to keep down the people. Ramsay MacDonald then rose to his feet. 'The British People never invited the Tsar to come here; they did not want him, and he was an unwelcome guest', he thundered.

He refuted the idea that refusing to receive the Tsar would be an insult to the Russian people. The case was exactly the opposite, he maintained, for the 'Tsar was at war with his own people and welcoming him to the Isle of Wight would be an insult to the Russian people'.

Keir Hardie proposed that everyone who was opposed to the Tsar's visit should wear a piece of black clothing on Monday 2 August, the day of the Tsar's arrival in Cowes. If they were Socialists, they could also add a dash of red to their clothes. The demonstration continued till 5pm, when a resolution was passed which declared, 'This mass movement offers the People of Russia its fraternal greetings… but emphatically protests against the Tsar being received by the King and Government in the name of the British people; it declares that his presence here is offensive, and that he is an unbidden and unwelcome guest.'

The demonstration in Trafalgar Square reflected a palpable sense of anger and frustration amongst many people in Britain at the fact that the British government and the King had invited Nicholas II to make a visit. In the month prior to the Tsar's visit, meetings to protest against this invitation had been held in working men's clubs and church halls up and down the country. The Trafalgar Square event marked the culmination of all these protests.

The last major protest occurred two days before the Tsar's arrival. On 31 July, Keir Hardie addressed a Labour demonstration at Sutton in Ashfield in Nottinghamshire, attended by thousands of protestors. He again repudiated the actions of the Government 'in welcoming to our shores the Tsar as Head of Russia'. In colourful language, he denounced the Russian pogroms and the killings of reformers and stated that Nicholas had personally invited the perpetuators of these crimes to his Palace in St Petersburg, decorated them and called them friends of Russia. There were cries of 'Shame! Shame!' from the crowd.

25

Promoting a new friendship

In contrast to this storm of popular indignation, there were also voices starting to speak out in favour of the Tsar's visit, encouraging people to learn more about the positive developments taking place in Russia and expressing a view that the relationship between the two countries was improving. This new rapprochement was soon to be reflected in a series of visits by Russian civic and professional delegations to Britain. There was also a growing interest in Russian art and culture, and mass-circulation British newspapers began to promote Russian style, food and literature. Russia was set to become fashionable, particularly amongst the upper and middle classes in a way that had not been the case since the visit of Tsar Alexander I in 1814.

This new mood of friendly reconciliation was perfectly summarised in a speech given by the British ambassador to Russia, Sir Arthur Nicholson, to members of the English Club in St Petersburg in December 1908. He declared, to widespread approval from his audience, that the relationship between Britain and Russia had never been so cordial and intimate as during the previous year. He recognised, though, that this relationship needed deepening in a more permanent way, and that this could not be done until the peoples of both countries got to know each other. He argued for the creation of an Anglo-Russian Council which could focus on developing these relations. He was enthusiastically hailed as the 'promoter of Anglo-Russian understanding'.

In the weeks before the Tsar's arrival, Russian delegations began to arrive in Britain. These delegations were carefully chosen from amongst Russia's professional and governing classes to create a positive image of the Tsarist regime, but they were also a genuine attempt to put into practice Sir Arthur Nicholson's plea to build stronger and more enduring links between the peoples of Britain and Russia. They were also clearly part of a Russian propaganda offensive ahead of the imperial visit. Their brief was to promote an image of a country where democratic government was being introduced and which was starting to prosper in economic terms.

A party of Russian Statesmen visited Edinburgh on 30 June, where they were entertained to lunch in the City Chamber by the Lord Provost, the grandly named Sir James Puckering Gibson. Gibson was also a highly-regarded Scottish Liberal politician, who had been successfully elected as the MP for Edinburgh East in April 1909. He toasted the health of the Tsar and said that everyone at the lunch regretted that there should be 'any question on the part of even a small section of the British people as to the reception of His Imperial Majesty on his projected visit to Great Britain'. He went on to reassure his Russian visitors that any opposition was entirely due, in his opinion, to misunderstandings, and he hoped that the Tsar would be received with unanimous approval by the whole of the British people.

The Russian delegation was clearly swept up by this mood of bonhomie. The leader of the delegation was Count Vladimir Brobrinsky, and he warmly welcomed the improvement in relations between the two countries. This visit to Britain had convinced him and his fellow delegates about the importance and value of strong representative government. Russia could only prosper, he noted, if it had effective democratic institutions like those that existed in Britain. In this spirit of overt cordiality, the Russians were ferried by motorcar first to Hopetoun House and then on to admire the engineering magnificence of the Forth Bridge. Democracy, engineering, and a Provost's lunch. This was a perfect start to the new relationship between Britain and Russia.

A few days later on 3 July, another Russian delegation was in Oxford, at the invitation of the Vice Chancellor Dr Herbert Warren. This was primarily an academic visit, and although it included mainly Russian scholars, the ubiquitous Count Brobrinsky was also part of the group. This time he went a stage further than he had in Edinburgh and to great cheers declared that the 'interests of England were the interests of peace and the wellbeing of mankind'. Statements like this, coming from a senior Russian political figure, would have been unthinkable even two years earlier.

In a rather more understated way, one of the leading members of the Russian delegation, Professor Pavel Milyukov, said that he spoke on behalf of all Russian intellectuals in acknowledging the debt that they collectively owed to eminent British lawyers such as Albert Dicey and William Anson in defining the basis for constitutional law and government.

Milyukov himself was an historian and a quixotic liberal politician who had fallen foul of the Tsarist authorities on more than one occasion. He was a founding member of the Constitutional Democratic Party, known as the 'Cadets', and had fled to Finland after the dissolution of the First Duma in 1906. It was here that he wrote what became known as the *Vyborg Manifesto*, which called on the people to resist the Tsarist regime by refusing to pay taxes or join the army. Despite its radical tone, Milyukov seems to have been forgiven by the Tsarist police. In 1907, he was elected to the Third Duma and two years later was clearly considered respectable enough to be sent as a member of the delegation visiting Oxford. There is a curious footnote to his career. In 1917, Milyukov was a member of the Provisional Government and took the lead in contacting Lloyd George to propose that the Tsar and his family be offered asylum in Britain.

Through July, arrangements for the Tsar's visit gathered momentum. On 7 July, it was announced that the armoured cruiser *Rurik* would escort the imperial yacht *Shtandart* to Cherbourg and Cowes. The *Rurik* was the finest new cruiser in the Russian Imperial Navy and had only been completed in July 1909. On 10 July, *The Times* reported that the Russian Ambassador had announced that the Tsar would be delighted to receive an address of welcome from the Corporation of Cowes when he arrived on the Isle of Wight. Two days later, it was confirmed that the Tsar would reach Cowes on Monday 2 August, in time for the Royal Yacht Squadron Regatta.

On 13 July, Portsmouth Town Council proposed that an address of welcome be presented to the Tsar and Tsarina in a gold casket. There were still hopes that the imperial family might visit Portsmouth, but if that proved not to be possible, the address would be presented on board the imperial yacht at Cowes.

The British press was now agog with the news of the Tsar's arrival. Despite the protests and demonstrations taking place against the visit, many people were fascinated and mesmerised by the glamour and gilded glory of the Russian Imperial Court. For a brief few summer days, much of the country lapped up every bit of news about the Romanovs. The four Grand Duchesses became a focus for media attention, an early example of the power of the press in shining a spotlight on those individuals around whom it wanted to spin myths of magic and beauty.

On the afternoon of the 30 July, King Edward VII and Queen Alexandra left Goodwood and proceeded to Portsmouth. There they embarked on the royal yacht, *Victoria and Albert*, and the following morning sailed for Spithead where they reviewed the British fleet, assembled in one of the greatest displays of naval might ever witnessed in English home waters. The most celebrated week in the summer yachting calendar had begun. The meeting of the Tsar of Russia and the King Emperor of the British Empire at Cowes would crown the 1909 Season with a special aura of imperial glory and, it was hoped, set the seal on the new alliance between Russia and Britain.

26

Cowes Week 1909

By 1909, Cowes Week was the largest yachting regatta of its kind in the world and along with the Ascot and Goodwood Races, it stood at the apex of Britain's summer social calendar. The Regatta had been in existence since 1826 and was patronised by Europe's royalty and aristocracy, who jostled at sea and on shore with top society figures, yachtsmen and amateur sailors. It also attracted people from every walk of life, who loved the fun, colour and vibrancy of the most important regatta of the summer season. Cowes Week was the great carnival of the sea, reflecting the rich and colourful palette of Edwardian Britain at play.

In 1909, yachts from across Europe and North America converged on Cowes. The German Emperor's steam yacht, *Hohenzollern II,* had been the largest royal yacht at the Regatta for many years. At nearly 400 feet in length, it was deliberately intended to create an image of German imperial power and majesty. The Kaiser himself had been a regular visitor to Cowes throughout the 1890s. In 1889 he was elected a member of the Royal Yacht Squadron and was an enthusiastic and highly competitive yachtsman. Since 1896, his racing yacht *Meteor II* had outpaced the smaller *Britannia* owned by King Edward VII.

This was greatly to the irritation of Edward VII, who lamented, 'The Regatta used to be a pleasant relaxation for me. But, since the Kaiser took command, it is a vexation'. Following the accession of Edward to the throne, the Kaiser had not been seen at Cowes, but his imperial yacht *Hohenzollern II* always appeared and in 1909 his new racing yacht, the 400-ton steel schooner *Meteor IV,* made its first appearance and was expected to win many prizes.

Cowes, however, was King Edward's show and he and his 4,700-ton royal yacht, *Victoria and Albert III*, dominated the social scene at Cowes every year. The King was a regular visitor to the Regatta, and a very keen and talented yachtsman. He was also the Admiral of the Royal Yacht Squadron and before becoming King in 1901, was Commodore of the Squadron, having been a member since 1863.

Edward's greatest triumph came in 1893, when he appeared at Cowes with *Britannia,* a 121 feet gaff-rigged cutter of 221 tons. The yacht set a new standard in yacht racing, and in her first five seasons *Britannia* took part in 219 races and won 147 prizes. She was the epitome of sleek yachting elegance, combining agility, speed and first-class design. The yacht had a high profile and a successful career and to the end of his life she was Edward's pride and joy. After his death she was refitted in 1920 by King George V and went on to win a succession of races throughout the 1920s. Like his father, George was devoted to *Britannia,* and his dying wish was that the yacht should be scuttled off the Isle of Wight, the scene of many of her greatest triumphs. After his death, in accordance with the King's final request, she was sunk into St Catherine's Deep.

The Royal Yacht Squadron's clubhouse, known as the Castle, was the focus for the high society of international yachting, and its gilded membership included kings and emperors, aristocrats, admirals and leading yachtsmen from around the world. It was the most exclusive of all the British yacht clubs. Nobody could ever apply to join. To become a member, a person had to be invited. This remains the case to this day.

In 1909, the Commodore of the Squadron was the Third Marquess of Ormonde, whose seat was Kilkenny Castle in Ireland. He had been a member of the Club since 1867 and Commodore since 1901. He was famous for his schooners *Koh-i-Noor* and *Mirage*, in which he made regular trips to the Arctic, going as far north as Spitzbergen.

The Vice Commodore was George Godolphin Osborne, the 10th Duke of Leeds who was widely known for his racing greyhounds and gambling debts. He was affectionately called 'Dolly', was never without a cigarette in his hand, and was a popular Squadron Flag officer, with a gentle touch, compared with the more disciplinarian approach of Lord Ormonde. He was elected as Commodore in 1919, a post he held until just before his death in 1927.

While the Royal Yacht Squadron was the most prestigious of the yachting clubs, there were other equally well known and famous clubs which sponsored their own regattas during Cowes Week. Amongst these were the Royal London Yacht Club, originally founded in 1838, the Royal Southampton Yacht Club, which was awarded its royal charter in 1875, and the Royal Thames Yacht Club, which was established in 1781 and is considered as the oldest continuously operating yacht club in the world. Each of these clubs offered their own prizes. The Squadron's was known as the King's Cup and was donated by the Sovereign. Winning this cup was considered the apogee of Cowes Week.

The King of Spain's new 15-metre racing yacht, *Hispania,* reached the Solent on 26 July. King Alfonso XIII was a prominent member of the Squadron and a patron of Spain's leading sailing club, the Real Club Náutico. His elegant cream and white hulled royal yacht *Giralda* became a regular sight in Cowes. However, in 1909, the King was prevented from attending the Regatta because of riots in Barcelona and uprisings in the Rif Mountains of Spanish Morocco.

Alongside the grand royal yachts, it was the racing yachts that would attract the most attention. The Regatta of 1909 hosted some of the most famous yachting names ever to grace the waters of the Solent. Amongst these were a group of sleek and dashing 23-metre and 'A class' yachts which were due to compete in all the races held by the major yachting clubs.

The most famous included the *Cicely,* owned by George Cecil Whitaker, and the *Shamrock,* which was the pride and joy of Sir Thomas Lipton. He had been born into a poor family in the Gorbals district of

Glasgow, but he had risen through his own efforts to create a famous brand of tea and a chain of over 300 grocery stores. Lipton was a keen yachtsman, and a good friend of King Edward VII. He was a regular visitor to Cowes, although, possibly because of his humble origins and suspicions about his sexual identity, he was only invited to join the Squadron shortly before his death in 1931.

Lipton liked to promote an image of himself as a 'ladies' man' and he was often described as the 'World's most eligible bachelor'. In fact, Lipton much preferred the company of young men. His partner of over thirty years, William Love, was one of his shop assistants. After they parted there was a succession of male companions, including a Cretan orphan and a mysterious Frenchman, Maurice Talvande, who styled himself the Count de Mauny Talvande. After his relationship with Lipton ended, Talvande went to live in an exotically-designed house at Taprobane, a small island near the coast of Sri Lanka.

White Heather II, which was owned by the American born Myles B. Kennedy, also became one of the stars of the 1909 season. Kennedy, who turned himself into the perfect English gentleman, was Vice- Commodore of the Royal Albert Yacht Club. He was well known for his range of glamorous boats with names like *Sybarita, Nyria and White Heather* and lived in great style in the heart of London's West End.

Four Spanish yachts owned by the Seventeenth Duke of Medinaceli, Luis Fernández de Córdoba y Salabert, sailed into Cowes a few days before the start of the Regatta. These included the 15-metre yacht *Tuiga,* which was an identical design to the King of Spain's yacht *Hispania.* This was done deliberately, so that they could then race on equal terms against each other. German and Russian yachts were also arriving, including the *Susanne* owned by Herr Oscar Huldschinsky, the German art collector and entrepreneur.

A witty but anonymous contributor to the August 1909 edition of *Yachting and Boating Monthly* described sailing down the Solent towards Cowes in the company of a numerous and cosmopolitan crowd, all of them heading for the Regatta. This crowd included 'three Spanish gentlemen, sallow of complexion, black-bearded and somewhat disdainful', who had brought their boats to race in the 15-metre class with the King of Spain's yacht, *Hispania*. Accompanying them were a 'couple of stout Teutons, voluble, guttural and determined that no detail should escape them that questions may discover'.

As they approached Cowes with its forests of masts, the anonymous writer was able to point out the 'lofty sticks of the two German schooners, *Meteor* and *Germania*', much to the delight of his Teuton companions. 'Ach, Der Kaiser's Jacht' they kept repeating with obvious pride and satisfaction.

On shore, the social pace was gathering. The newspapers were filled with news about the Society figures who were now arriving at Cowes and how they were passing their time. The Duke of Leeds was seen deep in conversation in the Royal Yacht Squadron's gardens with Lady Londonderry. It was reported that she was staying as a guest of Lady Ormonde at Avening Lodge. The socialite, Lady Evelyn Quinnone appeared dressed in black serge with a black straw hat, and rubbed shoulders with Lady Dorchester and her party, including Lady Boden and Nadine Beauchamp.

By the Saturday before the start of Cowes Week, all the first-class hotels were full, and every type of accommodation close to Cowes had been booked. Visitors poured in by launches and steamboats. Consuela, Duchess of Manchester and her party were ensconced in Egypt House, a large redbrick house built in 1880 that boasted a distinctive tower and spacious grounds. The Duke and Duchess of Somerset were at Holmwood Lodge, a favourite retreat of King Edward VII famous for its spectacular sea views. Lady Gort and Colonel Benson had brought over a large party of around twenty people, including Lord Fairfax and Lady Darcy de Knayth and they were all lodged at East Cowes Castle, across the River Medina from Cowes.

Anthony Drexel's beautiful yacht *Margarita* had been chartered for the week by Lady Paget and accompanying her were a glittering crowd, including Joachim, the Fifth Prince of Murat, Lady Sarah Wilson, and Lord Alexander Thynne. He was the youngest son of the Marquess of Bath, and he would be killed a few years later while fighting in France.

A host of other yachts were now crowding the seafront at Cowes, and these included the *Stella*, crewed by Sir Allen Young, the *Zaza* with Lord Anglesey on board and the elegant *Marcella* with Sir Simon and Lady Lockhart and the Duke of Somerset at the helm.

'Lady Charlotte', the pseudonym of a journalist writing for the *Daily Mail,* reported that 'Cowes Week is more fully packed with enjoyment than any other smart function of the year. The sea suits and the shore toilettes that are seen are immensely admired'. Serge cloth was all the rage for the 1909 Season, and 'Lady Charlotte' went on to recommend that it could be used in a variety of colours from marine blue through to purple, green, khaki, and soft grey. She particularly recommended purple, 'not a colour usually associated with the sea, it is however a most becoming choice, and when a good dye is used will resist the influence of the sun admirably'.

Alongside this glittering display of Edwardian High Society in action, Cowes week was also famous for its very diverse mix of visitors drawn from all sections of British society. One observer wrote how Cowes was 'the abiding-place of contrasts. No-where have I seen such beautiful specimens of English womanhood, such representative types of English gentlemen; yet around the corner are cheap-jacks, ring-tossers, the sweetmeat callers of Whitechapel and two fat men in top hats diving for coppers'.

Ordinary working people, who rarely left their home towns and cities, caught the paddle steamers every August from Portsmouth and Southampton in order to enjoy the spectacle of the Regatta. Here, in the narrow streets of Cowes, they could rub shoulders with kings, aristocrats and yachtsmen, glamourous people whom they normally only read about in newspapers and magazines. This vibrant social mix is what made Cowes Week such an exciting and sought-after experience. In August 1909, there was another even greater attraction. The Russians were coming.

All eyes in August 1909 were focused on the imminent arrival of the Tsar and his family and on the many Russian visitors now descending on the Isle of Wight. Waterford House was one of the main venues for the Russian diaspora. It was here that Prince and Princess Alexis Dolgoruky were staying, along with Prince Basil Dolgoruky and Countess Benckendorff, the wife of the Russian Ambassador. The Ambassador himself was staying at the Gloster Hotel, situated on the Parade in Cowes. He complained bitterly about the price of his accommodation and let everyone know that he thought there were few hotels of quality on the Isle of Wight.

Prince Alexis Dolgoruky was the descendant of one of Russia's most distinguished noble families and his distant ancestor had founded Moscow in 1129. His father had been Secretary of State to Tsar Alexander II and Alexis had been a Chamberlain to the Tsar, before moving to live in England with his English-born wife, Frances Fleetwood Wilson, now Princess Alexis Dolgoruky.

The couple were famous for their glamorous and lavish entertaining, both at their home in Mayfair, but also at their elegant, riverside house built for them by Edward Lutyens on the banks of the Thames in Taplow. This grand mansion they named 'Nashdom', the Russian for 'Our House'.

Other prominent Russian visitors included Baron and Baroness Meyendorff. The Baron had been elected to the Third Duma in 1907 and became its Vice-President in the same year. He was to flee into exile in Britain after the Revolution, where he became a senior lecturer at the London School of Economics for over ten years. Count and Countess Wrangel were also glimpsed alighting from a private yacht close to the Castle, the Royal Yacht Squadron's Club House. The Wrangel family were one of the most prominent members of the German Baltic aristocracy, who since the eighteenth century had provided the backbone of Russia's imperial government and administration.

The star of the Russian social scene that summer in Cowes was undoubtedly the Russian ambassador, Alexander von Benckendorff, and his wife, Countess Sophia Petrovna. They were accompanied by their attractive daughter, Lady Nathalie Louise, then aged twenty-three. Benckendorff had held the position of Russian ambassador to London since 1903 and was very popular both with the British ruling establishment and the King. In 1909 he was sixty years old and described as being 'tall and thin with a long, lugubrious face, and monocle. His moustaches were painstakingly curled'.

Benckendorff had been a key figure in the negotiations behind the 1907 Anglo-Russian Convention and he was an enthusiastic Anglophile. A sophisticated and intelligent diplomat, he did not have a particularly high regard for the Tsar and felt that Nicholas stood in the shadow of his uncle, Edward VII. Benckendorff felt that this disparity would be further emphasised during the Tsar's visit to the Isle of Wight. He was therefore unenthusiastic about the arrival of the Russian imperial family in British waters, and was observed walking about Cowes with an uneasy and anxious look.

None of this concern, however, affected the British press. As the time drew closer for the Tsar's arrival, newspapers were full of articles about Russian fashion, home life, and cooking. It was as though newspaper editors had suddenly woken up to the fact that Britain had a new friend and ally.

'English Women and the Cossack Cap' ran one bold newspaper headline on 3 August 1909, declaring that the Russian style hat with its 'compact mass of tiny ostrich feather tips with a spray of plumage fronds at one side is most becoming to a fair English face'. The journalist admitted that the milliners had decided to omit using fur, usual in a Cossack cap, because it was the height of summer and the sight of elegant ladies strolling along in fur hats on the Cowes seafront would not have seemed sensible. It was important though to flaunt a Russian look at Cowes and the adapted 'Cossack Cap' was recommended as the fashion item of the season.

Other newspapers praised Russian artistic skills in linen embroidery, enamelling, and in the creation of miniature trees and flowering plants in crystal. 'Beautifully formed Russian tiaras are now one of the most highly appreciated models in modern jewellery' fawned one journalist. Another wrote about how Russian diadems made of turquoise and azure gems were now influencing English brides in their choice of wedding crowns. Carried away by the exuberance of the moment, the same journalist then went on to recommend that children could be dressed in Russian peasant coats and blouses, in ways that would complement the fashions of their parents.

If Russian fashion was now all the rage, there was an equal interest in the daily life and culture of Russians. Several newspapers ran articles in early August 1909 describing how ordinary Russians passed their time at home. While the British public was more familiar with the lifestyle of the Russian aristocracy and gentry so richly evoked in the novels of Tolstoy, Turgenev and Chekhov, there was less familiarity with the daily life of the middle-class, people who were, in the view of one British newspaper, 'of growing importance to Russia'.

'Family Life among the subjects of the Tsar' was the headline in one newspaper, while another led with an article called 'A Day in a Russian home'. Russian houses were characterised by 'homeliness and solid comfort, which is one of the chief characteristics of the English home', wrote one correspondent. There then followed descriptions of the interiors of Russian family houses, with their large dining rooms 'where people partake of at least four and often five meals a day'. The Russian capacity for consuming large quantities of food and drink was clearly an aspect of Russian life that fascinated the British public. There were numerous references in the various newspaper articles to the samovar, the great steaming urn from which endless cups of tea were drawn, garnished with lemons. Russian food was described as 'excellent, though somewhat complicated and heavy'.

Furniture in a middle-class Russian home was 'extremely massive, with thick and beautiful carpets, and with curtains that are so heavy that they seem to be weighed down with lead'. On the walls hung family pictures in golden frames 'so intensely brilliant that they affect the eyesight'. These were complemented, British readers were informed, by portraits of the Tsar and Tsarina, and by small icons, generally framed in jewelled gold or silver.

This was a portrait of a country which was emerging into the twentieth century with a new energy, style and determination. The press agreed that Russia faced many challenges, but as one newspaper put it, 'The light of knowledge is entering and illuminating this great country'. The message was clear. Russia was no longer to be underestimated and a country which had often been viewed as primitive and backward was now transforming itself into one of Europe's great industrial and economic powers.

Most of the major newspapers agreed that it was time therefore to lay aside the suspicions and prejudices of the past century and welcome the Tsar and his family to British shores as allies of Great Britain and its Empire. For the first time in nearly a hundred years, the two countries shared many of the same international interests and concerns. They were united in a mistrust of Germany, both were linked to France through the Triple Entente, and they were collaborating over Persia and Afghanistan. British industrial and business investment in Russia was at an all-time high and there was a growing fascination in Britain with Russia, its culture and its people.

It was intended that the Tsar's visit to the Isle of Wight would set the seal on this new partnership. However, it would only survive for ten years, and the remainder of the twentieth century would again be marked by a return to the mistrust that had largely characterised the relationship between the two countries in the previous century.

27

Monday 2 August 1909

The parliamentary debates and political protests were now over. Britain and the Isle of Wight awaited the arrival of Russia's ruling family. At eight o'clock on the morning of Monday 2 August 1909, the Tsar and his family arrived in British waters aboard the imperial yacht *Shtandart*.

She was considered the largest and most glamorous royal yacht afloat. Built by the Danish firm of Burmeister and Wain and launched in 1895, she was a steel hulled vessel, 420 feet in length, 52 feet at the beam, and weighing in at 5,557 tons. Her two black and white funnels and three masts created a distinctive profile as she cut through the ocean waves at speeds of between eighteen and twenty-one knots. The *Shtandart* was also armed with eight Hotchkiss guns. The need for good security was always uppermost in the minds of the Russian imperial family.

The royal yacht was built with three decks in order to include a range of public and private rooms. The imperial day cabin was where the Tsar spent much of his time. Its walls were faced in panels of ash and birch, and these were hung with family photographs and paintings featuring nautical themes. There was a desk and comfortable chairs, where the Tsar could catch up with his correspondence and official duties.

The dining salon was situated next to the imperial day cabin. It was an elegant and richly upholstered room with a mahogany table and leather chairs that was able to accommodate up to eighty guests. There were five windows on either side, and a raised ceiling which ensured that the dining saloon was always flooded with natural light. In the evening, three crystal and ormolu chandeliers provided a soft, golden illumination. This picked out the Romanov double-headed eagle design which was finely etched onto the china plates and into the crystal wine and champagne glasses.

The imperial cabins were all located on the floor below. These included bedrooms, bathrooms and sitting rooms for the children, all furnished with plush carpets, comfortable chairs, and sofas covered in chintz. There were matching chintz curtains at the windows. The Tsar and Tsarina had their private suites on this deck, complete with the finest woodwork, leather sofas for the Tsar and a mauve chintz boudoir for the Tsarina. A private dining room for the Tsar and his immediate family was also to be found on this deck. Greg King, who has written extensively about the imperial yacht, describes the walls of the dining room as being 'faced in birch panels between contrasting cherry moldings and lit by three large windows and a ten-light crystal chandelier'.

The crew were accommodated across all three floors, many in very cramped conditions on the lowest deck, with a separate suite of rooms for the officers on the upper deck. The kitchens and galleys were also on the lowest deck, where an entire platoon of the Marine Guard was accommodated together with a special balalaika orchestra, the men of the ship's brass band, and a teak-lined stable with a cow that provided fresh milk.

Shtandart was one of the most luxurious vessels afloat, anticipating the style and elegance of the great White Star liners *Titanic* and *Olympic*, then under construction at the Harland and Wolff shipyard in Belfast. After the Revolution, she would be stripped of her fine interiors and used as a mine sweeper in the Baltic. She was then called the *Marti*, in celebration of the March 1917 Revolution which had overthrown the Tsar. In her final incarnation she became a training ship for young naval cadets, before being scrapped in Talinn in 1963, the year that would have marked the 350th anniversary of the Romanov dynasty.

On the voyage to Cowes in 1909, the Captain of the imperial yacht was Nikolai Pavlovich Sablin. He came from a prominent naval family. His father had been a Vice Admiral and his brother was Admiral Mikhail Sablin, famous for having survived the sinking of his ship, the *Oslyabya*, during the Russo-Japanese War.

Nikolai Sablin himself had had his share of dramas. He had been one of the officers on board the *Shtandart* in August 1907, when the vessel struck an unchartered rock close to the Finnish coast. The imperial yacht was badly damaged in the accident and took on a list of nineteen degrees. The situation was considered serious enough for the imperial family, who were on board at the time, to be evacuated and transferred to an accompanying escort cruiser.

On the trip to the Isle of Wight, there was a crew of over 350, including another *Shtandart* officer with the surname of Sablin. Nikolai Vasilyevich Sablin was not related to the Captain, but their shared surnames could on occasions cause some confusion. Nikolai Vasilyevich was a great favourite with the Tsar's children, particularly Grand Duchess Tatiana, who gave him the nickname 'Uncle'. After the Revolution he sought refuge in Romania, where he would write a memoir of his time at sea with the imperial family.

Accompanying the *Shtandart* was the imperial yacht *Polar Star*, which now belonged to Nicholas's mother, The Dowager Empress Maria. Although she had been present during King Edward's visit to Reval a year earlier, she had decided not to join the imperial family on their trip to the Isle of Wight.

The *Polar Star* was therefore being used to transport Alexander Izvolsky, the Russian Foreign Minister, and his bureau Chief, Alexander Savinsky, who was well known amongst the ladies at the court in St Petersburg for his good looks and dashing charm. A particularly important passenger was Alexander Spiridovich, the Head of Security for the Tsar. He was accompanied by members of the Okhrana, the Russian secret police. His evocative memoir *The Last Years at the Court of Tsarskoye Selo,* written in exile in Paris, tells a rich and entertaining story about the 1909 visit to Cowes.

The imperial yachts were accompanied by a Russian naval squadron, led by two armoured cruisers, the *Rurik* and the *Admiral Makarov*, and two destroyers, the *Emir Bukharski* and the *Moskvityanin*. At over 15,000 tons and with a crew of nearly 900, the *Rurik* had been built by Vickers of Barrow-in-Furness. She was considered the most advanced ship in the Russian navy, protected by Krupp steel armour and equipped with over fifty guns. The *Admiral Makarov* was smaller than the *Rurik* but built to similarly high specifications.

The *Emir Bukharski* and the *Moskvityanin* were both small destroyers attached to the Baltic fleet. The *Emir Bukharski* would be renamed the *Yakov Sverdlov* after the Revolution, in honour of the man widely suspected of giving the orders for the execution of the imperial family. The *Moskvityanin* was later sunk by the British in 1919 during the Russian Civil War.

The *Shtandart's* voyage to Cowes took her first to Cherbourg where the Tsar met with the French President, Clément Armand Fallières. An ardent left-wing Republican and a committed opponent of the death sentence, Fallières may well have been uncomfortable at hosting a visit by the Tsar. However, in the best tradition of pragmatic French diplomacy, he treated the Tsar and the imperial family with all the courtesy and honour that was required of him as President of France hosting a visit by France's most important ally.

The Franco-Russian alliance dated back to 1891 and was a key pillar of the foreign policy of both countries. There was increasingly close economic, military and naval collaboration. French financial loans to Russia bolstered the Tsarist regime and helped strengthen its economy and industrial and business expansion. The interests of the two countries were now closely intertwined.

Shtandart and *Polar Star* reached Cherbourg shortly after 1pm on the afternoon of 30 July. They entered the bay of St Anne. The two imperial yachts and their accompanying Russian squadron were escorted into Cherbourg by a division of four French cruisers and a dozen destroyers, to the thunderous salutes of the entire French Mediterranean and Northern fleets. They entered the Bay of St Anne and anchored close to the French cruiser Galilée, which was positioned near Fort de Chavagnac, a massive fortification which guarded the Western entrance to the harbour.

On board the *Galilée* and waiting to welcome the Tsar and his family was President Fallières, along with his genial but not particularly effective Foreign Minister, Stephen Jean-Marie Pichon. The President took a steam launch for the short trip over to the *Shtandart*, where he warmly greeted the imperial family. On board the imperial yacht things were not going so well. The sea was very rough, and both the Tsarina and the children were feeling sick, as their ship bucked the choppy waves.

It was therefore agreed that only the Tsar would accompany the President back to the *Galilée* for the review of the French Northern and Mediterranean fleets. This was a huge display of French naval power with over a hundred battleships, cruisers, destroyers, torpedo and submarine boats all lined up to greet the Tsar and the President. Nicholas was very impressed by what he described as the fine bearings of the French crews and the splendid appearance of the warships. He spoke in glowing terms about the development of the military forces of both Russia and France, which he stressed were dedicated to guaranteeing the peace of the world.

After the Review, the President and the Tsar returned to the *Shtandart*. Here the Grand Duchesses, who now seemed to have recovered from their bout of sea sickness, were eager to photograph the French submarines, then amongst the finest examples of underwater naval technology. Before doing this, they made a polite request to the President, asking his permission to bring out their cameras. He was reportedly enchanted by the charm and courtesy of these four attractive royal Princesses and immediately agreed, to a chorus of claps and cheers from all those on board the *Shtandart*.

In the evening, a state dinner was organised for the Tsar and Tsarina. This was held in a magnificent pavilion that was pitched on the quarterdeck of the French battleship, *Vérité*. There were place settings for eighty people on a horseshoe-shaped table which was decorated with roses, orchids and carnations, with a centre piece of glass covered with muslin, depicting the Russian coat of arms.

During the dinner there was a round of speeches and toasts which celebrated the Franco-Russian alliance, and which gave the Tsar the opportunity to mention his admiration for the French army and navy. The imperial couple were then treated to a spectacular light show. The ships of the French Northern and Mediterranean fleets were used as a backdrop for a series of innovative illuminations which outlined glittering shapes and designs. There were sea serpents, a dolphin pursued by a swarm of swans, and an enormous black and yellow grasshopper.

The centrepiece included a fantastic coloured light display of Lohengrin's swan escorted by two cygnets, together with a cock perched on a golden egg, dragging behind him a gondola. The Tsar was particularly impressed by one illumination which depicted a plane carrying a band of mandolin players, surrounded by a flock of geese.

For all the glamour of the State dinner, the magic of the illuminations, and the magnificence of the naval review, there was also a palpable sense of fear encircling the imperial family during their time in Cherbourg. A tight security net was thrown around them.

The Tsar's yacht was surrounded by a double ring of ironclads and destroyers were constantly circling her. A journalist's boat that came too close was fired upon with blank shots. Submarines followed the *Galilée* as she carried the Tsar and the President on their inspection of the French fleet.

There was a large police presence in the port itself and over twenty people were arrested on the first day of the Tsar's visit, including two suspected Russian anarchists. Despite all these precautions, agitators managed to distribute thousands of leaflets to the soldiers at the Cherbourg garrison, protesting in very violent terms about the arrival of the Tsar in France. The police immediately launched an investigation but could not discover who was responsible for producing the leaflets. Every hotel was under surveillance and suspect individuals were shadowed.

The security cordon was so strict that even the Tsar's own Head of Police Alexander Spiridovich, who had gone ashore for meetings, was refused permission to return to the *Shtandart*. He eventually had to call on the Admiral Superintendent in charge of Cherbourg port and prove who he was. After this embarrassing incident, an officer from the port was sent to accompany him all the way back to the imperial yacht.

The Tsar himself exhibited a certain degree of nervousness about his personal security at various points during the visit. While on board the *Vérité*, he refused to allow a group of French press photographers to take pictures of him. This caused enormous disappointment and the President had to intervene to calm the situation. In a measured and kind voice, he explained to the Tsar that 'These gentlemen are simply compilers of the history of our two nations'. The Tsar smiled and at once gave permission to the photographers to proceed.

On Sunday 1 August, the imperial family attended a Russian Orthodox religious service on board the *Shtandart*, following which the Tsar received a delegation of veterans from the Crimean War. These aged pensioners greeted the Emperor and assured him of their warm friendship towards Russia. The Tsar in return distributed medals to the veterans. He and the Tsarina then embraced seventy-three-year-old Madame Renon, who had run the canteens for the French armies during the Crimean War. This piece of theatre was intended as a symbolic laying to rest of the enmity and mistrust that had characterised the relationship between the two countries for much of the previous century. The Tsarina was described as looking tired and careworn throughout the event.

The rest of that day was taken up with a series of private meetings between the Tsar, the President and their Foreign Ministers. A lunch was organised for ninety-five people on board the *Vérité*, attended by both Nicholas and Alexandra. That evening the Tsar reciprocated by organising a dinner for the President and his entourage on the *Shtandart*, while outside a firework display lit up the night sky, illuminating the imperial yachts, battleships and cruisers in a magnificent tribute to the Franco-Russian alliance.

The French President showered the imperial family with gifts. The Empress was given a Gobelins tapestry in wool and silk on a background of yellow damask. The Tsarevich was given twelve different models of rifles, together with miniature military drums and trumpets. Olga received a writing table in silver and blue enamel. A travelling clock in blue enamel was presented to Tatiana. Her younger sister, Maria, was given a fully furnished two-storey doll's house, complete with a lift and electric lights. Eight-year-old Anastasia received a magnificent doll's trousseau.

Shortly after six o'clock on the morning of Monday 2 August, the *Shtandart* weighed anchor. Together with the rest of the Russian squadron, the imperial yachts headed out into the Channel for the crossing to Spithead and Cowes, accompanied by their escort of French navy vessels.

French and Russian newspapers were unanimous in praising the success of the visit. Before leaving Cherbourg, Russia's Foreign Minister, Izvolsky, had given interviews to large numbers of journalists. Consequently, the papers in both countries were full of positive articles celebrating the value and importance of the Franco-Russian alliance and how it had been strengthened by the meeting between the Tsar and the President.

The *République Française* in Paris sang the praises of the 'Franco-Russian alliance which remains so dear to the hearts of all the patriots in both nations and is an instrument of European conciliation'. This was a view echoed across Russia and France. The British press had also followed the visit with great interest and published detailed reports on the Tsar's itinerary, as well as reporting sympathetically on the Franco-Russian alliance.

The German press however struck a sour note, with several newspapers commenting that the French had humiliated the Tsar by reminding him of the Crimean war. The right-wing *Post* reported that the French and Russians needed to be careful of the British and not fall under the spell of an Anglophile foreign policy. The *Germania* asserted that the speech of the Tsar at the State dinner was more cordial than that of the French President and stated that 'Russia's financial dependence on France caused the autocratic Tsar to make this deep obeisance before the Jacobin Republic, an obeisance that is not compatible with his dignity'.

As the Tsar's yacht departed from Cherbourg, three British battlecruisers, the *Indomitable*, the *Inflexible* and the *Invincible,* put out to sea steering a course towards Cherbourg. Sailing under a cloudy sky and riding grey and squally waves, the British ships sighted the Russian squadron and its French naval escort shortly after eight in the morning. As the British ships neared the *Shtandart*, the French warships fired a salute and returned to Cherbourg. The Tsar's visit to the Isle of Wight had begun.

The three battlecruisers led the way back towards the English coast. Cruising at just over twenty knots, they soon left the imperial yachts behind. The *Polar Star's* maximum speed was only seventeen knots. This was an embarrassing breach of protocol and orders were quickly given by the Captains of the British naval vessels to reduce speed in order to allow time for the *Shtandart* and *Polar Star* to close the gap.

Soon, the Isle of Wight and Portsmouth hove into view with the roadstead of Spithead directly ahead. Spithead stands at the entrance to Portsmouth harbour. It is one of the most sheltered areas of sea anywhere in Britain, protected by a sandbank called the *Spit*. This extends three miles out from the Hampshire coast and runs for fourteen miles parallel with the coast. Spithead provided safe anchorage for the Royal Navy and was always the traditional place for the Reviews of the British Fleet by reigning monarchs.

Here on 31 July 1909, two days before the arrival of the Tsar, King Edward VII inspected over a hundred and fifty British warships and scores of smaller naval ships that were assembled in three lines between the Isle of Wight and Portsmouth. Each line ran for six miles, so that there were eighteen miles of warships in total. There were twenty-eight Admirals present at the Review. This was an impressive display of British naval strength. It was a warning to all other countries that Britannia still ruled the waves and that her navy was both her refuge and protection and her greatest asset in any future war. The Fleet Review also served another purpose. It was a floating showcase of the numerical superiority and technological inventiveness of the British nation at sea.

The southernmost line, nearest to the Isle of Wight contained all the battleships and armoured cruisers of the Dreadnought class. They were led by the 18,000-ton battleship *Dreadnought*, which had given her name to an entire class of new naval fighting vessels. These included her sister ships, *Bellerophon, Temeraire and Superb.* Lined up behind these were the battleships and armoured cruisers, *Indomitable, Inflexible and Invincible,* followed by *Minotaur* and *Defence,* two of the most powerful cruisers in the Royal Navy. This was proudly described by *The Times* as 'by far the most powerful cruiser squadron anywhere in the world, a squadron which could hold its own against any five foreign battleships now in commission'.

The middle line of vessels was headed by the battleship *King Edward VII*, which was the lead ship of eight pre-Dreadnought battleships. These had all been launched between 1903 and 1905. All eight were present at Spithead for the royal review, along with the ships from the Second Cruiser Squadron.

The third northern line, which was closest to Portsmouth, consisted of the entire Atlantic fleet, headed up by its flagship, the 14,000-ton *Prince of Wales*. Behind the *Prince of Wales* came thirteen other ships including the *Queen, Implacable, Formidable, Drake* and *Duke of Edinburgh*.

The King's Review of the fleet went smoothly, apart from a tragic episode which occurred aboard the battleship *Temeraire* while she was firing her salute. One of the guns backfired, and this caused a violent explosion. Four men standing behind the gun were badly injured, and one of them, Able Seaman Foran, died in hospital the following day. The King was deeply shocked and asked to be kept informed about the condition of all those injured in the accident.

Now, two days later, the Tsar's yacht was approaching Spithead. Already steamboats filled with newspaper reporters were bobbing around on the sea, trying to get as close as they could to the *Shtandart*. At the sight of the three armoured cruisers bearing down on them, they all removed themselves to a safe distance.

Spiridovich described a dreary morning, 'A cold wind blew. The sea, inhospitable, was leaden on its entire surface'. The weather forecast for the day was stormy, moving towards fairer conditions.

King Edward and Queen Alexandra were now anchored off Ryde on the Isle of Wight, on board the *Victoria and Albert*, awaiting the arrival of the *Shtandart*. They were accompanied by George, the Prince of Wales, and by Arthur, the Duke of Connaught. The Russian Ambassador, Count Benckendorff was also on board the King's yacht, together with his wife and daughter, the Prime Minister Herbert Asquith, and the Foreign Secretary Sir Edward Grey.

At midday, the two imperial yachts and their accompanying Russian and British escorts were sighted. The entire Naval fleet hoisted the Russian ensign and fired a royal salute of welcome. The *Shtandart* now emerged into full view, flying the imperial flag of Russia at the main, the British white ensign at the fore, and the Russian ensign at the mizzen.

The Tsar's yacht dropped anchor immediately to the south of the *Victoria and Albert*. The rest of the Russian squadron grouped around it. On the beaches and cliffs of the Isle of Wight, thousands of people strained their eyes or used binoculars to try and see what was taking place on board the two yachts. Destroyers patrolled the waters of the Solent in order to keep the idle and the curious at a respectable distance.

King Edward and Queen Alexandra boarded a small launch, which ferried them across the two hundred yards that separated the two yachts. On board the *Shtandart,* the King and Tsar warmly embraced. The King was diplomatically dressed in the costume of a Russian Admiral, although he had had trouble squeezing into it as he had clearly put on a lot of weight since he had last worn it. The Tsar was attired as a British Admiral of the Fleet, but clearly did not enjoy the experience. He later complained that he had been trapped in the costume for six hours.

The young Grand Duchesses lined up demurely in their matching white frocks and straw hats and were presented to their British relations. When the Prince of Wales came on board everyone was immediately struck by the facial similarity between him and his cousin, the Tsar. The Tsarina and Queen Alexandra exchanged cordial greetings, but many commented that the Tsarina looked pale and tired.

The Tsarina was now in increasingly poor health and was rarely seen at any public events in Russia. She had withdrawn into her own private world of suffering and religious devotion and would spend long hours in her mauve boudoir at the Alexander Palace. Occasionally, she would travel to the Crimea where she would sit on the terrace at Livadia Palace. Here she would spend hours looking at the sea or being wheeled around on short walks in a specially adapted bath chair. Alix had suffered from sciatica since she was a young woman, but the pain in her back and in her legs had worsened with age, and with the psychological strain that preyed on her mind and spirit. She believed that it was her destiny to be unhappy and refused all offers of medical help.

What memories must have crowded in on this fragile and anxious woman as she saw the Isle of Wight for the first time since her marriage to Nicholas in 1894. The Island was very familiar to her, but this time her beloved grandmother would not be there to greet her. Alexandra had not visited Britain since the death of the Queen in 1901 and returning to Victoria's favourite seaside retreat must have added another level of poignancy and stress to her visit. She was also acutely aware that Osborne House, where she had spent so many happy summers, was no longer owned by the British royal family.

The meeting of the two royal families on the *Shtandart* did not last long. Twenty minutes later, the King and Queen returned to the *Victoria and Albert* accompanied by the Tsar and Tsarina, and lunch was served at 2pm. On board were a host of British statesmen waiting to meet the Tsar. These included both the Prime Minister, Herbert Asquith, and the Foreign Secretary, Sir Edward Grey. The Russian Ambassador, Count Alexander Benckendorff, was now at the Tsar's side. He was constantly on edge, believing that the Tsar was no match for his skilled and sophisticated British hosts. He confided to a friend that he thought that the Tsar created the image of a well-intentioned, diffident and rather dull English country gentlemen.

There were, in fact, major international issues to be discussed during the Tsar's visit to Cowes. The responsibility for making progress with these talks fell mainly to the two Foreign Secretaries, Grey and Izvolsky, but Nicholas also made sure that he was involved. He was keen to stress to the King and Asquith how much he valued the Anglo-Russia Convention of 1907. The Tsar emphasised that he would go to great lengths to ensure that Britain and Russia did not come into conflict over Persia and Central Asia.

Soon after three in the afternoon, the *Victoria and Albert* slipped her moorings. To a thunderous cavalcade of guns from the fleet, she entered the lines of the assembled naval ships, followed closely by the *Shtandart,* the *Polar Star*, the two Russian cruisers, *Admiral Makarov* and *Rurik,* and their accompanying destroyers. New paintwork gleamed on the Russian ships as the crews had spent the time since their arrival in applying fresh coats of paint to the decks and woodwork.

King Edward and the Tsar stood on the bridge of the royal yacht, with Edward still in his Russian Admiral's uniform and Nicholas in his British Admiral's outfit. They were surrounded by what commentators described as a 'brilliant assemblage of dignitaries'.

The review of the fleet followed the same route as that taken by the King on the previous Saturday. The weather, though, was less auspicious. The sky was heavily overcast, and the sunshine appeared only fitfully, breaking through the clouds to reveal a grey and turbulent sea. The ships passed smoothly along the lines to a great chorus of hurrahs from the sailors on board the British ships. Amongst the cheering, the music of the imperial anthem 'God Save the Tsar' rang out loud and clear. The Russian sailors responded to the hurrahs of their British hosts with equal energy and enthusiasm.

On board the *Polar Star,* Spiridovich admitted to 'feelings of jealousy at the sight of this admirable tableau. If only we had something similar!' He was particularly overawed by the sight of the Dreadnoughts. This class of ship was unknown in Russia and he described the ships as looking like 'gigantic and monstrous irons, that pressed down, compressing the entire surface of the sea'.

He went on to remark that the scale and sheer size of the British fleet made him realise why the Tsars were so much in love with their navy. 'In effect it is in the fleet that the military power of the state is expressed with astonishing simplicity and in a truly tangible and visible manner', he wrote.

It was towards the end of the afternoon that a disaster was narrowly avoided. The royal yachts had successfully managed to manoeuvre around the battleship, *King Edward VII*, but the *Rurik* took the turn rather more sharply than she should have done. In a matter of minutes, she was on a collision course with the bows of the *Dreadnought*. The captain of the *Rurik* gave immediate orders for the Russian cruiser to stop and put its engines into reverse. It was a heart-stopping moment and caused a momentary flutter of fear amongst those watching on the surrounding ships. The King and the Tsar were completely unaware of what had happened, as the royal yacht had by then left the *Rurik* far behind.

The review lasted more than an hour. Shortly after five in the afternoon, *the Victoria and Albert,* followed by the two Russian imperial yachts and their accompanying squadron, cut through the line of naval battleships and headed directly for the Cowes Roads. They were greeted on arrival by a salute from the Royal Yacht Squadron's battery and dropped anchor close to one another.

The *Polar Star* and the Russian cruisers were allocated berths a little further out, in line with the British naval vessel *Enchantress*. Festive buntings were hung out on the rigging and masts of all the ships. Spiridovich was enchanted by the sight of the sea covered with yachts and small boats bobbing around on the waves around them, 'a genuine forest of masts, with flags flying from the tops of the boats'. He recorded, 'it was a happy and gay sight'. The Romanov Regatta had begun.

A special honour awaited the Tsar. The Royal Yacht Squadron, by unanimous acclamation, had voted to invite him to become a member. Suitably attired, the Commodore and Vice Commodore of the Royal Yacht Squadron, the Marquis of Ormonde and the Duke of Leeds, accompanied by the secretary of the Club Mr Pasley, boarded the *Victoria and Albert,* and announced to the Tsar that he had been selected for membership. In the world of yacht clubs there was no more coveted membership and Nicholas was clearly very touched. Although he was in no way an active sailor, he enjoyed the sea, and the time that he spent on his imperial yachts.

Meanwhile on board the *Polar Star,* the Tsar's entourage were now eager to get ashore and explore Cowes. The Isle of Wight occupied a special place in the Russian imagination, and those on board the *Polar Star* were consequently keen to soak up the atmosphere of the place.

The Foreign Minister, Count Izvolsky, assumed a haughty and impenetrable appearance as he gazed across at Cowes. With a monocle in one eye he gave Spiridovich the impression of being so repressed that 'he might explode with all the secrets that he was hiding'. His bureau chief, Savinsky, had an 'air of impeccable elegance and resembled a photograph from a fashion magazine'.

In order to prepare themselves for their Cowes visit, the military men on board the *Polar Star* had taken off their uniforms and were now decked out in civilian clothes. It was clear, though, to any casual observer that this transition was not going smoothly. Several of them wore ill-fitting and rather crumpled looking suits, with trouser legs that were either too long or too short, or else did not fit the current style of cut. In his memoirs Spiridovich recalls, 'They cursed their Russian tailors. The diplomats on board gave them condescending and pitying looks'.

As soon as an authorisation signal was received from the *Shtandart* that they could disembark, the passengers all tried to crowd into the first boat that was leaving for Cowes. Izvolsky alone remained aloof, keen to show that he was in no hurry to join the scrum.

The most high-ranking civilian on board was Prince Serge Belozersky and he duly gave the order to set sail for the shore. The pilot of the boat set a course to follow the official route into the harbour. This involved a detour because of the large number of yachts at anchor at the entrance to Cowes. Seeing this, the Prince became impatient and ordered the young pilot to change direction and take the most direct route. The pilot protested that he could not do this. The Prince now became angry. He told the young sailor that this was a military order. There could be no questioning of his command. Spiridovich picks up the sorry tale of what happened next.

'The sailor obeyed. We went out for a few seconds in a straight line and then we heard a dreadful crash. The pilot had been right. The Prince was really mad. His companions told him to stop getting involved in things he did not understand and that the pilot knew full well what to do and how it should be done'.

The boat had fortunately not been badly damaged, and so after several attempts at reversing and then going forward, the pilot managed to free the boat and navigated it carefully towards the quayside in Cowes where the Russians all tumbled out, much to their relief.

On shore, the bemused Russian visitors mingled with the summer crowds surging up and down the Parade and along the High Street. Several of them tried to practice their newly acquired English language skills on people they met in the streets and were met with equally bewildered responses. One woman explained very politely after a question had been put to her in a heavily Russian accented English, 'Pardon, but I do not speak French'.

Monday 2 August was a public holiday, so the town was much more crowded than usual. The Russians were surprised to find that a public holiday in England meant that all the shops remained closed. They deemed this to be a rather quaint British custom but soon realised that there was plenty to keep the eccentric British amused and entertained without resorting to shopping.

Cowes Week had officially opened with the annual Bank holiday Regatta of the Royal London Yacht Club. There were four races scheduled, and the first of these was a race for the 23-metre and 'A' class schooner yachts. Due to the presence of the naval fleet at Spithead, the course for all the day's races was altered and the yachts headed out to the west of Cowes. There was a strong north-westerly breeze blowing and so the races were completed in record time.

The 23-metre and 'A' class yacht race took a route from Cowes to Lymington Spit and back. It was dominated by two German yachts, the Kaiser's new *Meteor IV,* sailing for the first time in British waters, and its sleek rival, *Germania.* This was owned by Gustav Krupp von Bohlen, the owner of the armaments industry conglomerate Friedrich Krupp AG, the company which would later equip the German army in the First World War.

Germania was in the lead for the entire race but disqualified herself in the final moments by sailing on the wrong side of the committee boat which was responsible for judging the winner. *Meteor IV* which was sailing close behind her therefore won the race, the only victory for the Kaiser's yacht during the entire 1909 Regatta season. *Cicely* won the second prize. *White Heather* and *Shamrock,* both favoured by the British public, gave up the race halfway through, as they had fallen so far behind the leading yachts.

The 15-metre yacht race was the next big race of the day. The star vessel of the race was to have been the King of Spain's *Hispania,* but for unknown reasons she never appeared. This was something of a disappointment. The race was won by the British yacht *Ostara,* owned by W.P. Burton, who had also won the previous year. The Spanish yacht *Tuiga* was a close second. The four Spanish yachts taking part in the race felt that *Tuiga* had saved their national reputation, let down by the failure of *Hispania* to take part in the race.

In Cowes, all eyes were on the Russian visitors, particularly the elegant Princess Alexis Dolgoruky, attired in a costume of dark blue serge braided in black silk. She strolled nonchalantly, arm-in-arm with the Countess Benckendorff and Prince Basil Dolgoruky, fully aware of the interest that they were attracting.

The social hub of the 1909 Cowes Week was, as in past years, the Castle: the club house of the Royal Yacht Squadron. The large marquee erected in its gardens offered tea, coffee, cocoa and other light refreshments. Seats were set about on the lawn and there were little mats to protect people's feet from the dew and dampness of the grass. The Austrian violinist and bandmaster Julian Kandt and his Blue Hungarian Band played a selection of popular waltzes and Hungarian gypsy music. Dominating the musical scene that summer were songs from Monckton and Talbot's popular comedy *The Arcadians*, which ran in London for over 800 performances. It became the most popular British musical of the early twentieth century. In the evening the grounds of the Club house were brightly illuminated with coloured lamps, as guests listened to the lilting music from the mythical land of *The Arcadians*, conjuring up an island of beauty, gentleness and innocence.

Access to the Royal Yacht Squadron Gardens was highly sought after. Each club member had the right to give away five guest badges, three for ladies and two for men. The demand for these badges was so high that many people - even those who considered themselves part of the smart Cowes Week set - were inevitably disappointed.

The arrival in Cowes of the Tsar and his family meant that security around the Isle of Wight was now at an all-time high. The *Shtandart* was moored half a mile from the shore, sheltered between the *Dreadnought* on one side and the *Victoria and Albert* on the other. Both these ships were ringed by picket boats with armed crews which continually circled the sea around the imperial yacht.

At a short distance from this inner circle of protection there was a cordon of police launches, so that nobody could approach the *Shtandart* unless they had a permit which had been both signed and countersigned by the Police authorities. Callers were not allowed to board unless they had been thoroughly vetted on shore. The Tsar's programme was not made public. There were rumours that he would set foot on the Isle of Wight, but very few people knew this for certain and there was no advance briefing to the press.

Cowes was thronged with police detectives. They made it their business to watch everybody who was arriving on the Island. Suspicious characters were instantly arrested. Russian visitors came under very close scrutiny, however aristocratic or official their names and positions might sound. There was a real fear that anarchist terror groups might subvert and infiltrate the security surrounding the Tsar. This could be done by somebody who looked completely innocent and innocuous. A sharp lookout was also kept for seditious literature and anti-Tsarist postcards, such as had appeared in London in the days before the arrival of the imperial family. Despite regular searches, nothing was ever found on the Island.

The *Manchester Guardian* reported that 'a considerable proportion of the visitors to Cowes this week are Scotland Yard police officers, all wearing correct yachting costumes, with white slips to their waistcoats and white tops to their caps'. The article went on to state, 'there are hundreds of them on duty and they watch every approach to the Island, the steamboat piers at Portsmouth and Southampton, and all the landing places on the Isle of Wight, even to the tiny stairs where ships' dinghies put down their passengers. This vigilant and unsleeping watch seems particularly incongruous in the holiday atmosphere of Cowes Week'.

This level of security had never been seen before in Britain and it shocked and disturbed many observers. The local police confessed that they felt overwhelmed by it. Scotland Yard detectives also commented that the security precautions were unprecedented.

Russian secret police also patrolled Cowes and its environs, by agreement with the British police. They were dressed like yachtsmen in double-breasted blue jackets, with white-covered yachting caps. Two of them haunted the parade between the Royal Yacht Squadron's Club house and the pier. One was described as a burly man with a slight stoop, with half closed eyes and tattooed hands. This last feature was considered by many who saw him to be particularly sinister.

Other Russian secret police were seen out and about in the streets and country lanes around Cowes. One elderly lady reported falling off her bicycle into a ditch after being suddenly surprised by a man she swore was a Russian spy popping up in front of her.

'Jimmy' was a well-known character who lived on the Isle of Wight, and he earned his living by playing his mouth organ on the local ferries. While walking near the pier, he was suddenly stopped by two Russian policemen who secured him very tightly and then began a full body search. His precious mouth organ, which was in the breast pocket of his coat, had obviously made a suspicious bulge which they were keen to investigate.

Highly indignant at the way that he was being treated, Jimmy hit out at the two men and a tussle then took place. This soon drew people's attention and a couple of pier officials, who fortunately recognised him, rushed to his defence. They explained to the Russians who Jimmy was and requested that he be immediately released. After a lot of muttering, this was reluctantly done. Jimmy retreated along the Parade in a state of high dudgeon.

It was as though the paranoia of Tsarist Russia, with its panoply of secret police, surveillance and state-sponsored terror, had been suddenly imported into the heart of a small and innocent English island. Cowes Week was all about pleasure, relaxation, and sportsmanship. Instead, a dark and monstrous mirage had been summoned up, a window into another world in which assassination and revolution haunted the land.

The holiday crowds on the Isle of Wight, who were used to seeing their King and Queen move freely around with minimal security, were puzzled by the strange absence of the Tsar. 'Cowes has seen nothing of the Tsar yet', wrote one disappointed newspaper correspondent. 'It has seen his travelling squadron, it has heard the thunder of the guns, which saluted him; it is now looking upon his yacht and royal standard. But it wonders in vain what kind of man he is, knows nothing of who is on board the yacht, and is sublimely ignorant of when, if ever, he will come ashore and when he will depart'.

One opportunity cropped up unexpectedly to penetrate the suffocating security surrounding the imperial family. After the Tsar's review of the Fleet, several excursion steamers packed with day trippers set out from Cowes to make a tour of the great naval ships lined up in the Solent. Whether by accident or design, they managed to sail very close to the *Shtandart* and were not turned back by the patrolling police boats. The passengers on board were rewarded by the sight of the young children of the Tsar on the deck of the imperial yacht. The Grand Duchesses and the Tsarevich kissed their hands and waved to the excursionists, who all cheered and clapped loudly. The Russian sailors and officers returned the greetings of the sightseers with great warmth.

The first day of the Tsar's visit was drawing to its close. That evening, King Edward and Queen Alexandra hosted a welcome banquet for the imperial couple aboard the *Victoria and Albert*. The guests sat at a long table, the King and the Tsar facing one another, Queen Alexandra at the right hand of the Tsar and the Tsarina at the right hand of the King.

The banquet table was decorated with pink roses and gold plate, complemented by two massive silver gilt presentation vases. These had originally been given by the Patriotic Fund to Admiral Nelson's widow and Admiral Collingwood, after the Battle of Trafalgar in 1805.

King Edward gave the welcome speech.

'Your Majesty, as well as my dear niece, are no strangers to England, especially to the Isle of Wight' he began, 'and I trust that your memory will carry you back to years ago when the hospitality of my beloved mother was extended to you both'.

The King then went on to say how pleased he was that the Tsar had had the opportunity of seeing the most powerful and largest fleet that has ever been assembled. He also recalled the recent visit by the Deputies from the Russian Duma and how delighted he and the Queen had been to meet them. He hoped that visits like this would increase the good feeling existing between the two countries.

The Tsar responded with equal warmth. It was clear that unlike Cherbourg, he felt at home on the Isle of Wight. He paid tribute to what he described as 'the magnificent review which bears full testimony to England's greatness. The grand sight of the Home and Atlantic fleets has deeply impressed me'.

In a touching reference to the memory of Queen Victoria, he remarked that, 'Fifteen years have passed since last I came to Cowes. I shall ever bear in mind the happy days spent with your beloved and venerated mother, Queen Victoria, and the affection that she bestowed upon me as Emperor and upon the Empress, her granddaughter.'

The part of his speech which made the greatest impression on those Russians listening to him, was his reference to the visit by the Deputies of the Duma. It was rare that the Tsar ever made any reference to the Duma, a body that he disliked. However, he did so tonight. He thanked the King and Queen and the British people for their warm welcome to the members of the Duma and said how touched he was by this gesture of support. These words would soon echo across the whole of Russia and were interpreted as a positive commitment by the Tsar to the Empire's recently established consultative assembly.

Nicholas then raised a toast to the King and Queen, and to what he described as the 'growing cordial relationship between our two countries founded on common interests and mutual esteem'. Everyone knew that this flowering of the Anglo-Russian relationship was fragile and newly hatched. It would need to be nurtured, if it was to survive the challenges and strains of the coming year. It was possible to hope that this visit did indeed mark a new beginning.

At nine in the evening, a signal gun was fired from the flagship of the fleet, and all the ships of the fleet were outlined with thousands of electric lamps, creating a lavish spectacle for the two royal families and for the many spectators crowded on to the foreshore and promenade at Cowes.

As the royal yachts lay under a clear and starry sky, surrounded by the backdrop of the illuminated battleships, the Tsar authorised the local Reuters agent to issue a special message. This expressed his deep appreciation of the splendid welcome given to him and the Empress and how impressed he was by the magnificent appearance of the British fleet. Nicholas was letting the world know the importance he now attached to the burgeoning alliance between Russia and Britain.

28

Tuesday 3 August 1909

As the King and Tsar slept, the battleships of the great fleet slipped their moorings and dispersed into the misty dawn of an early August morning. These ships had dominated the sea lanes off the Isle of Wight for the previous three days, but their departure passed almost unnoticed. When people on shore and on the royal yachts awoke it was as though what they had seen the night before, the great, glittering outlines of over a hundred and fifty battleships and cruisers, was an illusion: a trick conjured up by a fantastical magician.

The Atlantic fleet, followed by the Fifth and Fourth Cruiser Squadrons, were the first to leave shortly after six in the morning, making their way out through the Solent towards the Needles on the west coast of the Isle of Wight. The Second Division of the Home Fleet went next, followed by the Second Cruiser Squadron. Finally, the First Division of the Home Fleet put to sea, setting a course for Spithead.

The dispersal of such a huge fleet in a quiet and efficient way was a marvel of naval planning and organisation. The few people who were awake to watch it taking place were overawed by the sight of the great battleships and cruisers steaming gracefully away over the horizon. Four warships, *Bellerophon*, *Indomitable*, *Inflexible* and *Invincible*, remained to guard the King and the Tsar, together with the four ships of the Russian squadron.

All that day, expectations were riding high in Cowes that the Tsar and his family would make a visit to the town. Little knots of sightseers and journalists gathered at Trinity Wharf in East Cowes and at the Royal Yacht Squadron landing stage in Cowes, hoping to catch a glimpse of the Russian royal family.

The Tsar and Tsarina remained at sea all day. They spent much of their time on board the King's cutter, *Britannia*, as guests of the King and Queen. The Tsarina was joined by her elder sister, Princess Victoria Battenberg. The *Britannia* set sail towards Ryde soon after midday and returned to Cowes at six in the evening.

It was a perfect day and the sun shone warmly out of a cloudless blue sky. The King wore a blue serge coat and white trousers and the Tsar was described as looking 'spick and span in blue serge'. The Queen and the Tsarina sat in cosy red-cushioned basket chairs side by side on the deck. The Tsarina was dressed in a graceful white dress, her hat tied with a gauze veil. The Queen kept to the Cowes nautical colour of blue serge.

The main race of the day was the King's Cup, organised by the Royal Yacht Squadron. This event launched the Squadron's Regatta and was the high point of Cowes Week. All those on board the *Britannia* were elegantly positioned to watch the race. Twelve yachts took part, and all were owned by members of the Squadron. Only full members were permitted to compete for this most prestigious of yachting prizes. Sailing conditions were described as ideal. Given the different types of yachts taking part in the race, ranging from the 400-ton schooner *Meteor* to the 40-ton cutter, *Bloodhound*, a handicap system was introduced. This gave the smallest yacht a fifty-two-minute differential to the largest yacht.

The Kaiser's yacht, *Meteor IV*, took the lead as the vessels swept past Osborne bay and headed towards Ryde. After turning at the Bullock Buoy and returning towards Cowes, *Meteor* was overtaken by *White Heather*, owned by Mr Myles Kennedy. He was a newly elected member of the Squadron and there were great cheers all round when he came in first, with *Cicely* in second place and *Meteor* taking the third. The Germans had invested great hope in the Kaiser's yacht winning the King's Cup. Their disappointment was matched by the delight of the King, who was greatly relieved not to be awarding the Squadron's prize cup to a boat owned by his greatest yachting rival.

The race for the 15-metre class of vessels ran from Cowes round to the Warner lightship and then to the East Lepe buoy, and back to Cowes. It was twenty-three miles in total length. All ten yachts competing that morning were cutters, and included the King of Spain's boat, *Hispania* and the Duke of Medinaceli's *Tuiga*. After being closely shadowed by the *Tuiga* and the *Ostara* for most of the race, the *Hispania* opened up a clear lead on the final stretch and came in six minutes ahead of the *Ostara*.

The Tsar expressed his sorrow that the King of Spain had not been able to come to Cowes for the Regatta but was delighted that his yacht had won the race. He would have sympathised with the reasons for the King of Spain's absence. There had been rioting in Barcelona for five days: crowds had erected barricades in the streets, churches and convents had been set on fire. Other cities in Catalonia had followed Barcelona's example. Anarchists, socialists and republicans had allied with the working classes to confront the army and the police in a series of violent uprisings that became known as 'La Semana Trágica', or the 'Tragic Week'. Memories of the 1905 Revolution in Russia must have crowded in on the Tsar as he heard about the events in Catalonia.

While the Tsar and Tsarina were being entertained at the yacht races, British journalists had been invited to look around the *Shtandart*. After his unfortunate brush with French journalists in Cherbourg, the Tsar was keen to create a favourable public image in the British press. The Russian Embassy in London had therefore been given permission to extend invitations to accredited journalists from all the major British newspapers.

The *Daily Mail's* special correspondent covering Cowes Week gave his readers an entertaining and spirited account of his tour around the imperial yacht. He was impressed by the warmth of the welcome that he received from the Russian crew, and by the scale and size of the ship which he described as 'a great handsome glistening vessel, which for the most part, appeared easy and luxurious'. He noted how it was equipped with every modern convenience, but it was not, in any way, showy or ostentatious. An understated sense of class and refinement were its defining characteristics.

The visitors were amused by the sight of numerous small sailor boys, who were standing to attention in their smart uniforms and trying very hard not to laugh as the journalists filed past them. When he enquired why there were so many boys on board the ship, he was told that they were the choristers for the services held in the royal chapel, and they were highly talented in singing both the Orthodox liturgy and Russian hymns.

This seemingly relaxed and light-hearted atmosphere came to an abrupt end, when the journalists came face to face with the guards standing outside the Tsar's private apartments. One of the guards was described as 'stolid of face, but watchful of eye, his hair cropped close, a loaded rifle resting in his right hand, his left hand, as if by practice, nestling near a pocket where a loaded revolver was concealed'. Another giant guard with 'a ponderous breadth of shoulder, a ruminating eye, and an easy slouch of posture' brought home to the journalists the full extent of the massive security presence that surrounded the imperial family.

The visitors were escorted around the salon where the Tsar and Tsarina were due to host the evening dinner for the King and Queen. Several journalists described it as rather a 'plain, modest apartment'. One was fascinated by the sight of a small but delicately painted icon of St George and the Dragon, which stood at one end of the salon. This moved him to comment that St George was both the patron Saint of England and Russia, a fortuitous emblem of the new alliance between the two countries. Along the corridor were piles of the Tsarevich's small shoes, a reminder that the yacht was both a family home and a floating palace to promote Russian imperial diplomacy.

That morning, the Tsar's children had all gone ashore, landing unexpectedly at Trinity Pier in East Cowes, where their arrival took both the police and the waiting crowds by surprise. Further confusion ensued when the four Grand Duchesses, dressed in matching white skirts, dark jackets and straw hats, insisted that they wanted to walk all the way to Osborne. The police were equally insistent that they travel there by car. After lengthy discussions with members of their entourage, they and the

Tsarevich were finally persuaded to ride in two landau carriages to the beach at Osborne Bay.

There they met the Princess of Wales and her children, who were staying at nearby Barton Manor. The royal cousins played together for about an hour on the beach, digging and gathering seashells. This was the same beach where Nicholas and Alexandra had spent their last day together in July 1894, before Nicholas returned to Russia to be confronted by the death of his father and his accession to the imperial throne.

The children returned to the *Shtandart* at about midday, after stopping off to pay a visit to King Edward's new yacht, *Alexandra,* a small, two-funnelled steamer which was moored in East Cowes. Here they ran around the decks for a few minutes. There was a touching innocence and naivety about the imperial children, anxious to snatch moments of happiness and fun whenever they could find it.

In the afternoon, the two oldest Grand Duchesses, Olga and Tatiana, decided to return to Cowes. What had been intended as a low-key shopping trip would transform them into early twentieth-century media stars. They would become amongst the first examples of the way in which the press would create public interest in royalty and celebrity.

The two young Princesses, then aged fourteen and twelve, led sheltered and isolated lives. They had scarcely ever ventured outside the secure confines of the imperial palaces in Tsarskoye Selo and Livadia. They were protected by parents who had largely withdrawn from public and court life. They knew very little about the realities of the world around them. A short trip to Cowes therefore seemed a perfect opportunity to sample a little bit of freedom, in a town where they felt sure they would be completely safe and would not be recognised.

Olga and Tatiana, accompanied by two ladies and two gentlemen from the imperial suite, landed at Trinity Wharf shortly after two in the afternoon. One of these gentlemen was Dr Eugene Botkin, the imperial doctor who would later die with them at Ekaterinburg.

They were delighted when they discovered that they could walk from the Wharf without having to take a carriage, as had been the case earlier in the day when they visited Osborne. The two girls were both dressed in light grey pleated skirts, buttoned up jackets, and straw hats. They carried tightly rolled black umbrellas. They could easily have been mistaken for a couple of local schoolgirls on a holiday jaunt. Their entourage agreed to follow them at a discreet distance, so as not to attract any public attention.

The Chief Constable of the Isle of Wight Captain Adam Connor and his Deputy, Mr Gallaway, kept the party under close observation but at this stage did not introduce themselves to the two Princesses. Olga and Tatiana were in a cheerful and carefree mood and, with lots of laughter and animated chatter, they headed directly to the chain ferry that crosses the River Medina and connects East Cowes with Cowes.

The ferry which the Grand Duchesses boarded was very new. It replaced an earlier model and had been operational for only two months. It was built of steel and the ramps were operated by steam power. An attractive feature was an upper viewing deck, which passengers greatly enjoyed during the warm August weather.

Settling themselves on board, Olga and Tatiana mingled freely with the other passengers, and paid a halfpenny each for their own tickets. This was a novel experience for two girls who normally never needed to carry money around with them. Once the short trip was over, they hurried off the ferry to begin their afternoon of shopping and sightseeing in Cowes.

The Times reported that their route took them along the High Street where they inspected 'very commonplace shop windows with much eagerness and excitement. There was much joyful exclamation when they came across a shop selling picture postcards'. They plunged into the shop and excitedly began asking the two surprised attendants all about the postcards. Although they were speaking in English, it was clear to the two attendants that they were foreigners, probably Russian, given the large numbers in Cowes that summer. If they did suspect that these were the Tsar's daughters, the shop attendants never let on.

They left the shop clutching postcards of their mother and father, of King Edward and Queen Alexandra, and a composite card with portraits of over thirty Princes and Princesses. The two girls then continued their walk along the High Street. They stopped at Beken, the Pharmacist, where they bought up most of the shop's supply of perfumes and hairbrushes and commented on how friendly and courteous everyone was in Cowes.

It was soon after this that their private adventure began to turn into a public spectacle. As they made their way down the street, they recognised a group of Russians in a carriage which had stopped in front of the Post Office. They ran across the road and laughingly called out in Russian to the passengers. At the sight of the two Grand Duchesses, the men stood up and removed their hats. One of the men then produced a large camera and tried to photograph the two girls. At this point both Olga and Tatiana realised the mistake that they had made and hurried back across the street.

It was too late. People in the surrounding area noticed what had happened and concluded that the two girls must be very important people. Soon a rumour began to spread that the Tsar and Tsarina were shopping in Cowes and the road was blocked by a huge crowd determined to catch a glimpse of Russia's imperial rulers. The Grand Duchesses and their entourage were now being followed down the High Street by a steadily growing number of people. Neither of the girls seemed particularly worried at this point, but members of their entourage and the police were already concerned at the potential security issues.

They then stopped to admire a window display at a jewellery shop called Benzie and wanted to go inside and make some purchases. Several women pursued them inside the shop and the police decided to intervene. Both the Chief Constable and the Deputy Chief Constable stood in front of the doorway, preventing anybody else from entering. Half a dozen policemen took up positions across the street, thus dividing the crowd in two.

The larger part of the crowd, however, remained with the Grand Duchesses and showed no sign of abandoning their royal prey. In a matter of moments, the two young princesses had been transformed from two unknown visitors wandering around Cowes into royal celebrities. Everyone wanted a small part of the magic, mystery and allure which they represented.

The excited crowd encircled the two girls, and despite the police presence began to press ever closer towards them. People were largely good natured, and several of them raised a cheer for the Grand Duchesses.

Olga and Tatiana acknowledged these good wishes with broad smiles and displayed a remarkable sense of calm and composure, despite the crush of people all around them. This was more than could be said for the members of their entourage, who showed signs of increasing fear and panic.

A decision was now taken that the royal party should make an immediate return to the chain ferry and cross back to East Cowes. The way ahead, however, was completely blocked. The girls were therefore taken down a narrow passageway which led them through the back streets to the ferry. The police stopped all access to the passageway, so that nobody else could follow the party.

After running into another large group of people whom the police this time managed to hold back, the two girls boarded the ferry and once again paid in cash for their halfpenny tickets. They seemed remarkably unperturbed by their adventure in Cowes and were in no mood to return to the *Shtandart*.

It was suggested that they might like a drive to the Royal Church of St Mildred at Whippingham, a mile from Osborne House. This idea was warmly welcomed by the two girls. After being hemmed in by the crowds in Cowes they were ready for a ride out into the open countryside. They were also curious to see the royal church where their great-grandparents Victoria and Albert had regularly worshipped, and where their mother had spent many hours in prayer.

Soon after moving to the Isle of Wight, Queen Victoria decided that the existing church at Whippingham needed to be rebuilt in a much more magnificent style. Construction work started on the church in 1854, and this was finally completed in 1861. Prince Albert took a keen interest in the design of the building. The new St Mildred's contained several brilliant rose windows and a large octagonal lantern. Its crowning glory, though, was its large square tower with five pinnacles, giving the impression of a German castle that had been conjured up from the banks of the Rhine. The royal church stands on a hill with sweeping views down to the River Medina and is surrounded by woodland and fields, creating an image of rural peace and tranquillity.

Two horse-drawn carriages were immediately summoned to take the

Grand Duchesses to St Mildred's. One was a comfortable open landau for the Princesses and the other was a wagonette for the English police officers. Demonstrating their newly found independence, Olga and Tatiana announced that they would much prefer the wagonette, claiming that it would give them a better view of the route to Whippingham. Somewhat surprised by this request but seeing no reason to oppose it, the police agreed to the plan. Several police officers crammed into the landau, while the two girls, accompanied by their entourage, made themselves as comfortable as possible on the hard-wooden seats of the wagonette.

In later years, long after the memory of those carefree days at Cowes had receded into history, people who were strolling around East Cowes that afternoon recalled the curious sight of two carriages passing them at a brisk speed on the road up to Osborne and Whippingham. The smarter one was filled with a rather disorderly collection of policemen while the other, a rougher looking wagon, rather incongruously contained a group of elegantly dressed ladies and gentlemen, attired in the latest high society fashions.

Bizarre though this sight was, what many of them remembered were the two young girls in straw hats and grey dresses, sitting near the front of the wagonette. There was something strange about the look on the faces of these girls, as though they were filled with happiness and joy, the warm summer breeze blowing in their faces. The two Romanov Princesses were indeed experiencing an intoxicating sense of freedom and adventure that was denied to them in their stultifying and constrained existence in Russia.

As the two carriages raced up the road to St Mildred's, they overtook Canon Clement Smith who had been Honorary Chaplain to Queen Victoria from 1893 until her death in 1901. He happily agreed to show the two girls and their party around the church. Olga and Tatiana showed great interest in the many memorials erected to the memory of Queen Victoria, little realising that within a few years, a plaque would be erected in the very same Church to the memory of them and their family. They were described by Canon Smith as staring 'wide eyed at the chair in which Queen Victoria used to sit when she attended services at St Mildred's'.

They were then taken to see the tomb of Prince Henry of Battenberg, the husband of Princess Beatrice. He was a member of the ruling family of Hesse and a cousin of the Tsarina. Queen Victoria's fierce possessiveness towards Beatrice, who was her youngest daughter, had meant that she wanted to keep the newly married couple as close to her as possible. In 1889, Prince Henry was made Governor of both Carisbrooke Castle and the Isle of Wight.

Chafing at his cramped lifestyle, and clearly craving a military adventure, Prince Henry managed to persuade Queen Victoria to allow him to take part in the expedition being planned against the Ashanti Empire in West Africa. In 1895 he was appointed Military Secretary to the Commander-in-Chief of the expedition.

As the British army moved towards the Ashanti capital of Kumasi, Prince Henry fell ill with malaria. He was taken on board HMS *Blonde*, then anchored off the coast of Sierra Leone, and died at sea in January 1896. He was only thirty-eight years old. His death was a terrible shock for Princess Beatrice. She buried him in a sumptuously-carved white marble tomb at Whippingham Church, in what would later become known as the Battenberg Chapel. Fifty years later, she was buried alongside him.

The two Grand Duchesses returned to Trinity Wharf at around five in the afternoon. They had been ashore for over three hours and were still in a very happy and excited mood. *The Times* Correspondent described them as 'laughing and talking' as they boarded the launch that would take them back to the *Shtandart*.

That evening, their parents held a dinner on board the imperial yacht in honour of King Edward and Queen Alexandra. It was an intimate occasion. No speeches were made but the Tsar raised a toast to his British hosts and Edward responded in kind. Nicholas was again dressed in the uniform of a British Admiral and Edward had squeezed back into his Russian Admiral's costume.

A five-course meal was served. There was a mock turtle soup, with a rich red wine sauce and small pastries. This was followed by a fish course of trout in a lobster and mustard sauce. The meat course was duck served with a Cumberland sauce, and a cider, gin and orange Victoria Punch. A dish of baby turkey was then offered with an artichoke salad, garden peas, and an ivory velouté sauce of chicken stock and cream. The banquet was rounded off with a selection of desserts including Neapolitan ice cream.

As the dark closed in, the royal yachts and their escort of British and Russian warships were illuminated in a scene of striking and almost ethereal beauty. It was a perfect night with scarcely a cloud in the sky and a full moon reflected over the calm surface of the sea.

The police launches protecting the *Shtandart* kept up their unceasing watch, as they had done throughout the day. The officers on board were armed with revolvers, with clear instructions that they were to be used only in case of an emergency. If any boat approached the restricted area, the Lieutenant in charge of the police patrols shouted, 'Keep outside the lines please!'

If these instructions were ignored, one of the cutters that lay astern of each police launch would cast off and forcibly remove the offenders. This had happened two or three times that day. On one occasion, the police officers were surprised to find a couple of nuns seated in a rowing boat. They were escorted back across the security lines with a stern but polite warning.

That evening, as the Tsar and Tsarina entertained their royal guests on board the *Shtandart*, Lady Eva Baring gave a masked garden party in the grounds of her home, Nubia Lodge, in Cowes. Her husband was Sir Godfrey Baring, then the Liberal MP for the Isle of Wight. Invitations were highly sought after and the party was judged to have been one of the high points of Cowes Week.

Conversation would doubtless have turned to the Tsar's visit, but also to one of the stories that was dominating the news that week, the raising of the sunken submarine HMS *C11*. This was one of the new C-class of submarines, only launched three years before at the Vickers yard in Barrow.

On 14 July 1909, the submarine was sunk in a collision with the collier *Eddystone*, in the North Sea near Cromer in Norfolk. Attempts were now being made to raise the submarine and recover the bodies of the twelve crew who had failed to escape. Over thirty steel hawsers had been fastened to the wreck, but all of them had snapped. In increasingly rough seas, six divers were working around the clock to try and attach new hawsers. The cruiser *HMS Vindictive* and two torpedo-boats stood ready to offer any assistance that might be required. Ultimately all these efforts failed, and the salvage work was eventually abandoned in the September of that year.

The British press continued to be fascinated by all things Russian. Food, alongside fashion, porcelain and jewellery attracted its share of newspaper articles. There were entire pages devoted to Russian recipes in the newspapers published on 3 August. Noting that the Russians enjoyed their food, and that both caviar and Russian salad were already well-known in Britain, one newspaper recommended that a fish soup called 'ukha' be tried. Readers were told that this was made from four types of white fish blended with celery, parsley, onions and lemons and accompanied by small patties called 'rastegal'.

It was recommended that the second course should be hazel hen, a type of small grouse that was very popular in Russia. The writer suggested that this be 'dished up with its own sauce de fumée with sour cream'. Kissel was the dessert of choice to complete the meal. This was made from potato flour combined with a selection of pureed or chopped fruit such as cranberries, strawberries and cherries. If readers were still hungry after all this food, a typical Russian sweetmeat was highlighted, made of 'monkey nuts' rolled up in hot caramel or toffee.

While the royal dinners, yacht races, and glittering social gatherings provided a glamorous backdrop to the Tsar's visit, they also created an important opportunity to strengthen the Anglo-Russian diplomatic and political alliance.

On the morning of 3 August, the Tsar asked the British Foreign Secretary, Sir Edward Grey, to call on him on board the *Shtandart*. In a memorandum written later that week, Grey recorded what he had discussed with the Tsar. 'The Tsar expressed great satisfaction' he wrote, 'that the Convention had stood so well the test of difficulties in Persia'. The British and the Russians both saw Persia as being central to their security and long-term interests in Central Asia and in India. In true imperial style, the Persian government was not consulted about this agreement and, much to their fury, only learned about it after it had been signed.

According to Grey's Memorandum, the Tsar was 'most cordial in his expressions of his pleasure that the Convention had confirmed and strengthened the good relations between us'. After the pleasantries were over, Grey asked the Tsar if he could speak freely on the Persian Question and Nicholas readily assented.

He told the Tsar that there was a section of British parliamentary and public opinion that was not well disposed towards Russia, believing that the Russians were determined to establish a military occupation in the northern part of Persia, which was within the Russian sphere of influence. The fact that no Russian troops had even been sighted there had temporarily quelled anti-Russian sentiments in Britain, but he wanted to warn the Tsar that these fears and prejudices existed and were a reality.

He also expressed concerns that these negative attitudes might cause a reaction in Russia, where 'a corresponding section of Russian opinion might be apprehensive that what had been happening in Persia might become unfavourable to Russia'.

The Tsar listened carefully to what Grey was telling him and reassured him that Russia would stand by the 1907 agreement between the two countries and had absolutely no intention of undermining it, so long as Britain honoured its commitments and obligations.

Later that day, the Tsar's Foreign Minister, Count Izvolsky, gave an important interview to a correspondent from the *Daily Telegraph* in which he justified Russian behaviour in Persia. He stressed the importance of the new cooperation between Britain and Russia in resolving areas of tension in Central Asia. The interview took place on board the *Polar Star*, where Count Izvolsky was staying during the Cowes visit. As the journalist entered the Minister's rooms, he noticed two bronze busts of King Edward and Queen Alexandra on prominent display. These had been presented to Izvolsky earlier that day by the King and Queen and the Minister seemed highly delighted with his new gifts.

Izvolsky said that he had had a very productive discussion with the British Foreign Secretary earlier in the day and that 'the understanding between Britain and Russia was grounded on the firm basis that while they had no conflicting interests, they had increasingly powerful interests in common'. He was confident that any diplomatic problems in Europe could be resolved through peaceful negotiations. He stressed that the two countries had an important role in working together to avoid a future war in Europe and that their alliance was a peaceful one and should not be seen as a threat to any other country.

Germany was the great spectre at the Cowes feast, but neither Britain nor Russia wanted to mention the country by name. The growing power of Germany haunted the waking hours of the King, the Tsar and their Ministers. Although the Kaiser himself was not present at Cowes in 1909, the sleek schooner yachts at the Regatta that summer - the Kaiser's *Meteor IV* and the Herr Krupp's *Germania* - were a constant and visible reminder of Germany's competitiveness and industrial might.

The *Daily Telegraph* journalist, once back on shore, ran into what he described as a 'group of distinguished Russians who were discussing with great enthusiasm the speech of the Tsar at the banquet on the previous evening'. They were unanimous in proclaiming that the single most important event to have taken place in Cowes that week was the Tsar's favourable mention of the Deputies of the Duma. They declared that they had not expected Nicholas to mention the Duma, but the fact that he had chosen to speak positively about its members was proof of his commitment to liberal reform. This was despite the daily pressures on him from the reactionary elements back home in Russia to suppress the Assembly. If Cowes had set the seal on the Anglo-Russian alliance, it was also the place where it appeared to many Russians that the Tsar was supporting and endorsing the country's newly-won democratic freedoms.

The newspapers in Germany published numerous reports on the Tsar's visit to Cowes. The conservative leaning *Kreuz Zeitung* noted that the Tsar had stressed the peaceful objectives of Russian foreign policy. This was contrasted favourably with the bellicose references that King Edward had made in his speech about the power of the British fleet.

The *Lokal-Anzeiger*, a newspaper which often expressed the official German government viewpoint, stated rather acerbically that 'it is curious that France was not mentioned at Cowes nor England at Cherbourg', seeing this as an attempt to disguise the true nature of the new emerging alliance between Britain, France and Russia.

The Liberal leaning *Vossische Zeitung* took a different position and saw no menace in the new alliance, 'as long as no serious attempt is made to isolate Germany, which by the way, would probably be futile'.

In Russia, all the newspapers were enthusiastic in their praise for the Cowes visit, except for the two pro-German papers, *Golos Pravdy* and the *Herold* which ran short, sour articles about the new friendship between Britain and Russia. The mainstream Russian press described the meeting as being of historic importance. The Russian Foreign Office issued a statement: 'Anglo-Russian friendship will be the basis of Russian foreign policy. All misunderstandings in Central Asia are definitely removed. The Anglo-Russian Entente will always be a guarantee of peace and progress in Europe'.

The French press was equally delighted by the success of the meeting taking place on the Isle of Wight. The *République Française* was clear that this built on the earlier Franco-Russian Alliance. 'Now that the Entente Cordiale has become the Triple Entente' it reported, 'equilibrium and conciliation in Europe is steadier than ever'.

British newspapers echoed French media enthusiasm for the visit. The *Pall Mall Gazette* praised the Tsar for 'striving to do his duty in difficulties which might well daunt the most consummate political genius who was ever called on to discharge so Herculean a task'. The *Daily Telegraph* stated that the English people bid 'the Tsar and Russia a hearty Godspeed upon the course to which destiny has called them'.

29

Wednesday 4 August 1909

That morning the haunting chant of the Russian Orthodox prayer 'Te Deum' echoed across the decks of the imperial yacht. This most sacred piece of Russian music was being performed in honour of the Tsar's mother, the Dowager Empress Maria, whose 'Name Day' it was on 4 August. Although she was not with them on this trip to Cowes, the entire imperial family gathered in the chapel of the *Shtandart* to join in a service of prayer and thanksgiving.

The chapel was equipped with a semi-circular iconostasis which held six painted icons on either side of the royal door opening onto the altar. Father Dobrovolsky of the Holy Synod led the prayers as the imperial family stood and kneeled around him. The verses, intoned in 'Church Slavonic', floated out across the calm waters of the Solent.

Later that morning, the Tsar received a deputation of officers from the Scots Greys on board the imperial yacht. He was wearing the full uniform of the regiment, in his role as its Colonel-in-Chief. This was an honour conferred on him by Queen Victoria when he had married Alix in 1894. Nicholas took his role very seriously, maintaining a close personal interest in the regiment and its activities. When he visited Scotland, in 1896, he made sure that he was dressed in the Scots Greys' striking scarlet, gold and black uniform. On that occasion, he was accompanied from Leith to Balmoral by a guard of honour drawn from the regiment.

In 1902, Nicholas had posed for a portrait in his uniform as the Colonel-in-Chief of the regiment. Holding his black bearskin hat in his left arm, the Tsar stands full square at the centre of the picture, staring confidently ahead. He seems to be making intense eye contact with the viewer. The artist was Valentin Serov, one of Russia's most successful portrait painters and a proponent of the Russian school of realist art. The painting now hangs in the regiment's museum in Edinburgh and is the only example of Serov's work anywhere in Britain.

The Tsar remained Colonel-in-Chief of the Scots Greys until his murder in 1918. To this day, his memory is honoured and held in great esteem. The Russian imperial anthem is still played at the regimental Christmas dinner and in the year 2000, an icon of the Tsar was presented to the Royal Scots Dragoon Guards, the successor regiment to the Scots Greys. It accompanied the Dragoon Guards into battle in Iraq in 2003.

While the Tsar was entertaining the officers of the Scots Greys, King Edward decided to go ashore in Cowes. This had always been his summer playground and he had been a regular visitor at Cowes Week since he was a young man. This year, his official duties in connection with the visit by the Russian imperial family meant that his usual social whirl had been more restricted than normal. He was determined, therefore, to make up for lost time.

The King landed at Trinity Wharf in East Cowes, arriving from the *Victoria and Albert* in a purple lined barge. His yacht, *Alberta*, was moored alongside the wharf and Edward climbed out of the barge and onto the *Alberta*. From here he made his way to the landing platform, where a crowd of around twenty ladies sitting on campstools were delighted to see him. They had been gathered there since the early hours of the morning in a spirit of what was described as 'quiet resolution'. They were a determined group and were eager to catch a glimpse of the two royal families, however long they had to wait. After a three-hour wait, their patience was finally rewarded. They gave the King a resounding cheer and he good-naturedly acknowledged their greetings. He then got into the royal car, with his favourite wire-haired fox terrier sandwiched between him and his equerry.

Edward's plan that morning was to make a call on Consuelo Montagu, the Duchess of Manchester, at Egypt House in Cowes. She was one of the most glamourous of all the King's inner circle, a Cuban-American lady who was well connected to both the Spanish aristocracy and American plutocracy. In 1892, she had married George Montagu, the eighth Duke of Manchester, a classic example of a rich American heiress marrying into the upper echelons of British society. Edward adored her and was devastated when she died in November 1909, only three months after their meeting in Cowes.

The King spent over an hour sitting on the lawn at Egypt House and chatting with Consuelo and her guests. He was persuaded to play a game of croquet, and appeared to be in the best of spirits, laughing and joking with everyone around him. He then returned to the royal yacht for a late lunch. The remainder of the day was going to be a busy one, as the Tsar and Tsarina had decided to go ashore and visit Osborne House.

Later that afternoon, a large racing yacht sailed up the Medina river towards Trinity Pier. Following closely behind it was the royal barge and a convoy of patrol boats. On board were the King, the Tsar, the Queen, the Tsarina and the Prince of Wales. The three men in the royal party were all dressed in identical yachting costumes, wearing white caps, navy-blue jackets, white drill trousers, and white boots.

News spread about the imminent arrival of the Tsar. The waiting crowds, including many journalists and the indomitable group of twenty ladies with footstools in hand, rushed to the gates of Trinity Wharf. All was expectation and excitement.

Outside the gates of the wharf, several motor cars were lined up, as if waiting to receive the royal guests. Sir John Fisher, the First Sea Lord, had also arrived wearing his full ceremonial uniform. It was clear to the crowd that this was the place where the Tsar was going to step ashore. People pressed ever closer and began to cheer with their cries ringing out across the waters of the Medina River. Then to everyone's surprise, and disappointment, the royal flotilla swept past them.

This had all been an elaborate security ploy. Arrangements had instead been made for the royal party to land at Kingston Wharf, the private landing stage of the Royal Naval College at Osborne, a mile upriver. The waiting cars and the presence of Sir John Fisher were a carefully-planned decoy. The journalists amongst the crowd rushed for their bikes in order to get to Kingston Wharf, but by the time they arrived it was too late. The Tsar and Tsarina had already left for Osborne.

Kingston Wharf provided perfect privacy and security. On landing at the wharf, three cars were waiting for the royal party. One was a cream coloured open car, and the other two were painted in black, one of which was totally enclosed. The Tsar and the King quickly clambered into the closed car while the rest of the party travelled in the other two.

There were only a few people around to witness the passing vehicles. At the crossroads, where the speeding cars had to slow down, there were a couple of men positioned wearing serge suits and yachting caps and trying very hard not to look like policemen. The cars entered the Osborne estate through the 'Captains' Gate'.

As this was taking place, a small launch from the *Shtandart* moored alongside Trinity Wharf. On board was the five-year-old Tsarevich and his four sisters. The Grand Duchesses were all dressed in matching white blouses and skirts, with light grey veils drawn around their straw hats. The Tsarevich was dressed in a white sailor suit and cap, decorated with the black and yellow striped ribbon of the *Shtandart*.

He was described by one newspaper correspondent as 'a chubby little fellow who is obviously the darling of his sisters' and by another journalist as 'a jolly looking boy, brown and merry'. At this time his haemophilia was not widely known outside close court circles and it would be another three years, after his near-death at the imperial hunting lodge at Spala, before rumours began to spread to the wider public about the fragility of the Tsarevich's health.

The children were helped ashore from the boat and, to the delight of the waiting crowd, spent a few minutes wandering around a small patch of ground near the pier entrance. They then climbed into a couple of cars that were waiting for them. The Grand Duchesses Olga and Tatiana were in the front car, which was an open saloon, and the Tsarevich followed in the second, fully-covered vehicle, together with Maria and Anastasia. A Scotland Yard detective rode on the running board of the Tsarevich's car.

As the two vehicles drove through the gate of Trinity Pier, the crowd erupted into enthusiastic cheers. These were warmly reciprocated by the imperial children. Tatiana acknowledged the greetings with 'a winning smile and the prettiest of bows'. The Tsarevich looked altogether more serious and as his car passed through the gate, he gave the crowd a salute, staring gravely at all the people gathered on either side of the road with wide-open eyes, full of curiosity.

As the two cars sped along the road towards Osborne Cottage, two of the girls produced cameras and began taking photographs of the scenes around them. All the Romanov children were great camera enthusiasts and systematically recorded every aspect of their daily lives, including their trips to the Crimea and their voyages on the imperial yacht.

Isolated in their own private world, the camera lenses became their eyes into an alternative reality. Their photographs survived their brutal deaths and remain today, as vivid testimonies to the hopes and thwarted dreams of five children for whom the twentieth century seemed to promise so much but delivered only tragedy and death.

Osborne Cottage stands on the edge of the Osborne royal estate, with an entrance leading from York Avenue. In 1909, it was home to Princess Beatrice and her children. It is an intimate and sheltered retreat, and the Romanov children happily played games on the lawn with Princess Beatrice, and Princess Patricia of Connaught.

Meanwhile, the Tsar and Tsarina were visiting the Naval College which then stood in the grounds of Osborne House. They were given a private tour by the Commanding Officer, Captain Arthur Christian, and by Prince Edward, the eldest son of the Prince and Princess of Wales. Twenty-seven years later he would briefly become King Edward VIII before abdicating in December 1936 due to his relationship with the American divorcee, Mrs Wallis Simpson.

Queen Victoria had stipulated in her will that Osborne House and its estate should remain within the ownership of the royal family.

However, nobody in the royal family wanted to live there, apart from Osborne Cottage, which became the property of Princess Beatrice, and Kent House, which became the home of Princess Louise. King Edward seems to have had few fond memories of Osborne House. In 1902, he bequeathed the palace and its grounds to the nation, although the private apartments of Queen Victoria on the first floor of the Pavilion wing were retained as a museum in her memory. The rest of the House was turned into a Convalescent Home for military officers.

The Royal Naval College was opened in 1903, and its buildings were constructed around the former stable block at Osborne House. Boys were admitted at the age of thirteen, following a rigorous academic test. They then completed six terms at the College as junior naval cadets, before continuing their education and naval training at the Royal Naval College in Dartmouth. The College had a tough reputation and many of its former pupils, including the young Prince Edward, did not particularly enjoy their time there.

Prince Edward had arrived earlier in the day by torpedo boat from Dartmouth, where he was now studying. Looking handsome in his cadet uniform, he had been driven straight to the Naval College to be warmly greeted by the two royal families.

The young Prince now proceeded to show the Tsar and Tsarina the gymnasium, his old bed and study, and the room where he used to do his school 'prep' work. They were both particularly fascinated by the dormitory where he used to sleep and asked a lot of questions. The Tsar seemed to be in his element and joked in English with a light-hearted fluency. The Tsarina was described by the British press as looking 'stately, handsome and dignified' during the tour though Prince Edward was struck by 'the sad expression on her face'. In later years, he remembered the visit with great vividness.

'This was the only time that I ever saw the Tsar', he later recalled. 'I do remember being astonished at the elaborate police guard thrown around his every movement. This certainly made me glad that I was not a Russian Prince'.

The Tsar laconically wrote in his diary that he 'had looked over the newly constructed Naval College' but as usual made absolutely no reference to what he really thought about the place.

The imperial children now joined the party. Prince Edward was struck by how the Tsarevich stared at him with 'large frightened eyes' and seemed to want to avoid talking to him. He was enchanted, though, by the pretty Grand Duchess Tatiana. She struck him as more sensitive and caring than her elder sister, Olga, and was clearly devoted to her young brother.

After the tour of the College, Nicholas and Alexandra visited Queen Victoria's private apartments. These were specially unlocked for the imperial couple. The Tsarina was particularly keen to see the bedroom where Victoria had died. This was now a shrine to the memory of the late Queen. It contained a huge bronze memorial plaque erected on the wall in her memory, and an altar constructed from a chest of drawers, draped with a cloth and supporting a cross and two candlesticks. The blinds were kept permanently drawn, which added to the funereal aspect of the room.

Alix lingered here for a while, lost in her own private thoughts. There was a tremor in her voice when she eventually spoke, recalling the happy times that she had spent at Osborne with her beloved grandmother. She said that she found it hard to accept that 'The Queen has gone and that we will never see her anymore'.

Before they left Osborne, the imperial couple visited the state apartments and the dining room, where Alix's mother, Princess Alice, had been married on 1 July 1862. This had been a gloomy wedding ceremony, overshadowed by the death in the previous year of Prince Albert.

The original plan had been for Princess Alice and Prince Louis of Hesse to marry in great pomp and style, but these arrangements were abandoned after Albert's death and a simple ceremony at Osborne was substituted. The dining room was cleared of furniture and an altar was set up beneath Franz Winterhalter's portrait of the royal couple and their children.

The Queen was overcome with grief throughout the wedding ceremony and wrote, 'I restrained my tears and had a great struggle all through, but I remained calm'. It was as though death stalked the feast, a portent of the tragedy which was to later befall Princess Alice. Thirty-two years later, Alice's daughter, Alix, would be married in St Petersburg. That wedding was similarly overshadowed by death and mourning, and would be by seen, by many Russians, as a sign of ill fortune for the Romanov dynasty.

On the wall of the Queen's dining room Alix saw the portrait by Heinrich von Angeli of the Hesse family, completed following the death of her mother in 1878. Both Alix and her sister, Elizabeth, appear in the painting, along with their parents and her brother, Prince Ernest. Alix paused in front of it, her head bowed, as if saying a quiet prayer.

Before their departure for Barton Manor, where the King was staying and where a royal tea awaited them, the Tsar insisted on signing the visitor's book at Osborne. His signature was delivered with a greater flourish and flamboyance than the bland words that he wrote in his diary that night. 'I saw the palace of the deceased Queen where I stayed fifteen years ago', is all that he recorded that night.

As they boarded their cars for the short ride to Barton, the Tsarevich suddenly displayed a great interest in the car belonging to Sir Edward Henry, the Commissioner of the London Metropolitan Police. He clambered all over it, tried to turn the steering wheel, and refused to leave the driver's seat. He was fascinated by the vehicle and insisted on travelling in it to Barton Manor. When asked to move into the official car, in which he was meant to be travelling, he refused every request to do so. At the age of five Alexei was already demonstrating the wilful stubbornness that was to become a feature of his character as he grew older.

In order to get the party moving, the Police Commissioner offered his car to the child for the rest of the visit, on the condition that he was accompanied by an official driver and by Alexei's sailor-nanny, Andrei Derevenko. The Tsarevich immediately agreed to this. Derevenko, a petty officer on board the *Shtandart*, had been looking after Alexei for two years by the time they visited Cowes. The Tsar and Tsarina had complete trust in him, and he was adored by Alexei.

Derevenko's main role in life was to ensure that no harm would ever befall the fragile heir to the throne. However, when the Revolution broke out in 1917, he quickly betrayed his former employers and, according to some reports, he used to take a delight in humiliating Alexei in front of former members of the court. The bewildered and frightened boy did not know how to respond.

In the summer of 1909, however, all this lay eight years in the future. As Sir Edward Henry's car pulled away from Osborne House and headed towards Barton Manor, the little Tsarevich could be seen sitting proudly in his seat, with Derevenko next to him, a protective arm around the boy's shoulder.

Barton Manor formed part of the Osborne estate. It had been owned by Winchester College for over four hundred years, but was sold to Queen Victoria in 1845 for £18,500. This was the same year that the Queen and Prince Albert acquired Osborne House. The entire house was remodelled to suit Albert's tastes and reflected his own personal sense of design.

The interior of the house was gutted, and new kitchens and farm buildings were added. Attractive terraced gardens were laid out, and these included a pond on which guests could skate during the winter months. The external walls and chimneys were largely preserved in their original style, with brickwork that matched the original as far as possible.

During Queen Victoria's reign, Barton Manor was mainly used to accommodate members of the royal household. The Queen herself never stayed there. However, after her death, King Edward decided that he would dispose of Osborne but retain Barton. It thus became his retreat on the Isle of Wight, a place where he used to enjoy entertaining his personal guests in privacy and seclusion.

All these factors therefore made Barton an ideal venue for hosting the Russian imperial family during their visit. The private location of the estate meant that the Tsar's security and safety could be assured with a minimum of fuss and bother.

The party spent the rest of the afternoon at Barton Manor. A Persian carpet was spread out on the terrace, and an Edwardian high tea was served. This included scones, strawberry jam and fresh cream, along with cucumber, salmon, and egg and cress sandwiches, Victoria sponge cakes, and mini sausage rolls. Comfortable wicker chairs were scattered across the lawn. A small blue and white pitched tent provided further shade, with a table on which stood cool jugs of lemonade and ginger beer. Refreshing cups of Darjeeling and Assam tea accompanied the food.

Formal photographs were now taken of the two families by Arthur William Debenham, a portrait photographer and miniature painter with studios in nearby Ryde and Sandown. These photographs have become iconic images of that final reunion between the ruling houses of the British and Russian Empires.

All the photographs were taken against the north-facing wall of Barton Manor, which still exists today and looks exactly as it did in the summer of 1909. In one of the photographs, the Tsar stands with a walking stick in his right hand, with Prince George at his side. The Prince of Wales holds the Tsar's right arm tightly. The two men are dressed in the same outfits with white trousers, dark blazers, and yachting caps. They look almost identical, something which greatly amused the Tsar.

Another photograph is entitled 'The Royal Gathering at Osborne', although it was taken at Barton Manor. This is easily the most famous image of the imperial visit to the Isle of Wight. The Russian and British royal families are grouped together with the Tsar and the King at the centre, the Queen next to the Tsar, and the Tsarina alongside the King. The four Grand Duchesses, dressed all in white, are in a cluster close to the Tsarina and Prince George. He has his arm affectionately around the Grand Duchess Maria. The Tsarevich sits at the feet of the King and the Tsar. On the far left of the group stands Prince Edward, wearing his full naval cadet uniform.

A third photograph shows the Tsar and Prince George, together with their two sons, Alexei and Edward. George's hands rest affectionately on the shoulders of the little Tsarevich, while the young Prince Edward leans in close to the Tsar.

It is hard looking at these photographs not to recall the events that happened less than a decade after this gathering at Osborne and Barton Manor. Here were two families, related through ties of blood and marriage, enjoying time together on a balmy August afternoon. It is difficult to believe that Prince George, who in the photographs appears to lavish so much affection on his cousins, would one day be complicit in denying the entire Romanov family sanctuary and refuge in Britain.

On the return journey to Kingston Quay, the King's car, with Edward and Nicholas on board, was nearly involved in a collision with a private vehicle car close to the Prince of Wales Hotel in East Cowes. Fortunately, the royal chauffeur skilfully swerved to one side and the car escaped without a scratch. The King and the Tsar took it all in good humour and smiled warmly at a very shaken policeman who was standing by the side of the road. He had also narrowly missed being hit by the other car.

During the afternoon, the news that the Tsar and Tsarina were on the Island had spread like wildfire. By the time that the royal party embarked at Kingston Quay to return to the *Shtandart*, both sides of the Medina river were lined with crowds of eager sightseers. Many people had also hired boats so that they could get a better view of the royal launch as it made its way back out to sea.

Cheers and waves greeted the Tsar from all sides. According to a reporter from the *Daily Mirror*, whose boat passed within a few feet of the royal launch, the Tsar looked very pleased with this warm reception and 'constantly raised his hat, bowing and smiling as he did so'.

That evening, King Edward, in his role as Patron and Admiral of the Royal Yacht Squadron, hosted a dinner on the *Victoria and Albert* in honour of the Tsar's election as a Squadron member. This was an important occasion for all the parties concerned and a large contingent from the Squadron turned up to celebrate their new colleague. Thirty-eight people sat down for dinner, including the Prince of Wales, the Marquess of Ormonde who was the Commodore of the Squadron, and the Vice Commodore, the Duke of Leeds. Many other senior members of the Squadron were also present.

While the Tsar was being feted and entertained by the King and the members of the Royal Yacht Squadron, the Tsarina hosted a private dinner party on board the *Shtandart*, in honour of Queen Alexandra and Mary, Princess of Wales. The menu included chicken consommé soup, saddle of lamb, parfait of foie gras with truffles, and a mousseline of pears for dessert.

It was described by one local journalist as 'the most illustrious dinner of its kind that has been given in Europe for a very long time'. He went on to conjure up a magnificent picture. 'A three-quarter moon threw its beams in the water in long glistening streams. On deck was the ship's company, brilliant staff officers all a glitter with gold and at a discreet distance groups of the Tsar's imperial guard, tremendously tall and powerful seamen, the gold and blue ribbed ribbon of the service dropping over their shoulders like women's millinery'.

Sitting next to the Tsarina that evening was Lord Charles Spencer, who was at that time the King's most senior courtier. He had a rather different impression of the evening. He thought that the Tsarina was 'tired and lacklustre' and that her conversation was desultory. He noticed that she only ate a few vegetables. The emotional and physical strain of the visit was clearly taking its toll on her. She was ready to return to her life of quiet and seclusion at the Alexander Palace in Tsarskoye Selo.

Wednesday 4 August was the mid-point of Cowes Week. The race to win the Royal Yacht Squadron Cup generated much excitement. This was a 46-mile race, and there were only two competitors, *White Heather* and *Shamrock*. This was a close duel between the two stars of the 1909 season. It looked, at first, that *Shamrock* would win, as she made a splendid start. However, *White Heather* pulled ahead and although closely pursued, she won the race by three minutes.

Another yachting highlight that day was the 47-mile long Emperor's Cup, a race that was sponsored by Kaiser Wilhelm II and organised by the Royal Yacht Squadron. Two German schooner yachts, the *Germania* and the *Susanne*, were the hot favourites to win the race. Although the *Germania* took the lead from the start, and retained it throughout the entire race, her handicap meant that the overall winner was the *Susanne*. The *Cicely* came in second.

On shore, the Cowes Week social scene continued its elegant whirl with gatherings in the gardens of the Royal Yacht Squadron, long lazy lunches by the sea, and strolls along the Parade and the High Street in Cowes. Pinnaces carrying messages and passengers sailed back and forth between the yachts moored in the Solent and the various landing stages along the seafront. Consuelo, the Duchess of Manchester, went off from her private landing stage at Egypt House to take lunch on one of the yachts, after the King had left her to meet the Tsar. The Duke of Leeds took a party of his friends on board his yacht *Aries* for a trip around the Island, bringing them back in time for dinner.

In the early afternoon, a group of Russians were at the centre of a minor nautical drama which drew huge crowds of sightseers. A journalist, writing in one of the national yachting magazines, described seeing a Russian steam yacht that had crashed 'right on to the stage of the Royal Yacht Squadron's landing platform and remained there for hours, almost overhanging the off-side edge, braced with hawsers and supported under her bilge by stout wooden struts'.

The amused journalist went on to conjure up a vivid image of the hapless crew, being berated by a succession of 'Muscovite functionaries, generally in pot hats and cut away coats'. The sailors, who were described as 'poor Ivans and Stepans', stood rigidly to attention while they were being harangued by these increasingly angry Russian officials. 'I fancy their reception when the tide did enable them to return to their ship was of a sultry nature as it was reported that they nearly drowned their Ambassador!'

This seems unlikely as the Ambassador, Count Benckendorff, was at that time comfortably settled in the Royal Yacht Squadron clubhouse. After several hours, the returning tide ensured that the luckless Russian yacht was finally able to float free from the landing stage.

Later that day, the Russian Foreign Minister, Count Izvolsky, issued an important statement to Reuters. 'Both Sir Edward Grey and I have agreed not to make any public declaration of our recent conversations but as to the outcome of this visit, I can assure you that the Emperor is highly satisfied'. Izvolsky went on to report that Anglo-Russian relations were now on a firm footing, as evidenced by the excellent cooperation over recent events in Persia, Afghanistan and the Balkans. He stressed that the aim of the Anglo-Russian alliance was to secure peace in Europe and around the world. 'If trouble does arise' he said, 'England and Russia will exert their influence in the same spirit, a determination to maintain the status quo'.

In a coded warning aimed at Austria-Hungary in particular, he stressed that 'the recent crisis over the Bosnia-Herzegovina situation, has been happily overcome, and so long as no European power manifests any particular ambition on this terrain, there is absolutely no reason to think that any complications may arise'.

As this statement was being issued, and as the King and the Tsar took tea with their families at Barton Manor, a gathering of army territorials was taking place on Salisbury Plain, fifty-five miles north of the Isle of Wight. This was the most important military gathering of the summer. There were infantry brigades from across the South of England, including from Hampshire, the South West and London, as well as a large contingent from the Junior Officers' Training Corps and five yeomanry regiments. Altogether this amounted to thousands of men on manoeuvres, accompanied by field artillery batteries, field ambulances, supply columns and corps of engineers.

It was an impressive display of the country's readiness for war, should such an event ever materialise. Izvolsky's statement, printed in all the major newspapers in Britain, Russia, Germany and France, would have assured most readers that a war in Europe was a distant and remote threat, an event that the major powers would manage to avoid as they had successfully done for most of the previous century.

The British press was much less sanguine, however, about the growing threat to British security posed by a new and confident Germany. Alongside the reports on the Tsar's visit to the Isle of Wight there were articles in all the major newspapers about German domination of the air. In that first week of August 1909, the giant airship, Zeppelin II, set out on its maiden flight from Frankfurt to Cologne with Count Zeppelin in command. At 450 feet in length, with a new aluminium frame, it had seventeen gas compartments, and was powered by twin Daimler motors. Another huge airship, designed by Professor Schutte of Danzig, was under construction in Mannheim with enhanced engineering features that enabled it to complete quick mid-air turns and stay in the air for thirty hours at a time.

This burst of advanced airship construction in Germany alarmed the British. On 4 August 1909, the government announced that the engineering company *Vickers and Maxim* of Barrow-in-Furness had been commissioned to construct an airship that would outperform its German rivals. At 600 feet in length and 100 feet in breadth it would be twice the size of the Zeppelin and the Schutte airships. In addition to the rapid construction of this huge airship, the War Office announced that it would press ahead with trialling the new Wright aeroplanes at Aldershot.

Izvolsky's statement from Cowes would certainly have reassured a wider public about the importance of the Anglo-Russian alliance. However, unlike the nineteenth century, it was no longer Russia that was the primary threat to Britain's global interests, but a newly resurgent Germany.

30

Thursday 5 August 1909

The day dawned fine and sunny, with hardly a breath of wind stirring the air. This was perfect summer weather, the sea as calm as a millpond. On the final day of the Tsar's visit both the Isle of Wight and the Solent were flooded in glorious sunshine.

At noon, deputations from various Corporations and Chambers of Commerce came aboard the imperial yacht and were received on the quarter deck of the *Shtandart*. General Baron de Fredericks, the Minister of the Imperial Household and Domains, announced the arrival of the Tsar and Tsarina. The Tsar was in the uniform of a Royal Navy Admiral of the Fleet, while the Tsarina wore a white dress with a waistband of pink roses and a white hat trimmed with a large ostrich feather.

The first delegation to make its presentation to the imperial couple was that from the Corporation of the City of London. The Recorder, who gave the speech, warmly welcomed them both to Britain and recalled 'with pride the occasion, now more than 35 years ago when your revered grandfather, Tsar Alexander II, was graciously pleased to accept at the Guildhall, an address of welcome from the City of London'.

He went on to express his confident belief that 'this visit is a happy augury of a firm and lasting continuation of the friendly relations now existing between Russia and Britain. We pray that this happy unanimity may prevail for all time'. The address was enclosed in an 18-carat golden casket, which was then handed to the Tsar by the Lord Mayor of London.

The casket itself was decorated with a miniature jewelled replica of the Russian coronation crown, supported by four Russian eagles. The emblem of the City of London was represented on the casket by the City Dragons, and there were also the emblazoned arms and enamelled views of the Guildhall and Mansion House.

The Tsar expressed his delight with the sentiments in the speech and said that he and his family would greatly prize the beautiful casket, in which a scroll of the address had been carefully rolled up. He thanked the British people for the warm welcome that he and his family had received during their visit. He hoped that the new spirit of cooperation between the two countries would strengthen peace and civilisation throughout the world.

These were no pious sentiments. Nicholas was a firm advocate of promoting international peace. He had been instrumental in launching the First Hague Peace Conference, which had opened in May 1899 and was responsible for setting up a permanent Court of Arbitration to resolve international disputes, as well as setting out a detailed code of behaviour for combatant armies in times of war. This outlawed the execution of soldiers who had surrendered and the bombing or looting of undefended cities. The subsequent Hague Peace Conference of 1907 built on the work established by the 1899 Conference and both events prefigured the later work of the League of Nations and the United Nations.

Following this, it was the turn of the Corporation of Portsmouth to deliver a short address. There were only four people in the delegation, including the Mayor. He said how delighted the town had been to welcome a visit by Russian battleships, as well as a delegation from the Duma. This was followed by addresses from the Chambers of Commerce in London and Liverpool, two cities which both had long standing commercial relations with St Petersburg.

The growth in the Russian economy and the rise of a new urban middle class meant that British manufacturers and trading companies now looked forward confidently to a major expansion in business links between the two countries. Before the delegations left, the Tsar and Tsarina shook hands with their visitors and signed their names in the autograph books that were eagerly proffered to them.

At this point, the Tsar conferred Russian imperial decorations on over thirty British courtiers, naval commanders and civic officials who had been involved in his visit. These included the Lord Chamberlain - Lord Althorp - who received the Order of the White Eagle, and Admiral Sir William May, the Commander-in-Chief of the Home Fleet, who was awarded the Imperial Order of Saint Alexander Nevsky.

Alongside giving high-level decorations to the admirals and courtiers, the Tsar did not overlook the police who had protected the imperial family during their visit. He presented the Chief Constable of the Island, Captain Adam Connor, with the Order of Saint Stanislaus, and gave him a gold cigarette case, with the imperial arms set in precious stones. The Deputy Chief Constable of the Isle of Wight, Superintendent Gallaway, was given a similar award and a pair of gold and diamond cufflinks. The Tsar also conferred silver medals on four officers from the Water Police Force of the London Metropolitan Police, who had all been employed on guard boat duties during the Russian imperial visit.

The Tsar gave a donation of £1,000 (around £115,000 in today's money) with instructions that this should be distributed amongst the poor on the Isle of Wight. The Russian Ambassador, Count Benckendorff, wrote to the Chairman of the Cowes District Council, Charles Brown, informing him that the Tsar was giving £600 to the poor of East Cowes and Cowes. A second letter went to the Mayor of Newport, with a cheque for £400, asking him to distribute this in Newport and other towns on the Island.

It was three in the afternoon by the time that the *Shtandart* was ready to depart on her long journey back to Russia. Sailors from the British cruiser *Bellerophon* came across to unshackle the Imperial yacht's bridle. A journalist from *The Times* watched this happening in the middle of what he described as a typical Cowes scene, with 'the sun shining brilliantly, the races in progress, and scores of graceful yachts in motion or at anchor'.

It seems that the Tsar was in no rush to leave Cowes. In celebration of his visit, he had decided to award the first, second and third prizes for the 15-metre Royal Yacht Squadron race. He was therefore keen to know who had won the race before his departure. This was a 23-mile race around the Warner Lightship and back from the Eastern Mark. The King of Spain's yacht *Hispania* was in the lead for the first half of the race, but eventually lost to *Ma'oona*, a nimble sailing ketch built by the Scottish shipyard of James McAlister and Sons and launched in 1907. The Spanish yacht *Tuiga* took second place and another Scottish-built yacht, *Mariska*, came in third.

Shortly before half past three, signals were exchanged between the two royal yachts, *Shtandart* and *Victoria and Albert*, indicating that it was now time for the imperial family to depart. The Tsar and Tsarina appeared on deck, with the Tsarevich and a couple of his sisters. One of them had a camera and was busy taking photographs of the *Victoria and Albert*. The King and Queen, together with the Prince and Princess of Wales, stood on the upper deck of the *Victoria and Albert*, as the propellers of the *Shtandart* began to turn and the Russian yacht edged away from her moorings.

Three British naval cruisers, *Indomitable, Inflexible* and *Invincible,* were the official escorts for the *Shtandart* and its Russian convoy. They now positioned themselves with their bows facing towards Spithead. The *Bellerophon* fired a royal salute of twenty-one guns, which the *Admiral Makarov* returned with gusto. There was cheering and cap waving from the sailors on both the Russian and British naval vessels. The British national anthem was played on board the *Shtandart* and the Russian imperial anthem on the British ships.

This stately nautical procession now moved into the Cowes Roads and then headed out towards Spithead and the open sea. In the lead were the three British cruisers. Behind them followed the *Shtandart*. Immediately behind her came the second imperial yacht, the *Polar Star*. The two Russian destroyers, *Admiral Makarov* and *Rurik,* positioned themselves on either side of the *Shtandart*.

It was a magnificent and stirring sight, and one never to be witnessed again. Thousands of visitors on the Isle of Wight lined the coast to watch the departure of the Russian imperial family. Though nobody knew it, this was Britain's farewell to the Romanov dynasty. It was the last time that a Russian imperial yacht would sail in British waters and the final time that a Tsar would be a guest on British soil.

The Romanovs' final glimpse of Britain would have been of the coast of the Isle of Wight, with its seaside resorts, wooded hills, sandy beaches and rocky bays, and racing yachts skimming across the blue waves of the Solent. As the cortège of ships moved ahead at a speed of fifteen knots, there were royal salutes from the ships anchored at Spithead and, from the nearby military fort, the guns thundered out, the echoes fading and the smoke evaporating in the silvery summer air.

A journalist from *The Times* conjured up a poetic and elegiac description of this last voyage, described the sea as being 'shot with ever changing gleams of green turning into gold, as it caught the beams of the setting sun, and its surface was so calm, that as the great warships ploughed their way onward, the bow waves raised by them seemed to stretch away on either hand to a distance that seemed endless to the eye'.

As the late afternoon sunshine turned into the dusk of early evening, a parting between the British and Russian ships took place. The British cruisers made a complete turn so that they faced in the opposite direction to the Russian convoy. A last royal salute of twenty-one guns was fired. The two groups of vessels were within a mile of each other and as each of the British cruisers passed the *Shtandart*, the band of the imperial yacht played the Russian national anthem and her crew cheered lustily. The Tsar stood on the bridge and acknowledged the farewells of the British ships.

The fine weather that blessed the Tsar's departure from the Isle of Wight was seen by many as a positive sign for the future of the relationship between Britain and Russia. Several newspapers in both Britain and Russia described the visit to the Isle of Wight as a 'Happy Omen'.

The Tsar also clearly felt that this was the case. In a message issued to the British people on his departure from Cowes, he stated that he had been deeply impressed by his visit to Britain and was grateful for the 'affectionate welcome accorded to him and the Empress by the royal family, and the reception given him by the magnificent naval force which saluted him at Cowes. The attitude of British statesmen, people and Press, are all happy auguries for the future.'

The statement went on to say, 'It is the Emperor's firm desire and belief that this all too brief visit can only bear the happiest fruit in promoting the friendliest feelings between the governments and peoples of the two countries'. This message set the seal on the importance to the Tsar of his visit to the Isle of Wight. There is no doubt that, in his view, it marked a high point in the growing partnership between Russia and Britain in the early twentieth century.

The Tsar's departure from Cowes did nothing to dampen the lively yachting and social events taking place that day both at sea and on land. In the afternoon, as the Tsar's yacht slipped its moorings, Sir Whittaker and Lady Ellis gave a garden party at Solent Lodge in Cowes. The garden afforded fine views over the sea. This gave the many guests who dropped by the chance to watch the departure of the *Shtandart*. Sir Whittaker had been Lord Mayor of London and the first Mayor of the London Borough of Richmond. Lady Ellis welcomed their guests on the lawn, wearing a dress of mauve muslin and lace trimmed with broderie anglaise, and a large mauve straw hat with matching plumes.

Much of the conversation that day in Cowes was about the success of the Tsar's visit and the new British alliance with Russia. However, there were other stories dominating the news. The Blue Anchor luxury liner *SS Waratah* with 211 passengers and crew on board was officially reported to be missing off the coast of South Africa, while on a voyage between Adelaide and London. The ship was never seen again.

A news story that the Russian Embassy did not want to get into the press appeared on 5 August in all the British papers. A Russian steamer, the *Irkutsk,* had arrived in London from the cholera infected port of St Petersburg. The Captain, Peter Omero, was warned by medical officers from the London Port Sanitary Authority not to permit any of the passengers to disembark. He allowed all of them to leave the ship without any health checks. The Captain was summoned to Tower Bridge Police Court, and in his defence pleaded that he did not understand English

and therefore had been unable to read the notice from the Port Sanitary
Authority. He was fined £20.

31

Aftermath

Friday 6 August was the final day of the Royal Yacht Squadron's Regatta. It was another very hot day across the whole of Britain, with temperatures touching 85°F in parts of the country, and scarcely a breath of wind on the Solent. In Southern Russia, temperatures were reported as reaching 122°F and people were perishing from sunstroke. The fashionable resorts on the Crimean coast, normally packed at this time of the year, were largely deserted as visitors returned to the cooler climates of St Petersburg and Moscow.

There were five racing events in Cowes organised that Friday, and those yachts taking part were all scheduled to compete against vessels in their own class. The schooners had their own race, as did the 23-metre, 15-metre, 8-metre and 7-metre yachts. The King of Spain's cutter, *Hispania*, won the 15-metre race, her second win of the week. The schooner race excited a lot of interest and attention. There was only one second difference between the *Germania* and the *Cicely*, but they both lost to the *Julnar*, built in Southampton in 1909 and owned by Sir Maurice Fitzgerald, the twentieth Knight of Kerry, one of the oldest hereditary peerages in Ireland.

One of the high points of the final day was the race between the two great adversaries of the 1909 season, *Shamrock* and *White Heather*. The two schooner yachts were locked in a continuous duel, with first *White Heather* leading, then *Shamrock* overtaking her. *White Heather* then passed her off Ryde, only to be overtaken by *Shamrock* as they both sailed around the Warner. *White Heather* then made a final pitch for victory and briefly overtook *Shamrock*. However, she was finally beaten by *Shamrock,* in the last minutes of the race.

The King and Queen spent much of the day cruising in the *Britannia.* They left the Cowes Roads around midday and sailed eastwards towards Ryde to get the best views of the yacht races taking place. They returned to the *Victoria and Albert* just before six in the evening. The King was in a relaxed and genial mood as he no longer had to worry about entertaining the Tsar and Tsarina and was therefore able to do exactly as he pleased, with a minimum of protocol and security.

Shortly before the King returned to the *Victoria and Albert*, he and many others were fascinated by the sight of Charles Rolls, one of the founders of the car manufacturer Rolls-Royce, making a balloon ascent from a boat in the Cowes Roads. The intrepid balloonist disappeared towards the mainland. Less than a year later, Rolls was the first person to be killed in a plane accident in Britain, when the tail of his Wright Flyer aircraft broke off during a flying display in Bournemouth.

The Grand Finale of Cowes Week was a splendid firework display which took place on the seafront by the Royal Yacht Squadron and on the barges that were moored further out to sea. It was a lavish and colourful show, culminating in portraits of the Tsar and Tsarina, which dramatically appeared in the dark night sky, 'depicted in lines of fire draped with the Russian national emblems'. Thousands of people crowded on to the seafront to watch the display, while parties and celebrations took place aboard all the yachts in the Solent, illuminated with electric lights and Chinese lanterns of various colours and hues.

One of the most sought-after invitations was to the dinner party hosted by Lady Paget on board the *Margarita.* This was a glittering occasion and the guests included the Princess of Liechtenstein and Admiral Lord Charles Beresford. The witty and entertaining Mr Montagu Guest was also a prominent attendee. He was one of the notable characters at the

Royal Yacht Squadron, described as a great hunter and shrewd collector of many fine paintings, prints, and cameos. He was a beloved member of the Squadron and no summer season was complete without him and his colourful tales.

The firework display and the elegant yachting dinners were described as a fitting end 'for one of the most, if not the most, successful and brilliant Cowes Weeks that has ever been known'.

As fireworks lit up the portraits of the Tsar and Tsarina, and as the *Shtandart* ploughed its way through the grey waves of the North Sea, the Russian War Office announced that successful experiments in wireless telegraphy had been completed between St Petersburg and Sevastopol in the Crimea. This development now opened the way for the construction of wireless stations from the Ural Mountains to the western frontiers of Russia. The War Office in St Petersburg added that these 'may prove very important for military purposes'. The German High Command noted with concern that Russia's military technology and capability was rapidly improving and that there may only be a few years left in which Germany could successfully win a land war against Russia.

On Saturday 7 August, Kaiser Wilhelm II and the Tsar met in Kiel, a major port on Germany's Baltic coast. Since 1865, it had been home to the German Imperial Navy and in 1909 was also well known for its prestigious Imperial Yacht Club. This had originally been founded in 1887 as the Marine-Regatta-Verein but changed its name to the Imperial Yacht Club when the Kaiser became its Commodore in 1891. The Kaiser was a strong supporter of the Club and moored his own yacht, *Meteor,* in the Club's marina. Since 1882, the Club had organised Kiel's annual yachting week, a summer rival to Cowes Week.

The German High Sea Fleet which had just returned to Kiel after its Atlantic cruise was ordered to take up position outside the harbour in honour of the Tsar's visit. The *Shtandart* reached Kiel after sailing along the 60-mile canal which links the North Sea with the Baltic. The Kaiser was keen to give the Tsar a warm welcome and to assure him that Germany's intentions towards Russia were honourable and peaceful. He was also acutely aware that the visits to both Cherbourg and Cowes had both been highly successful and he therefore needed to show the Tsar that Germany could also be a reliable partner for Russia.

Relations between the two countries had deteriorated since the 1890s. The Kaiser had little respect for the Tsar, whom he described as a 'ninny' and a 'whimperer' and as somebody fit 'only to grow turnips'. The Tsar in return saw Wilhelm as a bully and a narcissistic adventurer, and he had no desire to overturn his friendship with France and Britain in favour of restoring Russia's nineteenth-century alliance with Germany.

The meeting in Kiel was therefore a courtesy call. The Tsar was passing through German waters and it would have been rude of him not to accept the Kaiser's invitation to meet. The discussions were brief, and there was none of the warmth that had characterised the meetings with the French and the British in Cherbourg and Cowes. The German press tried to put a brave face on the encounter in Kiel and many of the newspapers ran bland reports about 'friendly sentiments and the strengthening of peace and friendship between the European family of States'.

Back in Cowes, the yachts and the parties were starting to disperse. It was announced that the King and Queen would return to Portsmouth on the Monday and that the King would leave soon afterwards for Marienbad in Austria-Hungary, where he would take the waters and join the royal and aristocratic social set that was now gathering there for the summer season.

On Wednesday 11 August, a specially convened meeting of the East Cowes and Cowes District Councils took place in the Town Hall in Cowes. Officials made a public announcement about the Tsar's gift of money to the poor of both towns. George Fellows chaired the meeting and declared that 'The Tsar's visit to Cowes would always be remembered and had contributed to the most successful Cowes Week ever'. He went on to say that 'His munificence would be forever gratefully remembered by the poor of both towns'.

Both Councils decided to vote on a formal resolution that would be sent to the Russian Ambassador for forwarding to the Tsar. This would thank the Tsar for his gift to the poor. It rejoiced that 'His Imperial Majesty's short stay at Cowes was attended by such favourable weather and we venture to hope that it may not be long before a visit which leaves such pleasant recollections may be repeated'.

The resolution was approved, but only after a heated debate, when a Mr W. Cochrane, a member of the East Cowes District Council, described in the local press as a 'Socialist dissident', furiously protested and refused to support it. He stoutly maintained that the Tsar was an oppressive tyrant and should never have been made welcome on the Isle of Wight. Eventually he was overruled by the other Councillors and the resolution was passed.

On Saturday 14 August the *Illustrated London News* published a leading article on the Russian imperial visit to the Isle of Wight entitled 'Friends: The British and Russian Sovereigns and their heirs'. The centre pages were devoted to photographs of two royal families at Barton Manor and on board the *Shtandart*. In the same edition of the magazine, there was a cut-away illustration of the hull of one of the new giant luxury liners then being built by the White Star Line in Belfast. Under the heading 'A Floating Town', the article went on to say, 'Every time a new giant liner is launched, the vessel in question is said to mark the limit for size, speed and comfort, yet its successors invariably go a stage further. The liner *Olympic* is such a case and its new sister ship is to be called *Titanic*.'

On 10 April 1912, less than three years after this article was published, the *Titanic* sailed past the Isle of Wight on its maiden voyage to New York. It followed a similar route to that taken by the *Shtandart*, sailing past Cowes and Ryde and then out to the open sea. Five days later, the *Titanic* lay at the bottom of the Atlantic Ocean, together with more than 1,500 of its passengers and crew. The celebrated Isle of Wight photographer, Frank Beken, who took such evocative photographs of the *Shtandart* and other famous yachts during Cowes week 1909, was also on hand to take the iconic photograph of the *Titanic* as it steamed confidently through the Solent, unaware of its impending rendezvous with fate.

The collapse of Imperial Russia has sometimes been compared to the sinking of a great ocean liner. An entire society, with a gilded and entitled aristocracy at its head, sank to the bottom of the sea as completely as did the passengers on the *Titanic*. There is a strange and fearful parallel between the fate of those who sailed in the Solent on the *Shtandart* in the summer of 1909 and those who travelled in those same waters on board the *Titanic* in 1912.

The publishers of the *Illustrated London News* must have deliberately decided to print the two articles in the same edition, in order to associate the luxury and style of the new White Star liners with the power and imperial grandeur of Romanov Russia. The connection between the two eventually had a different and ultimately more tragic association.

In a final irony, the *Illustrated London News* article on the Romanovs referred to the close security that surrounded the imperial Family on the Isle of Wight. It also included a paragraph in its article about the *Titanic* which informed readers that 'modern devices for safeguarding ocean liners could guard passengers and make the liner as safe as home'.

PART

VIII

THE COLLAPSE OF
IMPERIAL RUSSIA AND
THE END OF THE
ANGLO-RUSSIAN
ALLIANCE
1914-1918

32

War and Revolution 1914-1917

The immediate years following the Tsar's return from the Isle of Wight seemed to mark a calmer and more optimistic phase in Russia's history. The Tsar managed to reconcile his authoritarian and anti-democratic tendencies with the need to co-exist with the Third Duma, although it was a more conservative body than its predecessors. Until his assassination in 1911, the Prime Minister, Pyotr Stolypin, proved to be a steady hand at the helm of government and did much to steer the country - and the Tsar - in a more productive direction.

There was also positive news on the economic front. Although the traditional view is that the Russian economy stagnated in this period, there is now evidence to show that certain sections of the economy grew significantly in the years before the First World War and that per capita income was increasing, particularly in the rural areas and amongst the middle classes in cities and towns. In the last decades before the Revolution, average Russian industrial growth was reaching nearly 6% a year, which put Russia ahead of Britain, the US and Germany.

The revolutionary fervour of the 1905-07 period and the anarchist terror of the first years of the twentieth century appeared to have dissipated. Much of this may have been due to the successful suppression of terrorist and revolutionary groups inside Russia by the Okhrana. There does not appear to have been any lack of interest or support for radical political movements and ideologies, but much of the energy for this was now channelled into new forms of expression, particularly in the arts, literature, and theatre.

In this more open environment, a sense of renewed and vigorous creative energy began to emerge. This was the era which saw the arrival of poets like Anna Akhmatova, and Nikolay Gumilyov, and writers such as Maxim Gorky. The composers, Sergei Prokofiev and Igor Stravinsky, made a huge impact on both the Russian and international musical scenes. The pioneer of abstract art, Wassily Kadinsky and the painter and costume designer, Léon Bakst, were acclaimed as pathfinders of a new generation of radical artists bold and confident enough to challenge long-established artistic traditions.

If there was one area in which Russia excelled in the last years of Tsarist rule it was in ballet. Sergei Diaghilev, Léon Bakst and Alexandre Benois founded the *Ballets Russes*, which opened its first season in Paris in 1909 and went on to take the world by storm. The Company never performed in Russia but did more to spread the influence of Russian dance, art, and music than any other Russian cultural activity of the time. The dancers of the *Ballets Russes* were originally drawn from the Imperial Ballet of St Petersburg and trained to meet its exacting standards. Diaghilev merged this fine tradition of classical ballet with innovative dance techniques, costume design, and music, to create a sensational artistic offering. Highly talented and well-trained dancers like Vaslav Nijinsky and Michel Fokine raised the popularity of the *Ballets Russes* to new heights.

It is tempting, when looking back on the final years of Tsarist Russia, to speculate that a revolution was not in fact inevitable. In many ways, it seems that the country was heading in the right direction. There was growing economic prosperity, greater political and personal freedom, a flourishing artistic and cultural scene. Many have blamed the First World War for the destruction of Imperial Russia. They argue that if it had not been for the violent shock and stress that this imposed on the country, the Tsarist regime would have survived and perhaps evolved into a liberal constitutional monarchy.

Over a hundred years after the events of 1917-18, it is hard to know in which direction Russia might have developed without the First World War. In 1913, when the Romanov dynasty celebrated 300 years on the throne of Russia, it looked possible that the regime would survive well into the twentieth century. The reality, though, was much less positive, and many people in government and amongst the ruling elite were growing increasingly concerned about the way the Tsar and his government were running the country. Amongst a wider section of the population, there was growing frustration with the Tsar's limited commitment to democratic reform, and a sense that he was not serious in wanting to create a more liberal society.

Economic growth was unevenly spread, and large parts of the population felt that they were not benefiting from the growing prosperity in the country. There was widespread discontent in the rural areas and huge poverty amongst the industrial workers in the cities. Revolutionary movements may have been less visible, but many students, intellectuals, peasants and workers still felt the attraction of violent political agendas. This was a country which was not at peace with itself, and where social and class resentments may have been muffled, but were still very present. The Romanov dynasty was sitting on a volcano that was ready to erupt.

Pyotr Stolypin had been appointed Prime Minister of Russia in July 1906. He was one of the Tsar's most capable Ministers and understood very clearly the challenges that were facing the country. On taking power he immediately dissolved the First Duma, because of its radical nature and stubborn refusal to work with him and his government. When some of the more radical members fled into exile in the Finnish town of Vyborg and issued a manifesto calling for public resistance and tax evasion, he allowed the authors of the manifesto to return to Russia without any immediate retribution. However, sixty members of the First Duma were eventually sentenced to between three and six months in solitary confinement, some of them in grim conditions with cholera outbreaks due to overcrowding.

A second Duma was appointed, but again this proved to be resistant to working with Stolypin and his government. It was dissolved in June 1907. A third Duma was elected, which drew heavily for its membership on the nobility and the propertied classes. It was a much more conservative body, and finally provided Stolypin with the kind of parliamentary assembly with which he could do business. The Prime Minister was a firm believer in the value of representative government, but he was also a realist and felt strongly that Russia was not ready to adopt a Russian equivalent of the British parliamentary model without significant political, social and economic reforms.

Stolypin therefore began to quietly implement these reforms. He focused on new policies to assist land reform and worked hard to create a class of smallholding landowners who had a stake in the rural economy. He also sought to improve the status of urban labourers and to improve the power of local governments.

Stolypin had survived a vicious assassination attempt on him and his family at his private dacha in 1906. Both his son and his daughter were seriously injured. Thereafter, he took a tough line on terrorism, and he was responsible for introducing a much speedier court system for dealing with suspected terrorists. This led to an increase in the number of executions and a sharp reduction in the number of terror attacks across the country. This had a negative impact on Russia's reputation internationally and led to protests against the Tsar, in both Britain and France, prior to his visits to Cherbourg and Cowes in 1909.

Stolypin was widely disliked by the more reactionary factions at court, who resented his plans to reform the economy and his willingness to work with the Duma. He had also made an implacable enemy of the Tsarina, who by this time was completely in thrall to Grigori Rasputin. Stolypin actively disliked the Siberian holy man and told the Tsar that the man was a rogue and should not be trusted. The Tsarina was infuriated by these accusations and from then on waged a constant war of attrition against Stolypin, even demanding his dismissal.

Nicholas stood his ground and refused to sack his Prime Minister, although he put a stop to the investigations that Stolypin was carrying out into Rasputin's private life. Rumours of wild parties with prostitutes, orgies at the homes of some of the monk's wealthy aristocratic patrons, and frequent drunken escapades were beginning to spread through St Petersburg.

The growing influence that Rasputin now exercised over the imperial family was becoming a matter of real concern not only to Stolypin but also to many members of the Romanov family. The Dowager Empress, Maria, was particularly worried, and felt that the scandals surrounding the Siberian monk posed an existential threat to the future of the dynasty. She raised these worries with her son on several occasions, but he was not prepared to take any action that would upset his wife, or which might threaten the welfare of the young Tsarevich.

The reality was that Rasputin had now become the emotional prop on which the fragile Tsarina depended both for her own spiritual and mental sanity and the health of her son. His critical role was confirmed when Alexei fell seriously ill with a severe haemorrhage at the royal hunting lodge at Spala in Central Poland in October 1912. The imperial doctor, Dr Botkin and Serge Fyodorov, the top surgeon in St Petersburg, had abandoned hope that anything could be done to save the child.

The Court prepared to release official news reports announcing the death of the heir to the throne. In her desperation, the Tsarina sent an urgent message to Rasputin who was then at his home in Siberia. He immediately set out for Spala. Before he did this, he sent a telegram requesting that all conventional medical treatment on the Tsarevich should stop. 'The illness will not be dangerous', he reassured the distraught parents. 'Do not let the doctors make him tired'. In a second telegram he said that all would be well with their son. He had prayed to God, and God had heard his prayers and would save Alexei.

Within a few hours of receiving this message, the bleeding stopped and the Tsarevich began to make a steady recovery. Rasputin's position of trust at the heart of the imperial family was now firmly secured, with ultimately tragic consequences for both the Romanovs and the country over which they ruled. The Tsar's head of Police, Spiridovich, wrote that Spala was a turning point for the Tsarina. After this her faith in Rasputin 'was unshakeable and there was no force in the world that would ever alienate the monk from the friendship of the imperial family'.

By the time that this event took place, Stolypin had been dead for over a year. On 14 September 1911, the Prime Minister decided to attend a performance of Rimsky-Korsakov's *The Tale of Tsar Saltan* at the Kiev Opera House. The Tsar and his two eldest daughters, Olga and Tatiana, were also present. Although protected by ninety security guards, a young man called Dmitry Bogrov, who was supposedly a left-wing revolutionary, managed to enter the theatre. He shot Stolypin twice.

As he collapsed, Stolypin turned towards the imperial box and made a sign with both hands, as if to warn the Tsar to leave the theatre. Some believed that he made the sign of the cross, as if in a final blessing, but this seems unlikely. At this point, Stolypin did not know how serious his injuries were. He died three days later, lucid and conscious to the end.

Bogrov was suspected of being in collusion with the Secret Police and was hung within a few days of the assassination. At the time there were rumours that the murder had been carried out on the orders of a reactionary faction at Court, but this was never proved. Certainly, Stolypin's reforms had angered many conservatives, who resented his liberal policies.

Stolypin's successor was Vladimir Kokovtsov. He was appointed Chairman of the Council of Ministers and Prime Minister. A moderate conservative, he worked hard to stabilise the economic situation in the country, as well as ensuring that better social protection was afforded to Russian workers. He also tried hard to restrict the influence of Rasputin and in 1912, he had planned to exile the notorious holy man to Tobolsk. The Tsar absolutely refused to countenance this.

In 1912, the fourth and last Duma of Imperial Russia was elected. The first session opened in November. It would sit till 1917, when it was officially disbanded by the new Provisional Government. The fourth Duma was essentially a conservative body, although as the First World War progressed, it became increasingly radical and critical of the Tsar and the way in which he was conducting the war. Between 1912 and 1914, the Russian Empire and the Romanov regime seemed to be bathed in a final sunset of imperial glory. There was growing economic and social prosperity. Few people would have predicted the storm that was to burst upon the nation.

One event, which took place in April 1912, did however portend the looming clouds of revolution that were gathering. Workers at the

Anglo-Russian owned Lena Goldfield Mine in Siberia went on strike in April 1912 in protest at harsh working conditions, low salaries, and the appalling safety record at the mine. Government troops were sent in to restore order. All members of the strike committee were arrested. Several thousand goldmine workers marched in protest at this arbitrary action and were fired on by the soldiers. This led to a tragic massacre in which over 270 demonstrators were shot dead. Public opinion both inside Russia and abroad was deeply shocked.

A huge embarrassment for the Tsarist regime was that the shareholders in the Lena Gold mining company included the Dowager Empress Maria Feodorovna who had made huge profits from her shares in the mine. British business and investment, now widespread across Russia, also came in for criticism as 30% of the owners of the company were British. Joseph Stalin announced that 'The Lena shots broke the ice of silence, and the river of popular resentment is flowing again'. In the years that followed the Lena massacre, strikes and protests by workers began to increase across the Russian Empire. In 1914, the avante-garde Russian artist, Kazimir Malevich, produced his painting *An Englishman in Moscow*, which is an exploration of futurism and the rejection of rationality. The strange symbols make artistic references to the English business connection with Russia and the events at the Lena mine. A new, angry world was dawning.

In 1913, Russia celebrated three hundred years of Romanov rule. There were festivities and celebrations across the whole country. St Petersburg was festooned with coloured lights, the imperial flag fluttered from every main building. There were portraits of all the Tsars stretching back to the founder of the dynasty, Michael Romanov. Crowds filled the streets, which were crammed with stalls selling Romanov flags and souvenirs. There were free concerts in the parks and circus artists paraded through the streets. As dusk fell across the city, all major buildings and fountains were illuminated. The celebrations and the parties went on till dawn.

In February, the Tsar and his family attended a service of thanksgiving in the Kazan Cathedral in St Petersburg. White doves fluttered down from the dome of the Cathedral during the service and hovered over the heads of Nicholas and his son. This was widely interpreted, not least by the

Tsar himself, as a blessing on the House of Romanov.

In May of that year, the imperial family embarked on a tour of some of the cities of ancient Muscovy. The weather was poor, with rain and cold winds. The crowds along the route were sparse. The imperial family were warmly greeted by the local nobility and imperial officials. Many others who turned up to cheer the Romanovs did so more out of curiosity, rather than because they were passionate about the dynasty. A high point of tour was a visit to the Ipatiev Monastery in Kostroma, where the young Michael Romanov had first been offered the crown of Russia three hundred years earlier. In his diary entry for 20 May 1913, Nicholas records how people in Kostroma lined the riverbank and even waded into the river up to their knees, to get a glimpse of the 'Little Father Tsar' and his family.

Kostroma was the original home of the 'Feodorovskaya Icon' of the Mother of God, the patron icon of the Romanov family. Tsar Michael had prayed in front of this icon before leaving for Moscow. Many copies had been made of the icon but by 1913 the original painting was scarcely visible. It was blackened with age. In contrast to the good omen of the white doves, the darkening of the original Feodorovskaya Icon was believed to be a bad sign for the future of the dynasty. Some said that the Virgin was hiding her face from the imperial family.

After the tour, the Romanov cavalcade made a grand entry into Moscow. The Tsar's sister, Grand Duchess Xenia, described the magnificent procession which wound its way through the city's streets to the Archangel Cathedral in the Kremlin, where the Tsar lit a lamp at the tomb of Michael Romanov. Afterwards there were a succession of splendid balls and parties, while the crowds in the city cheered the imperial family and showered their guests with rose petals and confetti.

During that final year of European peace, it must have seemed that the Romanov dynasty would last for ever. There were many people who were happy to accept another three hundred years of imperial rule. The newspaper *Novoye Vremya* declared, 'in every soul there is something Romanov. Something from the soul and spirit of the House that has reigned for three hundred years'. Lenin, in exile in Austrian Poland, gloomily predicted that there would be no revolution in Russia in his lifetime. The end of Imperial Russia was in fact only four years away.

At the end of May, Nicholas went to Berlin for the wedding of Princess Victoria Louise, the only daughter of Kaiser Wilhelm. This was the last time that the Tsar would meet with the Kaiser and with his cousin, King George V. The wedding was the final gathering of the crowned heads of Europe, before war and revolution would overwhelm and destroy the Romanovs, Hapsburgs and Hohenzollerns.

The winter season of 1913-14 in St Petersburg was the most glamourous and frenzied that anyone could ever remember. It was as if there was a looming presentiment of something unknown and unsettling drawing ever closer. Greg King describes how 'St Petersburg sparkled as never before. In that last season the city revealed its full glory as an immensely rich playground of artistic, culinary and sensual delights'.

The imperial family withdrew to the seclusion of the Alexander Palace at Tsarskoye Selo, with an occasional foray into St Petersburg to see close family members. The Tsarina was frequently ill and took to her bed. She actively disliked the lively social scene in the capital, the back-biting and the gossip. The Tsar's four daughters were now growing into elegant young ladies but were viewed by many of the court as being gauche and awkward. They were largely content with their own company, and they did not mix with people outside their narrow family circle.

On Christmas Eve 1913, Nicholas noted in his diary that he and his daughters went to Church in St Petersburg with his sister Xenia and her children, then back to the Anichkov Palace where 'there was a Christmas tree in the blue drawing room, followed by a family meal. We returned home at ten-thirty in the evening. Then Alix and I had our own Christmas tree'.

On 9 February 1914, the Romanov family gathered for the wedding of the Tsar's only niece, Princess Irina Alexandrovna, the daughter of his sister, Xenia. Irina was then considered to be the most eligible woman in Russia. The marriage had caused a major uproar in the imperial family, as Irina's choice of husband was Prince Felix Yusupov, a descendant of one of Russia's wealthiest noble families. He had a reputation for having an ambiguous and controversial private life and it was widely rumoured that he was bisexual. The marriage eventually went ahead, but many in the Romanov family foresaw disaster. Two years later in December 1916, Yusupov, together with his close friend Grand Duke Dmitri Pavlovich, a young man with whom he may have had a romantic relationship, murdered Rasputin at the Yusupov Palace in St Petersburg. In one of his last acts as Tsar Nicholas exiled Felix to the remotest of the Yusupov family estates in western Russia. Dimitri was sent to the Persian front.

On 28 June 1914, Archduke Franz Ferdinand of Austria, the heir presumptive to the Austro-Hungarian throne, was assassinated in Sarajevo. A month later, on 28 July, Austria-Hungary declared war on Serbia. The interlocking web of European alliances made it inevitable that the other major powers would be drawn into the conflict. The First World War had begun. Russia backed Serbia. The shelling of Belgrade on 28 July led to the partial mobilisation of the Russian army. This was followed by a full Russian mobilisation on 30 July. Two days later Germany and Austria-Hungary declared war on Russia. On 2 August, France ordered its army to mobilise in support of Russia.

The German army first planned to strike at France, before turning its attention to Russia. This had been the long-established strategy of the German High Command. In order to invade France, the German army needed to cross Belgium. A request was therefore put to the Belgian government, demanding that German troops be given free movement across Belgian territory. This was refused. Germany invaded Belgium on 4 August.

The Belgians appealed for help to Britain, invoking the 1839 *Treaty of London* which guaranteed British protection of Belgian sovereignty. On 4 August Britain declared war on Germany. This was followed by a declaration of war against Austria-Hungary on 12 August.

Britain, France and Russia were now military allies in a war against Austria and Germany. This was the first time that Britain and Russia had fought together on the same side since the Napoleonic Wars. Sixty years earlier they had been enemies, as they clashed violently in the Crimean Peninsula. Now, they were allies in what would become one of the most destructive conflicts ever to befall the European continent.

The British declaration of war on Germany was greeted with huge relief by the Tsar. He wrote in his diary, 'In the morning we heard the good news. England has declared war on Germany because the latter has attacked France and violated the neutrality of Belgium and Luxembourg in the most shameful way'. From Siberia, Rasputin sent an urgent telegram to the Tsar warning him not to take Russia to war. War, he believed, would end in the destruction of the Empire and the dynasty. Nicholas was angered by what he described as an unwarranted interference by Rasputin in the affairs of state.

King George V sent a letter to Nicholas. 'Both you and I did everything in our power to prevent war' he wrote, 'but alas we were frustrated, and this terrible war which we have all dreaded for so many years has come upon us. Anyhow Russia, England and France have clean consciences and are fighting for right and justice'.

The war unleashed a wave of patriotism across Russia. Vast crowds cheered the troops as they set out for the front. The imperial flag garlanded public buildings, and renditions of the imperial anthem 'God Save the Tsar' rang out at numerous public meetings. In an emotional act of national zeal, the Tsar agreed that St Petersburg should be renamed Petrograd.

In late August 1914, the Russian Second and Third Armies advanced into the German province of East Prussia. It looked as though the Russians might be in Berlin by Christmas. However, the Russian armies turned out to be poorly equipped and badly trained, with a crippling lack of shells, rifles and uniforms. This was the largest army in Europe, but it was not ready to fight a modern, twentieth-century war. At the Battle of Tannenberg which took place between 26 and 30 August, the Germans destroyed the Russian Second Army. 78,000 men were killed and wounded, and another 92,000 others were made prisoners of war. Only 10,000 soldiers escaped. The Commander of the Second Army, General Alexander Samsonov, committed suicide shortly after the battle.

A week later, the Russian First Army was destroyed at the Battle of the Masurian Lakes, with the loss of 70,000 men killed or wounded and 45,000 men taken prisoner. These were colossal and shocking military defeats, which weakened the morale of both the Russian government and people.

The war against Austria-Hungary on the south-western front went better for the Russians, at least initially. Lemberg, the capital of the Austro-Hungarian province of Galicia was captured, along with the strategic Hapsburg fortress of Przemyśl. In May 1915, German and Austro-Hungarian troops launched a counter offensive, and recovered the Austrian province of Galicia. However, Germany then invaded and occupied Russian Poland, Lithuania and large parts of Belorussia, bringing the war directly into Russian territory.

In July 1915, a Danish offer to help negotiate a separate peace settlement between Germany and Russia was rejected by the Tsar, who felt strongly that he could not betray his allies. A month later, Nicholas removed his cousin, Grand Duke Nikolai Nikolaevich, from his position as Supreme Commander-in-Chief of the Russian armies and assumed overall command of the Russian war effort, supported by General Mikhail Alekseyev. The Tsar left Petrograd and moved to the military headquarters, or 'Stavka' of the Imperial Army, at Mogilev in Eastern Belorussia. It was here that Nicholas now spent more and more of his time directing military operations. In doing this, he unwisely removed himself from the day to day running of his government in Petrograd.

The Tsar had no direct military experience and his decision to assume control of the overall Russian war effort was not a sensible one. It clearly terrified him. He wrote in his diary at the end of August, 'I signed the mandate concerning my assumption of the High Command yesterday. Lord, Help and Guide me!'. He knew how ill-prepared he was to take on this role. The Tsarina, who now represented Nicholas, was left in charge of political affairs together with an increasingly unpopular government. This was another mistake. Alexandra increasingly relied on a small coterie of advisers, including Rasputin, to support her, and they began to play a powerful role in her daily decision making.

Nicholas continued to correspond regularly with his cousin, King George V. In September 1915, he wrote to express his thanks that the British submarine E-8 had joined the Russian naval forces in the Baltic

Sea. He also sent his condolences over the loss of the E13 submarine, which was attacked by the Germans in the Baltic with the loss of fifteen of her crew.

In 1916, there appeared to be an improvement in the fortunes of the Russian armies fighting in south-western Europe. General Alexsei Brusilov led a brilliant campaign against the Austro-Hungarians and the province of Galicia was recaptured. Romania joined the war on the side of the Allies. The Austro-Hungarians sustained huge losses, and their war effort seemed to falter. During a few brief weeks in June 1916, it looked as though the Hapsburg army might even collapse under the pressure of so many defeats.

The Germans reacted quickly and sent reinforcements to bolster the morale of the Austro-Hungarians. Much of Romania was then overrun, and the Russians had to divert forty-seven divisions to support the Romanian army. This came at a time when their own military resources were over-stretched on the other war fronts. Fierce battles followed in Transylvania and along the Black Sea coast. There were heavy casualties on both sides.

Meanwhile, the British had decided to increase their direct military support to Russia. In June 1916, an important military and political mission set out from London. Its aim was to identify ways in which Britain could support the Russian war effort more effectively. Leading the mission was Field Marshal Herbert Kitchener, then the Secretary of State for War, and at the time the most famous soldier in Britain. His walrus-moustached face stared out from innumerable recruiting posters, accompanied by the thundering words 'Your country needs YOU!'

Kitchener was accompanied by a group of senior military advisers and civilian experts on Russia, including Hugh O'Beirne, who had worked at the British Embassy in Petrograd before the war. He was considered a rising star in the British diplomatic service and was greatly valued for his insights about Russian political life.

On the afternoon of 5 June, Kitchener and his party boarded the naval cruiser *Hampshire*, which was riding at anchor in Scapa Flow in the Orkney Islands. The weather was atrocious, with a force nine gale blowing from the north west. In order to avoid the worst of the storm, the Captain of the ship decided to take a westerly route out of Scapa Flow, rather than the safer easterly route. This was a major error of judgement. This route had not been swept clear of German mines and at 7.40 in the evening, the ship hit a mine which blew out one of its large boilers. It sank within fifteen minutes.

Only twelve crew members out of a total complement of 735 men survived the sinking and the entire mission to Russia including Kitchener and O'Beirne perished in the icy cold waters of Scapa Flow. Ironically, the two escort ships which had been accompanying the *Hampshire* had turned back to port a few minutes earlier as they could not keep up with the faster cruiser, which was increasing speed in order to escape the storm. If they had been alongside Kitchener's ship when it struck the mine, there is a good chance that there would have been many more survivors.

Rumours abounded after the sinking of the ship, the death of Kitchener and all his mission members. These included reports that German agents or Irish republican terrorists had been seen boarding and had craftily planted explosives in the part of the ship where the most damage would be caused. The most far-fetched of the conspiracy theories was that this was the work of Russian revolutionaries who had wanted to prevent any British assistance reaching the Tsar. Tempting though it was to lay the blame for the tragedy at the door of enemy agents, this was a case of appalling weather, over confidence, and bad judgement.

Kitchener's death on the *Hampshire* was a huge shock to the British government and public. One man in Yorkshire committed suicide when he heard the news and many others believed that this event marked the beginning of the end for the British war effort. It was viewed as a national tragedy.

There were no further British attempts to mount military missions to Russia and plans to send military assistance to the Tsar's regime were abandoned. Russia was still receiving financial loans from its allies, and it was therefore able to bring in some military equipment, but the blockades in the Baltic and the Black Sea were preventing any significant imports of food and medical supplies.

Isolated at the Stavka headquarters in Mogilev, Nicholas was unaware of the growing unpopularity of the war amongst the Russian public, and the dislike felt by many sections of the population for the Tsarina and the imperial government. In Petrograd, scurrilous stories abounded about the relationship between Rasputin and Alexandra. Vicious cartoons circulated depicting the Tsarina in the lascivious embrace of the holy man. The Tsarina was also widely mistrusted because she was German and was thus suspected of being in league with the Kaiser.

Oblivious to all this, Alexandra and her two eldest daughters, Olga and Tatiana, spent much of their time helping soldiers who had been wounded in the war. They visited hospitals in St Petersburg and set up their own private hospital in the grounds of Tsarskoye Selo, where they personally tended the injured men. For Olga and Tatiana, this was their first real experience of dealing with the outside world and working in the hospital gave them the chance to meet young men of their own generation in a less restricted and controlled environment.

This allowed a first intense romance to blossom between Olga and Dmitri Shakh-Bagov, a Georgian adjutant in the Life Grenadiers of the Erevan Regiment whom she called 'Mitya'. Tatiana meanwhile fell in love with Vladimir Kiknadze, a young lieutenant in the Third Rifles Guards Regiment. Tatiana affectionately called him 'Volodya'. These were innocent affairs but deeply meaningful to the two young Grand Duchesses.

In Petrograd, political tensions were rising. The Tsar had allowed the Duma to reconvene in July 1915. It demanded more control over the government and the army and was prorogued in September. The Duma met again in February 1916. By now there was a strong Progressive bloc amongst the Duma's members. Many of them were open in their attacks on the Government Ministers and demanded constitutional reform.

Rasputin and Alexandra now insisted that the Tsar should temporarily close the Duma and not permit it to meet again until February 1917, at the earliest. The Deputies in the Duma responded by calling for the resignation of all the government Ministers and they openly attacked the Prime Minister, Alexander Protopopov. The situation was getting out of control. On 16 December a formal decree was issued by the Tsar, closing the Duma until January 1917.

The British and the French governments were becoming increasingly worried by the turn of events inside Russia. It was clear that the Tsar's government was unstable, and that the Russian war effort was not going well. Sir George Buchanan, the British Ambassador, warned the Tsar that he should grant constitutional reform in order to fend off revolution.

In January 1917 Buchanan told Nicholas that he felt that it was his duty, as a friend, to warn him of the abyss that lay ahead if he did not agree to support the Duma's reform plans. He enquired how the Tsar proposed to regain the confidence of his subjects, to which he received the following blunt reply from Nicholas: 'Do you mean that I am to regain the confidence of my people or they are to regain mine?'

Buchanan was highly suspicious of the way that the Tsarina was interfering in the process of government. He confided in Mikhail Rodzianko, the President of the Duma, that he was worried that Alexandra was an unwitting instrument of the Germans. He said that he found it increasingly difficult to get an audience with the Tsar.

By early 1917, Russia was on the verge of total economic collapse. Fifteen million men had been taken from the land and drafted into the army. Agricultural production had stalled in many areas and food prices had soared. The economy had been placed on a war footing and therefore everything was geared to supplying the armies at the front. This meant that the transportation system was not prioritising the needs of the civilians living in the cities. There was a severe shortage of grain and other basic commodities in the shops.

On the streets of major towns and cities there was increasing disorder throughout the autumn of 1916, with demonstrations against food and fuel shortages and regular strikes, even in key industries. More worrying for the government was the fact that many of these strikes seemed to be politically motivated. On 23 February 1917, International Women's Day, the frustrations of ordinary people living in Petrograd burst out into the open. Food shortages, hunger and the bitterly cold weather all combined to create a lethal cocktail of grievance and discontent.

The demonstrations were initially led by thousands of women textile workers and housewives, angry about the bread shortages in the capital. Nobody expected that these demonstrations would lead to a revolution, but they were to become the catalyst for the events which followed.

Over the next few days, the women were joined by striking workers and by students and members of the middle classes. The French revolutionary anthem the *Marseillaise* was openly sung, and red banners were unfurled. Crowds chanted, 'Down with the German Woman! Down with Prime Minister Protopopov! Down with the War and Down with the Tsar!'. Rioting broke out and food shops were attacked with widespread looting.

Nicholas had recently returned to the front at Mogilev and when news reached him about what was happening in Petrograd, he gave orders that the army should suppress the rioting. Alexandra was isolated from the reality of what was taking place around her, snowbound at the Alexander Palace in Tsarskoye Selo.

On 25 February, the Tsarina wrote to reassure Nicholas, 'It is a hooligan movement, young boys and girls running about and screaming that they have no bread, only to excite, then the workmen preventing others from work. If it was very cold, they would probably stay indoors. But, this will all pass and quieten down if only the Duma would behave itself'.

The following day, the Tsarina's tone was more cautious. She admitted that there were disorders in Petrograd and that over 200,000 people had taken to the streets. Her attitude was still combative: 'Our people are idiots. A poor gendarme was killed by the crowd, a few other people too'. She criticized the 'gaping public, well dressed people, wounded soldiers, girl students, who egg on others'. In order to seek reassurance, she took the Grand Duchess Maria with her to kneel and pray before the grave of Rasputin, who had been murdered only a few weeks earlier. 'I felt such a peace and calm on His [Rasputin's] dear grave. He died for us'.

Meanwhile events in Petrograd were spiralling out of control. Soldiers loyal to the Tsar fired on the crowds and over two hundred were killed. However, other army units decided that they would no longer support the government. Soldiers and officers in four elite regiments, Volinsky, Semonovsky, Izmaylovsky and Preobrazhensky, all mutinied. An estimated 170,000 soldiers joined the insurgents. Prisons and police stations were attacked, and symbols of the Romanov regime were torn down by the crowds.

On 26 February, Rodzianko, the President of the Duma, sent an urgent telegram to the Tsar informing him of the critical situation in the capital. 'The government is completely paralysed, and totally incapable of restoring order where it has broken down', he wrote. 'Your Majesty must without delay summon a person whom the whole country trusts'. There was no response from the Tsar, who had decided to return to his family in Tsarskoye Selo and take personal control of the situation in Petrograd.

Events were now moving too fast even for the Tsar's train to catch up with them. On 28 February the new 'Provisional Committee' of the State Duma declared that, in view of the serious situation facing the country, it was now taking over control of the government. It asked for the people and the army to give it their support. The Tsar had effectively been deposed, though he did not know it yet.

In Petrograd, a Soviet of Workers and Soldiers was now formed, and sent its representatives to meet with the Duma at the Tauride Palace. Rodzianko took the lead in negotiating with the Soviet, which agreed to support the 'Provisional Committee'. Prince Georgy Lvov was appointed as Prime Minister. The Soviet demanded that Alexander Kerensky, one of the most outspoken critics in the Duma of the Tsar, should be made Minister of War. The regimental commanders in charge of the mutinous soldiers agreed to support the new 'Provisional Committee'. Tsarist Ministers, Police Chiefs and Generals were all arrested and imprisoned.

The Tsar's train was now halted at the small town of Pskov, about 160 miles south-west of St Petersburg. When the Tsar discovered that the railway line to the capital had been blocked by revolutionaries, he decided to head to Moscow, believing that this would be a good base for him, as it had not yet declared for the Revolution. News was then brought to him that Moscow was in the hands of rebel soldiers, so this plan also had to be abandoned.

On 1 March the Tsar received a series of messages from his loyal Generals, telling him that the situation in St Petersburg, the Baltic regions and Moscow was completely hopeless, and that Tsarskoye Selo was also in the hands of revolutionary troops. This news worried the Tsar more than anything else, as he feared for the safety of Alexandra and their children.

The Provisional Committee of the Duma and the Petrograd Soviet had now come to an agreement that the Tsar must abdicate. It was decided that he should be succeeded by his son, Alexei. Grand Duke Michael would act as Regent during the minority of the young Tsar. A new government would be formed and there would be elections for a new Constituent Assembly. The aim was to preserve the Romanov dynasty and to continue prosecuting the war, though the Petrograd Soviet took some persuading on both these points and it was Alexander Kerensky, the newly appointed Minister of War, who finally won them over. Everyone agreed that the discredited Tsar and his government must go. A committee of Duma members left for Pskov to persuade the Tsar to accept these proposals.

Marooned in his train, Nicholas dithered about what to do. He was aware that there was little support for him remaining in power as Tsar. He toyed with the idea of throwing himself on the mercy of the army of the north, commanded by General Nikolai Ruzsky who was based in Pskov. He even wondered whether he might march with Ruzsky's loyal troops against Petrograd. He realised, though, that this would plunge the country into civil war and would very likely imperil the lives of both Alexandra and his children. He therefore abandoned this idea. He then fell into a passive and fatalistic state of mind, in which he is reported to have said that he would give everything up and go and live in Livadia in the Crimea, because he loved flowers.

It was General Ruzsky who finally persuaded Nicholas to abdicate. He was in touch with Rodzianko and knew the hopeless nature of the situation in Petrograd. There were reports, after the event, that Ruzsky browbeat a reluctant Nicholas in to signing the Manifesto of Abdication. Others state that the Tsar did it willingly, once he realised the desperate situation in which he and the Romanov dynasty now found itself. Nicholas initially agreed to Alexei being named as his successor, but after consulting with various doctors who confirmed that the Tsarevich's haemophilia was incurable, he decided to abdicate on behalf of both himself and his son.

He named his brother Grand Duke Michael as his successor. The Tsar signed the Manifesto of Abdication on 2 March 1917. His last words as Tsar were an appeal to his brother, to 'govern in the closest concert with the representatives of the nation who sit in the legislative assemblies and to pledge them his inviolable oath in the name of the Beloved Country'.

Nicholas's decision to abdicate came as a shock to his brother, as the Tsar had had no time to warn Michael about his plans to give up the throne. On 3 March, Michael met with Prince Lvov, Rodzianko, Kerensky and other members of the Provisional Committee. They persuaded him to turn down the offer of the throne, pending a new constitutional settlement. In responding to the offer, Michael stated that he would only accept the position of Tsar 'if it is the will of our great people'. After 304 years, the Romanovs had departed the throne of Russia with scarcely a whimper. Nicholas was horrified when he heard what his brother had done and accused him of 'Kowtowing to the Constituent Assembly', stating that the agreement he had reached with the Provisional Committee was 'rubbish'. By this time, nobody was interested in the former Tsar's opinions and they were not reported in the press.

Nicholas re-joined his family at Tsarskoye Selo on 9 March 1917. From that moment on, they became prisoners in their own Palace. The children had been ill with severe measles for much of this period and were therefore shielded from the reality of what was taking place outside their bedrooms. It was now time to break the news to them that their father was no longer Tsar of Russia and that they were prisoners. It was a painful moment for Nicholas and Alexandra, and there were sobs and tears and expressions of incredulity from the children at this fateful downturn in their fortunes. They were now guarded by soldiers who had no great love for the imperial family. Their long-standing and loyal Palace guard had been dismissed and the men who replaced them were surly and uncooperative, following the Tsar and Tsarina around the Palace, and making aggressive and unpleasant comments to their faces.

33

Refusing a refuge to the Romanovs

The new Provisional Government was becoming increasingly aware that the family's situation was precarious. Radical elements in the Petrograd Soviet were already calling for the trial of the Tsar. It seemed safer, therefore, to remove the Romanovs from the country entirely. The Russian Foreign Minister, Pavel Milyukov, approached the British Ambassador Sir George Buchanan with a request for Britain to provide asylum for the imperial family. This was a reasonable request. Russia was still an ally of the British in the war against Germany, and Nicholas and George V were first cousins. The Tsarina was a granddaughter of Queen Victoria and therefore closely related to the British royal family.

The Provisional Government also had in its possession a telegram sent by George V to Nicholas, dated 6 March, which read, 'Events of the last week have depressed me. My thoughts are constantly with you and I shall always remain your true and devoted friend as you know I have been in the past'. This message was never passed to the former Tsar, but Milyukov noted the strong sentiment of affection and support for Nicholas expressed in the King's words. He had no doubts that the British would offer asylum to the former Tsar and his family.

Initially, the Russian request seemed to be well received. There were a few questions asked from the British side as to whether the Russian government would pay for the cost of the upkeep of the imperial family. There was also some discussion about where they would stay when they came to Britain. Osborne House was even considered, but it is possible that Barton Manor, also on the Isle of Wight, and then still owned by King George V might have been designated as their future home. This was in a secure and private location and could have been easily protected.

Both the King and the British government, led by the Prime Minister David Lloyd George, were in favour of responding positively to the Russian request. Sir George Buchanan was therefore instructed to inform Milyukov that the former Tsar and his family would be welcome in Britain. If the Russians were agreeable, a British cruiser could be sent to Port Romanov, now called Murmansk, to evacuate the family.

Given the deteriorating political situation, an immediate departure was clearly sensible, but Nicholas and Alexandra were anxious not to leave immediately as their children were still not well. There is some evidence that this delay may have suited Nicholas, who harboured a strange delusion that he could continue living safely in Russia as an ordinary citizen.

The Provisional Government was becoming increasingly worried that any delay in the departure of the imperial family might make it impossible to get them away safely. Bolshevik political leaders and soldiers were already threatening to block any attempt by the Tsar to leave the country. Travelling to Port Romanoff would have required complicated transport planning in order to bypass revolutionary guards' units that were positioned around the capital.

Pierre Gilliard, who was the tutor to the imperial children, wrote in his memoirs, 'Our captivity at Tsarskoye Selo did not seem likely to last long and there was talk about our imminent transfer to England. Yet, the days passed, and our departure was always being postponed'.

The fact was that the British offer of asylum had been withdrawn almost as soon as it had been issued. This decision had been made at the request of the Tsar's own cousin, King George V, the man who had warmly welcomed the Romanov family to Cowes eight years earlier.

In later years, when the truth finally began to emerge about what had happened during this period, there would be accusations that King George had colluded in an act of great family betrayal. The background to this, and to the cover-up that took place around it, are complex.

On 17 March 1917, Lord Stamfordham - who was then the King's Private Secretary - sent a private and confidential message to the Foreign Secretary, Arthur Balfour. 'The King has been thinking about the Government's proposal that the Emperor Nicholas and his family should come to England. As you are doubtless aware, the King has a strong personal friendship for the Emperor and would therefore be glad to do anything to help him in this crisis. But His Majesty cannot help doubting, not only on account of the dangers of voyage but on general grounds of expediency, whether it is advisable that the imperial family should take up residency in this country'.

Lord Stamfordham played a key role in the King's decision to withdraw the offer of asylum to the Romanovs. He appears to have exercised a strong influence over the King, having been Private Secretary to Queen Victoria for six years and then made Private Secretary to the young Prince George in 1901. He was to remain in this role till his own death in 1931.

It was Lord Stamfordham who persuaded the King in July 1917 to change the name of the royal family from Saxe-Coburg-Gotha to Windsor, as he was worried that anti-German sentiment in the country might turn against the royal family. He was sensitive to any perceived threats to the monarchy and was quick to identify possible areas of risk. Preserving the future of the *House of Windsor*, at all costs, was his main goal in life and he pursued this task with dedication and a single-minded ruthlessness. It appears that the King was ambivalent about whether to accept the Romanovs. It was therefore relatively easy for Stamfordham to convince him that rescinding the offer of asylum was in the royal family's best interests.

In Stamfordham's opinion, there was a serious risk to the future of the monarchy if the King were to bring the Tsar and his family to Britain. The Tsar had never been popular with Socialist and Liberal elements in the country, and there was growing opposition from these quarters to offering any form of asylum to the Romanovs. There were more and more articles appearing in the popular press which denounced the former Tsar. Stamfordham was convinced that political and popular opposition could begin to directly threaten the position of the British royal family. He shared these concerns with the King and with the Queen, Mary of Teck.

It was rumoured at the time that Queen Mary was not impressed by the Russian imperial family, and that she had resented the way that she had been treated by the Tsarina. She felt that the Tsarina looked down on her being from a very minor German Princely House, and she was convinced that she had been snubbed by Alexandra on the various occasions when they had met in England or Germany. Whether this was in fact the case, or whether this was due to Alexandra's crippling shyness, the perceived slight was never forgiven or forgotten. Queen Mary was therefore not likely to oppose Stamfordham and insist that Britain offer asylum to the Romanovs.

The King was alarmed by Stamfordham's warnings and, in this mood of doubt and uncertainty, he changed his mind about the asylum offer. He may well have consoled himself that other countries would be likely to provide the Russian imperial family with a refuge. It might also be argued that he also did not realise the danger that the Romanovs were facing in an increasingly volatile and unstable Russia. King George was not a very imaginative man and he had probably not reflected on the lessons of history: King Charles I and King Louis XVI, two deposed monarchs, had both been executed during the English and French Revolutions.

Stamfordham's message to the Foreign Secretary Arthur Balfour, suggesting that the offer of asylum to the former Tsar be reconsidered, received a cool response. He quickly wrote back to Stamfordham that both he and the Prime Minister felt that 'it is now not possible to withdraw the invitation that has been sent, and they therefore trust that the King will consent to adhere to the original invitation, which was sent on the advice of His Majesty's Ministers'. This reveals that the British Government was fully behind the invitation and did not believe that welcoming the Tsar to Britain would cause problems for the King.

Stamfordham was not going to give up so easily. A few days later, he again contacted Balfour, making the King's opposition to the asylum offer very clear. 'Every day the King is becoming more concerned about the question of the Emperor and Empress of Russia coming to this country', he wrote. 'As you know the King has thought that the presence of the imperial family, especially of the Empress, would raise all sorts of difficulties'. The reference to the Empress was a clear warning to the Foreign Secretary that the King and Queen wanted to distance themselves from any possible German associations. The letter continues to inform Balfour that the King was receiving letters from people of every class, saying how widely the matter was being discussed and that Labour members of the House of Commons were raising difficult questions about the proposal to bring the former Tsar to Britain.

Stamfordham wrote another letter to the Foreign Secretary later that same day. 'The King wishes me to write again on the subject of my letter this morning' he begins, hardly able to contain himself. 'He must beg you to represent, to the Prime Minister, that from all he hears and reads in the press, the residence in this country of the Ex-Emperor and Ex-Empress would be strongly resented by the public and would undoubtedly compromise the position of the King and Queen'.

He insisted in his letter that the British Ambassador in Petrograd should inform the Russian Foreign Secretary that opposition to the arrival of the Tsar in Britain was now so strong, it was imperative the offer of asylum be withdrawn immediately. In order to influence the government's thinking on this issue, he cited an article written by Henry Hyndman, blaming the King for inviting Nicholas and his family to Britain. This had been published in the British Socialist Party's weekly newspaper *Justice*.

Hyndman was a well-known Marxist with strong Republican views. The newspaper had a relatively small circulation and Hyndman's regular attacks on the British establishment did not usually worry the King or the government. It is strange, therefore, that Stamfordham chose to make such an issue of Hyndman's article. It points towards his utter determination to find any opportunity to withdraw the invitation to the Tsar and his family.

There was no reply from Balfour to Stamfordham's two letters. At the end of March, the King's Private Secretary decided that he would call on the Prime Minister at 10 Downing Street. There he berated Lloyd George about the asylum offer, explaining why it must be withdrawn as soon as possible. He stressed that it would be 'most unfair on the King, if their Imperial Majesties came here when popular feeling against their doing so is so pronounced'. He showed Lloyd George the article written by Hyndman and reported negative comments by other people, though he admitted, when pressed, that many of these comments were from unknown sources.

Lloyd George was taken aback by Stamfordham's tirade. It was now dawning on him that this was a much more serious issue than he had first realised. The King was clearly determined to renege on the original asylum offer. Lloyd George therefore decided that he would approach the French government and enquire if they would consider providing a refuge for the Romanovs.

After his blistering discussion with the Prime Minister, Stamfordham hurried over to the Foreign Office to see Balfour. He told him that Lloyd George was now reconsidering the asylum offer and warned Balfour that the King was very irritated that the asylum offer had not yet been cancelled.

The Foreign Secretary agreed to draft a telegram to the British Ambassador in St Petersburg, Sir George Buchanan, instructing him to do this. Later that evening the telegram was despatched with the approval of the Prime Minister. The British Ambassador realised that this might well seal the fate of the imperial family, as time was now running out for the Tsar and his family to leave Russia in safety.

Buchanan was evasive in the way he communicated the news to members of the Russian Government. Pavel Milyukov was informed that 'the British Government no longer insists on the Tsar's family coming to England', while Alexander Kerensky learned that 'the government of England does not consider it possible, while the war continues, to extend its hospitality to the former Tsar'. In later years the British would insist that it was the Russians who failed to arrange the departure of the Tsar when the offer had originally been made. Kerensky and his colleagues maintained to the end of their lives that the British withdrew their offer and thus prevented the Romanovs from leaving Russia.

It seems that Nicholas received the news that Britain would no longer offer him refuge with calm resignation. His fatalism and passivity in the face of danger were noted by everybody around him. It may well be that he was relieved, because part of him wanted to remain in Russia whatever the consequences. He believed, to the end, in the innate goodness of the Russian people and trusted in them to save him and his family. It was beyond his imagination to foresee the full horror that was now heading in his direction.

Sir George Buchanan never forgave himself for not doing more to try and save Nicholas and his family and was haunted all his life by their fate. While Lloyd George and the British government publicly accepted the blame for withdrawing the offer of asylum, Buchanan knew that it was the King and Stamfordham who had pushed for this. His health collapsed and he left Russia in December 1918. Shortly before his death in 1924, he decided to write his autobiography, *My Mission to Russia and other Diplomatic Memories*. In the original manuscript he wanted to tell the truth about what had happened. He was threatened by the Foreign Office with the cancellation of his pension and with being charged with a breach of the Official Secrets Act. Given this level of intimidation, he decided not to include any mention of it in his book.

In 1932, his daughter, Meriel Buchanan, published her book *The Dissolution of an Empire*, in which she stated that her father had been forced to redact those sections of his book relating to the withdrawal of the asylum offer. The role of the King and Lord Stamfordham in this tragic tale would not emerge till many years later.

34

Exile and death

Events in Russia now began to unfold with dramatic speed. On 8 July 1917, Alexander Kerensky succeeded Prince Georgy Lvov as Prime Minister. Russia was still involved in the war, despite growing opposition to it from the Bolsheviks. In August, Kerensky assumed the position of Supreme Commander-in-Chief of all military forces. He announced that Russia was a Republic on 2 September 1917. Grand Duke Michael wrote in his diary, 'We woke up this morning to hear that Russia has been proclaimed a democratic republic. What does it matter what form of government will be, provided there is order and justice in the land'.

The Tsar and his family heard the news formally marking the end of their dynasty in the remote Eastern Siberian town of Tobolsk. They had been sent there by Kerensky a month earlier on 31 July, in order to protect them from what he perceived as a growing threat from Lenin and the Bolsheviks. The imperial family hoped that there might still be a chance to leave for the Crimea but as the hot summer days drew towards early autumn, it became clear that even this route was closed to them. On the Isle of Wight, the Tsarina's elder sister, Victoria, began to prepare her plans to bring the imperial family to safety in East Cowes.

During their stay in Tobolsk, the Romanovs were housed in the former Governor's mansion in the centre of the town, where they spent the following autumn and winter. There were long days in the house with occasional forays into the yard or on to the roof of the mansion. It was a dull and dreary existence but at least they felt safe here. The guards treated the family with a measure of civility and respect.

Events in Moscow and Petrograd initially seemed to have little impact in Tobolsk. The townspeople were honoured to have the former Tsar and his family living amongst them, and small crowds would gather in front of the house to wave at the children. Fresh vegetables, meat and fish were delivered every day by well-wishers to the kitchen of the mansion. Nicholas was finally living the life of a country gentleman, albeit in a rather restrictive way, in an obscure and remote corner of his former Empire. It was an existence he had always believed would suit him very well.

In late October, everything suddenly changed for the worse. Kerensky and the Provisional Government were losing control of both the political and military situation. There were now daily riots in the streets of Petrograd and Moscow. Most workers were on strike and industrial production had virtually ground to a halt. The Bolsheviks successfully infiltrated the factories and the military regiments. Everything was in place for Lenin's Bolshevik coup.

At 9.40pm on the evening of 25 October 1917, the cruiser *Aurora*, stationed in the centre of Petrograd, fired shots at the Winter Palace. This salvo marked the start of the Bolshevik Revolution. Bolshevik militiamen began taking over key installations in the city, beginning with the Post Office, Telegraph Office and Telephone Exchange. There was no opposition from any of the military regiments in the city to this illicit seizure of power. The Winter Palace, where the Provisional Government had its headquarters, was attacked and all the government ministers who were present in the building were arrested. Kerensky fled the country.

Vladimir Lenin declared that the Provisional Government had been overthrown and that Russia would now be ruled by a new style of government, based on a Union of all the Soviets or Workers Councils. He agreed, though, that elections should take place as planned for a Constituent Assembly. This happened in November 1918, but the Bolsheviks gained only 25% of the popular vote. The dominant political grouping was the Socialist Revolutionary Party, with strong roots in the countryside amongst the rural peasantry. It commanded nearly 50% of the vote. The Russian Constituent Assembly met for the first time in January 1918, and it was immediately suppressed by Lenin on the grounds that it was a counter-revolutionary body. In March, Lenin declared that Russia would henceforth be ruled by the Communist Party.

In Tobolsk, news that the Bolsheviks had taken control of the government appalled the Tsar. He could not believe that Kerensky and the Provisional Government had been overthrown so easily and he was shocked that once-loyal Tsarist regiments, like the Preobrazhensky and the Izmailovsky, had not intervened to oppose the insurgents. He was already out of touch with events in his former capital and did not realise the extent to which many soldiers and officers had become radicalised by Bolshevik ideology.

Conditions in Tobolsk now deteriorated. The new Bolshevik government changed the soldiers guarding the Romanovs. Surliness and aggression replaced the more easy-going attitude of the men who had formerly overseen the imperial family. Winter had arrived. Heating in the mansion was inadequate, food was now rationed, and there was a distinct air of menace about the situation in which Nicholas and his family now found themselves. The Romanovs were issued with Ration Card Number 54, which permitted the family to have 10lbs of flour, 7 lbs of butter and 1/2lb of sugar every month.

Nicholas and his family worked hard to keep up their spirits during this bleak time. Secret messages were smuggled to them in Tobolsk, promising them that they would soon be rescued. Various monarchical organisations, including the shadowy Brotherhood of St John of Tobolsk, were active in planning rescue attempts. None of these would ever come close to realisation. The British Foreign Office was reportedly behind a plan to smuggle the Tsar and his family out on a British torpedo boat. King George V, in a belated show of concern for his Russian cousins, was reportedly supportive of this idea.

On 24 April, Pierre Gilliard, the tutor to the Tsar's children, wrote a gloomy entry in his diary. 'We are all in a state of mental anguish. We feel that we are forgotten by everyone, abandoned to our own resources. Is it possible that no one will raise a finger to save the imperial family? Where are those who remained loyal to the Tsar? Why do they delay?'

A day later, on 25 April, events took a more sinister turn. A Bolshevik revolutionary called Vasily Yakovlev turned up in Tobolsk, together with a hundred and fifty armed horsemen. He carried orders from the Central Executive Committee of the Communist Party to transfer the imperial family to Moscow, where it was presumed the former Tsar would stand trial. An air of mystery surrounds Yakovlev, who many suspected of being a double agent, working for both the Bolsheviks and the Monarchists. There were rumours that he was in fact planning to rescue the Romanovs and take them further east, where British agents were waiting to carry them to safety.

None of this seems likely. Yakovlev was almost certainly on a mission ordered by Moscow to make sure that the imperial family did not fall into the hands of more extreme Bolshevik groups in Siberia, particularly the Urals Soviet based in Ekaterinburg. Their leaders were already demanding the execution of the Tsar for his crimes against the Russian people.

The original plan had been for Yakovlev to remove the entire family from Tobolsk, but this turned out not to be possible. Two weeks earlier, Alexei had fallen seriously ill after suffering a serious haemorrhage in his abdomen, which had then spread to his groin and legs. Although he had made a slow recovery it was clear that he was in no fit condition to travel hundreds of miles across rough terrain to Moscow. It was finally decided that Nicholas and Alexandra would leave Tobolsk, together with the Grand Duchess Maria. The four other children would remain behind and join the rest of the family as soon as Alexei was fully recovered.

There were tears and sobs on the morning of the departure. It was not clear where Nicholas, Alexandra and Maria were being taken and whether any of them would ever see each other again. The convoy first travelled in horse-drawn farm carts to the railway station at Tyumen, about 220 miles from Tobolsk.

It was a rough and uncomfortable journey with the wagons crossing frozen rivers and becoming stuck in muddy ditches. No courtesy or help was extended to the former Tsar and his wife. They were treated like any other ordinary travellers, left to fend for themselves as they struggled through the icy river waters, or bedded down on cold stone floors.

When they finally reached Tyumen, the party boarded a train which, on Yakovlev's orders, set off in the direction of Omsk, 350 miles to the south-east of Tyumen. This seemed a very strange route to reach Moscow and aroused immediate suspicions that there was a rescue attempt under way. In fact, Yakovlev had decided to avoid taking the more direct route to Moscow through Ekaterinburg, as he had been warned that the Urals Soviet planned to seize the Tsar on his way through the city.

In the end, Yakovlev's evasive actions to avoid Ekaterinburg were to no avail. The Urals Soviet, hearing that the Tsar's train was heading towards Omsk, sent a detachment of troops to intercept the train at Kulomzino station, about seventy miles from Omsk. Here Yakovlev was forced to hand over his prisoners to the Urals Soviet. The imperial family was taken under close guard to Ekaterinburg, and housed in a mansion once owned by a merchant called Nikolai Ipatiev. It was ominously named 'The House of Special Purposes'. The building was screened from the road by a high wooden palisade, the windows whitewashed so that nobody could see in or out. This indeed was a prison with a sinister intention. It is an irony of history that it was in the Ipatiev Monastery in Kostroma that the Romanov dynasty had been born in 1613 and it was in the Ipatiev House in Ekaterinburg that it finally perished three hundred and five years later.

The city was already a hotbed of Bolshevik revolutionary activity. Hatred and anger towards the former imperial family was intense, particularly amongst the urban working and industrial classes. Five years earlier, during the Romanov Tercentenary celebrations, a new opera theatre had opened in Ekaterinburg with a performance of Glinka's paean of praise to the Romanovs, *A Life for the Tsar*. The theatre had been crowded out with the elite of the Urals, eager to demonstrate their loyalty and affection for the Tsar. By 1918, many of those who had been in the audience that evening were already under arrest, in hiding, or in exile.

There would be no life for the Tsar, or for the city's former ruling classes, in Bolshevik Ekaterinburg.

On 30 April, the Chairman of the Ural Region Soviet sent a message to both Lenin and the Chairman of the All-Russian Central Executive Committee in Moscow, Yakov Sverdlov. This stated, 'This day, I took charge from Commissar Yakovlev of the former Tsar, Nicholas Romanov, the former Tsarina Alexandra, and their daughter Maria Nicolaevna. They have all been lodged in a guarded mansion. Cable your questions and instructions to me'.

On 23 May, Alexei and his three sisters joined their parents in Ekaterinburg. It was a rapturous reunion. Nicholas wrote in his diary, 'It was an immense joy to see them again and to embrace after four weeks of separation'. The family had less than eight weeks to live. Despite the humiliations and the insults that they were now experiencing, the imprisoned Romanovs seemed to draw comfort and solace from being together under one roof. Religious devotions and biblical readings became a feature of their daily lives.

As Russia plunged into civil war in the summer of 1918, their hopes of an eventual rescue began to grow. Secret messages were smuggled into the Ipatiev house, which promised the family that help was on the way. Most of these appear to have been fake letters, sent by Bolshevik agents who wanted to build up evidence that the imperial family were conspiring with counter-revolutionaries. The Romanovs' replies confirmed to the Urals Soviet that the family were indeed a growing threat to the survival of the Revolution.

By June, a full-scale anti-Bolshevik uprising was under way in Siberia. A provisional national government had been established in Omsk by the White armies, those forces opposing the 'Red' Bolshevik government of Lenin. A Czech legion of 40,000 trained soldiers supporting the Whites had taken Samara and cut the telephone lines between Moscow and Ekaterinburg. It looked increasingly likely that the Czechs would soon reach Ekaterinburg. The distant gunfire of the advancing White armies could now be heard in the city. Lenin's great fear was that the Whites would free the Tsar and his family. Siberia would then become a base for a monarchist counter-revolution. It was obvious that this could not be allowed to happen.

In early July, as Czech legions surrounded Ekaterinburg, a new Commander was appointed to guard the Romanovs at the Ipatiev House. His name was Yakov Yurovsky. He was a hard line Chekist, a member of the security organisation established by Lenin to suppress opposition to the new regime. He treated the family with a detached and cool politeness, but he was also ruthless and cruel in the way that he insisted on getting them to obey his orders.

The decision to execute the imperial family was made by the Urals Soviet in Ekaterinburg on 29 June. A formal request was then sent to the Central Executive Committee in Moscow. Lenin, Sverdlov and five other members of the Committee agreed that the Urals Soviet could carry out the action at a date of their choosing, but they needed to get final approval from Moscow before they proceeded.

On 15 July, Yurovsky received confirmation from Moscow that the entire imperial family could now be eliminated. These orders came from Sverdlov and through him from Lenin. There were to be no exceptions. The entire family must die to save the Revolution.

In the early hours of 17 July, the imperial family and their remaining four retainers were roused from their beds. They were told that for their own safety they needed to move to the lower floor of the house. The city was in confusion and chaos. There was shooting taking place in the streets. The Tsar and the Tsarina, followed by their five children and their retainers, amongst these their family doctor Eugene Botkin, and the Tsarina's loyal maid Anna Demidova, descended the stairs into the courtyard. There was no sense of alarm, and no panic, amongst the small group.

They were then taken into a small ground-floor room, from which all the furniture had been removed. The Tsarina requested chairs for herself and Alexei. These were brought. Alexei's knee was improving but he could still not stand up straight. Yurovsky later commented that he had seen no reason why the heir to the throne should not die in a chair.

It was now 1.30 in the morning. Outside in the courtyard, the engine of a lorry could be heard revving up. It was there on a special mission, with the responsibility to carry the bodies of the imperial family to a remote location outside the city following their execution. Yurovsky informed the assembled group that he wanted photographs taken of them as proof that they were all still alive. Rumours were circulating that some harm had befallen the family, and the photographs would prove that this was not the case.

Yurovsky had begun planning the murders a day before, on 15 July. He decided that there needed to be an exact match of one executioner to one victim. This he hoped would make the process cleaner and less fraught. He later wrote, 'It's no easy matter to arrange an execution, contrary to what some people may think'. The dispassionate tone in which Yurovsky wrote this recalls the cold, rational indifference of Bazarov and the Nihilists. The monstrous spirit summoned up by Turgenev, on a storm-swept day on the Isle of Wight, had now achieved its final, terrible apotheosis in Ekaterinburg.

There were three hundred guards at the Ipatiev House. Yurovsky personally selected a small group of men whom he believed would not flinch from carrying out the murders. Two of them refused to be involved when they were told that that the royal women would be killed alongside the Tsar. The men who agreed to take part were then armed with Mauser and Browning revolvers.

The executioners burst into the room, which now became a cramped space with over twenty people in it. Yurovsky faced the Tsar and read out the family's death sentence. 'Nikolai Alexandrovich, in view of the fact that your relatives are continuing their attack on Soviet Russia, the Ural Executive Committee has decided to execute you'.

There was a stunned silence in the room and Nicholas turned to his family and exclaimed, 'What? What?'. These were the last words he ever spoke. There were muffled cries of shock and despair from the others. Alexandra tried to cross herself. The men raised their weapons and fired into the group.

The Tsar and Tsarina died immediately. It took longer for the others to be killed. In the confusion, any semblance of order was lost. The men fired randomly amidst the smoke, shrieks and cries of pain. The bullets bounced off the walls and for a moment the Grand Duchesses seemed to be escaping death and cowered in a corner of the room, begging for mercy.

Jewels had been sewn into their corsets which meant that the bullets could not reach their bodies. In the end the executioners were driven to stabbing them to death with bayonets and shooting them directly in the head. It was a gruesome and macabre end to Russia's greatest dynasty, an event which haunts the country to this day.

The bodies were taken by lorry to a disused mineshaft called 'Four Brothers' in the Koptyaki Forest outside Ekaterinburg. The disposal of the physical remains of the family and their retainers was chaotic. Yurovsky was infuriated by the poor planning of his colleague, Peter Ermakov, whom he had entrusted with the detailed implementation of this part of the operation. Ermakov was drunk, as were most of the men whom he had brought with him. They only had one spade between them and there was not enough sulphuric acid to completely dissolve all the bodies. The victims were stripped of their clothes, their belongings scattered on the ground, and attempts were made to chop up the corpses before burning them and then burying them in the mine shaft.

Yurovsky did not believe that the burial site was secure. The mine shaft was too shallow to disguise the dismembered and half-burnt bodies. Two days later, he decided that the remains should be exhumed and reburied in a more remote spot, at a copper mine deeper in the forest. The lorry stalled, however, on its way to the mine, in a meadow called 'Porosenkov Log' or 'Pig's Meadow'. The men were too exhausted to continue and so a pit was quickly dug, and the bodies tipped into it. They were covered with quicklime and railway sleepers were placed on top to disguise the site.

Porosenkov Log would remain the secret resting place of the imperial family until five of their skeletons were exhumed in 1991. After detailed investigations and DNA tests, which involved using DNA provided by the Duke of Edinburgh - one of the Romanovs' closest living descendants - the Russians declared the remains found in the meadow to be those of Nicholas, Alexandra, Olga, Tatiana and Anastasia. They were officially reburied at the Peter and Paul Cathedral in St Petersburg eighty years after their deaths, together with the remains of their four faithful servants. The remains of Alexei and Maria were recovered later, from a separate grave, but have still not been released for burial.

Over the next few weeks, other members of the Romanov family met similarly savage ends. On 18 July, four royal Princes and the Grand Duchess Elizabeth Feodorovna, the sister of the Tsarina, were taken to a mine shaft outside the town of Alapayevsk, where they were murdered with gun shots and explosives. Despite their brutal treatment, Elizabeth Feodorovna survived the initial assault and her voice could be heard singing psalms and hymns from the depths of the mine, until a further round of hand grenades silenced her forever.

The death of Elizabeth Feodorovna shocked many people around the world. Following the assassination of her husband in 1905, she had given away all her wealth and founded an order of nuns dedicated to helping the poor. She died alongside another nun, Sister Barbara Yakovleva. Both women had dedicated the last years of their lives to supporting the SS *Martha and Mary Convent* in Moscow where Elizabeth was Abbess. This was a place which had become a beacon of hope for the poor and dispossessed living in the city.

In the early hours of 28 January 1919, four Romanov Grand Dukes, all of whom were close relatives of the Tsar, were executed by firing squad in front of the Peter and Paul Church in St Petersburg. They were buried in a mass grave along with thirteen other people shot that morning. One of the victims was the eminent historian, Grand Duke Nicholas Mikhailovich, a committed liberal who had argued for radical political reforms. In his later years, he became fascinated by the reign of Tsar Alexander I and published fifteen books on the period. Maxim Gorky pleaded with Lenin to spare the Grand Duke's life, but was curtly informed, 'The Revolution has no more need of historians'.

Grand Duke Michael, Nicholas's brother and the man to whom he entrusted the future of the Romanov dynasty, was murdered a month before the imperial family. On 13 June 1918, he and his loyal private secretary, the Englishman Nicholas Johnson, had been driven to a forest outside the town of Perm, where both men were executed by a squad of Bolshevik secret police. As he died, the man who had abandoned the throne of his ancestors may well have reflected bitterly on his statement that he did not care which form of government Russia had, so long as there was order and justice.

35

Neverland on Wight

The story of the Romanov dynasty and its relationship with the Isle of Wight began in 1698 with Peter the Great sailing in the Solent. It ended there 220 years later. In 1918, the Tsarina's eldest sister Victoria, was living in Kent House in East Cowes, and planned to turn the Island into a sanctuary for the daughters of Nicholas and Alexandra.

Victoria was the eldest daughter of the Grand Duke of Hesse and his wife, Princess Alice. She was one year older than her sister Elizabeth and seven years older than her sister Alix. After the death of their mother in 1878, the motherless children were taken under the care and protection of Queen Victoria, and the Isle of Wight became a second home for the Hesse children.

Their first visit had been in 1868, when Prince Louis and Princess Alice arrived with their three eldest children. In 1875, they all returned for a second visit, this time with the young Alix. According to Michael Hunter, in his article *The Romanovs at Osborne*, Queen Victoria was smitten with Alix from the moment that she first saw her. In her diary she records that she 'tried to make a sketch of the adorable, splendid little Alix'. She described her as being 'very fidgety' and said, 'I don't like to be maked'. Victoria went on to write, 'she has the most beautiful colouring and deep large blue eyes'. The children used to enjoy going down to the Swiss Cottage, a fully-equipped and substantial playhouse which Prince Albert had built in the grounds of Osborne, where they took tea with the Queen, tended the gardens and planted trees.

In August 1878, Princess Alice made her last visit to the Isle of Wight. She brought all her children with her. Victoria was worried by how pale and thin her daughter looked. Four months later in December 1878, Alice was dead from diphtheria. Despite her own grief at the news, the Queen lost no time in inviting the whole family, including Prince Louis, over to Osborne. They arrived on 21 January 1879, and spent the next month staying with Victoria.

The Queen remained obsessed with little Alix, whom she felt was particularly fragile and needed extra cosseting. It was as though she sensed that a menacing shadow hung over the child. This fear would remain with Victoria all her life. On Sunday 2 February, she wrote in her diary, 'Alix looked very sweet in her long cloak. I feel a constant returning pang, in looking at this lovely child, thinking that her darling mother, who so doted on her, was no longer here on earth to watch over her'.

Over the next few years the Hesse children would return to Osborne on a regular basis, to spend long periods with their grandmother. These visits would usually last several weeks. The Queen would always await Alix's arrival with great delight. In July 1885 at the time of Princess Beatrice's wedding on the Isle of Wight, she wrote that Alix looked 'lovelier than ever and immensely grown'.

In 1887, the Queen celebrated the fiftieth anniversary of her accession to the throne. There were celebrations all over the country, but the moments that Victoria cherished the most that year were the weeks that she spent at Osborne with her favourite grandchildren, Victoria, Elizabeth and Alix. The three Princesses accompanied the Queen as she toured the Island in her open carriage, receiving loyal addresses from enthusiastic crowds in Cowes, Ryde and Newport.

In her journal the Queen recorded, 'there were endless kind inscriptions, flags, flowers, green boughs and festoons across the streets'. Memories of that glorious summer on the Isle of Wight must have returned to Alix as she travelled across Russia twenty-six years later, during the Romanov tercentenary of 1913.

For Alix, the Isle of Wight would always remain a place of comfort and safety, a sheltered retreat to which she could always return and find sanctuary in the arms of her beloved grandmother. It must surely have crossed her mind many times during the dark days of 1918, when her entire world was turned upside down, that this English island would be the one place her family might finally find peace and security.

Alix returned to Osborne in the summers of 1888 and 1889. It was here, in 1894, that she also spent time with her fiancé, the Tsarevich Nicholas, after their official engagement. Ten years earlier in 1884, Alix's sister, Princess Victoria had married Prince Louis Alexander of Battenberg, an officer in the Royal Navy and a relative of the Princess through a morganatic branch of her own German family. The couple made their home in Britain, apart from short assignments to the Mediterranean fleet in Malta. Prince Louis was a capable and well-regarded Naval commander and in 1912, he was appointed to the position of First Sea Lord and Chief of Naval Staff.

With two of her sisters married into the Romanov family, Victoria was a frequent visitor to Russia. She was confident and outgoing, keen to experiment with new ways of doing things, and a sharp judge of character. In this she was unlike her two younger sisters, the shy, retiring Alix and the religious mystic Elizabeth. Victoria thoroughly disapproved of Rasputin and his influence over her sister. She tried speaking with Alix about the need to rely more on conventional medicine in treating Alexei's haemophilia, but she had no success.

At the outbreak of war in August 1914, Victoria was in Ekaterinburg and made a hasty return to Britain. She first returned to St Petersburg where the Tsar quickly arranged for her to travel on to Norway, taking a safe route through the Grand Duchy of Finland. From Norway she sailed back to Britain from the port of Bergen. It was the last time that she would ever see her two sisters. In later years, Victoria would reflect on the sad irony that her last visit to Russia should have been to Ekaterinburg. As she drove to the city's main railway station, she had passed the Ipatiev

House where her beloved sister would be murdered four years later.

In Britain, the war provoked an ugly anti-German mood across the country. German shops and businesses were ransacked and the 53,000 Germans living in the country were widely suspected of being spies and potential traitors. All German men aged between seventeen and fifty-five were interned in prison camps. The German community was largely loyal to Britain, many of them having lived in the country for several generations. They felt accepted in their adopted country. None of this protected them when the war broke out, and popular rage was directed against them.

The Battenbergs, with their strong German family ties, also found that they were not trusted by sections of the British establishment. In late October 1914, the Navy Minister Winston Churchill requested that Prince Louis should resign his position as First Sea Lord. Although King George V opposed his resignation and made him a Privy Councillor, it was not enough to save him.

Louis and Victoria decided to retire to the Isle of Wight, where they spent the rest of the war in quiet seclusion. They moved into Kent House in York Avenue, East Cowes, which was given to them by Princess Louise, Queen Victoria's sixth child, on the death of her husband the Duke of Argyll. The Battenbergs lived there for the next seven years, until Prince Louis's death in 1921.

Kent House had originally been purchased by the Queen in 1864 from Thomas Caitlin, a London lawyer, and was a substantial building with over forty rooms, a carriage house and stables. It was surrounded by large gardens and was a perfect retreat for the Battenbergs. While they were in residence, Prince Louis significantly extended the house and even created the bridge of a ship in one of the attic rooms, to remind himself of his days at sea. Today the house still stands but little remains of its original grandeur.

On 17 July 1917, King George V, feeling under pressure due to his own German family background, formally announced that the royal name of Saxe-Coburg-Gotha would be changed with immediate effect to Windsor. He also requested that all his relatives anglicize their names. This included the Battenbergs, who agreed to change their name to the more English sounding Mountbatten. In order to compensate Prince Louis for all the indignities that he had suffered, the King conferred on him the title of Marquess of Milford Haven in November 1917.

While all this was taking place, Victoria, now the Marchioness of Milford Haven was becoming increasingly worried about the safety of her two sisters in Russia. There was little she could do for Grand Duchess Elizabeth, who refused to leave her convent in Moscow, but there might still be a way to rescue her youngest sister Alix and her family. The refusal of the British government to offer asylum to the Romanovs in early 1917 had appalled Victoria. It is unlikely that she knew the full story behind this and, to the end of her days, probably blamed the Prime Minister Lloyd George for what had happened. However, there are indications that she suspected that the King had not been as helpful as he might have been.

In her desperation to find a way of bringing at least some of the family to safety, she turned to the Foreign Secretary Arthur Balfour, a man whom she respected and whom she knew had expressed sympathies for the former Tsar. According to Helen Rappaport, the author of *The Race to save the Tsar*, the fact that Princess Victoria did this demonstrates that she had lost hope in receiving support from the King.

In a letter written to Balfour on 23 May 1918, Victoria pleaded that an attempt should be made to save the three youngest Romanov daughters, Maria, Tatiana and Anastasia. Already she feared that it might be too late for the Tsar, Tsarina and the Tsarevich, as it was unlikely that they would ever be released by the Bolsheviks. She also thought that the eldest daughter, Olga, might be retained as a hostage. In her view, though, there was hope for the other girls.

'They can be of no value and importance as hostages to a Russian government nor be an embarrassment to any other government in whose country they might reside. I desire greatly, if it be possible, to try and have these girls, the youngest of whom are nineteen and seventeen years old only, put under my charge'.

According to Rappaport, Victoria believed that the Isle of Wight would be an ideal refuge for the Romanov Grand Duchesses. It was a quiet and remote place. She described it as 'this out-of-the-way little Isle of Wight'. The girls could live 'a simple private life with me who am myself quite politically unimportant'. There they could live in total obscurity and be kept away from any Russians.

A sense of despair comes over very clearly in this letter. Here is an aunt trying to save her beloved nieces. She is beginning to fear the worst but is willing to make one last effort.

Arthur Balfour did try to get the matter discussed at a Cabinet meeting but was not successful in eliciting any positive response. On 25 May he replied to Victoria's letter, 'I regret that from all the enquiries that I have made privately from those best acquainted with present conditions in Russia, the difficulties in the way of such a proposal seem to me almost insuperable'.

There was no further correspondence on the matter and within two months, the entire Romanov family had been murdered and buried in a forest outside Ekaterinburg. Victoria would learn the dreadful news a few weeks later, though for a while she hoped that some of the children might have survived.

It is intriguing to speculate whether the Isle of Wight might have become a final refuge for the Russian imperial family. The Tsarina's sister was right in identifying it as a safe and secure place. Had the Tsar and his family been able to escape to Britain in 1917, the Island might well have made a suitable home for them. The fact that the Tsarina's eldest sister was already living there would have made it attractive to Nicholas and Alexandra. They both had very fond memories of the Island from their visits there to see Queen Victoria, and from the time that they had spent there with their family during the 1909 visit to Cowes.

The Island also contained a residence that could have provided appropriate accommodation for the Romanovs. This was Barton Manor, still privately owned in 1917 by the British royal family, and sufficiently large in scale to have housed the exiled Tsar and his modest court. King Edward VII had entertained the imperial family there in August 1909 and the memory of that visit would have given the house an added appeal for the Romanovs. If Victoria's desperate 1918 attempt to bring the three youngest Grand Duchesses to East Cowes had been successful, then the

Isle of Wight would perhaps have emerged as a final refuge for them and other surviving members of the Russian imperial family. The murders in Ekaterinburg prevented any of this from becoming a reality.

Several members of the Romanov family did however succeed in reaching Britain during these tumultuous years. King George V sent the warship *Marlborough* to rescue his aunt, the former Dowager Empress Maria, from the Crimea in April 1919. She was accompanied into exile by her daughter, Grand Duchess Xenia, as well as by two cousins of the Tsar, Grand Dukes Nicholas Nikolaevich and Grand Duke Peter Nikolaevich, and by several members of the Yusupov family.

The Dowager Empress initially spent time in Britain with her sister, Queen Alexandra, but decided that she did not wish to remain there and moved back to her home country of Denmark. She lived out her final years in her summer house at Hvidore on the coast near Copenhagen, supported by a pension from her nephew, George V. She died in 1928, half hoping till the end that Nicholas and his family had somehow managed to survive the Revolution. She was a sad and disappointed woman, who had witnessed the deaths of most of her immediate family and seen her entire life's work collapse before her eyes.

A final insult to her dignity was the arrival of her private belongings from Russia, shipped out in fifteen huge shipping cases and sent to her by courtesy of the Bolshevik government in late 1919. When the cases arrived, Sir Frederick Ponsonby, the Keeper of the Privy Purse, arranged for them to be opened in the grand Throne Room at Buckingham Palace. The first few cases were found to contain pokers, tongs and shovels, along with old railway guides and cheap novels. It turned out that there was nothing of any worth in any of the cases, and each one was filled with nothing but trash. This was intended to be a deliberate provocation by the Bolsheviks, who were making the point that the former Empress was considered as worthless as the rubbish which they had sent her.

Grand Duchess Xenia decided to settle in Britain but fell into poverty very quickly. She made the mistake of selling all the jewels that she had brought out of Russia to a man whom she believed was a jewellery expert. He had then disappeared without paying her for a single item. She was saved from total bankruptcy by George V, who agreed to let her stay in Frogmore Cottage and give her an annual pension of £2,400. Eventually she moved to Wilderness House, a modest property in the grounds of Hampton Court Palace, where she lived until her death in 1960, dying a few months before her sister Olga.

Those members of the Romanov family who sought exile in Britain were, in some ways, an embarrassment to the British royal family. They were a continuous reminder, by their very presence, of the failure of King George V to rescue his Russian cousins. It was also difficult for the British royal family to know where, or how, they fitted into the hierarchy of the contemporary British royal court. They were ghosts from the past, figures from an Imperial Russia that no longer existed. They were rarely invited to royal functions or celebrations and eventually as the years rolled by, they were largely forgotten.

It would take the collapse of the Soviet Union in 1991 before a rehabilitation of the Romanov dynasty could begin to take place inside Russia itself. A few years earlier in November 1981, the Russian Orthodox Church Abroad canonised the last imperial family and their retainers as new martyrs. All were declared to be victims of Bolshevik oppression. On the same date, Grand Duchess Elizabeth and Sister Barbara Yakovleva, along with the four Princes who had been murdered with them, were canonised as the Martyrs of Alapayevsk.

These actions caused considerable controversy between the two branches of the Russian Orthodox Church and amongst the wider public. Those who opposed the canonisation of the Tsar argued that he had been a weak ruler and that his incompetence had brought ruin and sorrow on the country.

In 1992, a year after the fall of the Soviet Union, the Moscow Patriarchate agreed to canonise Grand Duchess Elizabeth and Sister Barbara, two women whom they recognised as being of outstanding virtue and saintliness. They hesitated, though, about conferring this recognition on the Tsar and his family. In 1998, the remains of the last Tsar and Tsarina, together with three of their children, were buried in the St Peter and Paul Cathedral in St Petersburg with the Orthodox Church's official blessing. Two years later, the imperial family were declared to be Saints and Passion Bearers by the Moscow Patriarchate.

Since this announcement in 2000, the religious status of the imperial family has grown significantly, and icons of the last Romanovs are now to be found in churches across Russia and throughout the world. The Romanov Memorial Cross in East Cowes is a perfect example of this elevation of the imperial family into representatives of Russian Orthodox Sainthood.

Meanwhile, today's Russians seek to grasp the enormity of what happened as a result of the Revolution and the impact this event had had on their country during the twentieth century. The decision to restore the name of St Petersburg to Russia's second city revived an interest in the former ruling dynasty. This led to an outpouring of books, journal articles and television programmes which reappraised the legacy of the Romanovs and the contribution which they had made to developing Russia as a major European and Asian power.

This growing interest in Russian imperial history coincided with a recovery of national pride in Russia's spiritual and cultural mission, and the country's role as the standard bearer of Slavic and Orthodox religious values. The Romanovs were the perfect symbols for this movement.

On 16 June 2003, the 'Church on Blood in Honour of all Saints Resplendent in the Russian Land' was consecrated in Ekaterinburg. It stands on the site of the Ipatiev House, which had been demolished in 1977 on the orders of the Soviet Government. The Church contains a museum to the former imperial family and the main altar stands directly on the site of the basement where the Romanovs were executed in 1918.

In May 1996, I visited the site of the Ipatiev House. The construction of the new Church had not yet been started and the foundations of the original building were still visible. It was night when I entered the site, but a full moon illuminated the ghostly remains of the place where the last imperial family had met their brutal end. It was a strange experience to be standing in a place redolent with such memory and history. I threaded my way amongst the masonry and brickwork that still survived and saw the outline of what looked like a small basement room. Was this the place where the murders had taken place, I wondered? There was no answer, only silence, the long echo of lost lives and unfinished dreams.

At 2.30 am on 17 July 2018, the centenary anniversary of the massacre in the Ipatiev House, more than 100,000 people joined a thirteen-mile long procession led by Kirill, the Russian Orthodox Patriarch. It wound its way from the site of the executions to the *Four Brothers* mineshaft, where the bodies of the Romanovs were initially buried. In the same week, prayers were held in Churches across Russia to the memory of the Tsar and his family. Some Orthodox believers claimed that their prayers had been answered by the imperial family, who had interceded to cure their illnesses.

It is hard to know what this new veneration of the Romanovs signifies both for Russia in the twenty-first century and for the way in which the country needs to come to terms with its recent history. This may be a natural reaction to many years of Soviet propaganda and a rebalancing of the historical narrative. It may equally presage the creation of a new national myth, in which the last Tsar is accorded the status of a martyred and misunderstood ruler, who died for his people's salvation. A move in this direction may be needed to rebalance the distortions of the Soviet period, but equally it would be a mistake to believe that the Tsar did not contribute, in some ways, to the misfortunes that befell his country in the years that he was on the throne.

The unveiling of the memorial to the Romanovs on the Isle of Wight on 7 July 2018 reflected the challenge that is now facing Russia in its efforts to construct a new narrative about the Romanov dynasty. It is fitting that this memorial was erected on the island in the English Channel which has had such a long and close association with the dynasty and the Russian Empire.

Prince Rostislav Romanov, the great-grandson of Grand Duchess Xenia, the Tsar's sister, spoke at the ceremony in East Cowes. His speech was quiet and reflective. He did not refer to the long-standing mistrust and suspicion that had clouded relations between Russia and Britain since the nineteenth century. There was only a brief reference to the alliance that had emerged in 1909 between the two countries and which had been sealed by the Tsar's last visit to the Isle of Wight.

Prince Rostislav chose instead to describe the joy and happiness of the Tsar's children as they played on the beach at Osborne and wandered freely along the streets and lanes of East Cowes. The Isle of Wight had long been a retreat for the Romanovs and for a few days in August 1909, the whole family could believe that they had discovered a place of safety and security.

This is perhaps where we should leave the last Romanovs, in the golden light of the little island that might have become their last home, if events had taken a different turn. On the centenary of the family's murder, 17 July 2018, some of the Romanov family gathered in Ekaterinburg, while I took the road from East Cowes, past Osborne House, to the royal church at Whippingham.

In the shadow of the late afternoon, I searched for the small memorial that I knew existed in the church to Russia's last imperial rulers. It is not easy to find, as it is situated on a side wall in the Mountbatten Memorial chapel. It is a modest and largely forgotten tribute to a family who once presided over one of the most powerful Empires in the world and were finally abandoned by everyone who might have helped them, including their own British cousins. The one woman who fought valiantly to save them was Victoria, the Marchioness of Milford Haven, the Tsarina's beloved elder sister, and the grandmother of Prince Philip, the Duke of Edinburgh. It is no coincidence that she chose to be buried here. Her grave lies in the cemetery outside the church, close to the memorial to her murdered sister, nephew and nieces.

36

Epilogue and dedication

The fall of Tsarist Russia in 1917 and the Revolution and Civil War that followed destroyed the lives of millions of subjects living in Imperial Russia. People from every strata of society were suddenly condemned to living on the margins of a country that they no longer recognised, were denounced as public enemies, and declared to be 'Former People'. Many were murdered or disappeared into the totally alien environment of Soviet Russia. In desperation, hundreds of thousands fled the country, cast up as refugees on foreign shores and dependant on the generosity and kindness of people whom they hardly knew. My own family was part of this huge exodus. The Romanov family, or those members of it who survived the destruction of the Empire over which they had once ruled, were similarly scattered to all corners of the world.

Amongst the few photographs that my family managed to bring out of Russia was one taken of my grandfather in his official Tsarist uniform. He was photographed in 1909, the year that the Tsar visited the Isle of Wight. He is wearing a smart navy-blue jacket, with a stiff white shirt fixed at the collar with a bow tie. In the lapels of the jacket are two golden Tsarist eagles. He was the very image of the dedicated Tsarist public servant, who had dedicated his life to the Romanov regime and believed that this life would follow its prescribed and ordered pattern. In 1922, a very different photograph was taken. My grandparents had just reached the safety of Romania after their flight across the Dniester river in May of that year. They are both wearing threadbare clothes and their eyes are hollow and filled with pain. This is a photograph of despair and fear, a haunting glimpse into a world turned upside down.

This book is dedicated to my grandparents, to the nameless young woman with the floral scarf who drowned while trying to cross the Dniester river, and to the millions of Russians who believed in a bright and hopeful future for their country but in the end were destroyed by the collapse of the Romanov dynasty. It is also dedicated to the people of Britain, and to my mother and her family, who gave my father sanctuary, love and security when he fled the turmoil of Eastern Europe after the Second World War.

THE EARLY ROMANOVS 1613 - 1801

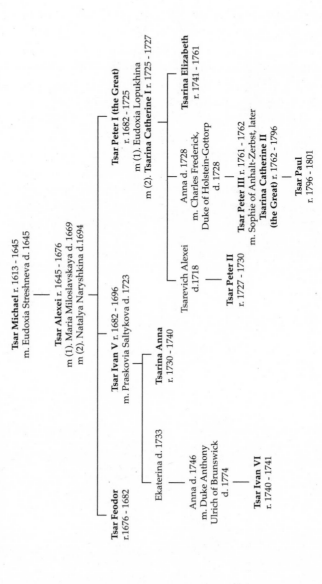

Tsar Michael r. 1613 - 1645
m. Eudoxia Streshneva d. 1645

Tsar Alexei r. 1645 - 1676
m (1). Maria Miloslavskaya d. 1669
m (2). Natalya Naryshkina d.1694

Tsar Feodor
r.1676 - 1682

Tsar Ivan V r. 1682 - 1696
m. Praskovia Saltykova d. 1723

Tsar Peter I (the Great)
r. 1682 - 1725
m (1). Eudoxia Lopukhina
m (2). **Tsarina Catherine I** r. 1725 - 1727

Ekaterina d. 1733

Tsarina Anna
r. 1730 - 1740

Tsarevich Alexei
d.1718

Anna d. 1728
m. Charles Frederick,
Duke of Holstein-Gottorp
d. 1728

Tsarina Elizabeth
r. 1741 - 1761

Anna d. 1746
m. Duke Anthony
Ulrich of Brunswick
d. 1774

Tsar Peter II
r. 1727 - 1730

Tsar Peter III r. 1761 - 1762
m. Sophie of Anhalt-Zerbst, later
Tsarina Catherine II
(the Great) r. 1762 - 1796

Tsar Ivan VI
r. 1740 - 1741

Tsar Paul
r. 1796 - 1801

THE LATER ROMANOVS 1801-1918

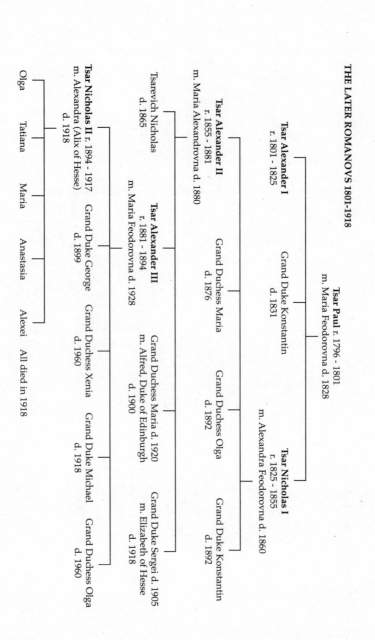

Tsar Paul r. 1796 - 1801
m. Maria Feodorovna d. 1828

Tsar Alexander I
r. 1801 - 1825

Grand Duke Konstantin
d. 1831

Tsar Nicholas I
r. 1825 - 1855
m. Alexandra Feodorovna d. 1860

Tsarevich Nicholas
d. 1865

Tsar Alexander II
r. 1855 - 1881
m. Maria Alexandrovna d. 1880

Grand Duchess Maria
d. 1876

Grand Duchess Olga
d. 1892

Grand Duke Konstantin
d. 1892

Tsar Nicholas II r. 1894 - 1917
m. Alexandra (Alix of Hesse)
d. 1918

Tsar Alexander III
r. 1881 - 1894
m. Maria Feodorovna d. 1928

Grand Duchess Maria d. 1920
m. Alfred, Duke of Edinburgh
d. 1900

Grand Duke Sergei d. 1905
m. Elizabeth of Hesse
d. 1918

Grand Duke George
d. 1899

Grand Duchess Xenia
d. 1960

Grand Duke Michael
d. 1918

Grand Duchess Olga
d. 1960

Olga   Tatiana   Maria   Anastasia   Alexei   All died in 1918

THE BRITISH, HESSE, DANISH & GREEK CONNECTIONS TO THE ROMANOVS

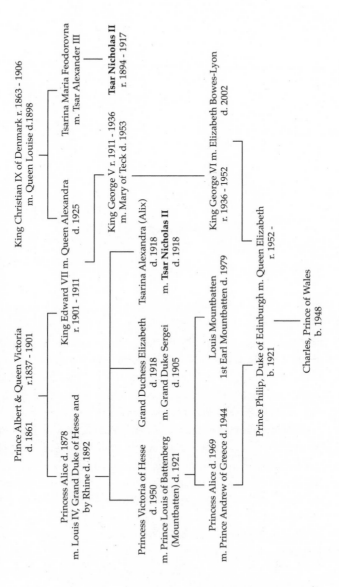

Prince Albert & Queen Victoria r.1837 - 1901
Prince Albert d. 1861

King Christian IX of Denmark r. 1863 - 1906
m. Queen Louise d.1898

Tsarina Maria Feodorovna
m. Tsar Alexander III

Tsar Nicholas II
r. 1894 - 1917

King Edward VII m. Queen Alexandra
r. 1901 - 1911 d. 1925

King George V r. 1911 - 1936
m. Mary of Teck d. 1953

Princess Alice d. 1878
m. Louis IV, Grand Duke of Hesse and
by Rhine d. 1892

Grand Duchess Elizabeth
d. 1918
m. Grand Duke Sergei
d. 1905

Tsarina Alexandra (Alix)
d. 1918
m. **Tsar Nicholas II**
d. 1918

King George VI m. Elizabeth Bowes-Lyon
r. 1936 - 1952 d. 2002

Princess Victoria of Hesse
d. 1950
m. Prince Louis of Battenberg
(Mountbatten) d. 1921

Louis Mountbatten
1st Earl Mountbatten d. 1979

Prince Philip, Duke of Edinburgh m. Queen Elizabeth
b. 1921 r. 1952 -

Princess Alice d. 1969
m. Prince Andrew of Greece d. 1944

Charles, Prince of Wales
b. 1948

Notes on Bibliographic Sources

PART I: THE PROLOGUE

The history of my family's flight from Russia to Poland between 1920 and 1922 survives through photographs, and the oral history handed down to me by my father's family, particularly my grandmother. She told me the full story of the journey through Russia and across the Dniester river when I made my first ever visit to Poland, in September 1977. I was twenty-four years old then, the same age as my father had been when, in 1944, he fled Vilna as the Soviet armies advanced westwards. My grandmother was ninety when I met her, but this in no way deterred her from climbing onto a table and singing me an old Russian love song, with a vodka glass in hand. She then described, in vivid detail, the events that had unfolded during the family's flight from Russia, and the kindness of the Romanian family who had saved them from almost certain death. We have copies of the documents issued by the Romanian authorities when my grandparents crossed the River Dniester and reached Soroca in Romania, in late May 1922.

In 1916, in an act of patriotic zeal, my grandfather had also invested most of his personal savings in Russian Imperial War Bonds. These bonds were repudiated by the Soviet government in February 1918. The only item that he managed to bring out of Russia was an antique, silver-framed icon of the *Feodorovskaya Mother of God*, the Black Virgin Mary of Kostroma and the patron icon of the Romanov family. This was handed down to him by his grandfather, Alexis Alexandrovich Romanovsky. It was lost during the Second World War.

Two good books on Russian emigration after the Revolution are:

Brown, Douglas, *Doomsday 1917: The Destruction of Russia's Ruling Class,* Sidgwick and Jackson, 1975

Smith, Douglas, *Former People: The Last Days of the Russian Aristocracy*, London, Macmillan, 2012

I have had a long-standing interest in the Romanovs, and I have read widely about the role that they played in both Russian and British history. In writing this book about the Romanovs and Britain, I consulted original sources which included personal diaries, letters, government and parliamentary papers. Newspaper reports from Britain, Russia, France and Germany were also a very good source of contemporary comments and views. There is now an increasing amount of secondary information available, both in print and digital formats, about the relationship between Britain and the Romanovs during the period 1613-1918. I will explore my main sources under each of the relevant chapter headings.

One outstanding book which covers the entire period of the Romanovs and their connection with Britain is *Russia: Art, Royalty and the Romanovs*, published in 2019 by the Royal Collections Trust to accompany the same-named exhibition at the Queen's Gallery in Buckingham Palace. It contains a foreword by HRH The Prince of Wales, with an excellent introduction by Stephen Patterson and essays by many other leading experts. It is a visually lavish account of the cultural and artistic relationship between Britain and Russia during the 300 years that the Romanovs were the imperial rulers of Russia.

I first visited the Isle of Wight in 1961, when I was eight years old. I have made many visits since then and in many ways consider the Island to be a second home. My publisher and friend, Peter Harrigan, lives on the Island and runs the Medina bookshop in Cowes. It was during one of my visits to see Peter that the idea for a book on the Romanovs and the Isle of Wight first emerged. I have now visited all the places and sites connected with the Romanovs on the Island. On 7 July 2018, I was privileged to be invited to attend the unveiling of the Romanov Memorial Cross in Jubilee Park, East Cowes, and met many of those involved in funding and erecting the Cross. These included Maria Harwood and members of the Grand Duchess Elizabeth Romanov Society, as well as David Hill, Karl Love and other representatives from East Cowes Town Council, and David and Sarah Burdett from the East Cowes Heritage Society. They have all worked tirelessly to raise awareness of the Romanov family's connections with Britain and the Isle of Wight.

The East Cowes Heritage Centre in East Cowes is a rich and valuable source of material relating to East Cowes, and all the places closely associated with the Romanovs that were in existence during their visits to the Island. The Heritage Centre has a wide range of books, pamphlets, newspaper archives, photographs and maps.

The Royal Yacht Squadron, housed in a building popularly known as the 'Castle', is located on the Parade in Cowes. The building looks very similar to what it did in 1909, when the Tsar was elected as member of the RYS. The Royal Yacht Squadron has an archive and library, rich in books, club papers and journals relating to the history of the Squadron, as well as photographs and paintings.

The Classic Boat Museum in East Cowes has a library with a lot of useful material on the Isle of Wight's yachting history, including boat journals covering the 1909 Cowes Week.

Osborne House has a good bookshop with a wide range of books and materials about the history of Osborne House during the reign of Queen Victoria and Prince Albert. There are also paintings in Osborne House linked to the Romanovs, including Heinrich von Angeli's famous 1879 painting of the Hesse family. This includes portraits of the future Tsarina Alexandra and her sister, Grand Duchess Elizabeth.

Osborne Cottage, where the Romanovs frequently stayed, is now a private residence, as are Barton Manor, where the imperial family was entertained to afternoon tea in August 1909, and Kent House, which was the home of Princess Victoria, the elder sister of the Tsarina.

Beken of Cowes is at 16 Birmingham Road in Cowes, and the shop contains a valuable archive of original photographs taken during the visit by the Romanovs to the Isle of Wight in 1909, as well as a rich collection of yachting photographs stretching back over 100 years. These include photographs of the Imperial yacht *Shtandart*, the Royal yacht *Victoria and Albert*, the Naval Review, and scenes on shore during Cowes Week. The original Beken Pharmacy shop which the Grand Duchesses Olga and Tatiana visited in August 1909 still stands on the opposite side of the road.

Benzie, the jewellers in Cowes which Grand Duchesses Olga and Tatiana also visited and in which they were besieged by a huge crowd of excited onlookers, is still operating at 61, High Street.

St Mildred's Church, Whippingham is located a few miles outside East Cowes and is open to the public. It contains the tomb of Prince Henry of Battenberg, and the chair used by Queen Victoria, which Grand Duchesses Olga and Tatiana saw during their visit, as well as the memorial to the Romanov family. This is in the Mountbatten family chapel. In the churchyard outside are the tombs of Prince Louis Mountbatten and his wife, Princess Victoria Mountbatten.

Ventnor, Blackgang Chine, and the Tsar Alexander I monument on St Catherine's Down are the other places on the Isle of Wight connected to the Romanovs. These are covered in *Notes on Sources Part III* and *Part IV.*

Key secondary sources

Burdett, Sarah and Prior, Margaret, *East Cowes; A Town of Ships, Castles, Industry and Invention,* Wimborne Minster: The Dovecote Press, 2011

Burdett, Sarah, *Victoria's Island Village Whippingham,* KSW Books, 2018

Hunter, Michael, *Romanovs at Osborne House* in *The Last Romanovs: Archival and Museum Discoveries in Great Britain and Russia,* London: Pindar Press, 2018

North, Mike, *The Royal Navy and the Royal Marines on the Isle of Wight,*
    The Isle of Wight Society, 2012
Turner, Michael, *Osborne: A Guidebook,* English Heritage, no publication
    date

PART II: THE EARLY ROMANOVS AND BRITAIN:
INSPIRATION AND DISENCHANTMENT 1613-1800

There is a wealth of material on both the early Romanovs and their relationship with Britain in the period 1613-1800. One of the first books published in England about Russia was Giles Fletcher's *The History of Russia, or, the Government of the Emperour of Muscovia with the Manners & Fashions of the People of that Countrey*, which was written in the late sixteenth century and re-published several times during the seventeenth century.

Lord Macaulay's *History of England*, which first appeared in 1848, contains an entertaining and colourful overview of Anglo-Russian relations and he focuses on the visit of Tsar Peter the Great in 1698. He uses vivid language to tell the story of Peter's travels around England and describes the Tsar as having 'an intellectual forehead, piercing black eyes, and a tartar nose'.

An oversized statue of Peter the Great and his dwarf servant stands in Glaisher Street, in Deptford, south-east London. It is an intriguing and bizarre sculpture and was erected to commemorate the Tsar's three-month long stay in England in 1698. It was designed by two Russian artists, Viacheslav Bukhaev and Mikhail Chemiakin, and was unveiled in June 2001 by Prince Michael of Kent. The Tsar lived in a house belonging to the diarist, John Evelyn, in Sayes Court in Deptford, and studied shipbuilding in a shipyard close to his present statue. The house no longer exists.

Joseph Nye, the Master Shipbuilder of Peter the Great, established a yard in East Cowes where he constructed naval vessels. It was here that he built up his reputation as one of the finest shipwrights of his generation.

Nye's shipyard was eventually taken over by J. Samuel White, the founder of one the most famous of the Isle of Wight's shipbuilding companies. It ceased to operate in 1981.

Josiah Wedgwood's famous Frog dinner and dessert service, commissioned by Catherine the Great in 1773, is now the property of the State Hermitage Museum in St Petersburg. However, one plate was retained in London. This is on display at the British Galleries in the Victoria and Albert Museum.

120 of the paintings from Sir Robert Walpole's famous art collection are now in the possession of the State Hermitage Museum in St Petersburg. A selection of them returned to Britain in 2013, where they were exhibited at their original home in Houghton Hall, Norfolk.

Key secondary sources

Cavendish, Richard, *The Murder of Tsar Paul I*, History Today, Vol 51, Issue 3, March 2001

Cross, Anthony, *In the Lands of the Romanovs: An Annotated Bibliography of First-Hand English-Language Accounts of the Russian Empire 1613-1917*, Open Book Publishers, 2014

Cross, Anthony, *Anglo-Russica: Aspects of Cultural Relations between Great Britain and Russia in the Eighteenth and Early Nineteenth Centuries*, Oxford: Berg Publishers, 1993

Hughes, Lindsey, *Russia in the age of Peter the Great*, New Haven and London: Yale University Press, 1998

Martin, Rob, *Joseph Nye: From East Cowes to St Petersburg Peter the Great's Master Shipbuilder*, Isle of Wight: Vectis Publishing, 2004

Montefiore, Simon Sebag, *The Romanovs: 1613-1918*, London: Weidenfield & Nicolson, 2016

Piotrovsky, Mikhail and Dedinkin, Mikhail, *The Hampton Court Albums of Catherine the Great*, Fontanka, 2016

Sweet, Matthew, *Wedgwood: The Empress and the Frog* in *Wedgwood Museum and World of Wedgwood*, September 2014

Tucker, Clara, *The Russians in the Channel Islands* in *Annual Bulletin of La Société Jersiaise*, 1968

Vaizey, Marina, *The Walpole Paintings at Houghton Hall: A Brief Homecoming*, Moscow: Tretyakov Gallery Magazine, Number 4, 2013

Williamson, George, *The Imperial Russian Dinner Service*, London, George Bell and Sons, 1909

PART III: TSARS ALEXANDER I AND NICHOLAS I: ALLIANCE AND CONFLICT 1800-1856

The monument erected in honour of Tsar Alexander I in 1814 still stands on St Catherine's Down, in the south-east corner of the Island. It is maintained by the National Trust, and it has recently been renovated. The inscription to the Tsar is clearly visible. The monument also contains a later inscription in memory of the British soldiers who died in the Crimean War of 1853-1856. Many of the places that Tsar Nicholas I visited during his time in England can still be seen. The Royal Arsenal in Woolwich, where he arrived and departed, has now been renovated and developed with a museum, restaurants and shops. Chiswick House, where a large celebration was held in the Tsar's honour, is now managed by English Heritage and is open to the public. Many of the finest of Roger Fenton's Crimean war photographs are owned by the Royal Collections Trust. Others are on display at the Imperial War Museum in London.

Original Sources

De Grellet, Étienne, *Memoirs of the Life and Gospel Labours of Stephen de Grellet,* Vol 1, London, 1860

Frampton, Mary, *The Journal of Mary Frampton from the Year 1779 until the Year 1846,* ed Harriot Georgiana Mundy, London, 1885

Queen Victoria's Journals contain important references to the visit of Tsar Nicholas I to England in 1844 and to events taking place in the Crimean War. All rights in *Queen Victoria's Journals* are reserved to HM Queen Elizabeth II, and the author and publisher are grateful for permission to use extracts from the *Journals* in this book.

Romanov, Grand Duke Nicholas (trans Henry Havelock), *Scenes of*

Russian Court Life, Being the Correspondence of Alexander I with His Sister Catherine, London: Jarrolds Ltd, 1917

Temperley, Howard (editor), *The Unpublished Diary and Political Sketches of Princess Lieven Together With Some of Her Letters*, London, 1925

The Times newspaper is a valuable source of contemporary news and comment about Tsar Nicholas I's visit to England in early June 1844. There are reports both about his visit and about the popular opposition to his visit. The editions of 4 June, 5 June and 6 June are particularly useful.

Punch, the popular satirical magazine which flourished in Victorian Britain, published several very good cartoons and short articles lampooning Tsar Nicholas I during his 1844 State visit. Many more were published during the Crimean War.

Key Secondary Sources

Baldwin, Gordon; et al, *All the Mighty World: The Photographs of Roger Fenton 1852-1860*, New York: The Metropolitan Museum of Art, 2004

Hartley, J.M., *Is Russia Part of Europe? Russian Perceptions of Europe in the Reign of Alexander I* in *Cahiers du Monde Russe et Sovietique*, 1992, 369-385

Kizilov, Michael, *Between Leipzig and Vienna. The Visit of Russian Emperor Alexander I to England in 1814 as Seen through the Eyes of Contemporaries*, published on www.academia.edu

Lieven, Dominic, *Russia against Napoleon: The Battle for Europe, 1807-1814*, London: Allen Lane, 2009

Lincoln, Bruce W., *The Emperor Nicholas I in England*, History Today, Vol 25 Issue I, January 1975

Riasanovsky, Nicholas V, *Nicholas I and Official Nationality in Russia 1825-1855*, Berkeley: University of California Press, 1959

Simon Sebag Montefiore, *The Romanovs: 1613-1918*, London: Weidenfeld & Nicolson, 2016

Sobolev, Olga, *The reception of Alfred Tennyson in Russia* LSE Research Online, November 2016

Temperley, Harold, *England and the Near East*, London: Longmans,

Green and Co, 1936

Tennyson, Alfred (Lord), *The Charge of the Light Brigade*, poem first published December 1854

Troubetzkoy, Alexis S., *A Brief history of the Crimean War,* London: Constable Robinson, 2006

Williams, David L. and de Kerbrech, Richard P., *J. Samuel White and Co Shipbuilders*, Cheltenham: History Press, 2012

Wright, Dorothy, *Michael Hoy, 1758-1828: Russia Merchant* in *Proceedings of the Hampshire Field Club and Archaeological Society*, Vol 47, 1991

PART IV: WIGHT RUSSIANS

Ventnor is closely associated with radical Russia and there are several streets and buildings in the town closely identified with political thinkers like Alexander Herzen and Pavel Annenkov, and writers such as Ivan Turgenev and Count Alexei Tolstoy. The house where Herzen stayed, St Augustine Villa, still stands close to the sea in Ventnor, while the site of Belinda House, where Turgenev rented rooms, is now marked with a blue plaque. Karl Marx lived at 1, St Boniface Gardens, where he wrote part of *Das Kapital*, a book which was to inspire several generations of Russian Marxists.

Close to Ventnor is Blackgang Chine, where Turgenev spent time on a stormy day in August 1860. His visit there inspired him to write his novel *Fathers and Sons* and conjure up the character of the nihilist Yevgeny Bazarov, who went on to haunt the soul of revolutionary Russia.

I am particularly grateful to Dr Sarah. J. Young for her article *In Herzen's footsteps: a visit to Ventnor*, to *The Slavonic and East European Review* for the article by Richard Freeborn, *Turgenev at Ventnor* and the article by James B. Woodward, *Turgenev's Phantoms*. I am also indebted to Faber and Faber for permission to use a short extract from Tom Stoppard's play *Salvage*, the third play in the *Coast of Utopia* series. One of the scenes is set in Ventnor at a time when it became a fashionable holiday destination for Russian political radicals.

Original sources

Herzen, Alexander, *My Past and Thoughts*, Vol IV, London: Chatto and Windus, 1968. This contains several letters between Herzen and Turgenev, referring to Yevgeny Bazarov, the leading character in Turgenev's novel *Fathers and Sons.*

Turgenev, Ivan, *Fathers and Sons*, Moscow: Grachev and Co, 1862. The first English language edition was published in New York in 1867 by Leypoldt and Holt.

von Meysenbug, Malwida (trans Monte B Gardiner), *Memoirs of an Idealist*, 1999. First published in German as *Memoiren einer Idealistin* in 1869

Key secondary sources

Carr, E.H., *The Romantic Exiles: A Nineteenth Century Portrait Gallery*, Harmondsworth: Penguin Books, 1949

Freeborn, Richard, *Turgenev at Ventnor*, in *Slavonic and East European Review*, 51, no 124, July 1973, 253-74

Partridge, Monica, *Herzen, Ogarev, and their Free Russian Press in London*, in *Anglo-Soviet Journal*, March 1966

Schapiro, Leonard, *Turgenev, His Life and Times*, Harvard University Press, 1982

Stoppard, Tom, *Salvage: The Coast of Utopia Part III*, London: Faber and Faber, 2002

Waddington, Patrick, *Turgenev and England*, Basingstoke: MacMillan, 1980

Woodward, James B., *Turgenev's "Phantoms": A Reassessment* in *Slavonic and East European Review*, 50:121, October 1972, 530-545

Young, Sarah J., *In Herzen's footsteps: a visit to Ventnor*, posted on Dr. Sarah J. Young's website *sarahjyoung.com*, November 2011

PART V: TSARS ALEXANDER II AND ALEXANDER III AND ROYAL FAMILY TIES 1856-1894

Many of the places that both Tsar Alexander II and Alexander III visited during their trips to Britain can still be seen. These include Osborne Cottage on the Isle of Wight, where Alexander III stayed in summer 1873 when he was the Tsarevich, together with his wife and two sons, the future Tsar Nicholas II and his brother George. Windsor Castle, where Alexander II stayed during his state visit in 1874 is open to the public, as is Virginia Water Lake, where you can see the reconstructed ruins of Leptis Magna, greatly admired by the Tsar.

Grand Duchess Maria's main home after her marriage to Prince Alfred of Edinburgh in 1874 still stands in Eastwell Manor near Ashford in Kent. It now operates as a country house hotel. Maria spent many summers at Osborne Cottage on the Isle of Wight, but this is now a private residence. From 1893, Grand Duchess Maria and Prince Alfred lived at the Schloss Ehrenburg in Coburg, when he became the Grand Duke of Saxe-Coburg-Gotha. The Schloss is used today as a Museum and is open to the public.

Original sources

Kropotkin, Peter, *The Conquest of Bread,* Penguin Random House, 2015 (first published in French in 1892)

Mandache, Diana, *Dearest Missy: The Letters of Maria Alexandrovna, Grand Duchess of Russia, Duchess of Edinburgh, and of Saxe-Coburg-Gotha, and of her daughter, Marie, Crown Princess of Romania 1879-1900,* Rosvall Royal Books, 2011.

The letters of Grand Duchess Maria to her daughter Crown Princess Marie of Romania cast a sharp eye on the Grand Duchess's relationship with Queen Victoria and her attitude towards Britain. Many of these are available in Diana Mandache's book *Dearest Missy.* The author and the publisher are grateful to Ted Rosvall of Rosvall Royal Books for permission to use extracts from Grand Duchess Maria's letters in this book.

Maylunas, Andrei and Mironenko, Sergei (trans Darya Galy), *A Lifelong Passion: Nicholas and Alexandra: Their Own Story*, London, Weidenfeld & Nicolson, 1996. This is a very important publication containing a range of private letters, diary entries, and official documents produced by the imperial family, the British royal family, and the Russian and British governments. The author and the publisher are grateful to Orion Books for permission to use extracts from *A Lifelong Passion* in this book.

Queen Victoria's Journals between 1839 and 1880 are an important primary source of material for her relationship with the Romanovs during this period. There are several entries covering Tsar Alexander II's visits two visits to England, the first in 1839 when he was the Tsarevich and the second in 1874 when he came as Tsar. All rights in *Queen Victoria's Journals* are reserved to HM Queen Elizabeth II, and the author and publisher are grateful for permission to use extracts from the *Journals* in this book.

The Times newspaper is an invaluable source of contemporary reports on the visit by Tsar Alexander II to Britain in 1874, with particularly good articles in the editions published between 12 and 14 May 1874, covering his delayed arrival at Dover, his visits to Windsor Castle, Frogmore Mausoleum and Virginia Water Lake, as well as his meeting with Benjamin Disraeli at Buckingham Palace.

Key secondary sources

Aronson, Michael, *The Prospects for the Emancipation of Russian Jewry during the 1880s* in *Slavonic and East European Review*, 1977.

Azar, Helen, *Queen Victoria and Tsar Alexander II: Would-be Romance and Mutual Descendants* in *TheRomanovfamily.com*, September 2015.

Collins, Ian, *Fabergé: From St Petersburg to Sandringham*, Norwich: Sainsbury Centre for the Visual Arts, 2018.

McCarthy, Kieran and Faurby, Hanne, *Fabergé: Romance to Revolution, Victoria and Albert Museum*, 2021

Montefiore, Simon Sebag, *The Romanovs: 1613-1918*, London: Weidenfeld & Nicolson, 2016.

Offord, Derek, *The Russian Revolutionary Movement in the 1880s*, Cambridge University Press, 1986.

Radzinsky, Edvard (trans Antonia W. Bouis), *Alexander II: The Last Great Tsar*, Free Press, reprint edition, 2006.

Rappaport, Helen, *Love Before Albert: Queen Victoria's Suitors* in *History Today*, 29 March 2018.

Smith, S.A., *Russia in Revolution: An Empire in Crisis, 1890 to 1928*, Oxford University Press, 2017.

Waldron, Peter, *The End of Imperial Russia 1855-1917*, Basingstoke: Macmillan, 1997.

Waldron, Peter, *Russia of the Tsars*, London: Thames and Hudson, 2011.

Yarmolinsky, Avrahm, *Road to Revolution: A Century of Russian Radicalism*, New York: Macmillan, 1955.

PART VI: BUILDING A NEW ANGLO-RUSSIAN ALLIANCE
1894-1907

Many of the places associated with Nicholas and Alix during their time in England during the summer of 1894 still stand. Cathcart House in Harrogate, where Princess Alix retreated in May 1894 following the news of her engagement to Nicholas, is no longer a boarding house and has been converted into private apartments. Elm Grove House, referred to by Nicholas as a 'cosy cottage', was where Nicholas and Alix spent several blissful days in June 1894. It is in Hersham Road, Walton-on-Thames. Nicholas also spent a couple of days at Sandringham House and the gardens, house and stables would still be recognisable to him today.

On the Isle of Wight, Nicholas and Alix stayed with the Queen in Osborne House, rather than at Osborne Cottage. As they were not yet married, Nicholas was given his own suite of rooms. These were located on an upper floor of the main wing of the house and are not generally open to the public. The rooms have magnificent views out across the gardens of Osborne House and towards the Solent. The beach at Osborne, where the couple spent many delightful hours together, is open to the public, as is the Swiss Cottage where Alix used to play as a child.

In September 1896, the imperial couple travelled to Scotland to stay with Queen Victoria. They landed at Leith Docks and were accompanied by a regimental guard from the *Royal Scots* up to Balmoral Castle, where they stayed ten days with Queen Victoria. Alix was delighted to be back with her 'grandmama' but for Nicholas the entire trip was an endurance test and he was glad when the time came to take the train back south to Portsmouth. Balmoral Castle is the private residence of HM Queen Elizabeth II and is not open to the public.

Reval, where King Edward VII and Tsar Nicholas II met in June 1908, is now called Talinn and is the capital of Estonia. The two royal yachts anchored in the sea close to Talinn, but the King and Tsar never came ashore during the visit.

Sites associated with Russian revolutionaries in Britain can still be traced. The *Three Johns* pub is where Lenin and other members of the Russian Social Democratic Labour party organised the famous 1903 Congress, which split the party into Mensheviks and Bolsheviks. This can be found in White Lion Street, Islington. The anarchist Prince Peter Kropotkin lived at Crescent Road in Bromley for thirteen years, before moving to Muswell Hill. Most Russian exiles and Jewish refugees in this period lived in Whitechapel, a district infamously associated with the Ripper murders of the 1880s. These murders were initially blamed on Russian refugees.

Original sources

Bunin, Ivan, *Russian Requiem, 1885–1920*, Chicago: Ivan R Dee, 1993

Grey, Sir Edward, *Letter from Sir Edward Grey to Sir Arthur Nicolson, dated 29 August 1907*. National Archives/Cabinet Office papers reference CAB 37/93/81

Hansard, *Parliamentary House of Commons debates on Visit to Russia, 26 May 1908 and 4 June 1908*. Contains Parliamentary information licensed under the Open Parliament Licence v3.0

Hardinge, Charles, *Secret Memorandum by H.M Ambassador on the King's visit to Reval, dated 12 June 1908*. National Archives/Cabinet Office papers reference CAB/37/93/81,

Maylunas, Andrei and Mironenko, Sergei (trans Darya Galy), *A Lifelong Passion: Nicholas and Alexandra: Their Own Story,* London: Weidenfeld & Nicolson, 1996. There are diary entries from Nicholas and letters between Nicholas and Alix covering their time in England in the summer of 1894, and during the Tsar's coronation in 1896. Letters and diary entries from other members of the Romanov family in the period 1894-1905 are also included here.

O'Beirne, Hugh, *Hugh O'Beirne to Sir Edward Grey, St Petersburg, 2 June 1908.* National Archives/Cabinet Office papers reference CAB/37/93/76

O'Beirne, Hugh, *Confidential report from Hugh O'Beirne to Sir Edward Grey about the impact on Russian opinion of the King's visit to Reval. St Petersburg, 18 June 1908.* National Archives/Cabinet Office papers reference CAB/37/94/87

Ponsonby, Sir Frederick, *Recollections of Three Reigns*, London: Odhams, Eyre and Spottiswood, 1951

Queen Victoria's Journals in the period 1894-1896 refer to the engagement of Nicholas and Alix, their time in Windsor and on the Isle of Wight in 1894, and their visit to Balmoral Castle in 1896. All rights in *Queen Victoria's Journals* are reserved to HM Queen Elizabeth II, and the author and publisher are grateful for permission to use extracts from the *Journals* in this book.

The Times, The King and the Tsar, Meeting at Reval, 10 June 1908

The Times, The King and the Tsar, significance of the meeting. Report on the King's visit to Reval, dated 11 June 1908

The Times, Great Britain and Russia, plea for closer economic relations, 27 June 1908

Key secondary sources

Erickson, Carolly, *Alexandra The Last Tsarina: The tragic story of the last Tsarina of Russia,* London: Robinson, 2001

Figes, Orlando, *A People's Tragedy: The Russian Revolution,* 1891-1924, London: Jonathan Cape, 1996

Geifman, Anna, *Entangled in Terror: The Azef Affair and the Russian Revolution*, Scholarly Resources (SR) Books, 2000

Montefiore, Simon Sebag, *The Romanovs: 1613-1918,* London: Weidenfield & Nicolson, 2016

Radzinsky, Edvard, *The Last Tsar: The Life and Death of Nicholas II,* London: Doubleday, 1992

Ridley, Jane, *Bertie: A Life of Edward VII*, London: Chatto and Windus, 2012

Rosenbaum, Martin, *London's Role in the Russian Revolution,* posted on *BBC news and politics* website, October 2017

Smith, S.A., *Russia in Revolution: An Empire in Crisis, 1890 to 1928*, Oxford University Press, 2017

Timms, Elizabeth Jane, *Tsarina's gift to her goddaughter sold at auction.* Posted on website *royalcentral.co.uk*, 3 March 2017

Waldron, Peter, *The End of Imperial Russia, 1855-1917,* Basingstoke: Macmillan, 1997

Waldron, Peter, *Governing Tsarist Russia*, Red Globe Press: Macmillan International Higher Education, 2007

Waldron, Peter-,*Between Two Revolutions*, Northern Illinois University Press, 1997

Waldron, Peter, *Radical Russia: Art, Culture and Revolution*, Norwich: Sainsbury Centre for Visual Arts, 2018

Walsh, Edmund A., *The Fall of the Russian Empire,* Boston: Little, Brown and Company, 1928

Welch, Frances, *The Imperial Tea Party*, London: Short Books, 2018. This book gives a comprehensive description of three meetings between the British royal family and the Romanovs at Balmoral Castle in 1896, Reval in 1908, and at Cowes in 1909.

Young, Sarah J., *Russians in London: Pyotr Kropotkin.* Posted on website *sarahjyoung.com*

Zygar, Mikhail, *The Empire Must Die: Russia's Revolutionary Collapse, 1900-1917,* New York: Public Affairs (Hachette), 2017

PART VII: THE 1909 RUSSIAN IMPERIAL VISIT TO THE ISLE OF WIGHT

East Cowes and Cowes, the Solent, and Spithead are the primary places associated with the Romanovs during their visit to the Isle of Wight in 1909. The family stayed on board their yacht, *Shtandart*, during the visit, with day trips into East Cowes and Cowes. The *Shtandart* was moored in the Solent, protected by police boats and British and Russian naval cruisers.

On his first afternoon in British waters, the Tsar reviewed the British fleet at anchor in Spithead. This was one of the largest naval reviews ever organised. Nicholas's one day ashore with the Tsarina was spent at the Royal Naval College, then located in the grounds of Osborne House. The College was closed in 1921 and the buildings were subsequently demolished. Nicholas and Alexandra also spent time looking at Queen Victoria's private apartments in Osborne House, and visited Barton Manor, where they had tea with King Edward VII and Queen Alexandra.

The imperial children made visits both to Osborne Beach and to Osborne Cottage, as well as joining their parents for tea at Barton Manor. In addition, the two eldest Grand Duchesses, Olga and Tatiana, spent time shopping in the High Street in Cowes, where they bought hairbrushes and perfumes from Beken, the Pharmacist. Their wanderings took them as far as Benzie, the jewellers, where they were trapped by a huge crowd. Accompanied by Scotland Yard police officers, they then had to beat a hasty retreat through a backstreet route to the Chain Ferry, once their identities became known. The two girls also made a visit to Whippingham Church, where a memorial was later put up in memory of the Romanov family by Princess Victoria Mountbatten. The route to Osborne and Whippingham goes past Jubilee Park, where a new memorial to the Romanovs was unveiled in 2018, on the centenary anniversary of their murders.

Original sources

Conrad, Joseph, *The Secret Agent*, London: Methuen Publishing, 1907

Daily Mail, Town full of detectives, 2 August 1909

ibid, *Guarding the Czar*, 3 August 1909

ibid, *A Russian meal*, 3 August 1909

ibid, *Englishwomen and the Cossack cap*, 3 August 1909

ibid, *A Day in a Russian Home*, 4 August 1909

ibid, *The Tsar ashore, merry party at Osborne, dinner scene in the Shtandart*, 5 August 1909

ibid, *Cowes Regatta, White Heather defeats Shamrock*, 5 August 1909

ibid, *The Czar's farewell, and happy auguries for the future*, 6 August 1909

Daily Mirror, The King and the Tsar meet off Spithead, 3 August 1909

ibid, *The Tsar entertains the King*, 4 August 1909

ibid, *The Tsar goes ashore near Cowes*, 5 August 1909

ibid, *Little Russian Princesses do some shopping in Cowes*, 5 August 1909

ibid, *The Tsar leaves Cowes*, 6 August 1909

Grey, Sir Edward, *Secret memorandum from Sir Edward Grey about his conversation with the Tsar on 3rd August 1909*. National Archives/Cabinet Office papers Reference CAB/100/108

Grey, Sir Edward, *Letter from Sir Edward Grey to the Russian Ambassador, Count Benckendorff, 12 August 1909*. National Archives, Foreign Office (FO) 800/73

Hansard, *Parliamentary House of Commons debates on the Tottenham Outrage and alien anarchists and alien immigration to Britain*, 18 February, 25 February and 1 March 1909. Contains Parliamentary information licensed under the Open Parliament Licence v3.0

ibid, *Parliamentary House of Commons debates on the Tsar's visit to Cowes*, 10 June, 15 July, 22 July, 23 July, 29 July 1909. Contains Parliamentary information licensed under the Open Parliament Licence v3.0

Illustrated London News, *Friends: The British and Russian sovereigns and their heirs*, 14 August 1909

Isle of Wight County Press, *The Cowes Week*, Saturday 7 August 1909. This is a detailed account of all the events during the week that the Russian imperial family were visiting Cowes.

Lady Charlotte, *Dresses at Cowes, Daily Mail*, 2 August 1909

O'Beirne, Hugh, *Letter from Hugh O'Beirne to Sir Edward Grey, 29 July*

1909, National Archives, Foreign Office (FO) 800/73

Spiridovich, Alexander, *Les Dernières Années de la Cour de Tsarskoye Selo,* Payot Paris, 1922. English translation by Emily Plank, Russia House Press, 2009

The Times, Anglo-Russian relations: Speech by Sir A. Nicolson, 1 January 1909

ibid, *The Shooting Outrage: Anarchist Society at Tottenham,* 26 January 1909

ibid, *The Russian Statemen at Edinburgh and Oxford,* 1 and 5 July 1909

ibid, *The Labour Party and the Tsar,* 26 July 1909

ibid, *The Royal Naval Review,* 31 July 1909

ibid, *The repression in Russia,* 2 August 1909

ibid, *Editorial welcoming the Tsar's visit,* 2 August 1909

ibid, *The Tsar at Cowes,* 3, 4 and 5 August 1909

ibid, *Russian comments on Tsar's visit to Cowes,* 4 August 1909

ibid, *The Cowes Week- Royal Yacht Squadron Regatta,* 5 August 1909

ibid, *The Tsar's departure: The tumult and the shouting dies, the Captains and the Kings depart,* 7 August 1909

ibid, *Cowes Week: The last day,* 7 August 1909

ibid, *The Tsar and the German Emperor,* 7 August 1909

Yachting and Boating Monthly- Numbers 40 and 41, Vol VII, August and September 1909

Key secondary sources

Atchinson, Bob, *Alexander Palace.* The website www.alexanderpalace.org is packed with documents and information relating to the Romanovs.

Geifman, Anna, *Entangled in Terror: The Azef Affair and the Russian Revolution,* Wilmington: Scholarly Resources (SR) Books, 2000

King, Greg, *The Court of the Last Tsar: Pomp, Power and Pageantry in the Reign of Nicholas II,* New Jersey: Wiley and Sons, 2006

Latvian History, *Latvian Anarchism: The Story of Peter the Painter,* Published on 5 January 2014 and available on www.latvianhistory.com

Rappaport, Helen, *Four Sisters: The Lost Lives of the Romanov Grand Duchesses,* London: Macmillan, 2014. This book has a good chapter describing the 1909 imperial visit to Cowes.

Slatter, John, *Our Friends from the East: Russian Revolutionaries and British Radicals, 1852-1917* in *History Today*, Vol 53, Issue 10, October 2003

Waldron, Peter, *The End of Imperial Russia, 1855-1917*, Basingstoke: Macmillan, 1997

Welch, Frances, *The Imperial Tea Party*, London: Short Books, 2018. This has a good section on the 1909 imperial visit to Cowes.

Young, Sarah J., *Russians in London: The anarchist threat.* Published on 31 Jan 2011 and available on sarahjyoung.com

PART VIII: THE COLLAPSE OF IMPERIAL RUSSIA AND THE END OF THE ANGLO-RUSSIAN ALLIANCE 1914-1918

Many of the places in Russia associated with the last Romanovs can still be visited. These include the Winter Palace and the Hermitage, as well as the Alexander Palace and Gardens at Tsarskoye Selo. In Siberia, the Governor's Mansion in Tobolsk where the family was imprisoned between August 1917 and April 1918 has been fully restored. It is now a museum to the memory of the Romanov family. In Ekaterinburg, the Ipatiev House, where the Romanovs and their servants were murdered in July 1918, was demolished in 1977 but the *Church on Blood in Honour of All Saints* now stands on the site of their execution.

The bodies of the imperial family were first buried in the forest outside Ekaterinburg in a place called Ganina Yama. A monastery now stands on the site, with a poignant memorial to the seven Romanovs in the form of seven wooden chapels. Their remains were quickly exhumed from here by the Bolsheviks, and they were then buried in a field called Porosenkov Log, about four miles from Ganina Yama, and were not discovered again until 1979. Following the fall of the Soviet regime in 1991, the Romanov family were officially buried in the St Peter and Paul Fortress Church in St Petersburg in 1998.

In Britain, Kent House on the Isle of Wight became the home of the Tsarina's sister, Princess Victoria, who lived there between 1914 and 1921. She and her husband, Prince Louis Mountbatten, are buried at nearby

Whippingham Church. At Hampton Court, Wilderness House was the final residence of Grand Duchess Xenia Alexandrovna, the Tsar's younger sister. She lived there from 1937 until her death in 1960. Neither Kent House nor Wilderness House are open to the public, but both can be seen from the outside.

Original sources

De Price, Kent, *Diary of Nicholas II, 1917-1918: An annotated translation*, University of Montana: Scholarworks, 1966

Gilliard, Pierre, *Thirteen Years at the Russian Court*, Leonaur Books, 2016

Maylunas, Andrei and Mironenko, Sergei (trans Darya Galy), *A Lifelong Passion: Nicholas and Alexandra: Their Own Story*, London, Weidenfeld & Nicolson, 1996. There are diary entries from Nicholas and letters between Nicholas and Alix covering the period up to their deaths in 1918. These include the 1913 Romanov Tercentenary, the Revolution and imprisonment in Tobolsk and Ekaterinburg. There is also valuable correspondence relating to the abdication of the Tsar and the decision by King George V and the British government not to offer the Tsar and his family asylum.

Yurovsky, Yakov, *Murder of the Imperial Family - The executioner Yurovsky's account*, dated 1 February 1934. Documentation Centre of the Social Organisation of the Sverdlosk (Ekaterinburg) region. Posted to the Alexander Palace website www.alexanderpalace.org

Key secondary sources

Erickson, Carolly, *Alexandra: The Last Tsarina*, London: Constable and Robinson, 2001

Figes, Orlando, *A People's Tragedy: The Russian Revolution, 1891-1924*, London: Jonathan Cape, 1996

Fitzlyon, Kyril and Browning, Tatiana, *Before the Revolution: A View of Russia under the Last Tsar*, London: Penguin Books, 1992

Harwood, Maria (ed), *Proceedings of the International Symposium: The Last Romanovs - Archival and Museum Discoveries in Great Britain and Russia*, London: Pindar Press, 2018

King, Greg and Wilson, Penny, *The Fate of the Romanovs*, New Jersey: Wiley and Sons, 2003

Massie, Robert K., *The Romanovs: The Final Chapter*, London: Jonathan Cape, 1995

Radzinsky, Edvard, *Rasputin: The Last Word*, London: Weidenfeld & Nicolson, 2000

Rappaport, Helen, *Four Sisters: The Lost Lives of the Romanov Grand Duchesses*, London, Macmillan: 2014

Rappaport, Helen, *The Race to Save the Romanovs*, London: Hutchinson, 2018

Service, Robert, *The Last of the Tsars: Nicholas II and the Russian Revolution*, London: Macmillan, 2017

Waldron, Peter, *The End of Imperial Russia, 1855-1917*, Basingstoke: Macmillan, 1997

Welch, Frances, *The Russian Court at Sea: The voyage of HMS Malborough April 1919*, London: Short Books, 2011

Acknowledgements

There are many books now available about the Romanovs, one of the most celebrated imperial dynasties in Europe's history. However, the 300-year long relationship between the Romanovs and Britain has been less thoroughly explored, particularly in connection with the Isle of Wight. This was an island which became the focus for many interesting and unexpected connections between Britain and Imperial Russia. A book on this subject therefore seemed well worth writing, in order to shed light on the way that the Isle of Wight found itself at the centre of some of the most important moments in the history of the Anglo-Russian relationship.

I am particularly grateful to my publisher, Peter Harrigan of Medina Publishing, for his unstinting enthusiasm for my book, his many creative and valuable suggestions, and for all the introductions that he made for me on the Isle of Wight. These have proved invaluable and without his support and encouragement, this book would never have seen the light of day. My editor, Eleo Carson, has been hugely helpful, acting as a critical friend and always steering me in the right direction through several drafts of the manuscript. Her knowledge of Russian history and of the UK publishing world has also been of tremendous value to me.

I should also like to acknowledge the contribution of Sherif Dhaimish at Medina Publishing, who has worked tirelessly on a whole range of issues connected with the production of the book, including negotiating rights for illustrations from a wide variety of rare sources. His patience and reliability have been instrumental in keeping me to the publication schedule.

On the Isle of Wight, I should like to pay particular thanks to Michael Hunter, the Curator of Osborne House, who has always shown a great interest in my book, and who has also provided me with valuable information about the Romanov connections with Osborne. David Hill and Karl Love of East Cowes, who together with Maria Harwood of the Grand Duchess Elizabeth Romanov Society, were responsible for the commissioning of the Romanov Memorial Cross in Jubilee Park in 2018, have proved to be energetic and enthusiastic champions of my book and of the Romanov relationship with the Island. I have greatly appreciated their support. A big word of thanks must also go to Lady Grylls of Bembridge, who has proved to be an amazing networker on my behalf, introducing me to a wide range of people on the Island who were able to support my research.

Sarah and David Burdett from the East Cowes Heritage Centre encouraged me to make use of the valuable materials held by the Centre. Their colleague, Jenny Kendall, was always on hand to help me identify relevant documents. Rosemary Joy, the Manager of the Cowes Classic Boat Museum in East Cowes, assisted me during my researches in the museum library, where I found a lot of very valuable material relating to Cowes Week 1909.

I should also like to thank Commodore David Hughes, the Honourary Historian of the Royal Yacht Squadron in Cowes, for giving me an excellent introduction to the history of the Squadron and for being an invaluable guide to the correct use of naval and yachting terms in my book. Thanks also to Janet and David McNeal of Ryde, who gave me a lot of useful information about Whippingham Church, where they are both active members. Kenneth Beken of Cowes gave me access to his valuable photographic archive covering the 1909 yachting Regatta and the visit of the Romanov Grand Duchesses to Cowes, for which I am very grateful. The story of his own Russian family history was also very entertaining.

Dawn Haig-Thomas very kindly showed me around Barton Manor and fielded my numerous questions about how the house would have looked during the Romanov family visit there in August 1909. It made the imperial visit seem suddenly very real when I saw the actual wall where the famous photograph was taken of the British and Russian royal families standing together.

In mainland Britain, Maria Harwood, the Secretary General of the Grand Duchess Elizabeth Romanov Society, has been a source of aid and encouragement during the writing of my book and I should very much like to thank her, and her colleagues at the Society, for all their support. Maria has also been a great help in making connections for me to the Russian community in the UK'

Dr Peter Waldron, Professor of Modern History at the University of East Anglia, reviewed my manuscript and provided me with a lot of useful comments, particularly on the accuracy of the Russian history sections of the book. Joyce Yarrow, a novelist and creative writing consultant living in Seattle, USA gave me very valuable observations on how to make the book more appealing to non-specialist readers. I am very grateful to both Peter and Joyce, for the time that they spent reading through and commenting on early versions of my manuscript. In Norwich, Ivor Kemp provided me with books and documents relating to Britain and Romanov Russia and introduced me to Dr Waldron.

I am indebted to the staff at the National Archives in Kew and at the British Library in London for all their help in accessing documents and papers relating to the Romanovs as well as to Julie Crocker, the Senior Archivist at the Royal Archives, for giving me permission to quote freely from the diaries of Queen Victoria. I should also like to thank Ted Rosvall, from Royal Books, for allowing me to use original source material, without charge, from the correspondence between Grand Duchess Maria and her daughter, Crown Princess Marie of Romania. Orion Books have also been very accommodating in allowing me to use quotes from original letters by Nicholas and Alexandra and other members of the Romanov family. I am also grateful to Frances Welch, the author of *The Imperial Tea Party*, for her permission to use information from her book when I met her in East Cowes in July 2018.

I should also like to thank Coryne Hall, for her help in identifying changes that needed making to the text of the first edition of the book. These changes have been incorporated into the second edition. Similarly, I am very grateful to Chris Hickey, Henry Greenfield, and John Doble, all three having taken time to carefully review my book and send me their helpful comments. Henry Greenfield also drew my attention to the important story of the Lena Goldfield Massacre in 1912 and its connection with the artist Kazimir Malevich and his painting 'An Englishman in Moscow'.

I have been very pleased with the positive response that I have received from members of the Romanov family, Prince Rostislav Romanov, Princess Olga Romanov and Prince Paul Kulikovsky, when I have told them about the book. I am very appreciative of their continuing interest in it.

Finally, I should like to say a huge thanks to my wife, Dorcas, and my children, Tom, Eleanor and Grace, who have lived every minute of this book with me as I researched and wrote it, and have given me unstinting encouragement and support over the last three years.

Index